Politics and
Urban Growth
in Santiago, Chile
1891-1941

Politics and
Urban Growth
in Santiago, Chile
1891-1941

Richard J. Walter

STANFORD UNIVERSITY PRESS
STANFORD, CALIFORNIA
2005

Stanford University Press
Stanford, California

Printed in the United States of America on acid-free,
archival-quality paper

Library of Congress Cataloging-in-Publication Data

Walter, Richard J.
    Politics and urban growth in Santiago, Chile, 1891–1941 /
Richard J. Walter.
p. cm.
    Includes bibliographical references and index.
    ISBN 0-8047-4982-5 (cloth : alk. paper)
1. Santiago (Chile)—Politics and government—20th century. 2. Chile—
Politics and government—20th century. 3. Cities and towns—Chile—
Santiago—Growth. 4. Urban policy—Chile—Santiago—History.
5. Urbanization—Chile—Santiago—History. I. Title.
F3271.3.W35 2005
983'.315063—dc22

                                                    2004003970

Designed by Tag Savage at Wilsted & Taylor
Typeset by Wilsted & Taylor in 10.5/14 Joanna

Original Printing 2005

Last figure below indicates year of this printing:
14 13 12 11 10 09 08 07 06 05

For Braden,

Brianna,

Corey,

Danielle,

and Isabella

Contents

Illustrations and Tables

Maps

Figures

Tables

Photographs (following page 144)

Preface

THIS HISTORY OF SANTIAGO, Chile's capital and its largest and most important city, was directly inspired and influenced by my previous work on Buenos Aires (*Politics and Urban Growth in Buenos Aires, 1910–1942*, Cambridge University Press, 1993). It covers roughly the same period of the early decades of the twentieth century, a time when both cities underwent rapid growth and experienced patterns of development and the emergence of urban problems that persist to the present. In the case of Santiago, however, the story begins earlier, in 1891, when elected municipal government was introduced for the first time. It ends in 1941 with the demise of the first Popular Front government, something of a watershed in Chilean political history.

As with Buenos Aires, a main focus in this work is on local politics and government in Santiago for this period and the role they played in the city's growth. While there is a substantial and ever-growing literature on various aspects of Latin American urban history, with a few exceptions, such as Michael Coniff's study of Rio de Janeiro (*Urban Politics in Brazil: The Rise of Populism, 1925–1945*, University of Pittsburgh Press, 1981), Diane E. Davis's examination of Mexico City (*Urban Leviathan: Mexico City in the Twentieth Century*, Temple University Press, 1994), and my work on Buenos Aires, relatively little attention has been paid to the details of local politics and administration, and the case of Santiago is no exception.

To some extent, this relative neglect is understandable. Usually, for example, in Latin America as in the United States, there is generally less public interest in most municipal elections as compared with national contests.

Moreover, there often exists a negative view of local governments as weak, ineffective, and corrupt. In addition, as we shall see in the case of Santiago, which is certainly not atypical of the region as a whole, the authority of municipal officials is often constrained, eroded, and marginalized, especially in capital cities where they share power with national governments. Nonetheless, in Latin America, as elsewhere, it is local government with which city dwellers commonly have the most direct contact and which most often has a direct influence on their daily lives. It is to City Hall that most citizens go, for example, to get permits to construct houses and other buildings, receive licenses to operate businesses, or to request direct assistance for a particular personal or neighborhood need. It is local government that is ordinarily primarily responsible for basic infrastructure development, such as sewer construction, street paving and improvements, and the extension of basic utilities supplying water, gas, and electricity. Local government, too, usually provides essential services like street lighting, cleaning, maintenance and repair, the collection and disposal of garbage and trash, and, in some measure, the protection of public safety. Local officials are also largely responsible for the overall appearance of the city, including the establishment and upkeep of public buildings, monuments, parks, and gardens. In addition, it falls on the local administration to develop and enforce the rules and regulations of city life, ranging from the proper location and procedures for street vending, to the correct dimensions and appearance of new buildings, to the hours when commercial establishments are allowed to remain open. And, it is to City Hall that the citizen must repair to pay fines for violating ordinances related to these and various other regulations.

Over the course of the twentieth century, one of the most persistent and perplexing problems for most large cities has been how to deal with the explosion of vehicular traffic of various kinds and how to provide for and to regulate various modes of public transportation. In this case, too, Santiago has been no exception. In recent years, the rapid expansion in the number of buses, taxis, and private automobiles has produced not only major problems of traffic congestion but also, combined with topographical and climatological factors, has made the air of Chile's capital among Latin America's most contaminated. Trying to resolve this problem has become a major priority for national and local authorities alike.

In this study, I shall focus on certain antecedents to this problem in the early twentieth century, with a major emphasis, as in my history of Buenos Aires, on the relations between the city and the main provider of public transportation in this period, a foreign-owned electric streetcar company. This relationship, which was one of almost constant contention between the two parties, was a major concern for virtually every Santiago administration and serves as a useful theme to explore the dynamics of politics and government at the local level. It is also significant due to the fact that most of the city's population continued to depend primarily on the streetcar as the main source of public transportation throughout the period studied, despite the introduction of alternatives. The availability of public transportation was a matter that directly affected the daily lives of most residents. Moreover, because the issue involved from the beginning the relationship between the city and a foreign-owned enterprise and monopoly, the story of this relationship also bears on the evolution of economic nationalism as a major political force and issue in the nation's twentieth-century history.

In addition to contributions to the growth of economic nationalism, there were other important connections between developments at the local level and the larger national stage. Participation in Santiago's local administration, for example, frequently served as an important training ground for numerous politicians of various parties who moved on to national legislative and administrative positions. Municipal elections often served as referendums on current national administrations and harbingers of possible future changes. The institution of elected municipalities in 1891 was an important ingredient in Chile's overall democratic development over the course of the twentieth century, a development of which Chileans were justifiably proud. On the other hand, as will be seen, local politics within the nation's complicated and fluid multi-party structure often bogged down in what many considered excessive partisanship and maneuvering, leading to frequent stalemates and seriously hampering the overall effectiveness of the city administration to provide essential services. This partisanship and resulting ineffectiveness provided ammunition to critics who argued for the suspension of democracy at the local level, as occurred between 1924 and 1935 and again under the dictatorship of Augusto Pinochet between 1973 and 1990 when local officials were appointed directly by the national government. The restoration of democracy at the local level has been one of the major goals and achievements of the post-Pinochet administrations.

An examination of the earlier period of local politics and government, therefore, helps to supply context and background to understand better these more recent developments. Another recent trend of some note in Latin America generally is the emergence of leaders of large cities as presidential candidates. Fernando de la Rúa, for example, was the chief executive of the city of Buenos Aires before being elected president of Argentina in 1999, preceded a year earlier by Andrés Pastrana of Colombia, who was mayor of Bogotá before becoming president of that country. Cuauhtemoc Cárdenas was the first elected mayor of Mexico City in 1997 but was unsuccessful in his 2000 presidential bid. Indeed, in Chile itself, at the time this book was being written, conservative Joaquín Lavín, who was narrowly defeated in the presidential election of 2000, was serving as the elected mayor of Santiago (having won over the wife of ex-president Eduardo Frei, Jr.). Previously, he had been the mayor of the nearby suburb of Las Condes and appeared likely to run again for the presidency in 2006. Given these developments in Chile and elsewhere, it seems opportune and useful to examine the historical context in which Santiago's local administrations have operated.

Two other factors justify a focus on the history of local politics and government in Santiago. First, an examination of local government, especially of the debates and discussions that went on within the city council, provides a lens with which to view the larger elements of the city's growth over these years. While a main focus will be, as mentioned, on public transportation matters, considerable attention will also be given to a wide range of other issues that reflected the patterns and problems of the capital's development in these years. Second, as the story is being told for the first time, it has, I hope, an innate interest of its own. In the mid-1930s, for example, the vote in municipal elections in Chile was extended to women and women were allowed not only to cast ballots for but also to participate themselves in local administration, as, in the case of Santiago, several did. While this may not have been unprecedented in Latin America, it was certainly not usual. In addition, in 1939, as will be shown, the president of the nation appointed the first female mayor to preside over the capital, a first not only for Chile but for the region as a whole. These and other noteworthy developments will be dealt with in some detail.

The presentation of Santiago's history follows the pattern of my book on Buenos Aires. It begins with a chapter that portrays the city in general terms at the turn of the twentieth century and is followed by chapters that detail in narrative and chronological fashion the role of local administration, with additional summary chapters describing the overall pattern of growth during particular decades. While the principal focus is on local affairs, attention is also paid to the larger national context in which these occur and to which they relate. As a considerable secondary literature exists on the national story, it will generally be presented only in summary form.

This study draws heavily on the same kinds of sources as my work on Buenos Aires. These include foreign travelers' accounts, national census reports, diplomatic correspondence, newspapers and magazines, and government publications. As with my examination of Buenos Aires, the transcribed minutes of city council meetings have been a major source, often buttressed by articles from the nation's principal newspaper, El Mercurio. And, when these minutes were not available, as was generally the case for the years 1911 to 1925, that newspaper in turn was the principal source for information on council sessions and other items related to local politics and government. Unfortunately, during the time when most of the field research for this study was conducted, between January and June 2000, the various other newspapers in Chile's national library, the main repository for such material, were in the process of being microfilmed and were unavailable for consultation. However, checking El Mercurio's reports with council minutes revealed that the newspaper, despite its frequent conservative bias, was generally accurate and comprehensive in its reporting.

A final comment is needed concerning a definition for Santiago. The main focus of this study will be on the capital city, for the period under consideration also identified as the comuna (literally, commune) of Santiago. To complicate matters, the city was itself divided into ten comunas for electoral and administrative purposes. The city was also part of the larger Department of Santiago, which included the capital and its surrounding suburbs, or what might also be called Greater Santiago. These units, in turn, were part of the larger Province of Santiago, with its center in the capital city. For most, the name Santiago is usually broadly applied to the general metropolitan area, but, to repeat, this study will deal primarily with the capital city, or comuna, of Santiago, although some attention will also be paid to its relationship with the surrounding suburbs and provincial authorities.

Acknowledgments

VARIOUS INDIVIDUALS AND INSTITUTIONS aided me in the research associated with this book. I would like to thank the staffs of the Library of Congress and the United States National Archives in Washington, D.C., the staff at the Biblioteca Nacional and the Biblioteca del Congreso in Santiago, Chile, and the staff of the Olin Library at Washington University for their assistance. Thanks also go to María Inés Zaldívar of the Washington University Program at the Universidad Católica in Santiago for kindly letting me share an office with her while most of the research on this book was being done. In Santiago, Thomas Kluboch and Nara Milanich were helpful and supportive fellow researchers in the Biblioteca Nacional. I owe a special debt of gratitude to Paul Drake for his insightful comments on the manuscript, and to the late Simon Collier, who shared with me both his enthusiasm for the project and his unparalleled knowledge of Chilean history when the manuscript was in its rawest form. I also have been fortunate to enjoy consistent support and encouragement from Vice-Chancellor and Dean of the Faculty of Arts and Sciences at Washington University, Edward Macias, and the chair of my department, Derek Hirst. Chris Kurpiewski and Ximena Basombrio C. aided me greatly in the preparation of the maps. Finally, as always, a special word of appreciation for my wife Susana, who suffered with me through many a chilly day in the Biblioteca Nacional in Santiago and who was always there when I needed her.

RICHARD J. WALTER
St. Louis, Missouri
August 2003

Politics and
Urban Growth
in Santiago, Chile
1891-1941

1 Santiago in the Early Twentieth Century

SPANISH CONQUISTADOR PEDRO DE VALDIVIA founded the city of Santiago, named for Spain's patron saint, on February 12, 1541. During the period of Spanish rule, it was the seat of colonial administration and the main urban center of the colony. Following independence in the early nineteenth century, Santiago became the national capital and consistently and continually strengthened its predominance over the rest of the country. By the year 2000, Greater Santiago contained roughly five million Chileans out of a national total of about fourteen million.

Santiago's predominance in Chile compares with that of Buenos Aires and many other Latin American capitals. However, throughout its history, the capital has shared importance with Valparaíso, the nation's main port (although recently challenged by San Antonio to the south) some eighty miles northwest of Santiago. Unlike the case of Buenos Aires, Montevideo, Rio de Janeiro (until 1961), and Lima, South American capitals with which the nation's leaders have compared their city, Chile's capital has not been also its main outlet to the sea.

Santiago is located at the northern end of the nation's fertile, productive, and densely populated Central Valley. And, as national borders were extended northward and southward, that location was more or less in the geographic center of a country with one of the world's most peculiar configurations, some 2,500 miles long and, at its widest point, 200 miles wide.[1]

The city's setting is spectacular. On the east are the snow-capped Andes, visible from most parts of the capital, while farther to the west lies the smaller coastal range separating the city from the Pacific Ocean. Santiago's terrain is mostly flat, although there is a gradual but definite slope from east to west. Two prominent hills punctuate the generally level terrain, Cerro Santa Lucía, in the heart of the downtown area, and the larger San Cristóbal, to the northeast of the city center. Running east to west through the city is the Mapocho River. Like many Andean-fed streams, the Mapocho is not much more than an average-sized creek in the summer, but often a torrent in the winter and spring.

Although Santiaguinos frequently complain about the weather, the climate is generally benign. At an altitude of about 1,500 feet, the city has a dry atmosphere, especially in the summer (November to April), characterized by warm but not terribly hot days and cool nights, a sharp contrast to the heat and humidity of the Atlantic capitals. The winter is rainy and often uncomfortable, made more so by the relative absence of central heating, but snow, ice, and freezing temperatures are rare. While nature has blessed Santiago (and Chile) in many ways, earthquakes have been and are a constant threat, although the capital has yet to suffer the kind of devastation from such seismic events that have virtually destroyed other Chilean cities.

Santiago experienced steady growth throughout the late colonial period and into the nineteenth century. By 1870, the city had a population of about 150,000 (7.2 percent of the national total), at that time somewhat less than Buenos Aires (187,000) and considerably less than Rio de Janeiro (230,000), but significantly more than Lima (100,000) and Montevideo (110,000).[2] Despite its growth, Santiago was much like the country overall, considered isolated from larger international currents and somewhat provincial and backward. The man who began the modernization of the capital was Benjamín Vicuña Mackenna, one of Chile's most notable nineteenth-century public men and *intendente* (governor) of the province of Santiago from 1872 to 1875. (It should be noted that the Province of Santiago is a separate jurisdiction that surrounds the capital, although the city itself is the seat of the province and the *intendente* has authority over the city as well.) Vicuña Mackenna laid out a plan to transform the capital, like so many others of the period, along Parisian lines. Two of his most lasting accomplishments were to turn the previously neglected Cerro Santa Lucía into a beautiful and much-admired public park and to begin work on the Alameda de las Delicias (today the Alameda Bernardo O'Higgins, named for Chile's main hero of the wars of independence), a tree-lined monumental avenue that served, as it still does, as the principal east–west thoroughfare of the city. Also in the 1870s, important public buildings such as the National Congress, the Teatro Municipal (Municipal Theater), and the Mercado Central (Central Market) were completed. French and Italian architects were brought in to help design these and other structures, but Chilean architects began to make their contributions as well.[3]

The transformation begun by Vicuña Mackenna continued into the early twentieth century. The Alameda was extended to the west to the new Central Railway Station (Estación Central), completed in 1900 and the principal terminus for a national system that connected the southern part of the country to Santiago. In 1913 work was finished on the Mapocho Station, located near the Central Market on the north side of the river for which it was named and serving as the main rail link to Valparaíso and points north as well as east across the Andes to Argentina.[4] At the turn of the century, French landscape artist George Dubois, who also worked in Buenos Aires, designed the Parque Forestal on land reclaimed from channeling the Mapocho River, and in 1910 the impressive Palacio de Bellas Artes (Palace of Fine Arts), the capital's main art museum, was inaugurated at the western end of the park.[5]

By the time of the national census of 1907, Santiago's population had more than doubled from the time of the previous census in 1870, to 332,724 (10.4 percent of the national total).[6] This growth was due primarily to the normal push-pull factors of internal migration common to much of Latin America at the time. On the push side were poor wages, poor working conditions, and poor living conditions in a countryside dominated by the wealthy landowning elite, inducing tens of thousands to seek a better life in the capital.[7] Fluctuations in the mining economy, mostly in the North, also sent thousands to Santiago. Among the pull factors was an expanding national government, which offered employment opportunities for provincial elites and a nascent middle class. In addition, public works and other construction projects, as well as the beginnings of industrialization in and around Santiago, provided jobs for skilled and unskilled workers.[8] Improvements in roads and railroads made it easier for migrants to reach Santiago, while expanded telephone and telegraph services as well as the growth and diffusion of newspapers and magazines enabled *provincianos* to learn more about the advantages of life in the capital.

In contrast to the Atlantic capitals, and more like Lima, foreign immigrants played a relatively minor role in Santiago's growth. Chilean leaders had ambivalent and frequently shifting positions about encouraging immigration, dictated by changing economic conditions and racial attitudes. Moreover, Chile's relative isolation, especially before the opening of the Panama Canal in 1914, made it difficult for many to reach its shores. These factors, along with the relative lack of economic opportunities and low wages when compared with other destinations, produced a net immigration of only 55,572 between 1889 and 1914, compared with 2,351,715 to Argentina for the same period.[9]

Despite the low numbers, foreigners were not an inconsequential part of Santiago's population. In 1907 the census counted 18,786 foreigners (12,219 males, 6,567 females) in Greater Santiago. The largest groups were from Spain (6,131), France (3,491), Italy (3,483), and Germany (1,313). Smaller in numbers but significant in other ways were 250 from Russia, presumably the core of Santiago's small Jewish community, 464 from Turkey, which probably included most of the Middle East, and 101 from China and Japan.[10]

As Carl Solberg noted, "The power and influence that the 85,000 [of a total 134,524 foreign-born in 1907] Europeans and Orientals held in Chile was tremendous and bore little relationship to their sparse numbers."[11] By 1914, according to Solberg, foreigners "owned nearly one-third of the nation's commercial houses ... [and] 49 percent of Chilean industrial establishments."[12] Spanish and Italian immigrants were often small shopkeepers and businessmen and foreigners in general enjoyed significant representation in middle-class occupations.[13] In Santiago in 1907, foreigners made up 14 percent of all *empleados* (employees, or white-collar workers) and *funcionarios* (functionaries, or clerks) and 17 percent of all *comerciantes* (merchants).[14]

Of even greater significance were the foreign names prominent in Chile's and Santiago's economic, social, and political elite. Among those of English and Scotch-Irish descent were some of the capital's most prominent families—Edwards, Ross, Walker, Cox, MacIver, Mackenna. The Edwards were probably the best known, with a fortune in mining, banking, and other activities as well as owning the country's most influential newspaper, *El Mercurio*.[15] In the twentieth century, two political dynasties, the Alessandris and the Freis, were descendants of Italian and Swiss immigrants, respectively.[16]

Less prominent, but still important, were immigrants from the Middle East, such as Benedicto Chuaqui from Syria and Juan Yarur, a Palestinian by way of Bolivia, who built important textile and clothing factories in the capital.[17]

The story of foreign-born influence and prominence among the middle and upper reaches of Chile's and Santiago's society is fundamentally similar to that of Argentina, Brazil, and Uruguay. At the lower levels, however, the contrast is clear. In the Atlantic cases, immigrants made up a substantial and in some instances overwhelming portion of the working classes, especially of the urban working classes. In Santiago, however, the lower orders of society were predominantly native-born. In Buenos Aires, for example, 71 percent of skilled workers in 1914 were foreign-born.[18] In Santiago, in 1907, only 4 percent in this category were from outside Chile.[19] Another contrast is in the sex ratio. In Buenos Aires in 1914, thanks largely to the fact that many more foreign males settled in the country than did females, men outnumbered women 849,970 to 726,844.[20] In Santiago, on the other hand, women outnumbered men 219,270 to 184,505 in 1907.[21]

Both foreign immigration and internal migration were helping to change Santiago's social class composition by the turn of the century. Information on occupations taken from the 1907 census for Santiago and presented in Table 1 has been organized according to categories used previously for Buenos Aires.[22] While the number of occupations listed is considerably smaller for Santiago than for Buenos Aires, and while the categories may not be strictly comparable, the groupings correspond roughly to more impressionistic evidence and estimates.

At the top of the social hierarchy are the professionals, who make up about 5 percent of the total. This category is dominated by native-born males, with, for example, only 3 female lawyers out of 856 and only 4 female physicians out of 291, a pattern similar to that of Buenos Aires. Women do, however, make up the majority of religious personnel and teachers. The foreign-born are only 7 percent of the professional category, but represent 16 percent of the architects and 15 percent of the engineers. Unfortunately, the census does not list *hacendados* (owners of large landed estates) and mine owners (often connected with landed families), the main components of the upper class.

Next on the social pyramid is an emerging middle class. According to

TABLE 1. *Social Structure of the City of Santiago by Occupational Category, Gender, and Nationality, 1907*

| | Native-born | | | Foreign-born | | | | |
	Male	Female	Total	Male	Female	Total	Total	%
Working class								
Unskilled and menial	7,647	25,825	33,472	244	75	319	33,791	17.2
Semiskilled service	6,268	24,556	30,824	81	255	336	31,160	15.9
Rural semiskilled	18,440	723	19,163	213	5	218	19,381	9.9
Skilled	32,112	3,422	35,534	1,577	57	1,634	37,168	18.9
Middle class								
Rural skilled	4,642	203	4,845	195	7	202	5,047	2.6
Low non-manual	21,297	7,233	28,530	2,819	162	2,981	31,511	16.0
Middle unspecified non-manual	17,773	2,545	20,318	2,604	285	2,889	23,207	11.8
Upper class								
High non-manual	874	86	960	134	19	153	1,113	0.1
Low professional	3,757	967	4,724	267	249	516	5,240	2.7
High professional	2,829	1,102	3,931	293	44	337	4,628	2.4
Miscellaneous	1,603	2,461	4,064	143	122	265	4,329	2.2
Total	117,242	69,123	186,365	8,570	1,289	9,850	196,215	

SOURCE: Chile, Comisión Central del Censo, *Censo de 1907*, 430–33.

the census figures, about 28 percent of the total could be classified as belonging to this group. This figure, however, may overstate the case. As Peter DeShazo has pointed out, one of the main occupations listed in this category, *comerciantes*, often consisted of "transient peddlers who scratched out a meager living on a sales commission."[23] The term *empleado*, or white-collar employee, is also problematic, covering a broad range of occupational possibilities. Moreover, the census does not provide specific information on education, except to record that literacy overall in the capital was at 57 percent of the adult population (the national figure was 50.3 percent), or on wages, which would allow for a more fine-tuned analysis.[24] Nonetheless, many have commented on the growth of a significant middle class in Chile in these years, a growth fueled in large measure by the expansion of the national government. According to one calculation, the number of government employees, many of whom were found in Santiago, grew from 3,000 in 1880, to 13,000 in 1900, to 28,000 in 1919.[25] Government employment, as mentioned, attracted many well-educated *provincianos* to the capital and was also the goal for an increasing number of university graduates, notably from the state-supported University of Chile, founded in the 1840s, and the private Universidad Católica, established in the late 1880s, and both located in the capital city. Also, as mentioned, foreigners were generally well represented in this category. In addition to their inclusion in the ranks of *comerciantes* and *empleados*, they were prominent among actors (24 percent) and artists (16 percent). Women, at least numerically, were important among *comerciantes* (13 percent) and *empleados* (27 percent).

The working classes made up the remainder of the social pyramid. By 1907, skilled workers, with the general classification of *artesano* (artisan) composing more than half the total, represented almost 20 percent of the city's workforce. Women (9 percent) and foreigners (4 percent) were scarcely represented in this category dominated by Chilean males. Farther down the ladder, however, as in Buenos Aires and elsewhere, women, mainly as dressmakers and seamstresses, made up 80 percent of the semi-skilled service category, and, as domestic servants and laundresses, 77 percent of the unskilled and menial category. In Santiago, however, unlike Buenos Aires, these women were almost all native-born.

In addition to basically urban occupations, the census also included categories that were labeled rural. This reflected the fact that even with the rapid growth of the capital, there were still pockets of rural activity on the outskirts of the city. The census listed some 5,047 *agricultores* (farmers), overwhelmingly Chilean males. Also predominantly Chilean and male were the 19,381 *gananes* listed in the rural semi-skilled category. *Gananes* were originally rural peons, known for their mobility, and who engaged in seasonal temporary work in Santiago, often as day laborers. Listing them in a "rural" category, therefore, reflects more their origins than the nature of their urban-based work activity.[26]

IN 1891 SANTIAGO, AS PART OF a larger national reconfiguration, was divided into new political jurisdictions. These included ten main districts, or *comunas*, further subdivided into twenty-seven *subdelegaciones*. The 1907 census has information that shows the significant growth of the western and northern districts, but does not provide the kind of data that allow for a more precise social mapping of the city. Other sources, however, help provide a general overall picture in this regard.

As was true at the time for many Latin American capitals, the elite concentrated in and dominated the main core of the downtown area. In Santiago, this meant the blocks adjacent to and surrounding the main square, the Plaza de Armas. A list of the city's leading property-tax payers and easily recognized members of the elite in 1899, for example, found Alberto Mackenna at San Antonio 214, Agustín Edwards at Catedral 1183, Ismael Tocornal at Huérfanos 1207, Francisco J. Subercaseaux at Ahumada 201, and Ramón Subercaseaux at Agustinas 934.[27] Tracing the residences of Chile's national senators and deputies in 1909, DeShazo found the same downtown concentration, with a substantial number of elite addresses along and near both sides of the Alameda.[28] As the city expanded westward, an area south of the Alameda, bounded by Avenida Blanco on the south, San Ignacio on the east, and Avenida España on the west, and including the Parque Cousiño (today the Parque O'Higgins, or O'Higgins Park) and the Club Hípico (racetrack), also became a decidedly upper-class neighborhood.[29]

Middle-class areas were more difficult to define. The fast-growing Yungay district in the western part of the city, perhaps best known for the statue of the heroic Chilean "*roto*" (the common man representative of the urban lower classes) in the Plaza Yungay, was also recognized for its middle-class character as well as its social diversity.[30] Nearby, Capuchinos, San Rafael, and Quinta Normal, as well as Ugarte in the southwest and Recoleta to the northeast, were also identified as containing numerous middle-class residences.[31]

Working-class districts were located mostly on the city's periphery, where housing costs were lower. In his study of the city's outskirts at the end of the nineteenth century, Chilean urban historian Armando de Ramón identified Arenal, northwest of the Mapocho, and Matadero and Escuela Italia to the south, as barrios of the "lower social sectors."[32] DeShazo also identified Matadero (including the municipal slaughterhouse, for which it was named) as a working-class neighborhood, along with the area bordering Avenida Matta, also on the south side of the city. While these were outlying districts, there were also working-class concentrations in the area just north and northwest of the main downtown (San Pablo) and just northeast of the Estación Central. Working-class districts also corresponded to the

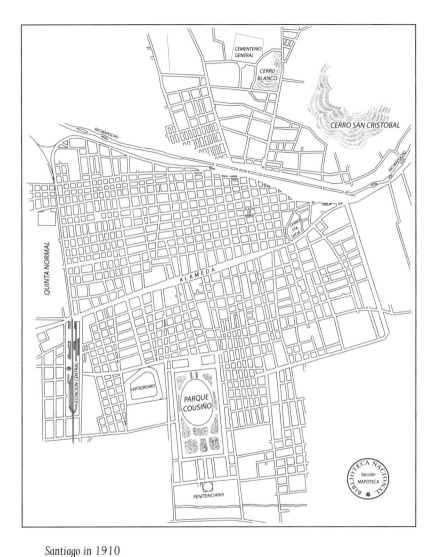

Santiago in 1910

SOURCE: Mapoteca, Biblioteca Nacional de Chile; adapted by Jeffrey Lancaster

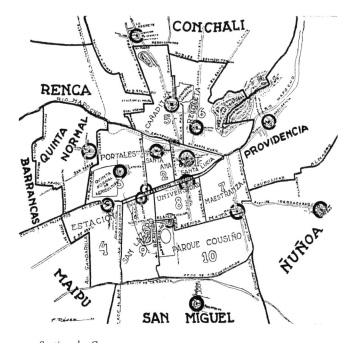

Santiago by Comuna
SOURCE: *El Mercurio* (April 3, 1938), p. 38

industrial growth of the period, with many workers living near their places of employment. By 1906, Santiago contained 1,100 industries, or 40 percent of the national total. Factories were scattered around the city, but many were located near rail lines and the main terminals.[33] As DeShazo observed, Santiago did not contain "a single working class neighborhood, but rather a series of them, some extensive, others small and isolated."[34] It appears, too, from general descriptions of the city, that while there were some clearly delineated wealthy and poor neighborhoods, there were also many parts of Santiago where there was considerable social diversity and where members of various classes lived within a few blocks (or on the same block) of each other. As in Buenos Aires and many other cities, some of the worst housing in Santiago could be found close by to some of the best.

IN MANY FUNDAMENTAL ASPECTS, the Chilean and Santiago upper class was similar to others of Latin America. Aside from the nineteenth-century immigrants from the British Isles, France, and Italy already referred to, most of its members were of Spanish descent and could trace their ancestry well back into the Spanish colonial period. Many upper-class families were prominent in the wars of independence. However, perhaps to a greater extent than in other Latin American countries, Basques predominated in elite ranks. One study found that 43 percent of 367 "aristocratic" names in Chile at the end of the eighteenth century came from the north and central-north of Spain. Two-thirds of those who arrived between 1751 and 1810 were from this area.[35] By 1882, there were fifty-nine millionaire families in Chile, with their fortunes based primarily on mining (gold, silver, copper, coal, nitrates), banking, commerce, industry, and land. In many cases, as with the Edwards, these families combined interests in various economic activities.[36] While the sources of their wealth lay primarily in the countryside, most, following the common Latin American pattern, lived in the capital in the areas already delineated. As the nation's economy expanded in the latter part of the nineteenth century, especially after Chile's victory over Peru and Bolivia in the War of the Pacific (1879–83) and the subsequent nitrate boom, the Santiago elite engaged in the conspicuous consumption of luxury items and, as with other Latin American elites, sought to imitate the lifestyles of the European aristocracy. One of the most visible and lasting aspects of this period of growth was the construction of some magnificent mansions in the center of Santiago, along the Alameda, and in the new upper-class district southwest of the Alameda. Similar to the upper-class residences found at the same time along Calle Florida and Avenida Alvear in Buenos Aires, these "palaces" were designed by European architects, usually French or Italian, and were filled with furnishings and decorations imported from the Old World. One of the most notable of these was the Palacio Cousiño, begun in the 1860s by Luis Cousiño, a Portuguese immigrant who had made his fortune in silver and coal mining, and completed in the 1870s after his death by his widow, Isidora Goyenechea. The Cousiño family sold their residence to the city of Santiago in 1941 to serve as a museum and to house visiting foreign dignitaries. French architect Paul Lathoud designed the mansion and Spanish landscaper Miguel Arana Borlca created the surrounding gardens.[37] The cost was two million dollars, "an unprecedented sum for the day."[38]

As in the rest of Latin America, the Chilean elite dominated most aspects of national life until challenged by new social forces in the early twentieth century. For most of this period, too, the aristocrats—or, less flattering, oligarchs—also dominated life in Santiago, where they controlled local as well as national government and largely determined and directed the capital's growth. The result was a city that was, at least in parts, very much theirs to enjoy, from the Teatro Municipal, with its dramatic and musical productions, to the Parque Cousiño, where, as in Buenos Aires's Parque Palermo, the upper class regularly paraded in elaborate horse-drawn carriages, to the Club Hípico, where horse racing became an upper-class obsession that eventually filtered down to the masses. While there were few explicit restrictions, many of the so-called "public" spaces created in these decades, including many new parks and plazas, were in practice "private" or by custom reserved for the elite.[39]

During these years, the elite developed, as one author put it, "complex social rituals" as part of their daily life in the capital. Mornings were occupied with strolling around the center of the city, stopping for an *"once"* (a snack taken at eleven in the morning, later transferred to teatime in the late afternoon) at a local bar or restaurant whose fashionableness and popularity with the elite fluctuated over time. Lunch was taken at home, then perhaps a siesta, and afterward, for women, visitors and tea while men frequented the stock exchange or their various clubs. When night fell, "the women dedicated themselves to home duties, or to devotions or pious activities, and the men began their 'night life,' which was scarce but monopolized by them [of the elite] . . . restaurants for late meals and clubs and gambling dens for gaming and systematic drinking," often followed by a visit to one of the capital's many brothels.[40] Another, tamer ritual took place in the late afternoon, when groups of young men congregated at the corner of Ahumada and Huérfanos, a block from the Plaza de Armas, "to watch the young ladies go by" and to offer flirtatious comments, a practice similar to one in Buenos Aires along the Calle Florida.[41]

For elite men, the most important of their downtown clubs, and the most exclusive, was the Club de la Unión, established in 1864 and comparable to the Jockey Club in Buenos Aires as well as others. In the 1890s the club was located at Estado and Huérfanos, again near the Plaza de Armas. In 1912 it acquired terrain on the Alameda, and when the new structure was completed in 1925 it became a major landmark of the city. In 1907 the rival Club de Santiago opened at Agustinas between Ahumada and Estado, also in the center of the city. It had a reputation for "racier" pursuits for a generally younger membership than its more staid rival.[42]

For most of the middle class, this upper-class lifestyle was a distant dream. Government employees, shopkeepers, clerks, students, and small businessmen often had to struggle to hide their genteel poverty. And, of course, they did not live in palaces but rather often rented rooms in boarding houses or *pensiones*. Over time, builders responded to middle-class housing needs with blocks of rather undistinguished and simple but affordable and reasonably hygienic dwellings in areas on the capital's periphery. Closer to the center appeared what were called *cités*, "a collection of small, two or three-room brick apartments which opened onto a small corridor leading to a single street entrance . . . [and which] normally contained a private bathroom and a place to cook."[43] While it is difficult to generalize about such a diverse social group, Chilean historian Gonzálo Vial Correa has argued that at the turn of the century a strong sense of middle-class resentment against the upper classes began to emerge, fueled by the significant disparity in wealth and lifestyle between the two groups as well as a clear aristocratic disdain for the parvenus who would aspire to their status. It was among the middle sectors, too, Vial asserts, that a xenophobic nationalism became most pronounced in these years.[44]

Whatever the gulf between the upper and middle classes, it paled in comparison to the distance between the elite and Santiago's working classes. Although they shared the same city, it was as though they lived in what were two different worlds. As was common at the time throughout Latin America and elsewhere, Santiago's working classes labored long hours for low wages in dangerous and unsanitary conditions with little protection and no "safety net" of benefits in case of illness or accident. In Santiago, as in Buenos Aires, the most common proletarian dwelling was the *conventillo*, or slum tenement. While Santiago's *conventillos*, unlike those of Buenos Aires, were not former homes of the elite, they had the same structure of a subdivided one- or two-story residence built around a central courtyard with a single entrance to the street. As in Buenos Aires, they usually lacked running water, adequate sanitary facilities, and proper heating and lighting. In 1925 the U.S. ambassador to Chile visited several *conventillos* in Santiago and wrote to Washington the following observations:

It is impossible to exaggerate in talking of the insalubrity and lack of sanitation of the great majority of Chilean houses. A vast number of the population live in *conventillos* . . . , where in rooms not over fifteen feet square are families averaging four persons, sometimes numbering eight, are [sic] huddled together. Rarely is there either gas or electric light or running water. The cooking is generally done on stoves placed on a platform in the narrow corridor used in common by all the tenants. The laundry is done in portable tubs put in the same corridor. Water closet facilities are limited to the maximum. On a recent visit . . . we noticed that the water closet facilities are two seats for one hundred and twenty people. The sanitary arrangements of these closets were almost unspeakable. The housing problem is the greatest that confronts Chile.[45]

In 1911 it was estimated that about 40 percent of Santiago's population lived in *conventillos*.[46] In 1906 a national mortgage office (the Caja de Crédito Hipotecario) was created to stimulate the development of public housing, and in 1911 two projects were inaugurated in Santiago. One was the Población Huemul, located about eight blocks south of the Alameda and a few blocks southeast of the Palacio Cousiño, and the other, the Población San Eugenio, west of the Club Hípico.[47] While noble efforts, these *poblaciones* accommodated only a few hundred families at most and went only a very small way to address a very large and continuing problem.

While workers in Santiago shared many of the same living and working conditions as their contemporaries in Buenos Aires, they also suffered disproportionately from some more severe social conditions to be described below. And, while conservatives in Chile, as in Argentina, debated the very existence of a "social question," working-class groups in Santiago, as in Buenos Aires under anarchist influence, began to organize to protest and to try to improve their situation through unionization and strike activity. Throughout the first decade of the twentieth century, Santiago, like Buenos Aires, was the scene of increasing labor agitation and militancy.[48]

MOST FOREIGN VISITORS TO SANTIAGO neither visited *conventillos* nor commented much on the social conditions of the poor. Instead, they described in generally favorable terms the ongoing modernization of the capital, especially in the main downtown area.

At the heart of the city, as it was in colonial times and remains today, was the main square, or Plaza de Armas. Following the pattern of such plazas throughout the Hispanic world, it featured the main cathedral with the archbishop's palace on its west side. On the north side was a distinguished group of governmental buildings originating, like the cathedral, in the colonial period. From east to west on the north side were the colonial governmental palace, remodeled in 1910 to serve, as it still does, as the main post office; the palace of the *audiencia real*, today the National Historical Museum; and the colonial *cabildo*, reconstructed in 1891 and serving then until the present as City Hall (the Casa Consistorial). On the remaining sides were arcaded buildings housing shops, restaurants, and hotels, with the Portal Mac-Clure on the east, and the Portal Fernández Concha on the south.

Foreign opinions of the plaza were generally positive. Writing in 1890 in *Harper's Magazine*, U.S. visitor Theodore Child enthused over the pleasant ambience of the plaza, with its "comfortable proportions and adorned with beautiful plants that provide an attractive aspect and an exquisite perfumed aroma."[49] In 1914 British visitor Francis J. G. Maitland commented that, "This square, with its vistas, east to the distant Andes, and west to the Cordilleras, with its well-designed central garden, is a charming spot, and conveys a distinctly good impression to the newly arrived traveler."[50] For Maitland and others, however, the buildings around the plaza lacked architectural distinction, which "by no means satisfy the fastidious taste." Maitland attributed this lack of style to fear of destruction by earthquake.[51] For fellow Englishman G. F. Scott Elliot, "The Plaza de Armas has colonnades along the side which are famous in Chilean history, but is possibly a little disappointing. Most of the other public buildings though fine and magnificent, do not show any very distinctive character."[52]

Foreigners were quick to note the plaza's role as social center for the capital's elite. Maitland wrote, "In the afternoon, from five to six, it is the rendezvous of the Chilean smart set, and 'tis here that those must come who would see the *beldades* (fair ones) of Santiago at their best."[53] Drawing the wrong conclusion, given the growing number of strikes in Santiago at the time, Elliot made the interesting observation that, "There does not seem to be much jealousy or ill-feeling between the upper and lower classes in Chile, for the masses keep to a different part of the Plaza, and do not intrude upon the pacing-ground of the richer, or better-dressed people."[54] This comment reinforces the notion of upper-class appropriation of supposedly public spaces in Santiago.

While reviews of the Plaza de Armas were sometimes mixed, foreigners were virtually unanimous in their praise of Santa Lucía Park and the Alameda. U.S. explorer Hiram Bingham, attending the First Pan-American Scientific Congress, held in Santiago in 1908, observed, "Santa Lucía is now a wonderfully attractive park with fine driveways, well-made paths that command splendid panoramas of the city, plain, and mountains, and a theatre and restaurant on its summit. The view is remarkably fine."[55] Bingham might also have remarked that every day, from the summit, a cannon was fired to mark the noon hour, a practice that continues to the present. With regard to the Alameda, British visitor W. H. Koebel, writing in 1913, described it as "a very fine street . . . [that] runs in a direct line for almost three miles and . . . must be one of the widest in the world. . . . Down the centre extends a broad belt of trees—oak, poplar, plane, and others of Chilean growth. The centre space thus pleasantly shaded—stocked moreover with statues, fountains and similar ornamentations—is in itself far wider than the average street of a city, and the outlook from the buildings on either hand is thus delightful."[56] Robert Mansfield called the Alameda "one of the finest avenues in the world."[57]

Along the Alameda, then as now, could be found some of the city's most important and finest buildings. The most famous, and most important, was the presidential palace, known popularly as La Moneda, since it had been formerly the colonial mint. Other attractive and notable structures were the main buildings of the National University and the Catholic University; the Church of San Francisco, the city's oldest; the previously mentioned Club de la Unión; and, completed in the 1920s, the Biblioteca Nacional (National Library) at the foot of Santa Lucía. Various private residences also graced the Alameda, including the neoclassical Palacio Errázuriz. Completed in 1872 and considered "the best residence of its era" at the time, it is today the Brazilian embassy.[58]

In this era, in addition to the Alameda, the streets leading into the Plaza de Armas also began to take on a more modern air. They became the sites of an increasing number of public buildings, banks, restaurants, hotels, theaters, movie houses, and commercial establishments. In 1910 the British-owned and -operated department store Gath y Chavés, also located in Buenos Aires, opened its doors to the public. Located at the corner of Estado and Huérfanos, a block from the Plaza de Armas, it was "the first multi-story construction in Santiago dedicated solely to commerce."[59] The *Baedecker of Chile of 1910* guide mentioned Gath y Chavés, as well as "Simon y Cía, Muzard, Burgalata, Pra, Novedades Parisienes, and many others where one can find all manner of goods, forming a nucleus of great commercial movement in the city center."[60] By that same year, Santiago had replaced Valparaíso as the commercial center of the nation.[61]

There were other signs of progress. Telephones, the telegraph, and national mail service had been introduced in the mid-nineteenth century, and in the 1880s the first electric lights brightened certain areas of the capital's downtown. By the turn of the century, most downtown streets had been paved with asphalt. Paving, however, did not extend much beyond the central core, and many commented on how dusty much of Santiago was. Paving issues were a main governmental concern and often a source of considerable political and public dispute when struggles occurred over which areas would be paved and when.

A major symbol of Santiago's advance was the introduction in 1900 of the electric streetcar, one of the first such systems in South America. The initial lines were inaugurated on September 2 of that year and by 1903 the city had 275 electric cars covering 97 kilometers of track, effectively replacing the old horse-drawn system installed in 1864.[62] Also at the turn of the century, the *ferrocarril de circunvalación* (circumferential railroad), providing rail transport in a belt around the city south of the Mapocho, was finished. By 1910, then, the combination of streetcars, trains, and horse-drawn vehicles on the outskirts had provided Santiago with a widespread and diversified system of modern public transportation. Nonetheless, reflecting an ongoing dispute, U.S. visitor Arthur Ruhl reported in 1908 that at least one newspaper editor with whom he spoke was "constrained to admit that the Electric Traction Company is giving abominable service."[63]

In 1910, Chile, like Argentina, celebrated the centennial of its independence from Spain. Santiago, like Buenos Aires, hosted international conferences and distinguished foreign visitors. Public buildings were refurbished and renovated, new parks and monuments were inaugurated to commemorate the occasion, and various social events marked the capital's and the nation's growth over the previous years.[64] Various foreign visitors, some commenting in the years prior to the celebration and others during and just after, were able to offer some comparisons between Santiago and other South

American capitals at the time. The aforementioned Arthur Ruhl, for example, writing in 1908, said of Santiago that, "It has many newspapers, the best quite as good as those of cities of similar size at home, a large university, many academies and schools, parks, and an art museum. Its citizens ride in trolley-cars, go to the theatre and opera and horse races, and talk to one another and Valparaíso over the telephone. There is at least one hotel well-kept and comfortable, and equal to what one would find in an average city of similar size on the Continent." Comparing Santiago with Lima, he found the Chilean capital more advanced, but suffering when matched against the progress achieved in Buenos Aires.[65] Visiting at about the same time, Hiram Bingham made much the same observation, arguing that, "In such matters as magnificent hotels, expensive restaurants, luxurious clubs, and showy automobiles, Santiago readily yields the palm to Buenos Aires."[66] While not comparing Santiago to Buenos Aires, England's Lord Bryce saw Santiago as being much advanced over Lima and La Paz and as a place where "prosperity and confidence are in the air."[67] Nonetheless, the competition with Buenos Aires was keenly felt among Santiago's leaders, and observations that placed it above the capitals of Bolivia and Peru offered little comfort.

Not all foreign observers were as complimentary as those quoted above. Juan Gabriel Serrado, whose *Visita a Chile en 1895* was published in Buenos Aires several years later, emphasized the lack of proper street cleaning, garbage collection, and sewage disposal in Santiago, leading at certain hours to the dispersion of "pestilent odors" in a city that was "supremely filthy."[68] Similar comments came from Albert Malsch, who visited the country from 1904 to 1906 and whose account, *Le dernier recoin du monde: Deux ans au Chili*, published in Geneva in 1907, advised travelers to skip Santiago altogether. There, he warned, one would find only 200,000 "*rotos*" living in the city's slums, as well as crime, drunkenness, and disease, along with *acequias*, or irrigation ditches, that ran through the city streets and served as depositories for waste matter. Except for the center, the rest of the city was, for him, "that indescribable sewer to which I already have referred."[69] An anonymous letter from a North American tourist, found by an enterprising journalist in a local bookstore, gave an account of a very unpleasant stay wherein the visitor, upon arrival at the Central Station, was soon covered with dust, insulted as a *gringo bruto*, and robbed in the street. He could not wait to leave Santiago and vowed never to return.[70] Finally, Robert Mansfield, in a work published in 1913, after commenting on the homes of the wealthy, observed that, "The life of the poor people in Santiago, the manner in which they live, their customs and habits, the misery and vice, the depravity, the disregard for law, and the low level of intelligence that prevails, form a sharp contrast to the picture presented in the homes of the rich."[71]

THE SHARP CONTRAST BETWEEN rich and poor was common to all Latin American capitals at the turn of the century.[72] Nonetheless, some of the social conditions prevailing in Santiago seemed particularly appalling, especially given Chile's generally "progressive" image, its relatively stable and democratic political system, and its aspirations, after the War of the Pacific, to be considered not only the dominant nation of South America's Pacific Coast but also a leader of Latin America generally.[73]

One of the most notable problems, both locally and nationally, was the prevalence of epidemic diseases. In the late nineteenth and early twentieth centuries, the capital was afflicted by periodic outbreaks of cholera, smallpox, yellow fever, and, most commonly and most persistently, typhoid fever, all of which took tens of thousands of lives. Childhood diseases such as whooping cough, measles, diphtheria, and influenza were also common killers, as were tuberculosis and syphilis.

The causes for disease were not difficult to find. The crowded and unsanitary conditions of the *conventillos* in which so many of Santiago's poor lived made for perfect breeding grounds for germs and unavoidable contagion. The capital lacked both a sure supply of safe drinking water and a comprehensive sewer system throughout the first two decades of the twentieth century. As Malsch noted, *acequias* were used as toilets. Garbage collection was sporadic at best. Often, what garbage was collected was thrown along the banks of or into the Mapocho, polluting the capital's main river. In other instances, garbage was burned in open fields, contributing to the dust and haze that were constant features of the Santiago skyline and helping to spread infectious microbes through the air. Personal hygiene, even among the well-to-do, left much to be desired. With regard to sanitation and hygiene in general, a publication in 1910 claimed that, "We do not believe that there exists today in the world a human agglomeration that finds itself in more horrible conditions than those that afflict the capital of Chile."[74]

There were attempts to deal with these public health problems through vaccination campaigns and the building of additional hospitals and clinics. In Chile, as in other parts of Latin America, however, there was some resistance to vaccination and hospitals served only to treat the symptoms not the causes of ill health. In 1904 the city government did create free public health clinics in each *comuna*, where patients could receive a doctor's care, and thousands did so. However, as DeShazo argues, while "some form of free medical care was available to working people, . . . few took advantage of it, either because they did not know that these services existed or because they were unwilling or unable to present themselves for treatment."[75]

Another contributing factor to poor health was the increasing cost and frequent scarcity of food. According to one account, between 1882 and 1912 the price of flour, bread, and butter in Chile increased by a little over 200 percent, that of rice 400 percent, beans over 700 percent, and potatoes a whopping 1,900 percent.[76] The reasons behind the increases were varied and complex. They included poor domestic food production due to the latifundia system, natural disasters, inadequate transportation facilities, monetary changes that increased the price of imported food or made exports attractive, leading to scarcities, and speculation by intermediaries. A constant complaint from consumers was the manner of buying, selling, and distributing foodstuffs from the municipally operated Vega Central on the north side of the Mapocho. There, wholesalers often brought large quantities of food, which they bought cheaply from producers and sold dearly in small lots to retailers, who charged their hard-pressed customers even more.[77] Whatever the reasons, the high cost of food made it difficult for many families, especially working families, to maintain a healthy diet. A related problem was the frequent lack and poor quality of milk, a particularly important issue for infant nutrition.

Alcoholism, especially among the working classes, was another major problem. The abundance and easy accessibility of cheap wine, the large number of bars and cantinas, the oppressive working and living conditions, and the lack of a proper diet all contributed to an environment that encouraged drunkenness. Sunday benders were so common that by the turn of the century one estimate had it that six out of ten workers were unable to report to their employers on Monday, which came to be known as another day of rest, or "San Lunes," Saint Monday.[78] Alcoholism was itself a disease and, in addition to its consequences for family members (it was mostly men who suffered from the affliction), made the alcoholic all that more susceptible to other diseases.

An additional social ill was prostitution. Brothels were prevalent throughout the city and attracted a clientele that included males from all social groups. A report from the Santiago office in charge of regulating prostitution in 1900 listed about 2,400 prostitutes in the city, which probably represented only 15 to 20 percent of the total. Of these, most were single, although a few were married or widowed. They were overwhelmingly Chilean and between the ages of 18 and 35. About two-thirds had been either seamstresses or domestics before becoming prostitutes, and about two-thirds were illiterate.[79]

A constant concern throughout this period was the prevalence of crime in Santiago, especially in peripheral, working-class neighborhoods. While the incidence of crime, especially violent crime, was less in the capital than in mining areas or the countryside, there was a generalized fear of attacks and robberies. As this excerpt from a Santiago newspaper indicates, there was little confidence in the police to control illegal activity: "The criminality in Santiago is awful; the police are still totally impotent to pursue and catch criminals . . . in our streets and homes, robberies and assaults are a daily occurrence, and, finally, there is no large gathering, be it a military parade or some other kind of celebration, in which the general public maintains the proper decorum, despite the efforts of our police in this regard."[80]

Of all Santiago's social ills, none were more heartrending than those that involved children, many of whom were from homes where mother and father were not legally married. For Chile as a whole, for example, in 1903, of 115,524 live births, 41,928 were illegitimate.[81] In that same year in Santiago, according to DeShazo, "49 percent of all births were illegitimate."[82] Due to the prevalence of disease, poor living conditions, inadequate nutrition, and ignorance, Chile had the highest infant mortality rate in Spanish America and one of the highest in the world. While there were some improvements in this regard over the first decades of the twentieth century, still, by 1928 one in four (as compared with one in three at the beginning of the century) live births in Santiago ended in death before the first year of life was completed.[83] Those who did survive often had to suffer abuse at home from alcoholic fathers, forcing them to join others in the open street. Vagrant and abandoned children were common sights in Santiago throughout these years. Others worked in low-paying and dangerous factory jobs.[84] Few had the benefit of any education beyond the rudimentary primary level, if that.

As this brief review of Santiago's social problems shows, the city was still far from the "civilized" and "modern" status to which its leaders aspired. While it was probably not as "progressive" as its admirers proclaimed, or as "backward" as its detractors stated, it was not yet the "Paris of South America" that many of its leaders wanted it to be. The primary responsibility for fulfilling those dreams and aspirations fell to both the national and local government. The following chapter will describe these efforts at the local level during a period when municipal politics and government underwent what were hoped to be some fundamental changes to address some of these problems.

2 The First Decades of Municipal Autonomy (1891-1910)

THE YEAR 1891 WAS AN EVENTFUL ONE in Chilean history. A violent and bloody civil war that began in January and ended in August overthrew Liberal president José Manuel Balmaceda and interrupted a tradition of peaceful presidential succession that had been established in the 1830s.[1] Constitutional normality was quickly restored, and for the next three decades the tradition of regular presidential rotation through election resumed. However, as a result of the war, impelled by opposition to Balmaceda's assertive use of executive power, most of these presidents were weak. The National Congress of the Senate and the Chamber of Deputies, in which various parties formed shifting coalitions and stymied presidential initiatives, dominated. The period came to be known, as a result, as that of the "Parliamentary Republic."[2]

At the local level, the most important consequence of the revolt against Balmaceda was the establishment of municipal autonomy. Prior to the 1880s, municipalities had been under the direct control of the national government, with presidentially appointed *intendentes*, or provincial governors, serving as their chief executives, and *alcaldes*, or mayors, relegated to minor administrative tasks. A law in 1887 had established the election of *alcaldes*, and in December 1891, promoted by Conservative José Miguel Irarrazaval, who in turn was inspired by Swiss and U.S. examples, the law of municipal autonomy had been approved as part of the general movement away from centralized national executive authority.[3]

For Santiago, the reform meant the election every three years of thirty *regidores* (councilmen, or aldermen), three from each of the ten *comunas* into which the capital was divided. From their own ranks, after being sworn in, they elected three *alcaldes* to serve through the first sessions of the municipality, sessions which ran from the first of May of one year until the end of April of the next, usually, but not always, with a substantial summer vacation break in January, February, and much of March. The First Alcalde (*primer alcalde*) served as the presiding officer and the capital's chief executive. If he was unable to preside, the Second Alcalde normally assumed that duty, and if he, in turn, could not be present, that responsibility fell to the Third Alcalde. If the First Alcalde should resign, the Second Alcalde became the presiding officer until new elections could be held. Upon resignation, the *alcaldes* simply went back to being *regidores*. Elections were held for *alcaldes* when the new sessions began each year in May. As we shall see, it was rare for *alcaldes* to be reelected.

What to call the local government poses some problems of nomenclature. When they assembled, the *regidores* constituted the Ilustre Municipalidad de Santiago (Illustrious Municipality of Santiago), and they often identified themselves during their deliberations as the Sala, or meeting hall. They were often labeled in the press as the Municipality, but that does not distinguish them from the larger city administration as a whole. In U.S. terms, they made up what we would call the city council or board of aldermen, with the office of First Alcalde corresponding to that of Mayor and the *regidores* corresponding to councilmen or aldermen. In this work, these terms will be used interchangeably.

While autonomy promised more authority, there were also important checks and balances. After 1891, the *regidores* had to share power with what were called Asambleas de Electores (Assemblies of Electors), composed "of all eligible voters within the commune [meaning the city as a whole]" and "charged with electing the municipal officials as well as with approving the municipal budget, municipal taxation and municipal loans. In addition, they had to approve all municipal agreements and ordinances sanctioning fines."[4] At the same time, however, municipal governments gained virtual total control over the election process at all levels, as they were "charged with registering voters, naming the polling officials, and administering the elections proper."[5] While such control gave the city government enhanced authority, it also proved to be quite time-consuming and contentious, as frequent partisan disputes colored almost every aspect of the registration, oversight, and balloting process.

Within the context of these changes, Chile's by now well-established multiparty system flourished, as various political parties vied for dominance at both the national and local level. Among them were the Conservatives, who traced their roots back to the early nineteenth century and represented the interests of the wealthy and the Catholic Church. The Liberals, also essentially representing the well-to-do, had battled the Conservatives historically over issues of church–state relations (they favored greater separation between the two) and centralized authority (they sought to weaken it) throughout the century. In the 1890s, they were divided into the mainline Liberal Democrats, the followers of Balmaceda, and the Nationals (or Montt-Varistas), who associated themselves with the regime of President Manuel Montt and his minister of the interior during the 1850s, Antonio Varas. The Radical Party, formed in the 1860s as a provincial reaction against the centralized control of Conservatives and Liberals in Santiago, had close ties to Masonism and was strongly anticlerical. As time progressed, it became the principal party to represent the evolving middle classes of Chile, similar to its counterpart in Argentina. Finally, organized in the 1880s, the Democratic Party sought initially to speak for and mobilize the working classes under artisan and middle-class leadership. Initially somewhat militant and confrontational, it gradually became more moderate and accommodationist. In some respects, it paralleled the Socialist Party of Argentina.[6]

The first elections for the municipality of Santiago under the new autonomy law in which these various parties could compete would not occur until 1894. In the municipal elections of 1891, however, held on October 18 concurrent with national elections for Congress and president, Santiago voters chose twenty-five *regidores* on a citywide basis. While the new law was yet to take effect, the 1891 election proceeded under a reform approved in August of the preceding year. That reform provided for a closely supervised registration of voters in subdelegations of no more than 150 citizens each, a cumulative vote for *regidores*, a secret ballot, and other procedures to safeguard against undue influence, as well as independent election boards (*juntas escrutadoras*) to supervise the process and to count the ballots. The purpose of the reform, crafted in Congress as part of the resistance to Balmaceda, was "to assure a complete independence of the electoral machinery from the Executive and his agents."[7]

Campaigning took place in a decidedly anti-Balmaceda atmosphere. (The ousted president, who had found refuge in the Argentine embassy, had taken his own life on September 19.) In the weeks prior to the election, all parties except the Liberal Democrats, associated with Balmaceda, held meetings, selected candidates, and engaged in active campaigning. The Democrats, in a manifesto to their followers, claimed they were not the kind of socialists who advocated the sort of class division and antagonism they alleged Balmaceda had promoted. During the recent civil war, they reminded the public, they had supported the Constitution and the law: "We believed that in those circumstances, we were neither a party nor partisans: we were Chileans." Their socialism, they averred, was that of defending "the sovereignty of the people, universal suffrage, freedom of the press."[8] The Democrats said nothing explicitly at this time about workers' rights or some of the pressing social issues of the day.

The Radicals offered a detailed program for these elections. They advocated municipal autonomy based on an adequate and independent financial base, the construction of a modern sewer system connected to every house, the overall paving of the city's streets, the creation of a professional police force, an extension and lowering of the price of potable water and public lighting, a uniform building code, municipal regulation of housing to assure its salubriousness, strict regulation of establishments that dispensed alcohol to assure that minors not be served, promotion of public gardens, the formation of registers for domestic servants to assure they were fairly treated and compensated, and the creation under municipal control of savings associations that would "alleviate the situation of the working class and defend them against the abuses of private businesses."[9] Signed by party leader Enrique Mac-Iver, the Radical program was notable for its specificity in addressing the city's main problems in a clear and straightforward manner. Reports of Liberal and Conservative rallies revealed no such attention to programmatic detail.[10]

While most campaigning was carried on by established parties, independent non-affiliated groups representing particular interests or neighborhoods also participated. For example, voters in Subdelegations 26 and 27 met on October 16 and endorsed the Liberal Alliance candidacy of Manuel Barros Borgoño, who would represent "the barrio and *industriales* [perhaps meaning "workers," in this context] of Matadero."[11] On the same page of the newspaper *El Ferrocarril* that reported this meeting was an ad that called for the supporters of Independent candidate Dr. Wenceslao Hidalgo to assemble for rallies on that Friday and Saturday (the election was on Sunday) at Alameda 263.[12] As it turned out, both Barros Borgoño and Hidalgo were elected.

This first post-Balmaceda election received high marks as a clean and fair contest. On election day, *El Ferrocarril* viewed it as "the first attempt at a free popular election under the safeguards of a governing committee [*junta de gobierno*], in which are represented all the historic parties of our political world, under the common banner of official non-intervention."[13] After the election, the same newspaper hailed it as the freest and fairest in the nation's history, carried out with "correct and satisfactory regularity," and "corresponding to the patriotic expectations that inspired the fundamental reform of our electoral system."[14] Chosen as *regidores* for Santiago, of those whose party affiliation could be identified, were fourteen Conservatives, three members of the Liberal Alliance, three Radicals, one Democrat, and one Independent. The leading vote-getter was Arturo Cousiño of the Liberal Alliance, who received 11,578 tallies. Most elected *regidores* averaged around 4,000 votes.[15]

The next municipal election took place three years later, under the provisions of the new autonomy law. It was held on the first Sunday in March, as would be all subsequent contests, and, as mentioned, candidates ran from *comunas* rather than citywide. Three candidates from each of the ten *comunas* were elected to serve, as in the past, for a three-year term. As the population of *comunas* and the number of eligible voters (literate Chilean males over the age of twenty-one) varied, it was possible to be elected with a relative handful of votes. In 1894, for example, Conservative Raimundo Valdés was chosen *regidor* from the Fourth Comuna with only 189 votes.[16] Valdés, moreover, was the only *regidor* from those selected in 1891 to be reelected. Among the notable features of this contest was the strong showing of the Balmacedist Liberal Democrats, who captured ten seats (see Table 2), paralleling an equally impressive performance in national congressional elections, where they won four senate and twenty-four deputy seats.[17]

TABLE 2. *Regidores of the Municipality of Santiago by Party, 1891–1909*

Party	1891	1894	1897	1900	1903	1906	1909
Conservative	14	9	10	6	8	7	6
Liberal		7		8	1	2	1
Liberal Alliance	3		1		2		
Liberal Democratic		10				6	6
Balmacedista			12				4
Liberal Errazurista			2				
Liberal Democrat Vicuñista				4			
Liberal Democrat Sanfuentista				1			
Moderate Liberal					4		
Independent Liberal							1
National			1			6	7
Radical	3	3	3	7	3	1	8
Democratic	1	1	1	3		6	2
Independent	1			1		2	
Unknown	3				6		1

SOURCE: BMS, 1891–1909.

One clear result of the 1891 reform was to make Santiago's municipal elections quite competitive. While Conservatives clearly dominated in that year, as Table 2 indicates, various other parties had substantial representation in the local government between 1894 and 1909 and often thereafter. Conservatives were reduced to just one other party among several keen competitors. Also, from 1894 forward it was fairly common for a number of the *regidores* to become well established in their particular *comunas* and to be rather regularly returned to the Casa Consistorial. The number of reelected candidates in these years ranged between six and ten out of the total of thirty. Liberal Julio Novoa Gormaz, for example, was reelected four times from the First Comuna after his initial victory in 1894. Liberal Democrat Pedro A. Herrera won election three times as a *regidor* from the Ninth Comuna between 1894 and 1900. Radical Rogelio Ugarte began a remarkable municipal career that would span almost half a century in 1900 with three straight elections as a *regidor* from the Seventh Comuna. It seems likely that the rate of reelection would have been even higher if leading *regidores* had not moved on to congressional positions, a common occurrence throughout this period.

Then, as now, municipal office was seen as a logical and important stepping-stone to the national stage.

While party and candidate interest in local elections was high, voter interest, at least in these years, was not. Generally, even though municipal contests in Santiago were held congruent with national contests, voter participation was generally lower. In 1897, for example, an editorial in *El Ferrocarril* lamented the fact that of the 150 voters registered at each polling place, only 60 to 80 had bothered to cast their ballots, leaving poll workers with little to do for most of the day.[18] The lower turnout in Santiago for municipal as opposed to national elections compares with the same phenomenon in Buenos Aires and elsewhere.

THE FIRST MUNICIPALITY ELECTED according to the 1891 provisions, that of 1894–97, established patterns that would persist. Installed on May 6, 1894, the new *regidores* elected Liberal Santiago Polloni as First Alcalde, Liberal Democrat Agustín Boza Lillo as Second Alcalde, and Conservative Raimundo Valdés as Third Alcalde.[19] While these three choices reflected the influence of the three major parties represented in the municipality at the time, they were not chosen according to numerical weight but rather, presumably, as a result of certain compromises and agreements among shifting coalitions. This would often be the case.

The First Alcalde, as mentioned, in essence served as the mayor of the city. One of his main duties was to preside over regular meetings of the *regidores*. These were held in the Casa Consistorial on the Plaza de Armas, usually at least once a week in the early evening and were open to the public. However, the assembled *regidores* could also vote to hold secret sessions on what they considered to be sensitive issues and the *alcalde* could also call extraordinary sessions, which could be either public or private. Extraordinary sessions were usually held to discuss particularly urgent matters and could take place on a daily basis when deadlines loomed. This was especially common during the annual consideration of the following year's budget, which often took place either at the end of December (the end of the calendar year) or in the last days of April, before the inauguration of the following year's sessions and the election of presiding officers.

Although the First Alcalde held office only temporarily, sometimes very temporarily, he was chief executive of a more permanent bureaucracy. This included two city attorneys, the municipal secretary, the city treasurer, and various department heads (Sanitation, Parks and Gardens, Water, Public Works, and directors of the Municipal Market and Slaughterhouse) and their respective employees. The *alcalde* could recommend the dismissal and replacement of members of the permanent bureaucracy, but at this time most of these personnel decisions had to be approved by the *regidores* as well as the Taxpayers' Assembly. Positions in the city government, as in the national government, were often highly coveted as secure and reasonably well-paying jobs, especially at the higher levels. Hence, appointments were subject to considerable partisan pressure, as the various competing parties sought to reward their "clientele" with municipal employment. These demands, in turn, subjected the First Alcalde to various countervailing pressures and often trapped him in a no-win situation. It was most often disputes over personnel and rewarding the party faithful that led to the resignation of the First Alcalde, a common occurrence in these years. Unlike the case of independently-selected or -elected executives, however, the former First Alcalde would not exit the scene completely, but rather he would commonly be returned to the ranks of the *regidores*, albeit usually somewhat embittered and disillusioned.

The 1891 law bestowed upon the city government of Santiago certain major responsibilities. Previously, the policing of the city had been under the authority of the Ministry of Interior. Now, it would be a local duty. In addition, as an editorial in El Ferrocarril of March 13, 1894, reminded its readers, the municipality would be in charge of "health, hygiene, beautification, and recreation; streets and public works; morality, security, and public order; construction on public streets; sanitation and industrial works, accident prevention, maintenance of good customs, regulation of spectacles and entertainments, the regulation and inspection of all services, the promotion of education and welfare, and the establishment and maintenance of all that which would encourage comfort, enlightenment, or development of the multiple elements of social activity and general interest."[20] All in all, a rather imposing list. In the same editorial, El Ferrocarril urged the various parties that made up the new city government to avoid partisan disputes and to work in common for the good of the capital so as to justify the confidence that had been placed in local administration as a result of the 1891 reform. This was a plea often evoked but seldom heeded.

One of the most significant consequences of the multiparty system within the city council and the partisan disputes that resulted was the difficulties they produced for the First Alcaldes. As mentioned, few *alcaldes* were able to keep a governing coalition in the majority and most were forced to resign before their three-year term expired. Some stepped down after only a few months. The case of Ignacio Marchant is fairly typical of many that could be cited for this period.

Marchant, a member of the National Party, was chosen First Alcalde in 1909 by a comfortable majority. During his first few months in office, the municipality agreed to contract a loan of 1,200,000 pesos to pay the floating debt of the city, approved new traffic regulations, and, in an attempt to deal with the continuing problem of alcoholism, issued a new set of regulations governing the operation of cantinas. At the end of the year, Marchant's supporters pointed to these and other accomplishments, including an increase in the number of street cleaners, new expropriations for street widening, and the hiring of only essential employees during his administration, as proof of his efficacy as *alcalde*. They also gave him credit for the fact that the National Congress had agreed to increase the rate of the capital's property tax from 2 pesos per 1,000 of assessed value to 3 pesos per 1,000, an important boost to the city's main revenue base.[21] Whatever the praise from his adherents, however, the voices of his critics had been sufficient for Marchant to present, and then withdraw, his resignation as the year drew to a close.

In late April 1910, Marchant submitted his budget proposal for the subsequent year. He proposed to let go more than 100 employees but those remaining would receive a salary increase of 11½ percent. More importantly, thanks to the new property tax rate, the city could be expected to bring in 3 million pesos more than in the previous year, with the prospect of a surplus rather than the chronic deficit that the city usually experienced.[22] Whether because of this good fiscal news or for other reasons, Marchant pulled off the enviable feat of being reelected as First Alcalde when new sessions started in May, only the second *alcalde* to have managed this over the previous two decades. The vote for him was a solid 22 to 1 with 5 abstentions. Spokesmen for the Conservative, Radical, and Liberal parties expressed their enthusiastic support and promised full cooperation. More ominously, however, Regidor Columbano Recabarren, of Marchant's own National Party, said that after initially backing the *alcalde*, he had broken with him over patronage issues and would keep a close watch over his future actions. Speaking for the Liberal Democrats, Augusto Vicuña Subercaseaux refused to join in either the praise for or attacks on the *alcalde*, but did observe that, in his opinion, Marchant "had not dedicated himself with enthusiasm to the administrative tasks of the Municipality, perhaps for lack of time to do so." So long as Marchant avoided a "government of friends" and did show enthusiasm for the job, Vicuña Subercaseaux and his party would lend their support. If this proved not to be the case, the Liberal Democrats would be the first to bring it to public attention.[23]

An opportunity to question the *alcalde* was not long in coming. On July 15, Independent Liberal Carlos Ureta introduced a motion of no-confidence in Marchant. In so doing, he pointed primarily to the manner in which the *alcalde* had submitted his budget in late April, which Ureta alleged had left no room for discussion, essentially forcing the budget down the *regidores'* throats. Ureta also argued that the municipality's finances were not as healthy as Marchant had suggested and that the proposed budget would leave the city with a 300,000 peso deficit rather than the surplus that Marchant claimed. While these matters had been passed over in Marchant's reelection, Ureta concluded, discontent against the *alcalde* had been growing like "a ball of ice" and the issues could no longer be avoided.

True to his word, Vicuña Subercaseaux joined the attack. In the same session, he charged that Marchant had made improper expenditures for improvements to the Teatro Municipal in preparation for the centennial celebration of Chile's declaration of independence from Spain. The *alcalde's* defenders called these charges unfounded. Conservative Armando Vergara L. asserted that Marchant had operated fully within his authority on the budget, which had to be approved quickly, and that "all the *regidores*" recognized the need for repairs to the Teatro Municipal. He also alluded to the inherent weakness of any *alcalde* in the current system: the more assertive and activist he was, the more likely he would be to offend members of the coalition that had supported him, as appeared to be the case in this instance. In his own defense, Marchant pointed to another inherent difficulty for any *alcalde*. If, in trying to address a contentious issue, he were to appoint a committee of *regidores* to study the question and suggest a solution, he would be perceived as procrastinating and weak. On the other hand, by acting on his own, he was being charged with trampling on the rights and privileges of the *regidores*. With regard to the budget, Marchant admitted to having made some last-minute changes, but he denied showing any favoritism with regard to salary increases for certain employees, as had been alleged.[24]

Unable to vote on Ureta's no-confidence motion on July 15, the *regidores* resumed debate at their next session three days later. Leading off, National Luis A. Moreno rejected Marchant's defense and asserted that the way the Alcalde had handled the budget discussion had indeed trampled on the *regidores*' rights. Moreover, in what may have been the crux of the whole controversy, Marchant's denials notwithstanding, he had, Moreno claimed, not only increased salaries for his friends but also had created positions for them. Overall, Moreno concluded, the Alcalde had shown disdain for the *regidores* and had acted outside the law. In support of Marchant, Radical Darío Roldán argued that from the beginning of his first term the Alcalde had had to deal with some tenacious opponents, who had, as in this instance, looked for any excuse to oust him. The Alcalde, he said, was experienced, honest, and dedicated to Santiago's well-being and had proceeded with "absolute correctness and legality" with regard to the budget and other matters. It did the image of the city little good, he concluded, to be engaged in this kind of partisan struggle on the eve of the centennial celebration. After Vicuña Subercaseaux denied that his opposition to Marchant was politically motivated, and after several other *regidores* were heard, the Ureta motion was ultimately defeated 14 to 12, with three abstentions.[25]

Although Marchant survived the no-confidence motion, it was obvious that substantial opposition to him existed and that he could expect to accomplish little if he stayed in office. Three members of his own National Party had voted for the Ureta motion and two more had abstained. Therefore, on July 20, Marchant submitted his resignation. Although the margin was narrow, the *regidores* accepted his resignation by a vote of 14 to 13, with one abstention. The *regidores* then unanimously approved a resolution affirming that the Alcalde's resignation in no way implied a censure of his actions, a sentiment that seemed more than a little hypocritical and probably offered Marchant little solace.[26]

*

DESPITE THE PARTISAN DIVISIONS that often hamstrung *alcaldes* and the municipality, the *regidores* often did agree on certain important matters. One was the problem of prostitution, the control and regulation of which was considered a municipal responsibility. Concerns about the spread of venereal disease had led the *regidores* in 1895 to craft a measure to regulate prostitution in the capital. When the measure was first introduced, on June 28, Conservative Moisés Huidobro, who favored total abolition, expressed his opinion that regulation in any form was "anti-Catholic, immoral, anti-hygienic, and illegal" and voted against it.[27] The opposition of Huidobro and other Conservatives notwithstanding, the regulation ordinance was approved on October 23 by a vote of 16 to 4, with the specifics discussed in secret session.[28] When the regulations went into effect the following year, they required prostitutes to register with the police and submit to regular medical examinations. They also prohibited the establishment of houses of prostitution within a certain distance (150 to 200 meters) of religious institutions, schools, and military barracks. As with many such ordinances, enforcement was spotty at best and, as the leading student of the matter has observed, "sexual commerce" continued to flourish in the capital.[29] Nonetheless, the city continued to issue new ordinances and regulations in an attempt to control and curtail prostitution, and these efforts continued throughout the first half of the twentieth century.

Another area of general agreement was on the need to regulate the *conventillos*. Consideration of an extensive ordinance in this regard began at the council session of July 8, 1901, when a Conservative *regidor* introduced the measure, observing: "Various are the causes that have converted this city into such an unhealthy one, but one of the most important contributing factors is the terrible condition of the proletarian dwellings called *conventillos*."[30] At the end of July, the regidores passed, without much apparent disagreement, an ordinance to regulate the construction and maintenance of the *conventillos*. Among its twenty-two Articles were provisions that required all *conventillos* to have potable water, sewer connections, proper receptacles for garbage, separate bathrooms for men and women, an adequate laundry room, and rooms for living of ample size and light with at least one window per room. The regulations also specified that *conventillo* construction should be of solid materials like brick and cement, that the units should be protected from flooding, and that walls and ceilings should be painted and/or whitewashed. Those who wanted to build *conventillos* would have to receive permission to do so from the city government, and those who already owned or operated them would have to register with the city and be prepared for regular inspections to assure adherence to the new regulations. Noncompliance would mean either fines or closure, but as a carrot, the regulations also provided certain tax breaks for owners who complied with the registration requirement and a commitment by the city to try to provide water to *conventillos* at a reduced rate.[31] As with the regulation of prostitution, enforcement of these regulations proved sporadic and mostly ineffective, despite various attempts throughout the years to close some *conventillos* that were in violation of these provisions.

Perhaps the most important item considered by the municipality's lawmakers during this period concerned the granting of a contract to construct an electric streetcar system. Once the contract had been let and the system established, both matters continued to be disputed within the municipality and absorbed a considerable amount of government energy and attention throughout the first decades of the twentieth century.

The original contract between the city and the Ferrocarril Urbano, which had initiated horse-drawn service in 1864, was due to expire in 1897, but by the early 1890s, dissatisfaction with this service was manifest. In 1888, for example, some members of an outraged Santiago public had burned several of the company's cars in reaction to a fare increase. Another public outburst against the company occurred on October 12, 1892, when the line's overcrowded and antiquated cars could not handle the large numbers of celebrants headed to the Quinta Normal, a popular park at the western edge of the city, to mark the four hundredth anniversary of Columbus's voyage.[32]

Criticism of the company became a constant theme in the municipality, and it involved representatives of various parties. At a session in June 1894, Liberal Democrat Rodolfo Salinas complained of the unsanitary and dilapidated state of the line's rolling stock. Fellow Liberal Democrat Pedro A. Herrera and Conservative Enrique Morandé pointed out the crowded conditions of the cars and the lack of limits on the numbers of passengers per car. Liberal Democrat Miguel Arrate Larraín, destined to become a major figure in this story, characterized the service on some lines as "detestable" and urged the Alcalde to force the company into compliance with requirements to provide sufficient cars for each line or to fine it for failure to do so. Democrat Francisco Landa criticized the shabby dress and discourteous behavior of the drivers, observing that the horses used were "thin and emaciated," and that delays and traffic jams were common. He particularly singled out the line's female drivers (a noteworthy feature of this system) for their slovenly appearance and "worse manners."[33] In a subsequent session, Radical Nicanor Moreno pointed out that the crowded conditions in the cars provided a perfect opportunity for pickpockets to rob passengers of watches, purses, and other valuables.[34]

The increasing number of complaints about deteriorating service was only one indication that the days of the horse-drawn system were numbered. As was becoming clear in many cities in Europe and North America, horse-drawn carriages had already outlived their usefulness. While few Santiaguinos were probably concerned about the inhumane treatment of the often sickly and malnourished horses that were compelled to pull the heavy cars containing up to forty passengers, even the most insensitive could not fail to appreciate the consequences for the already miserable sanitary conditions of the city when horse manure piled up in the streets and dead horses were left to rot alongside the tracks. And, by the 1890s, there existed a reasonable alternative for Santiago, as for others cities, one that promised a safer, more efficient, cleaner, faster, and more "modern" means of conveyance—the electrified streetcar.[35]

In 1893, entrepreneur and businessman Santiago Ossa, a member of one of Chile's wealthiest families, proposed constructing an electric streetcar system for Santiago. Consideration of Ossa's proposal had been postponed for several years while the *regidores* debated various alternatives. But, finally, in mid-1896, it was determined to open the concession for construction of a new system to national and international bids. After some delicate and controversial maneuvering, Ossa's proposal, now backed by the expertise of both a Spanish and a German engineer and the financial backing of the British investment firm Parrish Brothers, was accepted.[36] Soon thereafter, it was alleged by some, including persons involved with competing bids, that certain strings had been pulled—and perhaps illegal inducements had been offered—to convince the *regidores* to support the Ossa proposal. One such complainant concluded that the actions of the *regidores* had "profoundly wounded the honor and respectability of a body [the municipality] that should protect its dignity and should not succumb to the unhealthy influences of speculators and adventurers."[37] While nothing definite was ever proved in this regard, the hint of scandal surrounded negotiations between the streetcar company and the city from the beginning.

Once Ossa's bid had been accepted, the next order of business was to craft a contract between the city and Ossa's enterprise. This proved to be a lengthy and somewhat contentious process. The leading critic of the contract, objecting to almost every clause, was Liberal Democrat Arrate Larraín, who believed its provisions were too favorable to the company and did not provide enough municipal control over future operations. His objections, as well as those of several of his Liberal Democratic colleagues, perhaps reflected the incipient economic nationalism that was identified with Balmaceda and his party. In the end, they delayed final consideration of the contract for several months. During the course of the debate, the daily *La Tarde* published an open letter that was in tone and manner not atypical of exchanges between *regidores* and interested parties. The letter cast aspersions on Arrate's manhood, sarcastically praised him for being able "to speak for two hours without anybody understanding a word," and, more seriously, accused him of having a vested interest in seeing the current agreement with Ossa fail so that a rival consortium with which a relative was connected could get the concession.[38] Arrate rejected this accusation and argued that his concerns were with the well-being of the traveling public. "I am the first," he declared, "to want the implantation of electric traction and lighting, but I want at the same time that it be done in conditions of security and convenience for the Municipality."[39]

Whatever Arrate's motives, his objections failed to carry the day and the contract was ultimately approved by a substantial margin in April 1897. It went into effect on September 5, when it was signed by the municipal treasurer on behalf of the city. Seen in the context of the times, and Arrate's reservations notwithstanding, it does not appear to have been a particularly weak or unreasonable document, and it gave the municipality, at least in theory, a considerable amount of control over construction and operation of the system. Ossa's company was obligated to construct 100 kilometers of track, with the city having the final say in the layout of the lines. The fare schedule, which some critics thought too high, was set at 5 centavos for first class and 2½ centavos for second class between 5 a.m. and 9 p.m., with a doubling of these fares for night runs after 9 p.m. All fares could be doubled if the exchange rate fell below 15 peniques (pence sterling, at that time, 240 to the pound sterling) to the peso. To receive a fare increase, the company would have to petition the city for approval. This proved to be a major point of future disputes and confrontations. The company would also have to abide by all municipal ordinances related to its operation, and by all regulations drawn up by the *alcalde*'s office with regard to the movement of lines, the number of cars per class, the frequency of departures, the number of passengers per car, the manner of night service, and other details. At the end of the contract term, set for thirty years, the company would be obliged to sell its property and rolling stock to the city at a just price, as determined by an independent assessment. In addition to streetcar service, the contract also provided that the company develop its own source of electricity, which would serve residential and commercial customers as well as provide public street lighting. The company was authorized to purchase and use the rails and other equipment of the existing horse-drawn system, as well as to operate the old system until the new electric system could be established.

In return for these various obligations, the company would be granted exemption from all municipal taxes except those stipulated in the contract. Moreover, the city would petition the National Congress on the company's behalf to eliminate tariffs on those items that had to be imported to build and maintain the system, as well as for a 50 percent reduction in freight charges to carry these materials by rail from Valparaíso to Santiago.

In an effort to assure local control, Article 22 of the contract stipulated that the company would have its "domicile" in Chile. Furthermore, it would "submit itself absolutely to national jurisdiction and will renounce expressly and formally the right to solicit the intervention of the Government of the country to which it pertains with regard to administrative or judicial acts related to this concession." Article 34 obligated the company to have resident in Santiago a representative "with all of the authority necessary to deal with anything related to this contract, be it judicial or extra-judicial." Finally, an arbitration board with one representative of the company, one member of the municipality, and one independent member appointed by a local judge (*juez de letras*) would resolve "all questions of whatever nature related to the contract."[40] Although it was not explicitly stated in the contract, the agreement, in essence, guaranteed Ossa a virtual monopoly over streetcar service in Santiago. While other concessions were not precluded, in practice his company became the only provider of this vital means of public transportation.

As we shall see, disputes between the company and the city soon became the rule rather than the exception and the arbitration board was convened on many occasions to try to resolve them. Some of these disputes arose from flaws in the contract and the not unusual failure of such an agreement to foresee the unexpected. Others developed because of various unreasonable expectations on the part of municipal authorities with regard to the realities of constructing and maintaining a complex, expensive, and sophisticated tramway and electrical system. Still others, some would say the majority, arose because the company simply ignored contractual stipulations or interpreted them in ways that deviated drastically from the city's interpretation. Whatever the "rights" and "wrongs" of these competing positions, there is no question but that these disputes would take up an inordinate amount of the city government's time and energy over the next half century.

ALTHOUGH THE CONTRACT WAS SIGNED and work begun on the streetcar system soon thereafter, criticism of the agreement and of the company highlighted many subsequent municipal sessions. Throughout the late 1890s and into the early twentieth century, *regidores* of various parties, and a few *alcaldes*, complained of what they alleged was the slow pace of system construction, which after 1899 was under the direction of the Sociedad Chilena de Tranvías i Alumbrados (Chilean Society of Streetcars and Lighting), based in London. Then, in 1902, the company made the first of many attempts to have the municipality approve a fare increase. Citing unforeseen costs in construction and operation, it requested that fares for first-class passengers be raised from 5 to 7½ centavos, while leaving the second-class fare at 2½ centavos. In discussing the request, representatives of various parties pointed out that such an increase would unfairly affect the working classes, given the scarcity of second-class cars, a theme that would be often repeated. Liberal Democrat Pedro A. Herrera also claimed that the company had "intervened in the municipal elections to avoid careful oversight of the fulfillment of the contract," although he did not provide details.[41] The matter went to committee for a later report and recommendation.

At the same time that they were considering the fare increase, the *regi-*

dores also approved a new ordinance, containing fifty-three points, to regulate streetcar service. The ordinance began by laying out in some detail the
obligations of the company and its employees. Each car, for example, was to
be kept in clean and safe condition, with a driver and a collector who had
to be licensed by the city. Passengers also had responsibilities, including not
"bothering other passengers with rude words or censurable acts" and refraining from spitting or smoking within the cars. Other provisions laid out
rules and regulations with regard to hours of service, the frequency of trips,
and the behavior of the driver and collector.[42]

In July 1903 the committee considering the fare increase made its report.
To the surprise of many, the report recommended an even higher increase
than the company had requested: 10 centavos for first class; 5 centavos for
second class; and 2½ centavos for a proposed third class. The *alcalde* at the
time, Conservative Juan Enrique Subercaseaux, spoke in favor of the report.
The profits generated from the increase, he argued, would help defray the
costs to the city for the installation of electric street lighting and would reduce the burden of other city obligations with regard to electric service in
general. He also assured the *regidores* that he had personally examined the
company's books and had found their assessment of what was needed to
complete their project reasonable and accurate and justifying the increase.
His arguments, however, failed to convince, and the *regidores* rejected the increase by a vote of 17 to 3, with one abstention, on August 31, 1903.[43]

Following additional confrontations over the next two years, a revised
agreement between the city and the company was formulated after a series
of close votes in August and September 1905.[44] The new contract relieved
both the company and the city of their previous obligations with regard to
street lighting, as detailed in 1897. Under the new agreement, the company
would provide for the operation of eight hundred street lights free of charge
to the city for the length of the contract. For its part, the city would pay for
the basic installation of these lights. The most significant articles, however,
provided that the streetcar concession could be extended, by a unanimous
vote of the city council, for an additional twenty-five years beyond the thirty
years that had been agreed to in the 1897 contract, and that, in return, the
fares agreed to in Article 11 of the original contract would be maintained.
The new contract also reaffirmed the tax breaks that had been provided to
the company.[45]

While this agreement was being formulated, the company's British investors had transferred their capital into German hands, although management remained based in London and the company name, now "The Chilian Tramway and Electric Company," remained in English. As one observer noted, one result of the transfer was "the replacement of the antiquated British rolling stock for elegant German cars ... which made their appearance on line 19, to carry our aristocracy to the Parque Cousiño, where they enjoyed their *paseo* every afternoon."[46]

These changes did little to improve relations between the company and many of the *regidores*, however. In late 1906, citing a drop in the exchange rate, the company again pushed for a fare increase. This matter consumed much of the council's attention over the next few years and led to the resignation of at least one *alcalde*. Finally, in January 1910, by a vote of 19 to 3, the council agreed to an increase to 10 centavos for first class, 5 centavos for second class, and 10 centavos for night service. Helping to carry the day were the arguments that fares in Santiago, even with the increase, would still be lower than in most comparable cities and that higher fares would lead to expanded and improved service.[47]

Despite the new agreement, *regidores* of the Radical and Democratic parties, in particular, continued to express their opposition to the fare increase and their discontent with the quality of the overall service provided. While these discussions continued, the 1910 *Baedeker* guide for Chile commented favorably on the city's streetcar system. It counted twenty-six lines, covering a good part of the capital, with 280 cars. Electricity for the streetcars, and for the city generally, was provided by the streetcar company through six coal-powered plants built by English and Italian firms, and work on a hydroelectric project in the nearby Maipó River valley had begun. Overall, the travel guide implied, the streetcar company provided a modern system that served the city well.[48] Criticism of the company, its service, its cost, and its relations with the city, however, would continue to mark much of Santiago's public discourse in the coming decades.

BY 1909, FOR ALL ITS FLAWS, elected municipal government had become an established institution in Santiago. Moreover, for many who had ambitions for prestigious political careers, election to a municipal post offered an opportunity for experience and exposure that could well lead to higher office. Therefore, campaigns for *regidor* remained competitive and increasingly prominent features of life in the capital. The campaigns also became more sophisticated and more time-consuming for the parties involved as time progressed. By 1909, the parties were selecting their candidates for local (and national) office in open meetings, well in advance of the elections rather than at the last minute, as had often been the case previously. Active campaigning stretched over several weeks, with rallies, parades, and public speeches organized by local party committees in each *comuna* culminating in citywide demonstrations on election eve. *El Mercurio* described a Democratic Party rally prior to the 1909 elections in the following terms:

> In the small square of Cerro Santa Lucía were assembled, at the appointed hour, the Democrats of all the *comunas* of Santiago. There they organized a parade, in the midst of the greatest enthusiasm, led by a band of musicians playing marches. A long column of citizens, with banners, torches, and lanterns, traversed the streets of the city, passing by various newspaper offices, enthusiastically shouting out the names of the party's candidates. The good behavior of the demonstrators should also be noted.[49]

The press played an increasingly important role in these campaigns. The city's major newspapers gave ample coverage to the activities of all parties and provided detailed information on how citizens should proceed to vote, repeatedly listing polling places and their locations, as well as their presiding officials, for several days prior to the balloting. The parties, too, increasingly followed the practice of placing paid advertisements for their candidates in the major newspapers of the city. These often included a photograph as well as a brief description of what the candidate stood for. Prior to the 1909 election, for example, the Radicals placed the following *aviso*, which appeared enclosed within a prominent box outlined in red at the top of page one: "First Comuna, Santa Lucía. All those who desire as a member of the municipality a person with the following qualities—honesty, experience, a willingness to work hard—ought to vote for [Malcolm] Mac-Iver."[50]

The parties themselves created publications to promote their candidates and platforms. The Democrats, for example, employed their biweekly illustrated magazine, *Luz y Progreso*, to extol the virtues of Nicasio Retamales, elected as a *regidor* from the Fourth Comuna in 1906 and up for reelection in 1909. Retamales, the publication pointed out, was a mechanic by profession and had been active since the mid-1890s in the labor movement and party affairs. (He was probably the only *regidor* at the time with such a background.) Within the municipality, he had defended the interests of the working people of the city, seeking "to alleviate the miseries they suffer" by looking for ways to lower the price of meat and resisting the increase in streetcar fares. "His labors and his enthusiasm are an example for all, his morality a lesson for all," the article concluded. "For these reasons we commend him to the public."[51]

A somewhat similar publication, *El Santiaguino*, appeared on November 11, 1908. Claiming to be independent, it aimed to profile the municipal candidates and programs of all the parties. Among its first profiles was one for Augusto Vicuña Subercaseaux, a Liberal Democratic candidate. Born in Santiago in 1882, he had received his law degree from the University of Chile in 1905. He was recognized as a "young man of wealth and good family"—if all candidates were as well qualified as Vicuña, Santiago would have a "model municipality."[52] Vicuña would be elected in 1909 from the Ninth Comuna and, later, aside from his role in Marchant's resignation, he would serve as *alcalde* himself. As well, he would serve three terms as a national deputy from Santiago, as vice-president of the national Chamber of Deputies, and as vice-president of the Liberal and Liberal Democratic parties.[53]

Two ultimately successful Conservative candidates, Luis A. Santander Ruiz and Armando Vergara L., were also featured in *El Santiaguino*. Both were lawyers who were active in various Catholic social and educational institutions. Both were well traveled, having made the obligatory young aristocrat's tours of Europe. In accepting his candidacy from the First Comuna, Santander began by noting that the *comuna* housed representatives of "the most distinguished families of the republic" along with "the energetic worker who gains his daily sustenance with the sweat of his brow," and promised to work hard to fulfill the Conservative municipal program. For the 1909 election, that program sought to eliminate all municipal debts by suspending what were deemed unnecessary expenditures on "luxuries." It sought to focus instead on basic infrastructure development while holding the line on hiring new city employees until those already employed could receive a living wage. Addressing Conservative concerns about the "immorality" of the working classes, Santander promised to support the growth of popular theaters, which would provide workers' families with wholesome entertainment as an alternative to the tavern and brothel.[54]

Vergara, for his part, focused on the many deficiencies of the Third Comuna, where he was a property owner and which he sought to represent. Noting that the Third was the most "popular" *comuna* in the city, he observed as well that it lacked adequate paving, lighting, and cleaning, and he promised to work to provide these if elected. Echoing Santander, he pledged to develop a fiscally responsible municipality and to promote "honest and free diversions for our workers and comfortable parks and plazas for the young people" of the *comuna*. Finally, while he planned to run with pride as a local member of the Conservative ticket, he promised not to put partisan concerns above the overall well-being of the city.[55]

Conservative Eduardo Edwards Salas, of the powerful Edwards family, campaigned not only on future promises but also on past accomplishments. Having been elected three straight times from the Fourth Comuna and having served two years as First Alcalde, he boasted about the benefits he had had a hand in providing for both the *comuna* in particular and the city as a whole. These included the construction of the Estación Central and its surroundings, "today an active commercial area," the extension of the Alameda, improvements in the areas around Cerro Santa Lucía and the Teatro Municipal, and the beautification of the Parque Cousiño and other major parks and plazas. As *alcalde*, he claimed to have balanced the budget and to have maintained fiscal integrity. If reelected, as indeed he was, he would push for expanded streetcar lines into the Fourth Comuna and would work to have the rail lines that ran close to Avenida Matucana, a main north-south route, moved underground so that they would no longer pose a threat to the health and safety of the citizens of this fast-growing district.[56]

Successful Radical candidates in 1909 included Antonio Braga Castillo, Plácido A. Briones, Malcolm Mac-Iver, and Rogelio Ugarte. Braga, representing the Sixth Comuna, was a physician known for his services to the local fire department, mutual aid societies, and several working-class organizations and institutions.[57] Briones, of the Fifth Comuna, was a lawyer, teacher, and journalist who promised to work for the betterment of a district "that today finds itself in the most deplorable abandonment." In a letter published in *El Santiaguino*, one of Briones's constituents not affiliated with the Radical Party promised to vote for him because he was "the most perfect honorable gentleman."[58] Mac-Iver, son of a leading figure of his party and representing the First Comuna, was described as just the kind of young man the municipality needed because he would bring to it "new vitality and vigor" and "will form part of a good and healthy element ... inclined to work hard ... within the rules of morality."[59] Ugarte, born in Santiago in 1872, was a journalist and party activist. He was running for the fourth time as a representative of the Seventh Comuna. Like several of his colleagues, he served later as a national deputy from Santiago.[60]

A successful National Party candidate for the First Comuna was Emilio del Pedregal. A dentist and school director, Pedregal had distinguished himself during a general strike in 1906 by rallying others to defend property being threatened with destruction. In that same year, he had been deeply involved in philanthropic work following a major earthquake.[61] Liberal Democrat Carlos Silva Baltra, elected from the Second Comuna, where he had lived for twenty-five years, was a lawyer who had served as a judge for three years and in the Ministries of Interior and Industry for seven years. Described as one who "has defended warmly and energetically the interests of the working class and local progress," he pledged to increase and improve street paving in the comuna and to pay particular attention to expanding and beautifying Plaza Brasil as well as widening and modernizing the avenue of the same name. In carrying out his duties, he swore to do so "with an elevated vision and with strict accordance with the law, and having as my principal and only goal to serve the public good."[62]

Finally, Carlos Ureta would be elected as an independent Liberal from the Fourth Comuna. El Santiaguino predicted that Ureta, described as a young industrialist, would bring a spirit of efficiency and good administrative experience to the municipality. It also praised his willingness to run as an Independent, reflecting a general weariness with some of the excessive partisanship that characterized a local government where party affiliation and party loyalties too often seemed to prevail over the common good.[63]

This brief sketch of the eleven men above suggests a general profile of regidores in this period. First, most of these candidates, all of whom were elected, were relatively young men, most of them just embarking on political careers. Second, most were professionals, with lawyers predominating, but also including doctors, journalists, and at least one industrialist. Third, the Conservatives and Liberals came from well-established and well-known elite families—Edwards and Vicuña Subercaseaux, for example—while the Radicals were from somewhat less well-to-do backgrounds. Democrat Retamales, of course, stands out as coming from more humble origins and as the only one of the eleven with a working-class occupation.[64] Fourth, all seemed very well versed in the basic problems of their districts and of the city overall, and most laid out rather clearly what they intended to do within the municipality to address these matters. Fifth, throughout their campaign speeches and activities, the candidates had tried to stress their honesty, morality, and commitment to the common good—a clear response to a growing public criticism of the quality of the men elected as *regidores* and the partisanship that appeared to dominate their public behavior. Whatever the validity of these criticisms, on the face of it, most if not all of the candidates seemed by any objective standard to be quite well-qualified by background, education, and experience to serve effectively as *regidores*.

DESPITE THE PROFESSED GOOD INTENTIONS of the candidates and the enthusiasm generated by the 1909 municipal election campaign, as the first decade of the twentieth century neared its end, dissatisfaction and disappointment with Santiago's local politics and government were becoming increasingly evident. One problem had to do with the electoral process. After proclaiming the elections of 1891 and 1894 to be among the fairest and freest in the nation's history, *El Ferrocarril* had dramatically changed its opinion by 1900. Commenting on the contests in March of that year, the newspaper lamented the venality and bribery that had corrupted the whole process, with votes going to the highest bidder and with all parties involved. Senate candidates paid the most to get elected, national deputies almost the same, and the candidates for *regidor* "a little less." Instead of selecting the best qualified candidates, one editorial noted, parties chose those with the requisite financial resources to purchase the most votes.[65]

In addition to bribery, other fraudulent practices were used to assure victory. These were often carried out with the compliance of election officials selected by the municipality. *El Ferrocarril* charged that in 1900 such practices had favored municipal candidates Julio Videla (Liberal Democrat), Rogelio Ugarte (Radical), and Marco A. Tapia (Democrat) to the detriment of their opponents.[66] When the new municipality met in May to certify the elections and to swear in the new *regidores*, numerous challenges were heard. One involved the aforementioned Videla and his fellow Liberal Democrat Manuel Corvalán, both elected from the Second Comuna. A local citizen claimed that Corvalán did not meet the requirement of five years' residence in the capital and that both had benefited from officials "who had committed fraud to alter the free result of the election." "It is notorious," the complainant asserted, "that in that *mesa* [voting place] appear to vote persons who are absent that day from the capital and that adulterations have been of such a nature that they have given rise to a noisy protest to local judges, in which Sr. Videla, as the main author, has been deeply involved."[67] These claims notwithstanding, the election was ratified and both men were seated. Most such challenges were rejected, as parties maneuvered to help their own and to build their numbers. But successfully resisting these claims, which were a constant feature of initial municipal sessions following each election, did not mean that they were without foundation.

Press criticism of national and local elections continued throughout the decade. One of the loudest voices was that of *El Mercurio*, which had begun publication in Santiago in 1900 after having been founded in Valparaíso in 1827. Echoing *El Ferrocarril*, it observed that elections in 1903 were not true reflections of the popular will but rather the result of the efforts of those candidates who could best manipulate the electoral process.[68] In an editorial following the election of 1906, the daily was of the opinion that the only thing that made this contest different from the previous one was that the cost of the vote was now higher. It traced the by now ingrained practice of vote-buying to two basic causes: "first, the ignorance of the great masses of the people, who have not received sufficient education to be fully aware of their rights and duties; and, second, because of this same ignorance, a profound lack of interest to take part in electoral struggles." Parties were at fault as well, failing to select good candidates, lacking in ideas and coherent programs, and perpetuating the various corrupt practices that helped to undermine Chilean democracy.[69]

In addition to flawed elections, there was also the issue of what appeared to many to be an inefficient and ineffective local government. There were frequent criticisms, both from within the municipality itself as well as from outside it, that Santiago's elected officials were too busy squabbling among themselves to get much done with regard to the capital's most vital needs.

In an editorial prior to the elections of 1903, El Mercurio suggested that perhaps the law of municipal autonomy had been premature, that the citizens of Santiago and its parties were not yet ready to assume such a responsibility. It pointed to an excessive partisanship, wherein "political action absorbs all, corrodes all, vitiates all." Such partisanship at the local level severely weakened the alcalde, with various parties combining to elect a particular executive and then other parties, or some of the same, combining to bring him down a few months later.[70]

This was a widely recognized problem. During a discussion of the resignation of Alcalde Ignacio Marchant, Conservative Luis A. Santander commented with considerable insight on the matter. Every year that passed without an alcalde being forced to resign, he claimed, was a year of "glory" for the municipality, but unfortunately such years had been few and far between. Marchant, he argued, was a man of rectitude and accomplishment, but he had been brought down because of certain inherent flaws in the way the municipality was organized and operated. To stay in and maintain power, Marchant, or any alcalde, had to accommodate to the majority that selected him, even "in cases of absurd presumptions." Such dependence made the alcalde reluctant to act forcefully or to embark on bold initiatives, for fear of offending one or another component of his supporters. "How different things would be," Santander speculated, "if the alcalde had the security of office for one year without being concerned with majorities and minorities." Complicating matters even more, and at the root of many of the municipality's weaknesses, was a lack of adequate revenue. This, of course, made it difficult, if not impossible, for the alcalde to satisfy all the wishes of his supporters. Accordingly, it was no accident, Santander observed, that attacks on the alcalde would intensify at the end of the year so that someone more compliant with the wishes of new or old majorities might replace the incumbent and be in a position to determine how the funds collected for the coming year would be dispensed. As Santander put it, "It is logical that the alcalde's opponents want a crisis before January, because at that point funds begin to enter the city treasury, and thus they can meet the legitimate aspirations to improve their respective comunas, where everybody requests something, by being able to decree funds for the paving or repair of Comuna A or B of the triumphant majorities." Alcaldes, he asserted, were usually good and well-intentioned men trying to operate in a system with built-in limits on their freedom of action, and they were almost always destined to fail. "The people of Santiago know," he concluded, "that the *alcaldes* of the city never fall, generally, because they do not fulfill their duties, but, on the contrary, for doing just that."[71]

The lack of funds in the city treasury was a recurring lament. Usually, no matter what economies were practiced, the city ran a deficit, and periodically it had to ask the national government for a loan or for authority to contract for one in order to meet its obligations. *Regidores* and *alcaldes* often referred with envy to the much more generous and ample budget for the city of Buenos Aires as compared with their own meager revenues.[72] The comparison, of course, had to take into consideration the fact that Argentina was a significantly wealthier country and one undergoing at that time a remarkable economic expansion, but the point still had validity. In a study for a law thesis at the University of Chile in 1920, Silvestre Ochagavía Hurtado rather convincingly traced the weaknesses of local government in Chile to inadequate sources of revenue, which led to recurring fiscal crises. Basically, the city's revenue sources included a personal income tax of from one to three pesos that was earmarked for education, a tax on the sale of tobacco and alcohol, license fees for businesses and professionals, fines for the violation of municipal regulations, subsidies from the national government, revenues produced by municipally owned properties and enterprises, and, most importantly and usually producing more than half of all revenues, a property tax.[73]

Under the urging of Alcalde Marchant, as mentioned, the National Congress had agreed in 1909 to increase the property tax rate from two to three pesos per 1,000 of assessed value. Even with this new rate and a new assessment office, revenues still failed to meet needs. As Arturo Valenzuela has pointed out, local governments after 1891 were reluctant to impose and to collect new taxes, continuing to depend on subsidies from the national government.[74] Whatever the reason, the lack of fiscal resources contributed significantly to ineffective local government, which ultimately meant, at least in the case of Santiago, that, increasingly, many of the responsibilities bestowed on the city by the autonomy law of 1891 gradually came under the authority of the national government. These included certain aspects of local sanitation which were absorbed by the national Dirección General de Sanidad (General Sanitation Office), the construction of worker housing, which passed from the municipality to the Consejo Departamental de Habitaciones para Obreros (Department of Workers' Housing), created in 1906, and the provision of potable water, which gradually fell to the Interior Ministry.

In sum, by 1910 the promises of 1891 with regard to municipal autonomy had yet to be realized. There appeared to be little public confidence in elected municipal officials to address and resolve successfully the capital's many pressing problems, a number of which—especially the lack of adequate sanitation, the persistence of the *conventillos*, and insufficient attention to improving public health—seemed to be getting worse instead of better as the city grew. While some of the criticism of elected officials might have been exaggerated, it also contained a fair amount of substance, a fact that many *alcaldes* and *regidores* themselves recognized. As a result, as the first decade of the twentieth century came to a close, there were renewed efforts to reform municipal government so as to make it more responsive and more efficient, efforts that produced mixed results at best.

3 Municipal Reform and Its Results (1910-1920)

THE MOVEMENT FOR REFORM got its official start in July 1908 with the creation of the Junta de Reforma Municipal in Santiago. Its leaders were a virtual "Who's Who" of the Chilean elite. Members of the Club de la Unión were prominent figures in the *junta*, including its president in 1910, botanist and businessman Salvador Izquierdo. The president and principal spokesman of the *junta* was Alberto Mackenna Subercaseaux, a member of one of Santiago's wealthiest families and himself an unsuccessful candidate for *regidor* on the Liberal Party ticket in 1906.

Immediately upon its founding, the *junta* sent to the national Senate a petition requesting changes in the 1891 law. The petition emphasized the inefficiency of Santiago's local government, which was unable to provide "the most necessary services for its citizens"; the resulting poor hygienic state of the city, conducive to periodic epidemics; and the inattention to working-class neighborhoods that were centers of "infection and vice." "The actual condition of Santiago," it argued, was "unworthy of the level of culture our country has achieved, and we believe that it is in the national interest to remedy it." The root of the problem was not only a lack of adequate resources but also, as the petition delicately stated, "the instability of the main local authority [the *alcalde*] and the lack of a precise orientation in his tasks offered by our municipality [the *regidores*]." Beyond individual problems, the petition asserted, was a "confusion of local interests with the interests of general politics, a confusion that in the minds of those who sign this petition, deprives the municipality of its independence so that it might dedicate all

its efforts and energies to the attention of the services it should provide."
Therefore, the petition concluded, the resolution lay in modification in the
laws of municipalities, which would provide Santiago's local government
with the economic and administrative independence to carry out its functions properly and effectively.[1]

There was more to the junta's agenda, however, than concerns over good
government. To a large extent, the junta represented an anti-democratic movement fueled by upper-class concerns that it was losing its grip over the political system. Vote-buying and fraudulent practices had, in the eyes of these
upper-class supporters, gotten out of hand and out of control and local political bosses who could deliver votes had become too powerful. As Arturo
Valenzuela put it, "The principal aim of the movement was to break the
influence of parties as linkages between the municipality and the central
government, fostering 'neutral' local administration. Underlying the movement was a strong feeling that the masses were not prepared for political
participation and leadership."[2] In this regard, as a reform from the top down
that sought to limit the influence of local bosses, the junta bore some simi-
larity to the movement for municipal reform during the Progressive Era in
the United States.[3]

Various aspects of the junta's proposals aimed to strengthen the hand of
the alcalde vis-à-vis the regidores. In the petition submitted to Congress, the junta
recommended that the three alcaldes be chosen by popular vote, with their
order determined by the council. It also proposed that alcaldes could only be
removed from office by a vote of two-thirds of the regidores, and that the First
Alcalde should receive a set salary.[4] Balmacedist Regidor Carlos Silva Baltra
took a different tack. For him, the basic problem of municipal government
was the lack of an adequate revenue base. Insufficient resources, he argued,
was the fundamental problem that lay behind the resignations of former alcaldes and contributed to administrative instability. Part of the problem of inadequate resources was the failure of property owners to pay their taxes and
the inability of the local government, due to "no support from the judicial
authority" and "the inertia of the national administration," to enforce compliance. Silva then enumerated by name and address an impressive list of
well-to-do property owners and professionals who were delinquent in
paying their taxes and license fees, including quite a few members of the
Junta de Reforma. Among them was the father of junta president Alberto

Mackenna Subercaseaux.[5] Later, it was clarified that Mackenna had met his tax obligations, causing Silva to admit that he had been mistaken in that particular case, which he attributed to his having relied on faulty evidence.[6]

While various individuals pointed to various causes for local problems, the leaders of the *junta* became increasingly frustrated with the Congress's incessant delays in considering their suggested reforms. As Congress delayed, criticism of local government and pressures for change continued to build. For example, the *alcalde* at the time, the National Party's Luis A. Moreno, who had replaced Marchant at the end of 1910, was generally considered a well-intentioned executive but one who had also inherited a deficit of one million pesos and who did not have funds to provide even the most basic services, such as street paving. A poem entitled "Ese Pobre Alcalde" ("That Poor Alcalde") that appeared in the local humor magazine *Pica-Pica* in June 1911 commented on Moreno's dilemma. It depicted the Alcalde's sufferings as of such gravity that only the return of Christ to Earth would relieve them. Meanwhile, the capital was "full of mud, the irrigation canals overflowed and the dross spread a thousand pests in summer," while it was impossible to pass through the center of the city, which was "ugly, dirty, immoral, and horrible."[7] For the magazine *La Semana*, so long as the Municipality of Santiago continued to be "a center of abject peculations and miserable political shenanigans, this city, destined by its climate and surroundings to be a jewel, will remain much like the colonial village of a century ago."[8] In even harsher terms, Carlos A. Ibáñez (not related to the future president), one of the leaders of the *junta*, with some exaggeration proclaimed at the end of a rally, "We live in the foulest city in the world, so that whatever visitor who comes upon it will compare us with the most savage tribes of Africa."[9]

At the end of 1911, on Christmas eve, the *junta* held a "meeting of notables" in the Salon de Honor of the University of Chile to pressure Congress to consider their proposals. *Junta* president Mackenna set the tone with an apocalyptic vision of what would happen to Santiago if the reforms were not approved. "The hour is grave," he told the assembly. If things continued as they were, "the representatives of brothels, gambling dens, and cantinas, all that Santiago has that is impure and abject," would sink their claws deeper into the municipality. These interests, in turn, would artificially increase property assessments and taxes, to create "new sources of revenue to satiate their unchecked and rapacious appetites." After other speakers chimed in with their own variations of these themes, the meeting concluded with the approval of a new petition to Congress and a promise to continue the fight if Congress failed to act.[10]

The points made at the meeting gained force from a growing scandal involving several prominent members of the current local government. On December 19, five days before the rally, charges had been brought by an official of the Supreme Court against Regidor Silva, accusing him, in essence, of having received a bribe involving the granting of a paving contract. Silva protested his innocence, saying that the charges stemmed from the grudges of "personal enemies," former municipal employees whom he had helped remove from their positions.[11] It may also have been more than coincidental that Silva, who had been prominent in trying to embarrass the leaders of the *junta* by pointing out their delinquency in paying property taxes, was now himself the target of charges. His protestations of innocence notwithstanding, the judge looking into the case ordered that Silva be held under arrest without bail while the investigation proceeded.

In early January 1912, the net spread wider. After interviewing various current and former city officials and employees, the investigating judge brought indictments against former *alcalde* Luis A. Moreno, the city treasurer, and fourteen *regidores* for the embezzlement of municipal funds in connection with the sale of season tickets to performances at the Teatro Municipal. The fourteen charged belonged to all the parties of the majority of the municipality. Also charged was Silva, who now added this new accusation to the charges that had already been lodged against him.[12] Later that month, the investigation was expanded to include alleged irregularities within the sanitation department, a branch of city government that was under almost constant scrutiny and criticism.[13] Also at the end of January Moreno was placed under arrest and imprisoned, while Silva was finally released, having paid 5,000 pesos in bail money.[14]

These events spurred the reform elements to renewed efforts. In February the Junta de Reforma held another rally to convince Congress to consider change, this one attended by an estimated 15,000 persons, including representatives of worker and student groups. Pleas were also made for the national government to intervene in the municipality, given its current state, and manage local affairs until reforms could be enacted, but they were ignored for the moment. In the meantime, the *junta* encouraged Santiago's citizens to boycott the elections to renew the municipality scheduled for March 3. "The honorable element of Santiago," the *junta* proclaimed, "should not take part in this coarse masquerade, prepared beforehand by political cliques, in which the electors are going to be ridiculously deceived."[15]

These pleas notwithstanding, all parties prepared to compete in the upcoming contest in the usual manner. After the normal processes of candidate selection and campaigning, the election took place as scheduled. The results were quite favorable to the Radicals, who won ten of the thirty seats contested. Five Nationals were also chosen. Among those elected were several individuals who were under indictment at the time.[16] For *El Mercurio*, the election, where turnout was low and fraud was prevalent, had produced *regidores* who, if they were not worse than those previously in office, "because that could not be," were just as bad. The concerns of Santiago's citizens, a post-election editorial claimed, would continue to be ignored by *regidores* "very well known among the social riffraff for their connections with gambling dens, houses of prostitution, and taverns."[17]

According to a report from the U.S. embassy, the elections had been the most fraudulent in Chilean history to that time, due to their having been held under municipal supervision, with the cities, in turn, "under the control of men of low standards." Under such men, every type of election trick imaginable had been practiced, from bribery, to stuffing ballot boxes, to throwing out legitimate votes, to falsifying returns.[18] The *South Pacific Mail*, the journalistic voice of the British community in Chile, made many of the same observations. Referring to municipal government, one editorialist wrote: "The evils of the present system have long been apparent. As things now stand, the mayors, even with the best of intentions, are unable to reduce municipal affairs to anything approaching order. They themselves are entirely at the mercy of the constantly changing majorities, and cannot even dismiss a messenger, or porter, without the fear of being themselves attacked and thrown out at the next session. The consequence is, a vast waste of public funds and an ever growing disinclination on the part of all, except the professional politicians, to become members of the local administration."[19]

Following the elections, protests by the Junta de Reform and others intensified. The *junta* organized more massive rallies and presented more petitions to Congress. Reflecting popular dissatisfaction, members of the Conservative, Moderate Liberal, and Liberal Democratic parties boycotted the opening sessions of the newly elected municipality in May. The general disgust with the elections and with the new city government was reflected in a sarcasm-laden poem that appeared in a local magazine near the end of the year:

> It cannot be denied: the regidores of 1912 are like cocky roosters.
> Elected by themselves through the most scandalous frauds and thefts, they cannot
>   foresee losing their jobs.
> So what if public opinion condemns them and they lack honesty and morality?
> What do they care?[20]

It was within this environment that conditions began to change. By order of the Supreme Court, the elections of March 3, 1912, were declared void and, as a result, the national government appointed the intendente of the province to manage local affairs until new elections could be held. Congress also began to address the junta's reform proposals with some seriousness. At the beginning of 1913, the president of the republic, through the minister of the interior, appointed a special six-man Junta Electoral de Vecinos (Citizens' Electoral Committee) to oversee new municipal elections to be held on March 31. The junta, presided over by Ismael Valdés Vergara, who, along with his other colleagues, was also active in the Junta de Reforma, encouraged all parties to put forth their most highly qualified candidates. In an effort to smooth over the partisanship that so deeply afflicted the city council, the junta also tried to get the contending parties to agree to an equitable sharing of the available candidate slots in a way that would fairly reflect their proportionate strength among the electorate. After intense negotiations, this effort ultimately failed, with the Radicals being the most notable but not the only party to refuse to limit its candidate list.[21]

The mainline parties selected their candidates and began campaigning in mid-March. Participating in the municipal elections for the first time was the newly formed Socialist Party of Chile, whose progressive program called for an elimination of the sales tax on basic consumer items, the promotion of ferias libres (farmers' markets), an eight-hour day, a minimum wage for city workers and employees, and affordable public housing, among other programs directed to the working classes.[22]

The election did not produce a particularly large turnout. The leading vote-getter, National Oscar Valenzuela, received only a little more than 11,000 votes. Nonetheless, El Mercurio, in its lead post-election editorial, claimed that this had been "the freest election in twenty years," thanks in large measure to the oversight measures of the special electoral junta.[23] The election itself was a major victory for the Conservatives, who won eight positions, and a major defeat for the Radicals, who gained only two. Some attributed the Radicals' poor showing to their unwillingness to compromise earlier on a fairer distribution of seats, while some Radicals placed the blame on better bribery efforts by their opponents. Twenty of the thirty men elected were associated with the Junta de Reforma, and two members of the Junta Electoral, Liberal Ismael Valdés Vergara and Conservative Abraham Ovalle, were among their number. In addition to the eight Conservatives and two Radicals, also chosen were five Nationals, four Liberals, four Balmacedistas, three Democrats, two Independents, one Independent Radical, and one Socialist, Manuel Hidalgo.[24]

The new council met on April 20 and chose Ismael Valdés Vergara as First Alcalde by 28 votes.[25] The municipality over which he would preside would be the last chosen under the 1891 provisions. Later in 1913, both houses of Congress would pass electoral reform measures that sought to redress the problems of fraud and corruption that had become so endemic. During debate for these measures in the Chamber of Deputies, Manuel Foster Recabarren, another leader of the Junta de Reforma, emphasized how municipal government, "now in the good hands" of fellow junta member Valdés, had been hamstrung in its efforts to effect improvements under the existing system. Particularly disturbing to Valdés was the growing contrast between the center of the capital, which was beginning to take on the appearance of a European city, and the periphery, where one found "stagnant, dirty water, garbage in the streets, smallpox in the houses, and drunks in all the shops and stores," sights that were sure to horrify visitors to an upcoming scientific conference to be held in Santiago the following year.[26]

Foster Recabarren's refrain was by now a familiar one. Santiago compared poorly with other capitals and its manner of local administration had to be changed to prevent it from falling even further behind. The argument clearly carried weight, as did the accumulated years of protest and the clear evidence of municipal inefficiency. Whether all the charges of corruption and fraud were true or not, they certainly helped to create a climate that made reform possible.

After negotiations between the Senate and the Chamber of Deputies, the new election procedures went into effect in early 1915 as part of a larger national electoral reform. Among the important changes was the removal of control of the election from municipal authorities and a separation of municipal elections from the national elections, with the hope that this might reduce some of the partisanship and party maneuvering that accompanied the combined contests. For Santiago, the number of *regidores* was reduced to thirteen, who would now be elected citywide instead of by *comuna*. The purpose of this reduction was to make it easier for the *alcaldes* to develop and sustain majorities, at least in theory, since there would be fewer *regidores* to accommodate. The citywide election reform was seen as a way to prevent the *regidores* from winning elections by bribing or coercing the relatively small group of voters in the *comunas*. Other changes gave the *alcalde* a bit more authority in handling expenditures, but the final reform measure did not provide the kind of clout that had been suggested by some of the initial reform proposals.

Historical interpretations of the significance and consequences of the reforms vary. For Chilean historian Julio Heise González, they represented "the most important step taken in the terrain of electoral legislation for the entire parliamentary period." Heise saw the reforms as significantly strengthening political democracy in Chile, pointing to provisions that helped to regularize and "purify" the electoral registries, the introduction for the first time of the secret ballot, and other measures to prevent fraud, including the establishment of fines and even imprisonment for committing irregularities and better national supervision of the entire process. He also argued that the reforms specifically benefited the Radical and Democratic parties, producing a major shift at the national level in electoral alignments and helping to produce the victory of the Liberal Alliance (Radicals, Democrats, and Dissident Liberals) in the presidential race of 1920.[27]

Fellow historian Gonzalo Vial Correa also had a positive view. For him, the cleaning up of the voter registries, with their many falsely inscribed voters, effectively reduced the power of the political machines that had feasted on such irregularities. At the municipal level, too, the Assemblies of Electors had been replaced with a more limited Assembly of Taxpayers which would oversee elections and supervise and control the local administration, a measure Vial viewed as helping to eliminate municipal corruption. On the other hand, he admitted that as a result of reducing the number of "phony" voters, the practice of vote-buying had actually increased after 1915, because "it was the only [political party] control over the electorate that remained untouched by the reforms."[28]

A less positive view was expressed during congressional debate over the reforms. Democratic Party founder and national deputy Malaquías Concha argued that the changes would restrict the choices of the electorate and limit popular sovereignty. Reducing the number of *regidores* and making the contests citywide, he claimed, would eliminate the representation of various parties and lead to the establishment of an "oligarchy" to direct city government.[29] More than half a century later, Arturo Valenzuela emphasized the reactionary nature of the reforms, which had slowed a democratizing trend begun in 1891. The "cleansing" of the registries every nine years under the supervision of the Taxpayers' Assembly, he asserted, had been intended to assure that suffrage remained at "reasonable," that is, manageable, levels for the parties involved. As a result, the number of registered voters had declined from 598,000 nationwide in 1912 to 185,000 in 1915, with a corresponding drop in turnout. This was something, he claimed, that had been desired by all the parties, which, having begun to mobilize the popular sectors then "seemed to realize that they would gain by restricting mobilization before it got out of hand."[30]

Whatever the point of view, the drop in registered and actual voters is telling. It is also interesting to note the contrasting experience in Argentina, where electoral reform at the national level, in 1912, and at the municipal level, in Buenos Aires in 1918, had greatly expanded the electorate and substantially stimulated and increased voter participation.[31]

While these reforms were being debated, the local administration under Valdés continued to wrestle with the capital's many problems. Among these was the question of how to regulate the growing numbers of taxicabs in the capital, many of whose drivers charged varying rates, often taking particular advantage of unwary foreign tourists. The municipality agreed on requiring that each taxi install a meter so that time and distance could be measured with some exactitude, but failed to agree on who should receive the concession to provide the meters.[32] This issue would continue to fester without resolution for several more years.

In the final months of 1914, both the national and local governments had to deal with repercussions from the outbreak of World War I in Europe. For the national government, a temporary fall in nitrate prices (Germany had been the largest purchaser) and a run on some banks at the onset of the war led to a reduction of government salaries, new taxes, and the issuance of paper money as stopgap measures.[33] In late August the *South Pacific Mail* reported that some two thousand unemployed workers and their families, mostly from the nitrate fields of the North, had descended upon the capital. There, the police had provided them with one peso each and they had found lodging in a large shed on the southern edge of the city.[34] One week later, it was reported that the Gath y Chavés Department Store had been forced to lay off 50 percent of its workforce due to a decline in receipts.[35] At the end of the year, the Conservative *El Diario Ilustrado* complained about the increasing numbers of beggars in downtown streets, which was attributed to "the lack of work and the difficult current situation."[36]

For the Municipality of Santiago, the major war-related issue was a by now familiar one. Claiming that the exchange rate had fallen below 9 pence per peso (there was some controversy over how this was calculated), the streetcar company requested an increase in fares, as the contract revision of 1910 allowed it to do, to 20 centavos for first class and 10 centavos for second class. The company asked the arbitration board first to intercede with the municipality to ensure its acquiescence to the increase. After six weeks of meetings involving representatives of the company, the arbitration board, and the city, the *regidores*, in secret session on December 30, 1914, voted 10 to 5, with four abstentions, against allowing the fare increase.[37] In response, the company threatened to resubmit its request directly to the arbitration board and, if the board denied the request, to suspend service altogether.[38] These actions touched off the most serious confrontation yet between the city and the company. And, as it developed, the confrontation took on features that would be repeated frequently in the years to follow.

Soon after the city's decision, an ad hoc group calling itself El Comité de Sociedades contra al Alza de Tarifas en los Tranvías (The Committee of Societies Opposed to the Streetcar Fare Increase) met to congratulate the ten *regi-*

dores who had voted against the increase, praising their "patriotic attitude."[39] A few days later, however, the streetcar company announced that it would be doubling its fares anyway, on January 15, while it awaited a decision from the arbitration board. Alcalde Valdés responded that the company's contract expressly excluded wartime crises as a pretext for raising fares, and he demanded that the company wait for the board's decision.[40] The following day, the municipality, by acclamation, again rejected the fare increase, voicing its strong support for the *alcalde's* position on the matter.[41]

True to its word, on January 15, 1915, the company then suspended service in Santiago. For their part, the city and private interests attempted to offer alternative means of transportation, including trucks, taxis, and horse-drawn carriages. However, they knew that such emergency measures could not fully meet the needs of a public that relied so heavily on the streetcar for daily transportation. Accordingly, a series of meetings were held involving representatives of the municipality, the streetcar company, the *intendente*, and, through the Ministry of the Interior, the national government. Complicating matters further was the estrangement, due to the war, between the company's management in London and its investors in Berlin, which led some of the company's opponents to argue that it currently had no legal standing and therefore any fare increase was unacceptable on those grounds.[42]

While service was suspended, the city imposed fines on the company for failing to meet its obligations. Finally, after ten days, a compromise settlement promoted by Valdés was accepted. The streetcar company would be allowed to collect the 20 centavo proposed fare in first class day and night but only 5 centavos in second class by day and 10 centavos at night. The agreement was to be temporary until the arbitration board reached a final decision. As might have been expected, even with the agreement things did not proceed smoothly. Once service was resumed at the new fare, the public, in essence, boycotted the first-class cars and crowded into second-class accommodations. On the many double-decked cars, this meant riding in the open air on the second stage. The company, in apparent retaliation, only slowly moved to restore full service and, it was claimed, began to limit the number of second-class cars in circulation. In the meantime, the third member of the three-man arbitration board had resigned in the face of complaints from the city's attorneys as to his impartiality and it took several weeks to find a replacement. While these events were transpiring, the Democratic Party held a large rally on the Alameda to protest the fare increase, which, they argued, fell disproportionately on the working classes during a time of economic crisis. The rallyers, speaking for "the people of Santiago," sent a message to the *alcalde* objecting to the higher fare and reaffirming the boycott of the first-class cars. They also called for an annulment of the existing contract, a city takeover of the company's assets, and the municipalization of its service.[43] These demands echoed similar proposals that had been introduced into the Chamber of Deputies by Democrat Malaquías Concha a week earlier.[44]

That a political party would try to take advantage of the controversy between the city and the streetcar company was not new. What was different this time, however, was the call for nationalization or municipalization of the service. While that solution would not come to pass for several decades, it now became a constant refrain in Chilean political discourse, repeated with increasing intensity during every subsequent confrontation between the Municipality of Santiago and the Chilian Tramway and Electric Company. It also reflected a growing sense of economic nationalism in these years, directed against various foreign monopolies like the streetcar company, a sentiment that would spread and deepen as time progressed.

Another new aspect in the dispute was the beginning of serious considerations of alternative means of public transportation. During discussion of a government takeover of the streetcars, for example, a local businessman petitioned Congress for permission to establish bus lines in Santiago and Valparaíso. Buses, he argued, had already proved practical and successful in Europe and North America. Even if the streetcar service were nationalized, he observed, it would still represent a monopoly. And if it were not nationalized, the competing bus service would have the advantage of being a Chilean-owned and -operated enterprise, without, as with the Chilian Tramway and Electric Company, "large sums of money going to foreign shareholders."[45]

In the last analysis, the introduction of buses was a much greater threat to the streetcar company than was the possibility of a government takeover. When the buses began to appear, their greater flexibility in terms of routes, if not always their greater comfort, brought serious and growing competition to the streetcar. As was the case in Buenos Aires and many other cities, the introduction of buses in Santiago, which today carry the great majority of those who use public transportation, spelled the ultimate extinction of the streetcar, which gradually became antiquated and inefficient. At the same time, the introduction of bus service posed its own set of problems and challenges for Santiago's officials. An effective bus system required improved paving on those streets that were already covered and added urgency to the need to extend paving even further into the rapidly expanding outskirts and suburbs of the capital. From an environmental perspective, paving helped to reduce the dust and mud that contributed to many of the public health problems of the capital. On the other hand, by facilitating the use of fuel-burning buses, private automobiles, taxis, and trucks, as opposed to electric-powered vehicles, the city also laid the groundwork (literally) for the noxious air contamination that has become such an overwhelming problem in recent years. These types of conveyances also require regulation, regulation that was often quite difficult to enforce. With the streetcar company, the city had been dealing with a single entity. With the proliferation of other types of vehicles, confrontations over rules and regulations and the setting of fares became more complex.

In 1915, however, these were problems for the future. Of immediate concern was a resolution of the fare increase dispute, which dragged on through February and well into March, complicated by delays in naming a third member of the arbitration board. Finally, with a third member in place and after having heard extensive arguments from both the city and the company, the board, by a vote of 2 to 1, determined on March 16, 1915, that the fare increase was not justified according to its interpretation of the law and the contract. Alcalde Valdés then immediately ordered the company to restore the fare of 10 centavos in first class and 5 centavos in second class.[46] Obeying this order, the company reluctantly reverted to the mandated fares the following day, but it also threatened to appeal the board's decision to the Supreme Court and refused to renew full service on some lines. In the face of these delays, the *alcalde* continued to levy fines on the company for noncompliance of its obligations. The company, in turn, refused to pay these fines, arguing that it was under no real obligation to do so, given the fare increase refusal.

WHILE THE CONFRONTATION BETWEEN the city and company continued to simmer, the capital's political parties prepared for the municipal elections slated for April 1915. These would be the first to be held in Santiago under the new electoral laws. They were to be preceded by the congressional contests, now held separately, in March. The new procedures, to "purify" the registries and the oversight of the municipal election by a Junta de Contribuyentes (Taxpayers' Assembly) seemed to have produced a fairer and more democratic result. But there were still instances of bribery and violence.

Overall, the congressional elections resulted in some subtle but significant shifts. In the Senate representatives of the Liberal Alliance came to enjoy a slim advantage over the Coalitionists (Conservatives, Liberal Democrats, and Nationalists), who maintained a sixteen-seat advantage in the Chamber of Deputies. There were growing signs that middle-class and even working-class voters were beginning to have an impact, and the Liberal Alliance began to make concerted efforts to attract their support. A noteworthy result in Santiago was the election to the Chamber of Deputies of two former *regidores*, Viterbo Osorio and Agustín Gómez García, who ran as Independents and who defeated, respectively, two well-known and well-regarded Liberal and Conservative incumbents, in the process accumulating the highest vote totals of any candidates.[47]

In preparation for the municipal elections in Santiago, slated for April 11, the Radicals met in assembly on March 16 and chose four candidates.[48] About a week later, the Junta de Reforma met and announced that it would support a list of candidates from the various parties who subscribed to their goals of "a good municipal administration that will invest tax revenues in works of sanitation, beautification, welfare, [and promote] lower-cost foodstuffs, education, and public morality."[49] Other parties also formed their lists and campaigned actively. Voting took place on April 11 without much commotion, or much interest, and the results were known soon thereafter. The three top vote-getters were all Radicals. In addition, two Democrats, two Nationals, one Liberal Democrat, one Independent Liberal Democrat, one Independent National, one Conservative, one Independent Conservative, and one Independent Liberal were also chosen. The leading vote-getter, Radical Washington Bannen, received 11,009 tallies, reflecting the disappointingly low turnout in a city of half a million.[50]

El Mercurio bemoaned the lack of interest and the results. Even though quite a few of the candidates endorsed by the Junta de Reforma, which the daily favored, had won, the election overall was, a lead editorial claimed, "frankly unpleasant for Santiago," since "many elements who inspire distrust" had triumphed, while others, more worthy, had been defeated.[51] Other disappointments followed. The hopes of those who had foreseen citywide elections and the reduction in the number of regidores as ways to limit partisan wrangling were soon dashed. Party competition and jockeying for position in the process of certifying the election results and forming the new municipality proved to be as intense, if not more so, in 1915 as it had been before the reforms. Indeed, limiting the number of positions may have had the unintended result of complicating coalition-building even more than usual. Party fragmentation, highlighted by the number of elected regidores who combined party labels with the adjective "Independent," seemed more pronounced than ever, as factions within parties fought to have their representatives on the ballot. The persistent problems in developing working and viable coalitions within the municipality, which the reforms had hoped to resolve, would continue with equal if not intensified force in the years to come.

The weeks following the election and installation of the new municipality of Santiago brought a complex and bewildering set of negotiations to determine the new alcalde. Drawn into the fray was soon-to-be president Juan Luis Sanfuentes (1915–20), whose home served as a meeting place for representatives of the Conservative Coalition. Finally, on May 3, the regidores agreed on Radical Washington Bannen as the new alcalde, after several other candidates had turned down the office and fellow Radical Horacio Manríquez had been rejected for the position.[52]

Bannen was the first member of the Radical Party to serve as alcalde. He was relatively young (having been born, in Santiago, in 1881) and inexperienced, and had been elected to his first post as regidor in the same year he was chosen alcalde. He did, however, have a law degree from the University of Chile, and he was the son of a Radical activist. He also belonged to the Cuerpo de Bomberos (Volunteer Fire Department), the Club de la Unión, and was active in the Club Hípico.[53] Despite his lack of experience in elected office, he proved to be reasonably adept at political maneuvering and managed to survive the usual criticisms directed at the First Alcalde, serving longer than some of his predecessors. Ultimately, however, after eighteen difficult months in office, he too submitted his resignation.

Bannen's main accomplishment was to resolve yet another dispute with the streetcar company in late 1916. The nub of this disagreement was debts the city owed the company and vice versa, with the company shutting down operations on several lines to force a resolution. After Bannen negotiated a compromise with the company, the *regidores* unanimously approved the agreement that led to a full restoration of service on October 25, 1916.[54] While many praised the *alcalde* for his efforts, it was not enough to repair the strained relations that had developed with his own Radical Party supporters over personnel matters, a circumstance similar to the situation that had forced Ignacio Marchant's resignation several years earlier. Having lost his majority, Bannen cited "health" and "personal" reasons, an increasingly familiar refrain of failed *alcaldes*, and resigned his post on November 2, 1916.[55]

On November 9, the *regidores* chose the National Party's José Víctor Besa to succeed Bannen. A former national deputy and *alcalde* elsewhere, Besa was experienced, well qualified, and generally well regarded. Although he was able to maintain a modicum of support and remain in office for the rest of the municipality's term, Besa was no more successful than his predecessor had been, however, in registering any significant achievements. Several months into his term, press commentary became scathing. In March 1917 the *South Pacific Mail* reported that "the gross ineptitude of the civil authorities [in Santiago] is once more arousing the indignation of the citizens." While this was nothing new, the *Mail* observed, it was causing special irritation at a time when it seemed apparent that other large Chilean cities—Valparaíso, Concepción, and especially Antofagasta—were being effectively managed.[56] At the same time, a series of editorials in *El Mercurio* claimed that the local government was "bankrupt," that city services were virtually nonexistent as a result, and that consideration should be given to replacing the elected *regidores* with a citizens' committee (Junta de Vecinos) appointed by the national government. "The Municipality of Santiago," one editorial concluded, "serves for nothing."[57]

As in 1915, critics of the municipality expressed the hope that the municipal elections of 1918 would produce better candidates and a more efficient government. Also as in 1915, all parties began to choose their candidates early in the year. Reflecting efforts at the national level, Conservatives and Radicals tried to form coalitions with like-minded partners, but without success. Ultimately, each party put forth its own list and the elections proceeded as scheduled. Again, turnout was low, with the leading candidate, Independent Enrique Phillips, garnering 19,090 votes and Liberal Democrat Pedro Marín, last on the list, receiving 9,901.[58]

A few days after the election, a streetcar strike brought public transportation in the capital to a virtual standstill. The strike, involving most of the workers in the company's machine shop as well as drivers and collectors, revolved around demands for an eight-hour day and higher wages. It was part of a growing number of such protests in Santiago and elsewhere during this period and marked the beginning of the strike actions of the streetcar workers themselves as a complicating factor in the company's request for higher fares. The company, which was again pushing for a fare increase, argued that workers' demands could not be met without the increased revenue such an increase would provide. The workers were wary of supporting a fare increase since the burden would fall most heavily on the working class as a whole. On the other hand, it was difficult to disentangle their demands from the company's request. This tension would persist. In the meantime, the provincial *intendente* was able to craft a resolution that was reasonably satisfactory to all parties and full service was soon resumed.[59]

As the streetcar strike came to an end, so, too, did the Besa administration. In an interview as he left office, the departing *alcalde*, without naming names, expressed his astonishment at what he called an unimaginable campaign of "systematic disparagement" that had been directed against the municipality during his tenure.[60] When the new municipality assembled, prospects were dim that Besa's successor would enjoy a kinder fate. The April elections had produced an even split among twelve elected *regidores*, with six for the Alliance and six for the Coalition, and with Independent and leading vote-getter Enrique Phillips holding the balance. After several weeks of uncertainty and negotiation, during which time Minister of Interior Arturo Alessandri, who would soon be the Liberal Alliance's presidential candidate, was drawn into the fray, the *regidores* finally agreed on Radical Rogelio Ugarte as First Alcalde.

Under Ugarte, the city's second Radical *regidor*, the municipality began to meet with some regularity and to deal effectively with certain issues. These included approving new regulations to assure sanitary conditions in bakeries, the extension of street paving to the city's outskirts, and the conversion of street lighting from paraffin to natural gas or electricity. The council also began to consider new regulations to assure the purity of milk sold in the capital, a perennial problem. At the same time, Ugarte revealed plans to create a new city office to keep a lid on skyrocketing prices for food and other basic necessities, and he met with the heads of municipal departments to discuss ways to make it easier for the public to pay taxes and fees. He also encouraged these officials to be more active in enforcing the laws and ordinances regulating cantinas, many of which were being ignored and violated. While engaged in these activities, Ugarte was not shy in attacking what he called an "obstructionist" minority on the council, which he blamed for the ongoing difficulty of achieving a quorum for regular sessions and for reflexively opposing almost any measure he suggested. The obstructionists only offered counterproposals that were, in Ugarte's words, "bombastic and impossible to realize."[61] The opposition responded in kind, accusing Ugarte, in rather contradictory fashion, of either insufficient attention to his job or, when he did act, of doing so in a high-handed and authoritarian manner.

These divisions became manifest when, at the end of July, Ugarte fired the head of the city's office in charge of regulating prostitution. In justifying his action, Ugarte described how he had personally inspected houses of prostitution, in the company of other city officials and the press, and that, contrary to existing laws and regulations, alcohol was being freely served in them. Although many prostitutes were able to show him the required city-approved health certificates, Ugarte noted, many others still obviously were carriers of venereal diseases. Personally, he believed that prostitution should be totally eliminated, but until that happened at the least it should be properly regulated. And since that was not happening under the current director, he had had no choice but to remove him from office and replace him with someone who could do the job.[62] These remarks, however, did not assuage those *regidores*, mostly Conservatives, who supported the director.

The issues raised in this case did not disappear. Enrique Phillips, one of the most outspoken and active *regidores* on the council, used the debate to raise numerous larger questions and complaints about the efficacy, or lack thereof, of inspectors and regulators throughout the administration. The city, he charged, lacked a sufficient number of "honest" inspectors, the majority having been appointed for personal and/or political reasons rather than by merit. Most of these, too, he alleged, did "what they felt like doing."

And they often succumbed to the influence of a "sweet bribe" (*coima dulce*). The result was, for example, continued "deplorable" conditions in the *conventillos*, which were supposed to be inspected and regulated on a regular basis but were not. The same was true for public transportation vehicles, which were filthy and germ-ridden because they were not inspected and cleaned as required. Most appalling, in Phillips's view, was the city's failure to properly regulate beverages and food, producing a situation where, "instead of liquors are sold poisons and other concoctions that kill our people; bread could not be filthier and more impure, butcher shops are full of flies and rats . . . and fish are sold after being treated with drugs to hide the foul odor." Moreover, at night, clandestine gambling dens, cantinas, and houses of prostitution flourished, attracting "minors of both sexes." To remedy these problems, Phillips recommended various reforms that were designed to streamline administration and to enhance the authority of the *alcalde* and department heads, which would attract "serious and suitable personnel." If these changes were not implemented, he warned, pressures to replace the elected municipality with an appointed *junta* of *alcaldes* would continue to grow.[63]

Ugarte did his best to respond to Phillips's concerns. On the very day of Phillips's presentation, the council agreed to the *alcalde*'s dismissal of the Inspector Técnico de Automóviles (Technical Inspector of Automobiles) because, according to Ugarte, he had been partly responsible for a growing number of traffic accidents in the capital.[64] In a related move about a week later, the *alcalde* decreed a reduction in the maximum speed limit for automobiles from 30 to 15 kilometers per hour in areas of heavy traffic congestion and 20 kilometers per hour in the rest of the city.[65] In practically every session of the council for the rest of the year, the mayor's office reported the closing down of half a dozen or so houses of prostitution as well as a somewhat smaller number of *conventillos* for violations of the city ordinances.

Ugarte maintained his majority and continued to serve as First Alcalde throughout the following year. For the most part, the problems and issues he faced in 1919 were carryovers from 1918. As usual, throughout the year relations with the streetcar company occupied a good deal of the *alcalde*'s time and attention. During this year, ownership and management of the company passed from German back to British hands. Despite this change, the basic issues with the city remained. Although it had made a profit during the previous year or so, the new representatives of the company met with Ugarte several times in April to push again for a fare increase, arguing that such an increase was the only way the company could meet the obligations it had incurred in the resolution of yet another strike by workers the previous January who had demanded higher wages and improved service overall.[66]

This request touched off considerable political maneuvering. In an open note to the *alcalde*, Conservative *regidores* encouraged him to oppose the company's request. A report from the city attorney suggested that the streetcar company had hidden the true size of profits earned and recommended that the municipality take over its operations. Then, in mid-June, the ever-contentious *regidor* Enrique Phillips sent a note to the director of the recently formed Federación de la Clase Media (Federation of the Middle Class), which had been organized to promote the interests of white-collar workers. Phillips claimed that Ugarte and other members of the municipality were meeting secretly with company representatives to agree to a doubling of fares. In a sharp response, Ugarte and the *regidores* of the majority labeled the charges "capricious and slanderous," claiming they were part of a campaign by Phillips "to demolish the prestige of the municipality ... [and] break the present majority."[67]

Ten days later, on June 24, Ugarte and the majority issued another statement in which they denied any collusion with the streetcar company to raise fares. They also assured the public that they were looking after the "legitimate interests" of all the capital's citizens and, in a not-so-subtle swipe at Phillips, asserted that the floating of rumors to the contrary was merely the "poor fruit of a mind out of control."[68] The following day, June 25, the Federación de la Clase Media sent a note to Ugarte thanking him for his clarification of the majority's position on the fare increase and for encouraging the municipality to meet in an extraordinary session to reject the company's proposal.[69] That session took place on June 26, at which time the *regidores* unanimously approved a committee report that recommended rejecting the fare increase. At the same time, Phillips took the occasion to register his strong objections to what he called "unjust charges" by some of his colleagues that he was somehow mentally unbalanced in his efforts to fight against the increase.[70] About a month later, the arbitration board reinforced the council's decision by determining that the streetcar company's claims for a fare increase did not meet the contractual standards established for such action.[71]

IN A REVIEW OF HIS TERM PUBLISHED in 1920, Ugarte pointed to the many difficulties and frustrations he had experienced as *alcalde* in trying to enforce decrees and regulations that he described as "a hodgepodge of truncated and often contradictory dispositions."[72] Like many of his predecessors, he did the best he could to make sure that city ordinances were observed and to address persistent problems within the fiscal and legal constraints imposed upon him. By most accounts, criticisms from Phillips and others notwithstanding, he was seen as an honest and well-regarded *alcalde*. However, like most of his predecessors, he was also subject to criticism that the general state of the city had not much improved under his administration. There were still abundant complaints—and considerable evidence—that sanitary conditions in the capital bordered on the catastrophic, that transportation, both public and private, operated in a reckless and dangerous manner and posed a constant hazard to pedestrians and passengers alike, and that the city's various efforts to deal with the increased costs of basic necessities like food, clothing, and shelter were ill-conceived and largely ineffective.

As these difficulties persisted, there were renewed calls for reform. Again, Alberto Mackenna Subercaseaux took a leading role. In late July 1919 he met with a number of other "aristocrats" who had been promoting municipal reform since 1908. They formed a special committee to advocate once again for national government intervention in local affairs. Two weeks later, the minister of the interior, at the committee's request, approved for submission to Congress a "law of exception" for Santiago, meaning that the proposed law would only apply to the capital. According to its terms, the president of the republic would appoint three *alcaldes* for terms of six years, with the possibility of unlimited reappointment and with the assurance of "adequate remuneration" for their services. Other provisions called for strengthening the hand of the First Alcalde by making it more difficult to remove him from office and easier for him to maintain majority support. The proposal also provided for eight *regidores* to be chosen by direct popular vote. The Preamble to the proposal pointed out that the measure, if approved, would put Santiago more in line with Buenos Aires, where Argentina's president appointed an executive, called the *intendente* and similar in his charge to the First Alcalde, who served with an elected council.[73]

The National Congress began to consider the "law of exception" for Santiago in late December. Although a majority seemed to favor it, a minority of Radicals and Democrats strongly opposed it, objecting especially to what they considered its anti-democratic features and limitations on municipal autonomy.[74] While the measure languished in Congress, the behavior of the Santiago municipality over the next year provided further ammunition for those who advocated reform.

In February 1920, battered from all sides, Rogelio Ugarte offered to resign as *alcalde*. As with Bannen, he had lost the support of members of his own party, at least one of whom, Regidor Horacio Manríquez, was reported to have ambitions of his own to succeed him.[75] When a new majority was formed against him, Ugarte officially resigned on February 18, 1920. On March 4, all thirteen *regidores* elected a new *alcalde*, the Conservative Eduardo Larraín, who defeated runner-up Manríquez.[76] This election, however, did little to make the municipality less partisan or more efficient. Over the next few months, political maneuvering within the council brought virtual paralysis to the local administration. Much of this maneuvering was related to the hotly contested presidential election between Arturo Alessandri of the Liberal Alliance and Luis Barros Borgoño of the now renamed Coalition, the Unión Nacional. While there was not always a direct correlation, the component parties of these two contending factions struggled mightily to control the municipality as the national elections proceeded. At the national level, Alessandri finally triumphed in the June 25 voting, drawing substantial middle- and working-class support. Nonetheless, he did not receive a majority of the popular vote and only a slim majority of the electoral vote, producing a situation of uncertainty that persisted until the end of the year, when he was finally installed as president.[77]

At the local level, matters became complicated when in August criminal charges involving misuse of municipal funds were brought against Larraín, leading to his arrest and resignation from office in a manner that paralleled the fate several years earlier of Silva.[78] Liberal Democrat Pedro Marín, who was chosen to succeed Larraín, inherited an administration that could only be described as in total shambles. Marín's main accomplishment was to finish out his term without being forced to resign. In the words of a biographer, this was an "incredible and seemingly unattainable achievement at a time when personal interests and ambitions gambled with men's honor and municipal funds."[79] Contemporary critics were less kind. An article published in the October 10, 1920, edition of El Mercurio claimed: "In the population of the capital, in all circles, without distinction of social classes or political ideas, exists the intimate conviction that the current municipality is the worst that could be expected."[80] While the "law of exception" remained stalled in Congress, the best critics could hope for was that the contesting parties would select better candidates than they had in the past for the upcoming municipal elections in April 1921. While there was nothing very new in either the criticisms or the hopes, these elections would take place under the supervision of a new national administration that had promised to bring fundamental change to Chilean political and social life. Whether this would make much of a difference at the local level remained to be seen.

4 Santiago in 1920

THE NATIONAL CENSUS OF 1920 illustrated the significant growth that had occurred in and around Chile's capital over the previous thirteen years. Overall, the population of the city of Santiago had grown from 332,724 in 1907 to 507,296 in 1920, representing 13 percent of the national total. Growth had been most pronounced in the outlying areas of the capital and less pronounced in the central districts.

Equally significant was the rapid growth in the same period of the *comunas* that surrounded the capital. Directly to the east, the *comuna* of Providencia, increasingly a desirable place of residence for the elite and the middle class, more than doubled in population, from 11,028 to 23,130. To the southeast, Nuñoa, also a desirable location for the established and the upwardly mobile, had grown from 17,880 to 26,756, while to the south the population of the predominantly working-class *comuna* of San Miguel had almost doubled, from 7,256 to 13,234. To the west, Quinta Normal had seen its population nearly triple, from 6,932 to 19,711, while to the north Conchalí had increased from 8,997 to 11,951. Overall, the nineteen *comunas* that, along with the capital, made up the Department of Santiago, had grown in population from 127,237 in 1907 to 178,771 in 1920.[1]

As had been the case earlier, most of this growth was due primarily to natural increase and internal migration. Foreign immigration played only a minor role; 28,909 foreigners were counted in the entire Department of Santiago, which represented 24 percent of the national total.[2]

Among the population as a whole, literacy continued to grow, with 67 percent of the adult population in the department listed as able to read and write in 1920, compared with 57 percent in 1907.[3] Again, this was slightly ahead of the national average of 63 percent.[4]

For the purpose of comparing changes in the size of social groups in Santiago, the census of 1920 offers the advantage of listing many more occupations than that of 1907. However, it has the disadvantage, for comparative analysis, of listing these occupations for the entire department rather than for the city alone, as was the case in 1907, and therefore the census data produces some inevitable distortions. Moreover, while the data for 1920 are richer with regard to the number of occupations, certain categories used in 1907, most notably that of *empleados*, were not used in 1920. Nonetheless, the available data provide at least a rough approximation of Santiago's social structure at the time.

As Table 3 shows, the working class continued to be represented in about two-thirds of the occupations listed. In comparison with 1907, there was a sharp drop in the numbers of unskilled and menial workers and a sharp rise in the numbers of semiskilled workers. Within that group, female seamstresses and cooks provided a healthy proportion of the total. Adding substantially to the male component, however, were occupations in transportation, notably among taxi and carriage drivers and streetcar and railroad workers. Skilled workers also showed an increase, from 19 percent of the total in 1907 to 27 percent in 1920. There was also a substantial increase in the rural skilled category for the same period, from 2.6 percent to 8.4 percent, undoubtedly due to the fact that the Department of Santiago contained many more areas devoted to agriculture than did the Municipality of Santiago, especially in 1920.

The most striking anomaly can be found in the middle-class categories. Whereas in 1907 these composed 31 percent of the total, by 1920 they were only 22 percent, running contrary to all impressions and observations concerning the growth of this group in these years. Again, the fact that these figures are for the department as a whole rather than just for the capital city, along with the omission of the *empleados* category, as previously mentioned, most likely explains this result.

The gender divisions within these groups evident in 1907 persisted in 1920. Women, especially domestic servants and laundresses, made up the bulk of the unskilled and menial category and predominated within the

TABLE 3. *Social Structure of the Department of Santiago*
by Occupational Category, Gender, and Nationality, 1920

	Native-born			Foreign-born				
	Male	Female	Total	Male	Female	Total	Total	%
Working class								
Unskilled and menial	4,194	8,692	12,886	48	49	97	12,983	7.0
Semiskilled service	23,452	29,372	52,824	671	593	1,264	54,088	29.2
Rural semiskilled	3							
Skilled	41,073	4,892	45,965	3,221	106	3,327	49,292	26.6
Middle class								
Rural skilled	14,532	699	15,231	364	12	376	15,607	8.4
Low non-manual	3,485	538	4,023	819	53	872	4,895	2.6
Middle unspecified non-manual	8,409	4,730	13,139	6,708	664	7,372	20,511	12.0
Upper class								
High non-manual	3,841	2,169	6,010	429	117	546	6,556	4.0
Low professional	5,316	1,393	6,709	599	370	969	7,678	4.0
High professional	3,794	1,828	5,622	575	225	800	6,422	3.5
Miscellaneous	2,872	3,731	6,603	379	204	583	7,186	4.0
Total	110,971	58,044	169,015	13,813	2,393	16,206	185,221	

SOURCE: Chile, Dirección General de Estadística, *Censo de 1920*, 464–67.

semiskilled service category. For the most part, females were absent from the transportation occupations, with only two females among the 2,422 listed categorized as *choferes*, for example. An exception was among the *tranviarios* (streetcar workers), where 482 women were listed within the total of 1,673. The presence of female conductors and collectors on Santiago's streetcars was a feature frequently commented upon by foreign visitors.[5]

Women were still only a small proportion of the skilled working class. Within the middle non-manual category, however, the number of female *comerciantes* grew from 2,826, or 12 percent of the total, in 1907, to 5,363, or 27 percent of the total, in 1920. It should also be mentioned that this was the category wherein foreigners were most heavily represented, with 7,355 (6,691 males and 664 females), or 37 percent of the total, although an even greater number of foreigners, 8,838, were listed as being "without occupation."[6] Within the high non-manual and professional groups, there were a significant number of nuns, nurses, midwives, and teachers listed. Among the more prestigious professions, however, there were no female architects, only 8 female lawyers out of 1,000, and 15 of 310 physicians.

The locational patterns suggested for certain social-economic groups for 1907 seemed to persist in 1920. Using information on property values, René Millar Carvacho, in his detailed study of the 1920 presidential elections, provided a map of Santiago that determined the social-economic charac- teristics of each sub-unit, or *sudelegación*, into which the city was divided. According to his analysis, the upper class continued to predominate in the central districts and near the Parque Cousiño. Middle-class districts were ad- jacent to these. The remainder, mostly extending from the Alameda and the Río Mapocho to the capital's outer limits, were the domain of the working classes.[7]

By 1920, various components of the social-economic groups described above had become organized and institutionalized. Beginning at the turn of the century the working class had begun forming unions and larger con- federations and had become increasingly active in the capital. The number of university students in the capital also grew substantially in these years. In 1906 the Student Federation of Chile had been created to represent student interests, and by 1920 it had become a major presence in Santiago, joining in various labor protests and working actively in the campaign to elect Ar- turo Alessandri president.[8] The Federación de la Clase Media appeared as well, to promote middle-class interests and to place pressure on both local and national governments to respond to the group's particular demands.

Industrial growth in Santiago seemed to level off during the 1910–20 pe- riod.[9] For the nation as a whole, however, the effects of World War I helped to spur industrial production, especially for domestic consumption, as im- ports were cut off and the national government began to institute some pro- tectionist policies.[10] An industrial exposition held in Santiago in 1916 dis- played a wide range of items from enterprises that produced food and drink products as well as clothing and general household items. One observer re- ported in 1918 that "over 90 percent of the furniture sold in Chile to-day is manufactured in the country" and that "great improvement is also noted in the textile industry, there being at present 7 knitting mills in Santiago work- ing at full capacity."[11]

In 1883 the Sociedad Fomento de Fabril (Manufacturing Promotion So- ciety, or SOFOFA) had been formed by Chile's industrialists to promote their interests. In 1918 another organization, with similar aims, the Cámara Industrial de Chile (Industrial Chamber of Chile), appeared and began to publish a magazine to highlight Chile's industrial progress and potential. Most of the Cámara's 250 or so members were located in and around the capital and were owners of mostly small-scale enterprises. Among them were two women, Rosa Ahumada, who owned a factory for making women's hats at San Diego 273, and Celia Z. de Buscaglia, who owned a linen-and-silk clothing factory at Loreto 277, as well as the former *regidor* and *alcalde* Guillermo Tagle Carter, who was listed as owning a factory for producing fat (*grasa*) at Arauco 1084. Also listed were the Chilean Electric Tramway Company and the Compañía Alemana de Electricidad (German Electric Company) with their headquarters at the corner of San Antonio and Santo Domingo. Reinforcing DeShazo's point, the addresses listed for the members of the Cámara showed these to be mostly small-scale establishments scattered across the city, with no significant concentration in any particular area.[12]

By 1920 the various immigrant groups had also begun to organize. The French, Italian, British, German, Swiss, Syrian, and Yugoslavian communities had established or were in the process of establishing sporting and social clubs in the eastern suburbs, institutions that continue to exist to the present day. The Jewish community, while relatively small, by 1920 had organized the Federación Sionista de Chile (Zionist Federation of Chile). With two hundred members and assets of 60,000 pesos, the federation's magazine, *La Patria Israelita*, promoted "the restitution of the people of Israel to their homeland of Palestine." On the back page of the first issue appeared advertisements for various Jewish-run enterprises in Santiago, including the cap and hat factory "La Europea" at Avenida República 46; Petruschkin, Sigal and Company, Importers, at Moneda 833; the "La Torre" drugstore at Delicias 3347; the furrier "Londres" at Delicias 2284 and Avenida Brasil 389; and the manufacturer of agricultural implements, Robinovitch Brothers, at Sotomayor 347.[13]

As in most cities, sports were becoming increasingly popular in Santiago. During this period, established newspapers like *El Mercurio* began to give expanded coverage to such activities, and there appeared various magazines, like *Negro y Blanco* and *Variedades y Sport*, designed to appeal to the growing public appetite for information on athletic competition at home and abroad. Soccer, horse racing, and boxing were particularly prominent, as were tennis and golf. Motorized sports and aviation were also beginning to attract a following. In 1917 the national celebration of the May 21 holiday that commemorated the epic battle between the Chilean warship *Esmeralda* and its Peruvian counterpart *Huáscar* during the War of the Pacific, for example, attracted a large and enthusiastic crowd to the Parque Cousiño. There, the crowd also observed a motorbike competition, a motorcar race, a bold aviator's acrobatics in the monoplane *Valparaíso*, and a balloon ascent.[14] The celebration continued with a parade that passed by the house of the widow of the hero of the legendary battle, Captain Arturo Prat, and ended with an orderly disbanding in the Plaza de Armas in front of City Hall.

Not all such celebrations, however, were so peaceful. During the 1919 commemoration of Chile's independence, on September 18, public drunkenness in the Santa Elena district along the Avenida Matta led to a brawl that produced several serious injuries and the death of one celebrant. This incident provided Enrique Phillips and other critics of the Ugarte administration another opportunity to attack the municipality for its alleged laxity in enforcing rules and regulations concerning the public consumption of alcohol.[15]

CONCERN THAT SANTIAGO WAS GROWING too rapidly and without any regulatory plan for rational development dated back at least to the time of Vicuña Mackenna in the early 1870s. In 1892 the national government had approved the Proyecto de Transformación del Plano de Santiago (Project of Transformation of the Plan of Santiago), which proposed to widen the congested and narrow downtown streets and the construction of broader avenues similar to the Alameda and extending to the outskirts of the city.[16] The project aimed to improve traffic flow and to give the city greater cohesion and uniformity. However, efforts to initiate construction were halted by the outbreak of World War I and the economic downturn that conflict occasioned. Along with recovery in 1915 and 1916, however, the problem began to receive renewed attention.

In 1915 Alcalde Ismael Valdés Vergara appointed a special committee of congressmen, *regidores*, and interested citizens to draw up a new plan for Santiago's transformation. Playing a leading role in this process was Ismael Valdés Valdés, a prominent member of the Liberal Party, former president of the Chamber of Deputies, and in 1915 a senator from Santiago. Under Valdés's direction, a projected new "transformation law" was submitted to the Senate in late 1915. As subsequently described and explained by him in a series of articles in El Mercurio, the national government, through the president of the republic and an appointed Junta de Transformación (Transformation Board) would regulate and control the capital's future growth. These authorities would oversee such matters as the proper height, size, and material of future buildings; assure that aesthetic considerations prevailed in the construction of new streets, avenues, and parks; and guarantee the preservation of historical monuments and buildings. Funding for new construction would come from special taxes and, when necessary, expenditures from the federal budget approved by the Senate and the president. Similar plans, Valdés pointed out, had enjoyed considerable success in cities like Barcelona and Buenos Aires.

An important feature of the proposal was its attention to the consequences of rapid suburban growth, which was haphazard and totally unregulated. Too often, speculators would buy up agricultural land and then subdivide it into lots to be sold at reasonably low prices but without any thought to the provision of basic municipal services or to how these new barrios, often in isolated areas, would be connected with the rest of the metropolitan region. Under his proposal, each new neighborhood development would have to submit a detailed plan for its approval before it could proceed. "The advantage of having the Junta de Transformación review plans for all new neighborhoods that are annexed to the city," he explained, "is that it will provide a certain uniformity to an experience which up to now has gone forward too freely, without study, and without any concern of the relationship of one neighborhood to another."[17]

From a practical point of view, Valdés's proposal made a lot of sense. Most major cities, especially capital cities, were either operating under such plans or were in the process of creating them. Given the political and financial difficulties of the Municipality of Santiago, it also seemed reasonable to place the direction of the capital's transformation in the hands of the national government. The development of a greater Santiago metropolitan region that would extend well beyond the city's official borders and involve various jurisdictions also argued for a greater federal role. At the same time, however, if the proposal became law, it would further undermine the autonomy and the authority of the local administration and marginalize it even more in the eyes of the public.

An important ally of Valdés and another leading figure in the various plans to transform Santiago was Carlos Carvajal Miranda. Born in 1873, Carvajal had joined the Navy as a young man and later became a military engineer. After earning a degree in civil engineering in 1896, he became General Director of Architecture in the national Public Works Ministry, from which post he oversaw the construction of various public buildings in cities throughout Chile. Addressing the Pan American Scientific Congress that met in Santiago in 1908, Carvajal argued that most urban problems were fundamentally moral problems, and he specifically cited the influence of "special interests and habits and human ambitions and egoism" that prevented basic reforms from being implemented. Anarchism, he believed, was the principal threat to society, and he urged the public construction of decent and inexpensive individual housing for each and every working family to counter that trend. In 1912 Carvajal submitted his own plan for the transformation of Santiago, which included a belt highway (*vía de circunvalación*) that would encircle the city, the development of diagonal avenues that would connect the center of the city with the outskirts, and the development of new "garden cities" in the suburbs.[18] In 1915 he strongly endorsed the Valdés proposal, which, if approved, in his words "would convert into reality the aspirations of so many who desire that we not remain left behind in the modern progress of all the civilized cities of the world."[19]

As it turned out, the Valdés proposal did not become law, so that no overall plan was adopted for Santiago's growth during the 1920s. Nonetheless, various of the measures that had been suggested bore fruit, as evidenced by a plan in 1920 of Alcalde Rogelio Ugarte to construct an avenue that would provide a new transportation corridor linking the Alameda with Nuñoa. Carvajal, for his part, retired from government service in 1915 but continued to be a prominent advocate of public housing and urban planning. He converted the Comité de Transformación de Santiago, which he had founded, into the Comité Central de Urbanismo (Central Committee of Urbanism) and eventually into the Instituto Nacional de Urbanismo (National Institute of Urbanism), a professional organization of architects, engineers, and planners devoted to addressing urban problems. In Santiago, as elsewhere, the "science" of urbanism was becoming increasingly prominent, as various technical experts sought to resolve the many complexities and problems of rapid urban growth. In Chile, Carvajal was one of the principal pioneers of this new science.[20]

While there was no action on the various transformation plans, some progress was made in these years on a major public works project that would become a lasting monument in the capital. For some years, city and national officials had considered ways to transform San Cristóbal Hill north of the Mapocho into a public park similar to Santa Lucía. By 1919, a special committee had been formed to study that transformation. In December of that year Carlos Thays, the parks director of Buenos Aires, visited Santiago and, accompanied by city officials, toured the site, noting with enthusiasm the impressive panoramic view the top of the hill provided. Upon his departure, Thays made some suggestions as to how the hill could be turned into a useful and attractive park.[21] A few months later, another Argentine visitor, the architect Martín Noel, also toured the site, making additional suggestions as to the design of the proposed park and proclaiming that because of its unique features "Santiago has in San Cristóbal a true jewel."[22] Encouraged by these favorable comments from distinguished trans-Andean experts, the National Congress, in July 1920, earmarked 1,400,000 pesos to help cover the costs of turning San Cristóbal into a major public park.[23]

FOREIGN VISITORS CONTINUED TO HAVE a generally favorable view of Santiago. Writing in the *Bulletin of the Pan American Union* in 1918, for example, Edward Albes extolled the many virtues of what he called "Chile's Charming Capital." In an article replete with handsome photographs of old and new buildings, avenues, parks, and plazas, Albes commented in most complimentary fashion about the Plaza de Armas and its surroundings, the Parque Cousiño, the Parque Forestal, and Cerro Santa Lucía. With regard to Santa Lucía, he asserted, "No city of modern times, as far as the writer knows, has anything just like it. It is the culmination of things beautiful and interesting in the Chilean capital, and must be seen to be appreciated."[24]

According to Albes, the city was also a fairly healthful place. It enjoyed "cool, crystal-clear water" from the Andes, had undergone extensive sewer and paving construction over the previous few years, and was "noted for its hospitals." Albes also observed that "the administration of the municipal affairs of the capital of Chile is admirable," and that the "excellent" streetcar system ran on fares that were "remarkably cheap." Finally, he observed, while commerce and industry had grown, for him, Santiago would "always remain preeminently the delightful city of beautiful parks, of the splendid Alameda, of the only Santa Lucía in the world, and of the alluring, entrancing life of the Plaza de Armas."[25]

Most Santiaguinos had a much less rosy view of the city. El Mercurio, for example, never seemed to tire of cataloguing Santiago's many deficiencies and the very poor conditions in which many of its citizens lived. An article of November 9, 1915, described the area in the northwestern part of the city between Cumming, Matucana, San Pablo, and the Mapocho as containing eighty blocks full of "cités of the poor and the most miserable conventillos of this city in which are the most miserable dwellings in the civilized world." In this area, a reporter had observed a boarding house in which sixteen people of both sexes had been crowded into one small room. The chimneys of the electric streetcar factory loomed over one part of this district, providing some employment for its denizens. However, also in its shadow could be found "numerous filthy and barefoot children clustered together in this immense worm pit of vice and poverty."[26]

El Mercurio was also concerned with the bad impression such conditions would make on foreign visitors. One article remarked that any tourist making his or her way from the Mapocho Station to Downtown would have to cross Sama and Mapocho Streets, in the heart of the district described above, and would be fully exposed to all of its horrors.[27] While much of the focus of El Mercurio's attention was on the conventillos of the downtown area, it also noted the fact that similar concentrations of inadequate housing for the working classes could be found in the areas around slaughterhouses and "important industrial establishments."[28]

Despite some well-intentioned governmental efforts to improve these conditions, little progress was made over the course of the 1910–20 period. On a 1918 visit to two conventillos on Calle Mapocho, in the same district, another reporter also noted many of the by-now familiar crowded, overpriced, and unsanitary conditions that marked such tenements—in this case, one water closet for thirty residents and the most rudimentary cooking and cleaning facilities. While women worked, their children played in a common patio, with filthy water running freely all over the surface. "Their husbands could be found," the reporter observed, "in the nearby cantinas which openly ignored the legal restrictions against the sale of alcoholic beverages."[29]

The unhealthy state in which many Santiaguinos lived contributed to the continued high mortality rates overall and among children in particular. Cold comfort was provided by a study that showed that by 1916 one in four of the city's infants died before the age of one, even though, five years earlier, the ratio had been one in three.[30] A report in 1920 showed the mortality rate in Santiago outstripped the birth rate, and that during the first eight months of that year, almost half of those who had died were babies. In addition to the effects of epidemic diseases, a growing number of illegitimate births, and the resulting neglect they occasioned, added significantly to the totals that died. According to the report, "In the first eight months of the present year there have been 7,097 births registered of which 5,664 are illegitimate."[31] A report one year later estimated that there were 5,000 orphans and abandoned children in Santiago, another result of the high rate of illegitimacy.[32]

For El Mercurio, the main cause of the city's "demographic retrogression" was the continued high rate of alcoholism. In the daily's perhaps overstated words, alcoholism "is the source of all the ills of which our people complain, of the illnesses that affect the race and of their economic misery."[33] With regard to this problem, the U.S. embassy reported in September 1920, "The progress of prohibition in the United States is being watched with the keenest interest in Chile."[34] By the end of the year, pressure was being applied on recently elected President Alessandri to implement something similar to the U.S. restrictions on production and sale of alcoholic beverages. One of the first petitions the new chief executive received came from the Chilean Federation of Labor (FOCH), which claimed that alcohol consumption took 350 million pesos annually from the pockets of the working classes. The FOCH urged Alessandri to support the longshoremen of Arica and Antofagasta in the North in their refusal to unload shipments of imported liquor, and to press for other, more sweeping measures to discourage consumption.[35] With labor intensifying its pressure, a special subcommittee appointed by the government in January 1921 recommended a prohibition on the planting of new vineyards; a prohibition on the manufacture of drinkable alcohol; a tax that would, in effect, make it nearly impossible to import liquor; a dramatic reduction in the number of establishments licensed to sell alcohol; and a significant increase in license fees for those that did. Overall, the aim of these recommendations was to move gradually toward total prohibition.[36]

Chile, however, was not the United States. At the same time as the FOCH presented its petition, the recently created League for the Defense of the Wine Industry, while agreeing on the need to curb excess drinking, argued that a moderate intake of wine was generally good for a person's health. More fundamentally, Congressman Guillermo Edwards, a defender of the industry, proclaimed that while it would be acceptable to restrict the importation of hard liquor, wine production was simply too important to the overall economy of the country to be curtailed, much less eliminated.[37] According to the same El Mercurio that had labeled alcoholism "the source of all the ills of which our people complain," some 320,000 Chileans were involved in some way in the wine industry, including some 30,000 owners of vineyards of ten hectares or less. The capital invested, not including the value of land, amounted to about 300 million pesos (Edwards's estimate was 900 million).[38]

These hard facts forecast the ultimate fate of the special committee's recommendations. While all sides recognized the seriousness of alcoholism and its debilitating effects on Chilean society, there would be no successful campaign for outright prohibition in Chile as had occurred in the United States, if for no other reason than the power and importance of the wine industry in the nation's economic life. Meanwhile, the immense social consequences of the problem would persist, especially affecting the capital's and the nation's working classes.

AS 1920 DREW TO A CLOSE, El Mercurio published an interview with a Chilean who had lived in Europe and the United States over the previous nine years. The newspaper asked him how Santiago had changed in that time. For the respondent, as for many Santiaguinos, a number of the new public and private buildings were indeed impressive, as was the expansion of commercial and industrial activity and the increase in street life in general. Local services, however, still left much to be desired. Street lighting was antiquated and insufficient; paving, except in a few streets, was "simply detestable"; and many streets, especially in the poorer neighborhoods, were public eyesores, full of rotting garbage and pools of stagnant and filthy water. With regard to the tramway, most cars were old and dirty and the service was unreliable and accident-prone. The expatriate predicted that in Santiago, as in the European and North American cities he had known, buses would soon replace streetcars as the main form of public transportation, although he noted that at present the buses that were operating were "inadequate and ugly" in comparison with those that operated elsewhere.[39] In other words, while some significant growth had occurred over the previous decade, many familiar and persistent problems remained, in many ways aggravated and accentuated by the rapid demographic and physical expansion of the capital and its suburbs. Old problems and new challenges, then, awaited the newly elected city government of 1921.

5 The Municipality of Santiago and the First Alessandri Administration (1921-1924)

HOPES AND EXPECTATIONS WERE HIGH when Arturo Alessandri was finally installed as president of Chile in late 1920. A charismatic and able candidate, Alessandri had campaigned as the champion of the common man and avowed enemy of the conservative oligarchy that had dominated the nation for more than a century. The program of the Liberal Alliance upon which he had run promised for the first time to address seriously Chile's most pressing social and economic problems, especially those that affected the working classes. For the most part, however, these high hopes were not realized and little real change occurred. Although the electoral strength of the Alliance grew during the first four years of Alessandri's term, divisions and disagreements consistently weakened the governing coalition. These disagreements, coupled with fierce conservative opposition, made it difficult to achieve much in the legislative realm. Alessandri's relations with labor, problematic at best, gradually deteriorated over time, depriving his administration of the kind of popular-sector enthusiasm and support that it badly needed to prevail over the opposition. Ultimately, political stalemate in 1924 led to military intervention and the first major interruption of Chile's democratic and constitutional government in the twentieth century.[1]

Expectations for progressive improvement at the local level, that is, for Santiago's government, were not as high, but the results there were equally disappointing. To a large extent, the actions of the city's administrations between 1921 and 1924 were a repetition of those that had preceded them, marked by constant partisan bickering and stalemate and with little of significance being accomplished. As in the past, too, relations between the city and the streetcar/electric company provided many instances of confrontation and served as an important issue and leitmotif throughout these years.

Alessandri's tenuous position as a president elected without a majority of the popular vote was strengthened somewhat by the national congressional elections of March 1921. The results of that contest gave the Alliance a solid advantage in the Chamber of Deputies, with seventy seats as opposed to forty-eight for the National Union. The Conservatives, however, held on to the Senate by an advantage of twenty-two to fifteen. The Radicals and Democrats continued to gain, with the former's thirty-nine deputies easily outdistancing the second-place Conservatives with twenty-five. The Democrats elected eleven deputies along with one of the two senators from Santiago. In the capital, three Radicals and two Democrats were the leading vote-getters.[2]

With the national elections out of the way, attention turned to the municipal contests slated for early April. Up to that point, Congress had still failed to act on the "law of exception" for Santiago, and supporters of the law began to lose hope that it would ever be enacted. In the meantime, the various pro-reform, or what might be called "good government," groups worked to provide a list of candidates with no partisan interests or affiliations and who would be only committed, at least in principle, to what would be good for the city as a whole. Playing a leading role in these efforts was Alberto Mackenna Subercaseaux, the longtime champion of reform, who had been named by Alessandri as *intendente* of Santiago. The attempt to come up with a common list along the lines envisioned by Mackenna and others failed, however, as the established parties were determined to select their own affiliated candidates. One commentator, who observed that general citizen interest in local elections was not very high, claimed that the participating parties, as a result, did not produce the same quality of candidates as they did for national office, so that the newly elected *regidores* would not be "prepared for the administration of a great capital city." Given the failure to develop a non-partisan list, the writer urged the parties to select "the best" candidates possible so as to avoid "three more years of sterility" in local government.[3]

Whether these words were heeded was a matter of opinion. For the most part, the parties selected candidates who either already were serving as *regidores* or who had done so in the past. The Radicals, for example, chose Horacio Manríquez and Viterbo Osorio, from the 1918–21 municipality, while the Democrats chose Diego Escanilla and Nicasio Retamales, also from the same council. Running for reelection as Independents this time around were Radicals Rogelio Ugarte and José D. Gajardo and National Eduardo Almarza. These candidacies, as well as others, were chosen, as had been the case for some time, in open party meetings, often accompanied by boisterous debate and disagreement. Procedures, however, varied from party to party. The Conservative assembly, for example, was attended by three hundred adherents of the party, but the candidates of the party were selected by only 55 voting members, whereas 1,515 voting Democrats chose their party's leading candidate, Nicasio Retamales.[4]

The campaign followed the time-honored practices of rallies, marches, and speeches. Addressing a crowd in the Club Conservador, Conservative candidate Luis Alberto Cariola admitted that the administration of the city had failed to take advantage of the spectacular location and natural attributes of Santiago and that the capital lagged behind other South American cities in its overall development. He argued that providing the city with low-cost food was a complicated and difficult problem but one that he and his party were resolved to address with tenacity so as to produce a substantial reduction in costs. In this same vein, he noted that streetcar transport was "one of the very rare inexpensive services that we have," and since inexpensive service was so important to those of "scarce resources, it ought to be maintained, necessarily on the basis of the current fares. If, however, reasons of justice and equity suggest concessions to the company that provides this service, these should be remedies that, based on maintaining these fares, consider the company's legitimate interests."[5] Cariola's position on this matter would soon be severely tested.

According to *El Mercurio*, the April 10 elections proceeded "generally, in a peaceful manner."[6] Again, interest and turnout were low. The leading vote-getter, Democrat Nicasio Retamales, received 10,443 tallies, as compared with the 23,069 votes recorded for the top candidate for deputy in the national elections a month earlier.[7] In general terms, results at the local level reflected the gains of the Alliance at the national level. The top six candidates included two Democrats, two Radicals, one Independent Radical (Rogelio Ugarte), and one Liberal Democrat. Overall, the new council would be composed of four Radicals, three Democrats, three Conservatives, one Liberal Democrat, one Independent Radical, and one National. Five former *regidores* of various parties failed to win reelection.[8]

While the results of the election seemed to assure the predominance of the Liberal Alliance, the actual coalition formed proved to be a surprise. Instead of the expected Radical–Democrat government, it was a Democratic–Conservative coalition that prevailed when the new municipality met on May 1. The reasons for such an arrangement were far from clear, but, at least ostensibly, the Democratic leadership seems to have allowed its *regidores* considerable latitude in deciding what might be the best course to follow to assure good and effective government for Santiago. In a joint statement, both parties promised efficient and comprehensive tax collection and special attention to improving lighting, sanitation, and paving in the city. They also agreed to maintain in the city's employ all those who were "honest, competent, and useful," and to remove those who were not, "regardless of political affiliation." Moreover, they promised "to maintain the current fares of the urban streetcars." Signing the agreement were the three Conservatives on the council, as well as Liberal Democrat Arturo Ramírez, National Emilio Silva Espic, and Independent Radical Rogelio Ugarte. Two Democrats, Nicasio Retamales and Diego Escanilla, also signed, but Democrat Bernardo Quiroga held off until he felt more assured about his party's position on the agreement.[9] On May 8, in assembly, the Democrats of Santiago voted 409 to 354 to approve the pact. Accordingly, Quiroga then agreed to join the majority, which now numbered nine, with the four Radical *regidores* composing the minority.[10]

The new majority chose Conservative Luis Alberto Cariola as First Alcalde. Democrat Diego Escanilla was elected Second Alcalde and Radical Pedro León Ugalde, leader of the minority, Third Alcalde. Born in Santiago in 1875, Cariola had received his law degree from the Catholic University in 1896, where he also had served as a faculty member beginning in 1916. Prior to his election in 1921, he had enjoyed a successful career in journalism, including as editor of *El Mercurio* when it moved from Valparaíso to Santiago at the turn of the century. After serving as an editor of various other newspapers, he had abandoned journalism to become director of a coal company, enjoying similar success in this endeavor as well. Politically, he had been active in the Junta de Reforma Municipal and the Liga de Acción Cívica (League of Civic Action), which had been formed to promote the nonpartisan candidate list for the 1921 elections, prior to his own selection as a Conservative candidate and ultimate election to office.[11]

Cariola's term as First Alcalde followed a familiar pattern. It began with considerable energy, enthusiasm, and optimism, backed by a solid majority. Over time, however, Cariola's position gradually deteriorated in the face of political opposition, internal disagreement, and the frustrations and disappointments that came with the inability to resolve successfully what seemed to be intractable, ongoing problems. Ultimately, like so many of his predecessors, Cariola resigned from office well before his term was due to expire.

Issues involving traffic and transportation remained constant concerns. The proper regulation of taxicabs was one of these. Despite what appeared to have been a breakthrough on this matter in an earlier administration, a proposal to install meters in taxis and set standard fares continued pending. The notoriously independent drivers also objected to attempts to restrict their parking in the downtown area, as part of a larger effort to ease congestion. By the end of the year, various drivers, citing increased costs for gasoline and other materials, had presented a petition to the municipality requesting that they be allowed to raise their fares by 50 percent. Democratic *regidor* Escanilla indicated that he would support this petition, but other unnamed *regidores* voiced their opposition.[12] Cariola, for his part, recognized the importance of all taxis having meters regardless of the fare. He took the occasion to propose that instead of requiring the drivers themselves to bear the cost of the meters, as was currently the case, the city should undertake this responsibility. Acutely aware that the state of the city treasury made this impossible, he recommended to the *regidores* that they should approach the Senate for permission to borrow two million pesos for this purpose.[13] Given other pressing needs, however, it seemed unlikely that either the council or the Senate would agree to such a request.

The still unresolved taxi meter issue paled in significance when compared to the seemingly never-ending struggle between the city and the streetcar/electric company. Despite the much-heralded efforts of the streetcar company to improve relations with its workers, labor disputes continued to erupt. In April and July, Alessandri himself intervened directly to resolve two walkouts that had produced serious disruptions in service, a sign that the entire issue was becoming as much a national as a local governmental concern. These resolutions, however, were only temporary, as the company continued to press for a fare increase, arguing that it was the only way to meet workers' demands. But the municipality, under Cariola, steadfastly refused to grant this request. Seeking to increase the pressure, the company gradually cut back on the number of cars in operation and shut down some lines altogether.

In late October, in the midst of this renewed standoff, the company received governmental permission to reorganize. The former Chilian Tramway and Light Company, Ltd., a British corporation, now merged with the National Electric Power Company, formed two years earlier in Valparaíso under the direction of Chilean Juan Tonkin and U.S. engineer Norman Rowe. The resulting company was called La Compañía Chilena de Electricidad Limitada (the Chilean Electric Company, Ltd.). While a Mr. B. C. Pearson of London was made president of the new board of directors, the vice-president was Ismael Tocornal, a well-regarded Liberal Party politician and diplomat, who had served off and on as Alessandri's minister of interior in 1921 and 1922.[14] Other Chileans, including Tonkin, were prominent on the board.[15] Apparently, by changing its name, merging with a Chilean enterprise, and incorporating well-known and influential Chileans on its board of directors, the company hoped to change its profile as a foreign-owned monopoly with its directors and stockholders far removed from Santiago.

None of this mattered, since the Cariola administration in late 1921 still refused to show any inclination to accede to higher fares. In late December the arbitration board, to which the most recent dispute had been submitted, determined that the company should restore full service without the fare increase. The company, however, ignored this decision and continued operating at a reduced level. Despite direct intervention by Alessandri and his minister of the interior, attempts at compromise failed, as both the company and Cariola, speaking for the city, refused to budge from their respective positions. Finally, in May 1922, the minister of the interior determined to send the matter to the National Congress for resolution, a resolution that ultimately never came. In the meantime, the Santiago public continued to suffer the poor and reduced service that resulted from this latest confrontation.[16]

WHILE RESOLUTION OF THE STREETCAR COMPANY'S intransigence remained pending, Cariola faced a series of other difficulties that gradually eroded his political support within the council. Generally, throughout his first year in office, the majority he had enjoyed at the outset stood solidly behind him, especially on the streetcar issue. The possibility of division, however, had arisen in late April and early May 1922, when members of the Radical minority claimed that the *alcalde* had violated the rules concerning nepotism by allowing a relative of National Party Regidor Eusebio Silva Espic to be named as an employee in the city's sanitation office. At the session to discuss the matter, Cariola asserted that if he had known the employee was a relative of Silva Espic, he never would have allowed the appointment, while Liberal Democrat Arturo Ramírez argued that in this case the law allowed for the appointment. There was no final resolution of the matter, as the minority abandoned the chamber, preventing a quorum.[17]

Later in the year, Cariola twice left his charge in the hands of the Second Alcalde so as to visit other South American capitals. On both occasions, the *alcalde* in charge and a majority of *regidores* had made decisions to which he strongly objected. The first had to do with the city allowing a local firm to rent meters to taxi drivers, a measure that Cariola saw as unnecessarily expensive and that he overturned upon his return. The second occurred while Cariola was leading a delegation to Rio de Janeiro, as part of Brazil's centennial celebration, and concerned a decision of the council to allow the streetcar company to double all fares in order to provide more cars and service during a typhoid fever epidemic that the city was experiencing. Even before Cariola had returned to Santiago, he made his firm opposition to the council's decision abundantly clear. In a cable from Montevideo, he called the typhoid epidemic a "pretext" for the streetcar company to get its way, and he said agreeing to the proposal was tantamount to sanctioning "the shameful dominance of an enterprise that scoffs at the nation."[18] Back in his office, he reiterated his opposition, but to no avail. The majority of *regidores* continued to favor it, thereby undercutting Cariola's authority and shattering his support on the council. After a key vote went against him on October 13, he promptly resigned his office. In an interview, he reported that he was not entirely unhappy to be relieved of a duty that was "un gran labor" (a great burden) and promised to continue as *regidor* to work for the best interests of the city.[19]

AFTER A FEW DAYS OF DISCUSSION AND SPECULATION, on October 18 National Regidor Eusebio Silva Espic emerged as the new First Alcalde. His support came primarily from Radicals, with a scattering of others. Initially, Silva's relations with the council went fairly well. Meetings were held on a regular basis, with generally full attendance and little apparent disagreement. The majority approved most of his personnel appointments, including a reorganization of the city sanitary office, with little dissent. In late November the council gave preliminary approval to a proposal from Rogelio Ugarte to float a bond issue of seven million pesos intended primarily to construct modern garbage incinerators, a need Silva himself had highlighted on various tours of the city and that everyone agreed should be a top priority of the local government. In the first half of November, too, Silva and the *regidores* basked in the glow of triumphant visits from two distinguished Latin American visitors, the Mexican intellectual and education minister José Vasconcelos and the Brazilian aviator Santos Dumont, who had a street named for him in the district north of the Mapocho. The afterglow of the visits, however, would quickly fade. In late November the streetcar issue arose again. The new minister of the interior (reflecting the high turnover rate of Alessandri's cabinets), Luis Izquierdo, met with *regidores* and congressmen to inform them that the double fare for the streetcars that the city had agreed to would not be going into effect on December 1 as planned. According to the minister, the company had informed him that it did not have enough cars to put into circulation to meet its end of the bargain. According to Juan Tonkin, the company was awaiting final word from Congress on the September 22 accord before proceeding.[20] Whatever the truth of the matter, the postponement was a clear signal that the entire matter was far from settled. At the same time, it intensified the already growing public opposition to the fare increase. Most important for Silva, it set in motion a series of events that would lead to a steady erosion of his position and to his ultimate resignation.

On the evening of November 29, following the minister of the interior's announcement, opponents of the fare increase met to plan their strategy. Playing a leading role was the Democratic Party, and particularly Regidor Bernardo Quiroga, a consistent opponent of the increase. A member of the Radical Party indicated, too, that there was considerable dissatisfaction within its ranks with regard to the party's *regidores* who had backed the increase. A spokesman for the Liberal Democrats reported actions by members of his party to block the increase, and it was already well known that two *regidores* of the Conservative Party, most notably ex-*alcalde* Cariola, had strongly objected to the September 22 accord.[21] A little more than two weeks later, the protestors met in another assembly and named as co-presidents of their coalition of labor and political groups opposed to the increase the then current *regidor*, Quiroga, and the former *regidor* and gadfly, Enrique Phillips. Chosen as treasurer was the former Conservative *regidor* Eduardo del Campo.[22]

As public pressure against the increase grew, Silva tried to pursue his normal activities. It appeared, at least for the moment, that he would leave a resolution of the conflict up to the national government. This strategy was complicated, however, by the fact that City Attorney Aníbal Mena Larraín was an active member of the anti–fare-increase organization. In an extraordinary council session on December 14, called specifically to address the streetcar situation, Mena made a pointed attack on the company as "a real monopoly that absorbs the energies of the country," concluding that the agreement made on September 22 was both illegal and unconstitutional.[23] Soon thereafter, Silva suspended Mena for two months, alleging that in his presentation of December 14 he had shown "disrespect for the person of the First Alcalde." Mena denied that this was so and an unidentified member of the municipal minority argued that there was no justification for the suspension, which he saw as a maneuver "to justify the interest of the current majority to impede however it can continued consideration of the streetcar matter."[24]

This comment was only the opening salvo of what would be an incessant barrage from the minority against the *alcalde*. After several delays, the council met on December 21 to elect Radical Viterbo Osorio as Second Alcalde and to engage in a heated exchange between the proponents and opponents of the fare increase. These fireworks, however, were overshadowed by a charge from the minority that Silva had received a bribe to overlook the violations of city ordinances observed during one of his tours of the capital, a matter in which one of his relatives was allegedly involved.[25] Silva denied these charges, but the minority—Cariola, Ugarte, Retamales, Martínez, and Quiroga—demanded that the *alcalde* allow a "tribunal of honor," made up of leading citizens, to look into the matter. After some initial reluctance, Silva agreed to this demand, so long as the tribunal looked into the activities of previous *alcaldes* as well.[26]

By the end of the year, things could not have been much worse for Santiago. The local government was deeply divided over the fare increase and the *alcalde* was under investigation for malfeasance in office. At the national level, the Congress seemed deadlocked and ill-disposed to favor the higher fares for streetcars that would have conceivably broken the impasse. As *El Mercurio* observed, the city government had been absorbed by the streetcar issue for two years, with nothing resolved. In the meantime, the city, it claimed, found itself "in full bankruptcy and complete abandon."[27] The only alternative that many saw to relieving the burden of the beleaguered Santiaguino commuter was to encourage the further development of service via buses, which were described as "agile vehicles that quickly pass the crammed streetcars" and which, it was argued, seemed to be working well in Valparaíso and could easily become equally popular in Santiago.[28]

The first few months of 1923 saw a steady deterioration of Silva's position. By April 1923, a majority on the council had turned against him, formally censuring his actions as *alcalde* and accusing him of criminal behavior in his handling of municipal funds, which led to his unavoidable resignation.[29] While this wrangling continued, so, too, did the city's confrontation with the streetcar company. During January and February, the anti–fare-increase forces intensified pressure on both the national and local governments. This seemed to have an effect, at least so far as the city council was concerned. At a March 2 meeting chaired by the Third Alcalde (Silva, whose removal from office was to be considered at this meeting, being absent) and before a packed chamber, the *regidores* agreed to now declare null and void the accord reached on September 22, 1922, to allow the fare increase and to recommend that the National Congress suspend all consideration of such an increase. They also approved a resolution from Cariola demanding that the company meet its legal obligations by ensuring that at least six hundred cars were in service on the line. No roll call was reported, but these two measures appear to have received unanimous support.[30]

The company's response was immediate and expected. Declaring the council's action "illegal," it refused to implement full service until the fare increase was allowed. Moreover, the company announced that it would begin to enforce limitations on the number of passengers per car as mandated by law, which promised to aggravate matters further. Faced with this response, the national government, with Alessandri playing a leading role, determined to intervene again, primarily at first to avoid violence and then to develop a long-term solution. Various measures were tried. To avoid protests that might lead to attacks on streetcars and other company property, the intendente, the alcalde, and the company agreed to a temporary suspension of all service until a compromise could be reached. Such a compromise seemed to be at hand when on March 14 Chile's ambassador in London announced that he had reached an agreement with the company's directors there by which higher fares would be allowed in return for a guarantee that at least 420 cars would be placed in service and that special cars would be provided for workers at a fare of 5 centavos.[31] Service was restored the following day. Speaking for the city, however, Silva demanded that 600 cars be put into circulation at fares of 10 and 5 centavos, asserting that the city could not accede to an arrangement that ran counter to its decision of March 2.[32]

It seemed clear to many at this point that Silva and the regidores, in shifting their positions on the fare increase, were looking for partisan advantage. Nonetheless, they were also responding to what was a strong popular groundswell and a well-organized and well-articulated protest movement against the company and its actions. It was clear, too, that President Alessandri was feeling some of the heat. Following a public rally on March 16 against the fare increase, Enrique Phillips met with the president to urge him to reverse the decree stemming from the March 14 agreement that had allowed the momentary fare increase. Appearing to waffle on the issue when addressing the crowd that had accompanied Phillips, Alessandri became the target of some hostile remarks from several people in the audience.[33] Not coincidentally, the next day the minister of the interior announced that the earlier agreement to raise fares had been revoked.[34] As a result, the situation returned to what it had been before. The company restored its minimal service of about 230 cars at the standard fare. While suggestions had again been made in favor of either national or municipal intervention to take over and run the streetcars, this did not seem a realistic option. In the meantime, the long-standing confrontation between the city and the company seemed no closer to resolution.

SANTIAGO WAS NOT THE ONLY South American capital where resistance to streetcar fare increases was occurring. A similar struggle was taking place in Buenos Aires at about the same time, and the city councilmen's actions there to forestall higher fares seem to have influenced their Santiago colleagues.[35] During his term as First Alcalde, for example, Cariola had visited Buenos Aires and Montevideo at least twice to observe developments and to see how lessons learned from their experience could be applied to Santiago. His position with regard to taxi meters, too, seems to have been affected by his observations of how these were installed and how much they cost to rent in Buenos Aires. Moreover, he had returned from Montevideo with detailed plans and other information on the construction of modern garbage incinerators to be used for a similar project in Santiago.[36] City Attorney Aníbal Mena Larraín, a leading figure in the anti–fare-increase movement, drew explicitly on examples from Buenos Aires to support his position.[37] Reporting on his visit as a member of the delegation to Brazil in 1922, Democratic *regidor* Nicasio Retamales remarked that in Rio de Janeiro, "the streetcar service is very superior to ours. There, all is discussed and there is no difficulty of any kind in observing contracts." He added, however, that fares there were also higher, at 10 and 20 centavos for second and first class, respectively, double what they were in Santiago.[38]

Cariola's first visit as *alcalde* to Buenos Aires had been personal and unofficial. While such visits had previously been the norm for most city officials, increasingly, beginning in the 1920s and continuing thereafter, there were officially arranged reciprocal visits of delegations representing the local administrations of various South American capitals. In mid-April of 1922, for example, the city council of Santiago hosted an extensive visit by fellow councilmen from Buenos Aires and Montevideo. Aside from the normal hoopla and ceremony that accompanied such events, they also provided abundant opportunities for the sharing of ideas and information about common municipal problems and to compare how their respective capitals stood with regard to such matters as relative rates of progress and needs for improvement.

AFTER ALL THE UNCERTAINTY AND TENSION over the long and drawn-out struggle over Alcalde Silva, the *regidores* determined to place executive authority in the trusted and experienced hands of Independent Radical Rogelio Ugarte. Meeting on April 9, the council elected him First Alcalde by a vote of seven in favor, with two abstentions. The "new" majority was very much like the old, a Conservative–Democratic alliance buttressed by a Liberal Democrat and a National. The Radicals, who generally abstained, were conspicuous by their absence, although one of their number expressed support for Ugarte, "always so long as his administration follows faithfully the principles that he has outlined."[39]

While the sailing was not always smooth, Ugarte's second term in office was relatively successful and productive. Beginning with the usual burst of energy of new *alcaldes*, he toured the city to inspect conditions firsthand and soon sent a message to Congress urging the drafting of a new municipal law that would give the city the fiscal independence he believed it so desperately needed. On the streetcar front, by the end of the year, after continued strikes and negotiations between the city and the company, it appeared once more that the long-standing dispute over the fare increase might be resolved. On the afternoon of November 15, Ugarte and Cariola for the city and two representatives of the company signed an agreement that allowed for the requested doubling of fares. In return, the company agreed it would keep a minimum of 500 cars in service, with a total capacity of 12,000 seats, and it would extend and improve lines and update its rolling stock. It also agreed to restore service on certain lines which had been abandoned, and to make other capital improvements, including the installation and maintenance of 8,000 new streetlights.[40]

The announcement of the agreement was met with sighs of relief and general praise for Ugarte and Cariola. The accord, however, had to be approved by both the municipality and the National Congress. In an interview on November 16, Ugarte listed the many benefits the agreement promised for the city and expressed his confidence that both bodies would approve

it.[41] So far as the municipality was concerned, Ugarte's confidence was justified. After several sessions, with the Democratic *regidores* expressing the
strongest reservations and demanding certain revisions and amendments,
the city council approved the revised agreement (the revisions were minimal) on November 22, with only one Democrat and one Radical showing
any serious objections.[42] Congressional approval, however, would once
again prove to be a major stumbling block to any final resolution.

WHILE THE STREETCAR FARE MATTER remained pending in Congress, national elections to that body were to be held in March 1924. These produced
sweeping victories for the Liberal Alliance, giving it solid majorities in both
houses. Once these elections were completed, the various parties in Santiago
geared up to compete in the municipal elections scheduled for April. The
Conservatives, smarting from their defeat in the congressional elections,
campaigned hard at the local level. Choosing four well-educated and experienced candidates, they promised to extend basic services, including street
lighting and paving, to all areas of the city and to pay particular attention to
improving sanitation and sanitary conditions.[43]

The Radicals campaigned with equal vigor. In late March the Radical Assembly urged all party members to overcome any past divisions and to work
in a united and disciplined manner for the elections of its four candidates
to the council. The party also formed an alliance with the Democrats to establish a joint committee that would campaign against the buying of votes.[44]
Radical candidate Viterbo Osorio complained of the frustrations he had
felt over the previous three years as a member of the municipal minority
and promised that in this election the four Radical candidates would be
marching in step behind a common program. That program included strict
oversight of municipal finances, improvement of sanitation and clearing
services through modernization of equipment (as resources allowed), development of an orderly plan for street paving and lighting, "especially in
working-class *poblaciones* and popular barrios," and stricter regulation of the
growing number of buses in the capital.[45]

Although Rogelio Ugarte was nominally a Radical, he ran for reelection
as an Independent. Advertisements on behalf of his candidacy stressed his
accomplishments as *alcalde*.[46] During the campaign, Ugarte took an automobile tour of the city with "Roxane" (the pen-name for Elvira Santa Cruz

Ossa), an increasingly popular female journalist who frequently wrote on local matters. They passed by institutions that had resulted from Ugarte's initiatives, including the site of his proposed Universidad Municipal del Trabajo (Municipal University of Labor) that would provide free classes for workers, a historical museum, and various parks and playgrounds. As they moved from place to place, Roxane commented on "the backwardness of Santiago, so dirty, so poorly lit, so badly paved." Ugarte responded that little could be accomplished in these areas, given Santiago's meager budget when compared with those of capitals like Buenos Aires and Rio de Janeiro. Much of the blame for the city's problems he placed on the National Congress, where, he asserted, most elected officials were little concerned with public affairs and where initiatives such as his own suggested reform of the municipal law and the streetcar accord languished while an income tax law, which had detrimental effects for the capital, was enacted. The poor conditions of Santiago, he averred, could be laid primarily to congressional neglect, and "if the new Congress does not act, we shall continue being an embarrassment in the eyes of all those who visit us." In addition to congressional failures and neglect, he concluded that a good deal of the blame for the poor appearance of the city could be traced to a general public inattention to municipal affairs and to a "lack of civic culture" and pride in maintaining both private places and public spaces.[47]

Conservatives, Radicals, and Independents were not the only competitors. The National Party, two branches of the Liberal Democrats, two branches of the Liberals, the Democratic Party, and the Communist Party also presented candidates. While there were differences in emphasis, there was a general consensus among all participants on what needed to be done to improve local administration and on what the city's most pressing needs were. Whether this general agreement would translate into less partisanship and more cooperation was another question.

There were rumors prior to the election that the Liberal Alliance government was seriously considering replacing the elected municipality with a *junta de vecinos*. If that were the case, the idea was rejected because the elections proceeded with relative calm and order as scheduled on April 13. Again, public interest and turnout were low. Rogelio Ugarte was the leading vote-getter with 13,103 tallies (in a city of half a million), compared with the 21,314 votes for the leading vote-getter in Santiago's national deputy elections in March.[48] Overall, the Conservatives did well, with all four of their candidates elected, followed by three Radicals, two Democrats, one Independent (in addition to Ugarte), one National, and one Liberal Unionist. Except for Ugarte, Radical Viterbo Osorio, and Conservative Calixto Martínez, who had served on the council from 1918 to 1921, the rest were new faces.[49]

The new council met on May 4 and selected Conservative and former national deputy Gonzalo Echenique as the new First Alcalde. His election was the result of an alliance between the Conservatives and the Democrats. From the beginning, the Echenique administration took some interesting twists and turns. These reflected, to some extent, the partisan maneuvering and resulting political stalemate that marked politics and administration at the national level. The first regular session of the new council, for example, was dominated by the newly elected Radical Regidor Humberto Mardones, who called for a thoroughgoing investigation of municipal finances and who argued that the city could not afford to go ahead with such expensive projects as the proposed garbage incinerators or Ugarte's Universidad Municipal del Trabajo. Most importantly, however, Mardones claimed that the streetcar accord of November 1923 was "prejudicial" to the best interests of the city and its administration, and he introduced a resolution that the council should recommend to the Chamber of Deputies that it cease consideration of the agreement. The motion carried by a vote of 7 to 6, with the Radicals, Democrats, one Conservative, and one Liberal in favor and three Conservatives, including Echenique, two Independents, including Ugarte, and one National opposed. This vote followed on the heels of a sharply worded note from the Radical Assembly to the minister of the interior, accusing him of having used his influence to push for an accord that would favor the company to the detriment of the Santiago traveling public. The assembly also took Alessandri to task for having allowed the minister "to develop activities so contrary to the true and lasting public interest."[50]

Mardones was also a major player in a shift in the governing coalition that occurred at the end of May. Reacting to what they considered an unfair personnel decision, the Democrats withdrew from the majority in protest. After the usual round of intense negotiations, the Radicals, who just a month earlier had severely criticized what they called the "unnatural" Conservative–Democrat coalition, now took the place of their nominal Liberal Alliance partners to form a new majority. The new coalition promised, among other things, to press Congress for the passage of laws and the provision of subsidies that would promote the capital's progress.[51]

Continued partisan bickering helped make these promises almost impossible to keep. An idea of the type of partisan sentiment that was often present within the municipality is provided by an incident that took place at the end of June, when Liberal Regidor Enrique Ramírez Rodríguez, a member of the minority, advanced on Echenique with a raised cane and threatened to strike him unless he was allowed to speak. Restrained by his colleagues, Ramírez returned to his seat and, finally given permission to take the floor, accused the administration of making personnel decisions based primarily on partisan considerations, in this case, by removing employees of "many years of meritorious service" and replacing them with "political hacks of doubtful competence and morality," a not unfamiliar refrain. His motion to censure Echenique on this score was defeated by a vote of confidence in the *alcalde* that passed with seven in favor, one opposed, and two in abstention.[52]

Despite the often bitter disagreements within the council, the majority held and Echenique's term was not totally bereft of achievements. The *alcalde* himself was given high marks for an aggressive personal campaign to crack down on vice by making extensive and frequent tours of inspection and ordering the closing of brothels, restaurants, hotels, and gambling establishments that operated in violation of city ordinances. Little progress was made, however, on the vital issues involving public transportation. Consideration of the Ugarte–Cariola streetcar agreement remained stalled in a Congress that was doing little beyond debating pay increases for itself. In the face of continued demands by its workers for improved working conditions and by the city for better service, the company steadfastly stuck to its position that nothing could be accomplished in either of these areas without a fare increase. At the end of July, the company, in a note to Echenique, announced that it had given up hope that the Chamber of Deputies would approve the accord and that it was therefore officially withdrawing from its side of the agreement. Company spokesman Juan Tonkin, however, did state that the enterprise was fully prepared to consider a new agreement, so long as it was "equitable for both the company and the capital."[53] While Echenique showed some willingness to consider such an agreement, in the last analysis nothing was resolved on this matter during what would be his truncated term in office.

While buses increased in number and popularity, that service, too, was far from trouble free. There were frequent complaints, for example, that too many buses ran on the same lines and that the competition for passengers produced excessive speed and reckless driving. An article in *Zig-Zag* asserted that the buses operated in a manner that "sowed terror" among the population and called on the local administration to regulate routes and speeds so as to protect "the weakest—women, children, the elderly—among whom are found the majority of the victims" of the drivers' recklessness.[54] An article in the popular "Day-by-Day" column of *El Mercurio* claimed that fare collectors on buses "never wash their hands and their general appearance is repulsive," as was the general state of the interior of most buses, which were overcrowded and rarely clean. It was also common for buses to start up before passengers had fully descended or ascended. At one particular corner, there were so many buses operating that "the number of accidents that could occur is infinite and the only reason there have not been more is thanks to heavenly intervention."[55]

In response, the local administration began to take action. On June 16, the acting *alcalde* decreed that bus collectors could no longer simply shout out the schedules of their routes at each stop, a practice that usually produced mass confusion, but that instead they should have their routes clearly displayed in at least three prominent places on their vehicles, as was the case with streetcars.[56] At the same time, the local administration began to enforce new regulations that had been formulated earlier in the month concerning routes, speeds, licensing, and cleanliness of the vehicles. These regulations, in turn, led to protests from drivers that city inspectors were acting arbitrarily and imposing fines unfairly in enforcing them. On August 5, a group of drivers met with the acting *alcalde* to protest the suspension of licenses pursuant to the new regulations and threatened to go on strike if the suspensions weren't lifted. The acting *alcalde* agreed to move the date of compliance from August 4 to September 1, thereby avoiding this particular threat.[57] However, this would be far from the last of such confrontations between the city and the bus drivers.

SEPTEMBER 1924 WAS A DRAMATIC MONTH in Chilean political history. For the first time in the twentieth century, elements within the military intervened directly in national political life, forcing the resignation of President Alessandri on September 8 and replacing the chief executive, who went into exile, with a three-man military *junta*. While the *junta* was to govern the country only so long as it took to restore constitutional democracy and civilian rule, the immediate and long-lasting impact of these events would be considerable, and nowhere was this more true than with respect to the government of Santiago.[58]

On September 10 the *junta* ordered the dissolution of the National Congress. Over the next several weeks, it seemed only a matter of time before the Municipality of Santiago would suffer the same fate. Alcalde Echenique tried valiantly to stave off the inevitable. He responded in detail to some of the specific attacks on his own administration, publishing in the city's main newspapers lengthy descriptions of what he asserted were his major accomplishments, such as improving and "cleansing" the city's bureaucracy and overseeing the passage of new regulations to assure the hygienic quality of milk.[59] The cause of the elected council's defenders, however, was not much helped by its session of September 17. Beginning with approval of suggested fiscal reforms to be submitted to the new national government, the *regidores* then turned to consideration of specific traffic regulations, some of which aimed to control bus operations. Objecting to these, numerous bus drivers had crowded the chamber and they made their objections known through shouts and threats, creating what El Mercurio described as "an atmosphere of hostility and complete disorder" and forcing Echenique to call in the police to remove the protestors forcibly. Then, in a special nighttime session, the council approved the new traffic regulations, as well as an ordinance governing the sale of milk.[60] As it turned out, this would be the last session of an elected council for more than ten years. As it also turned out, its successor would have no greater luck in keeping protesting bus drivers from disturbing functions within City Hall.

On September 21 the governing *junta* made the expected announcement that it would be dissolving the municipal governments of Valparaíso and Santiago and replacing them with administrative boards called *juntas de vecinos*. According to U.S. Ambassador William Collier, reporting back to Washington at the time, "This drastic reform is generally commended by newspapers as terminating governments that were inefficient and corrupt."[61] That was certainly the case with El Mercurio, an early proponent of the measure, which it hoped would end a municipal regime that had been constantly preoccupied with partisan considerations and replace it with one that would be directed by "respectable and responsible citizens." The announced change, the newspaper reported, had "produced an excellent impression among the public at large," and the passing of the old system, it observed, was welcomed by all.[62] The *junta de vecinos* took over on September 25, ending a thirty-three-year period of municipal autonomy and democratic government and initiating an eleven-year period of centralized executive authority for the capital through a local administration selected by the national government. Whether this change would produce the more honest, more efficient, and less partisan government that its advocates promised was an open question.

6 Santiago under the Junta de Vecinos (1924-1927)

THE DEMISE OF THE ELECTED MUNICIPALITY in Santiago seemed to produce few mourners. Public reaction to the naming of the *junta de vecinos* was muted, and many critics of the former system saw the new form of local government as one that would finally provide Santiago with the kind of stable, efficient, and nonpartisan administration that many had advocated for several decades. The national environment in which this new form of administration would operate, however, at least for the next three years, was anything but stable, efficient, and nonpartisan. In late January of 1925 the military *junta* that had forced Alessandri into exile was itself removed by a group led by junior officers Carlos Ibáñez del Campo and Marmaduke Grove. They opposed what appeared to be a Conservative restoration and sought to promote the social and economic reforms of the Liberal Alliance. This new *junta* invited Alessandri to return to Chile and to resume his presidency, which he did on March 20. Preferring to rule by decree rather than by restoring Congress, Alessandri helped oversee the drafting and approval by popular referendum of a new constitution, one that strengthened the power of the executive and separated church and state, among other changes. At odds with his minister of war, Carlos Ibáñez, Alessandri resigned in October, before his term officially expired. Chosen as his successor in a special election that same month was a former vice-president, Liberal Democrat Emiliano Figueroa Larraín. A passive president, Figueroa eventually gave way to Ibáñez, who was elected president in May 1927. With Ibáñez, Chile would return to stability under authoritarian rule for the next four years.[1]

THE FIRST *JUNTA DE VECINOS* FOR SANTIAGO, appointed on September 25, 1924, was composed of five men. Chosen as chief executive, the office now called the intendente municipal, was Enrique Donoso Urmeneta, a former alcalde. Serving with him were Liberal Emilio Aldunate Bascunan, a physician; Domingo Santa María Sánchez, an engineer; Liberal Democrat Augusto Vicuña Subercaseaux, a lawyer; and Alberto Valdivieso.[2] All five had homes or offices in the center of the city and all were described by U.S. Ambassador William Collier as "men of high character, splendid position, great ability and civic consciousness."[3]

The decree which established the junta in Santiago, as well as in Valparaíso, gave its members the same authority previously enjoyed by the alcaldes. The intendente was to serve, as had the First Alcalde, calling and presiding over meetings of the junta. The intendente had the luxury of ruling by decree and, even though he needed a majority of the votes of the other four members of the junta to make these decrees effective, it was expected that getting such a majority from a limited number of like-minded members would be much easier than had been the case with thirteen elected regidores representing half a dozen different parties. The enabling decree also abolished the role of the Asamblea de Contribuyentes as a check and constraint on the municipality's budgetary authority.[4]

El Mercurio was predictably enthusiastic about the new junta. It saw the change as the successful culmination of the campaign for reform that had begun in 1908 and as offering the real possibility of consigning the "poor and corrupt administrations" of the capital to the past. The new junta would also be, the newspaper predicted, perhaps too optimistically, "free from all the political influences that obstructed the work of previous city officials." El Mercurio then laid out what it considered the main priorities for the new city government: "to clean up [sanear] municipal personnel, to eliminate useless employees, to balance the budget, to improve city inspectors and inspections, to adopt measures to protect the public from the rising costs of basic goods, to resolve the serious problems of sanitation, and to arrive at a just and reasonable agreement with the streetcar company."[5]

The first weeks of the junta's activity seemed to justify its supporters' optimism. Meeting practically every weekday, the *junta* did its best to deal with the items *El Mercurio* had placed on its agenda. At one of its first sessions, it was determined to reorganize the city inspector's office, reducing the number of employees there from thirty-one to twelve, with the promise of more personnel cuts to come. Donoso, as had his elected predecessors, spent much of his day visiting various parts of the city, personally ordering the closure of establishments that violated city ordinances, and inspecting both the Mercado Central and the city slaughterhouse to see what could be done to control and, if possible, lower the costs of foodstuffs, especially meat. In an interview two weeks into his term, Donoso reflected on how busy he had been and on how he had found the municipal government to be even more disorganized than it had been when he had previously served as *alcalde* in 1908. He also announced that the city could not afford to proceed with Ugarte's Universidad del Trabajo, that attention would be focused on the problems of garbage incineration and street paving, that contacts had been made with the streetcar company to resume negotiations on a potential fare increase, and that further personnel reductions to a level "strictly necessary" were more than likely.[6]

Also like his predecessors, Donoso spent a lot of time on traffic issues. Responding to widespread complaints, he and the *junta* devoted many sessions to formulating a new set of regulations for all forms of transportation. In the meantime, the *intendente* decreed that all traffic should proceed on the right-hand side of the street, making the rule uniform throughout the city. He also met with the provincial *intendente* and the local chief of police to consider the development of a special brigade to be assigned only to traffic regulation. On October 11 the *junta* decreed new rules governing bus collectors, requiring them to carry a *carnet*, or identification card, that certified they had no criminal record and had passed a medical examination that proved they were free of contagious diseases. They were not to permit onto their buses passengers who were drunk and disorderly, were not to allow passengers to ride on the running boards of their vehicles, were to treat the public with courtesy and respect, and were to turn in to the city traffic office any items left on the buses by their passengers.[7] One month later, on November 11, the *junta* issued orders that all taxis should be equipped with meters, a measure that had been tried and had failed several times in the past.[8] During this period, too, permission was granted to engineer Luis Lagarrigue to explore the possibility of constructing a subway in Santiago, one that initially would be designed to run under the Alameda de las Delicias, from the Central Station to Plaza Italia. It was estimated that construction would cost twenty million pesos and would be completed in two years.[9] As it happened, this was a project that would not be realized until the 1970s.

In addition to traffic questions, the *junta* dealt with a number of other familiar items. On October 7 it named a special committee, including some well-known upper-class women, to devise standards for reviewing films to determine which would be suitable for children.[10] On October 14 it unanimously approved the construction of new garbage incinerators, but at a lower cost and a different location from that recommended by the previous administration.[11] In that same month, it earmarked funds for capital improvements in the Mercado Central, introduced new regulations and methods of inspection of milk, and considered ways to encourage the development of new food markets in areas of the city lacking them. In the last three days of October it was announced that the city had closed down more than a hundred businesses that had failed to pay their license fees.[12]

Public health also received attention. On November 19 Donoso met with a committee of the *junta militar* presided over by Carlos Ibáñez to discuss ways to control more effectively the spread and treatment of venereal disease.[13] In response, the *junta* issued a new forty-one-point ordinance to regulate prostitution.[14] These moves were part of a larger national effort to deal with public health matters in general.[15] In late November the governing *junta* announced plans to centralize hygiene and health services at the national level. The *junta de vecinos* complained that these measures undermined their own authority and responsibility in this area, but these complaints had little effect. The national government already had contracted with a U.S. public health specialist, Dr. John Long, an assistant surgeon general, to study conditions in Chile and to help draw up a new sanitary code for the nation.

Once again, public transportation issues continued to be the most prominent and to cause the most headaches for Donoso and the *junta*. Throughout the final months of the year there were reports of extensive meetings between the *junta* and the streetcar company to try to negotiate a solution to the long-standing conflict over fares and service, but there were no major breakthroughs in this continuing impasse during the life of the first *junta de vecinos*. By this time, as mentioned earlier, buses were beginning to offer serious competition to the streetcar. Their appearance, however, was not an unmixed blessing for the city government. Often operating on a financial shoestring and frequently engaged in fierce competition for passengers, the buses began to pose an even more serious threat to the safety and welfare of Santiago's citizens than did the streetcars, which led to the regulatory efforts previously described. Like other groups of workers and white-collar employees during this period, the bus drivers and owners began to organize into associations and to use aggressive methods to protest what they considered unfair and burdensome constraints on their activities. The events of November 28, 1924, provide a dramatic manifestation of these developments. On that day, some fifty buses, belonging to the recently organized Asociación de Choferes de Santiago (Association of Drivers of Santiago), circulated in a constant procession around the Plaza de Armas and in front of the Casa Consistorial, sounding their horns and blocking traffic. After some of the drivers were led to believe that Donoso had refused to receive their petition of grievances, they began hurling stones at the City Hall, leading the police to intervene and detain at least one of their number. The protestors' main demand, which was in fact received by Donoso, was that he immediately replace the current city traffic director, Oscar Iribarren, who was charged, rather vaguely, with being "the cause of the anomalous situation that has been produced within our association."[16]

Donoso responded a few days later. Asserting that the root cause of the protest was not so much the behavior of Iribarren, against whom no well-founded charges had been brought, but rather a resistance to increased enforcement of new traffic regulations, Donoso refused to dismiss the city traffic director. While underscoring his desire to assure good bus service, he also warned the leaders of the movement that he looked with "full disdain on those who stir things up in such an unruly and pernicious manner, following their own personal and mean-spirited purposes." Others also pointed out that the protestors represented only a minority of the drivers and that most of the owners of the larger lines were opposed to such drastic action. While both Donoso and the leaders of the strike met separately with the head of the Junta de Gobierno, General Luis Altamirano Talavera, to try to resolve the conflict, the owners' association issued a statement claiming that the head of the drivers' association, Guillermo Piedrabuena, was acting out of unspecified "personal political" motivations.[17] In a letter published in El Mercurio the following day, the director of the Compañía de Autobús de Santiago (Autobus Company of Santiago) traced the disturbance to the explosion in the number of buses and resulting tensions between large-scale and small-scale operators. He agreed with the complaints of the protestors that city inspectors were poorly trained and often imposed fines in an arbitrary and capricious manner. He encouraged Iribarren and the *junta de vecinos* to address these issues, but he also urged the strikers to employ time and patience in solving the problems created by the rapid development of this service.[18]

Despite these words of caution, the protestors continued to push their cause. Seeking to broaden their base of support, the striking drivers expressed their sympathy and solidarity with the many city employees and workers who were slated to be dismissed at the end of the year, as part of a general bureaucratic housecleaning. Apparently responding to these and other pressures, the *junta de vecinos* determined, on December 5, to name a special committee to develop a new traffic regulation code within ten days and ordered the city attorney to investigate the allegations made against Iribarren, who in the meantime would be temporarily removed from his post.[19] Two weeks later, a group representing the bus drivers' association met with Donoso and threatened a general strike unless Iribarren were definitively dismissed. Donoso's response was to confirm that the investigation of the director was continuing and that, so far, none of the charges against him had been proven.[20]

Ultimately, this whole episode ended with more of a fizzle than a bang. The city's investigation found that the charges against Iribarren, which were never made public in detail, had no substance, and he resumed his duties in early January of 1925. That decision led to another brief protest, this time along the Alameda and ending at La Moneda. There, a delegation of drivers met with a member of the Junta de Gobierno to request that it intervene with the *junta de vecinos*. The drivers wanted Iribarren at least removed to another position, to be replaced by someone they could trust and with whom they could work.[21] The *junta*, occupied with more pressing matters at the time, ignored the request, and the drivers eventually abandoned their protest and went back to work. These events, however, were an important harbinger of things to come. While the city government had welcomed and even encouraged the development of bus service as an alternative to the

streetcar, its subsequent relations with the drivers and owners of these vehicles were often as contentious and rocky as they had been with the streetcar company. These relationships, too, were often complicated by the fact
that instead of dealing with a single enterprise, as was the case with the
streetcar company, the government now had to negotiate with a variety of
associations and organizations representing large and small companies as
well as individual operators and independent drivers.

THE CHANGE IN THE NATIONAL governing *junta* that took place on January
23, 1925, had profound implications for the first *junta de vecinos* of Santiago.
Immediately, the local *junta* offered to resign, an offer that was initially refused. Two weeks later, Donoso denied rumors that his resignation continued in the works, claiming that the *junta* enjoyed the full confidence of
the new national government and would maintain its dedication "to the
interests and advancement of the city, that more than ever requires the cooperation of good men of true public spirit."[22] Pressures against the *junta*,
however, began to build. On February 15 the Centro de Propaganda Radical (Center of Radical Party Propaganda) issued a series of charges against
Donoso and his administration, claiming that the current officials had acted
in an arbitrary and high-handed manner, particularly with regard to personnel matters. At about the same time, the Federación de Comerciantes de
Santiago (Merchants' Federation of Santiago) protested new regulations on
the sale of foodstuffs that had been issued by the *junta* on December 27,
1924, claiming that these were costly and excessive, and that the federation
planned to carry their protest to the national government.[23]

As other, similar complaints mounted, El Mercurio came to the *junta*'s defense. In an editorial on February 19 the paper asserted that most of the
charges against the *junta* were motivated by politicians and parties who had
lost power as a result of changes at both the national and local level.[24] On
the same day, the *junta* approved a new traffic code drafted by Iribarren. It
also considered a proposal from *vocal* (as the members of the *junta* were
called) Santa María Sánchez for a fifty-million-peso bond issue to invest in
the construction of new workers' housing in response to an ongoing rent
strike. The next day, however, the members of the *junta* once again submitted their resignations. The group rejected in some detail the charges
brought against the *junta* by the Radicals, claiming they had been the target

of a determined campaign by "some political groups that are desirous of re-turning to take part in the direction of local government." Resignation was the only option, the *junta*'s members concluded, since "under these circum-stances, our task has become very burdensome and is hindered by intrigues and movements of systematic and pre-meditated resistance."[25]

Initial reports indicated that the group's resignation would not be ac-cepted. While the governing *junta* deliberated its response, however, two important constituencies made their voices heard. First, representatives of the municipal employees met with the minister of the interior on February 20 to discuss measures to assure greater job security in the face of shift-ing political circumstances. They asserted that many of their number had been unfairly and summarily dismissed by the *junta*, only to be replaced by less-qualified personnel who had some connection, often a family one, to a member of the new local administration. They also announced plans to form a federation to represent their interests.[26] Second, on the afternoon of February 21, representatives of various workers' and consumers' groups held a rally on the Alameda to urge the national government to accept the *junta*'s resignation. The *junta*, they alleged, over the previous few days had been meeting secretly with representatives of the streetcar company to agree to a doubling of fares. Moreover, the charges that the *junta* had acted in an "immoral and excessively personalistic manner" and that it was composed of persons "with no ties to the popular classes and who do not understand the interests of these classes" were reiterated.[27] The protestors were unable to reach La Moneda before it closed in order to deliver their demands. A de-cision about the local *junta*, however, already had been made and was an-nounced later that same day, when the national government accepted the *junta*'s resignation. How much impact these charges and protests might have had on the ruling *junta* cannot be determined. However, the events of Janu-ary 23, especially the recall of Alessandri to the presidency and the reaching out to the Liberal Alliance, especially to Radicals and Democrats who had been generally excluded from local government after the first coup in Sep-tember 1924, undoubtedly played a role. As a result, the new *junta de vecinos* for Santiago would be somewhat larger and somewhat more diverse politi-cally than had been its predecessor.

IT DID NOT TAKE THE NATIONAL GOVERNMENT LONG to name the new *junta de vecinos*. On February 24 the names of the new members were announced, and the *junta* began to act officially on February 27. The new *inten-dente municipal* was Luis Phillips Huneeus, a relative of the outspoken Enrique Phillips and a successful businessman and banker.[28] He was joined on what was now a seven-man *junta* by José Manuel Balmaceda Toro, a Liberal Democrat, as well as another member of that party with a distinguished name, Patricio Vicuña Subercaseaux. Also named were attorney Pedro Avalos Ballivian, who, like his father, was a prominent member of the Radical Party, and Ramón Corbalán Melgarejo, about whom little biographical information is available. The most dramatic change in the composition of the *junta* was the appointment of two representatives of the "popular classes," Onofre Avendaño Flores and Manuel Hidalgo Plaza. Avendaño, a tailor by trade, had become a successful small businessman who remained active in and supportive of various labor organizations and was affiliated with the Democratic Party. Hidalgo, who as a young man had been a jeweler, was by the time of his appointment a well-known labor activist and member of Chile's fledgling Communist Party. Certainly, from the Conservative point of view the most controversial choice for the *junta*, Hidalgo was the only member to list an address in a working-class area, in his case north of the Mapocho at Maruri 375. The remaining members of the *junta*, like their predecessors, lived and worked in or near the downtown core of the capital.[29]

Among Phillips's first actions was attendance at an organizational meeting of municipal employees, held on February 28. In his address to the group, which was well received, he encouraged government employees to proceed with forming a federation to promote and protect their interests, but added that he hoped "such an institution will not be an obstacle to the actions of the local authorities."[30] Phillips may have had doubts about the development of an entity that could well frustrate—or at least make more difficult—any plans he might have had for removing personnel and renovating the bureaucracy, but he did not express them. Indeed, he showed a certain political sensitivity and flexibility by appearing to side with what, at that point, seemed to be the inevitable formation of a municipal employees' federation.

The new *junta* began its work in the midst of a major rent strike in the capital. This movement had begun with the formation of a tenant league in Valparaíso soon after the coup of January 23, 1925. Faced with dramatic food price increases, the league had called for a 50 percent reduction in rents and had urged its supporters to pay only that amount in the future.

The movement soon spread to Santiago and other major cities, with anarchists and communists playing prominent roles. Reporting on these developments, U.S. Ambassador Collier saw them as part of larger events and generalized discontent that might possibly foreshadow a socialist revolution. Nonetheless, he also agreed with the protestors that "there is probably no reform more greatly needed in Chile, for the housing conditions of the poorer classes have long been known universally as being almost intolerable."[31]

On February 13 the governing junta responded by passing a new law. The law stipulated the establishment of housing committees (tribunales de vivienda) made up of representatives of the national and municipal governments and the tenant leagues. The committees would determine for each ward of each city whether property was "unsanitary," and if, as a result, it was judged that this was the case, then rents would be lowered by 50 percent. Property owners responded with an organization and a protest of their own. They succeeded in having the law modified so that they were also represented on the tribunales in a way that allowed them to delay and deny most claims for rent reductions. Then, in September, with Alessandri back in office, the minister of justice shifted the adjudication process from the housing committees to the civil courts, effectively ending the renters' movement, although scattered protests continued.[32]

WHILE THE NATIONAL GOVERNMENT WRESTLED with the rent strike and housing problems, Santiago's junta de vecinos focused primarily on questions related to traffic regulation and public transportation. The major issue remained the unresolved matter of streetcar fares and service. This matter was brought to the fore again, as increasingly had been the case in previous years, by a strike of the company's workers. The protest began in late March when collectors and machinists demanded an eight-hour day, paid Sunday rest, and a substantial wage increase. Negotiations over these demands, with the national government once more playing a major part, dragged on for a month. Again, the company repeated its argument that only a fare increase would allow it to meet "the just aspirations of its personnel."[33]

At the end of April a temporary resolution was achieved. The company agreed to raise workers' salaries and restore service at the old fares, but with the understanding that the junta would ultimately agree to a fare increase.

Over the next few days, a series of meetings was held involving President Allesandri, the minister of the interior, the provincial *intendente*, the municipal *intendente*, and company representative Tonkin to hammer out the details of a final accord. Faced with the threat of a new strike, the *junta* met on May 5 and agreed to a new contract that allowed for the fare increase in return for guarantees on various aspects of the service.[34] The company, however, objecting to certain clauses in the new offer, rejected the proposal and rescinded its wage increases, leading to a new strike.[35] With the minister of the interior active as a negotiator, and faced with a total unraveling of the situation, the *junta* met on May 8 and formulated a contract more to the company's liking. In return for the fare increase, the company would abolish the so-called "imperial," or open, upper-deck cars, and would provide modern, enclosed cars. It would guarantee at least 300 cars in circulation (well below the 450 cars previously demanded), construct new lines, reestablish old lines that had been discontinued, and install 9,053 streetlamps. As in the past, the company would be free of city taxes and fees, although it would provide a "general compensation" of 2½ percent of its gross revenues to the municipal treasury.[36]

The company immediately accepted this new proposal. The majority of the *junta* supported it, with varying degrees of enthusiasm. Corbalán appeared to be its strongest supporter. Avalos, Vicuña Subercaseaux, Intendente Phillips, and Liberal Carlos Rivas Vicuña, who had replaced Balmaceda Toro on the *junta*, argued that while they were not pleased by the company's actions, they saw no other option than to accept the fare increase.[37] As could have been predicted, both Avendaño and Hidalgo, representing working-class parties and organizations that consistently opposed the fare increase (except for the streetcar workers themselves), were the most prominent opponents. During discussion, both engaged in impassioned exchanges with their colleagues that were reminiscent of the partisan charges and countercharges that had characterized the elected council. When it came to the final vote, both registered their objections to the agreement in general and voted in opposition to most, but not all, of the individual Articles.[38]

On the same day as the *junta*'s actions, May 8, President Alessandri issued Decree-Law No. 450 to put the agreement into effect. He justified this "extraordinary" action as necessary to resolve a problem that "for so much time has been producing serious public disturbances, and that affects vitally the interests of the population of this capital."[39] U.S. Ambassador Collier saw the company as the primary beneficiary of the new agreement, having astutely used the walkout of its workers (some claimed the company had even prompted the strike) "as a lever to force the authorities to concede to the demands of the company."[40] However, this was not the first time that a labor disturbance between the streetcar company and its employees had led to a serious shutdown in service, intensifying pressure on local and national officials to resolve the matter by allowing a fare increase. All such previous efforts had proved unsuccessful. What was different this time, as Alessandri himself noted in his decree, was the absence of Congress, which allowed the chief executive to act with a freedom he had not previously enjoyed. As a result, Santiaguinos began paying 20 centavos for a first-class streetcar ride and 10 centavos for second class, with the hope that they would now get better service for their money.

AS USUAL, ACTIONS AT THE NATIONAL LEVEL directly affected the activities of Phillips and the junta. Particularly pronounced in these months was the increasing centralization of authority in the hands of the federal government, which gradually eroded municipal autonomy and removed from local hands much of the power and responsibility it had once enjoyed over the management of local affairs. Although this erosion had been proceeding for some time, it was accentuated and accelerated by the coup of September 1924, the imposition of the two military juntas, and the restoration of Alessandri without a Congress as a counterweight. Indeed, the appointment of the junta de vecinos by the national government without the democratic consent of the citizens of Santiago was itself dramatic evidence of this centralizing tendency.

Phillips and the junta grew increasingly discontented by the steady chipping away at their authority, particularly in the realm of fiscal policy. While the overall budget picture looked brighter than it had in years, with the city treasurer actually forecasting a one-and-a-half-million-peso surplus by the end of the year, the junta had plans for even greater expenditures.[41] At its meeting of August 8 it approved a grandiose plan for the transformation of Santiago, a plan that would require financing a loan of two hundred million pesos.[42] As historically had been the case, permission to contract such a loan had to be received from the national government. Phillips, however, in an interview on September 15, indicated that he had personally contacted "foreign capitalists" who would provide loans under "favorable conditions" to carry out the transformation project.[43] Among these was Lawrence E. Bennet, representing Ulen and Company of New York, who had been in Santiago for two months trying to negotiate a loan with the municipality in the amount of from ten million to twelve million dollars for public works.[44] Whether these negotiations were being conducted with the knowledge and approval of the national government is not clear. But at this time the national authorities issued a new decree-law expressly forbidding any municipality from contracting a loan without federal approval. This decree was apparently an important factor leading Phillips and the *junta* to threaten to resign at the end of September.

Other developments added to the *junta*'s discontent. Faced with a severe food price increase, the national government had established the Dirección Nacional de Subsistencias (National Food Board), which placed control of all articles of "prime necessity" under the authority of the Ministry of Health and Social Welfare, headed by José Santos Salas. Phillips and the *junta* had themselves been trying to address the issue of rising prices and declining quality of food, and they saw Salas's move as further undermining their role. At a two-hour meeting on September 24, Alessandri reassured Phillips that the city's loan request would be approved and that adjustments would be made on the food control issue. As a result, Phillips and the *junta* withdrew their threatened resignations.[45] Ironically, Alessandri himself resigned from office on October 2, leaving executive authority in the hands of his former Conservative rival for the presidency, Luis Barros Borgoño. It was under Barros's interim regime that the new constitution, approved in a national referendum in September, went into effect on October 18. Then, a week later, Emiliano Figueroa Larraín was elected president, defeating the former minister of social welfare Salas, his principal opponent.

The new constitution provided for a return to elected municipalities beginning with elections in April 1927. In anticipation, Phillips submitted to the Barros administration a proposed new municipal governance law that had as its most distinctive feature a provision to extend the vote in local contests to taxpaying women and foreigners. The law suggested by the national government did not go so far; it extended the vote to foreigners but not to women. It also provided for an *alcalde* named by the president of the republic who would have enhanced authority. Under the new law, city employees would also be offered greater job security. The *juntas de vecinos* would remain in place until 1927, but in Santiago they would be expanded from seven to nine members.[46] Accordingly, at the end of the year Jorge Zamudio Flores and former Radical *regidor* Horacio Manríquez were added to the *junta*. They joined Manuel Salas Rodríguez, a future provincial *intendente*, who himself had replaced Carlos Rivas Vicuña, who had resigned on December 18 for personal reasons.[47]

Phillips met with Barros on October 13 to discuss pressing city matters. These included plans for Santiago's transformation, an extensive paving program, and permission to float another loan to pay for these and other public works. Phillips reported that his conversation had gone well and that Barros seemed receptive and sympathetic to the capital's plight, but the fact remained that he would be chief executive for only a brief period. In the meantime, more decrees and other measures at the national level continued to impinge on local authority. At the end of September, for example, the federal government established a national board to monitor and, if necessary, censor motion pictures, something that previously had been under municipal purview. At the end of October, the government issued new and even more stringent rules for municipalities that wished to contract loans, reaffirming the need to get national permission to do so and giving the ministry of finance total control over how the loans should be spent, albeit "taking into consideration the interests of the municipality."[48] On October 13 the Council of Ministers approved a new sanitary code drawn up by U.S. advisor John Long. Most of the sanitary measures to be imposed were to be supervised by a director general of health, appointed by the president, who would have considerable power to take the actions he believed necessary. The director general would have national authority but would also work with local boards of health—*except* in the case of Santiago, which he would supervise directly.[49] While these changes provided for improvements in the sanitary and health conditions of the capital, they were also further examples of the expanding limitations on local authority and responsibility. As an editorial that appeared in *El Diario Ilustrado* during the resignation crisis noted, if this erosion of authority continued the city government would soon have nothing more to do than clean the streets and pick up the garbage, if that.[50]

WITH THE NEW CONSTITUTION and the election of Figueroa Larraín, the national political and governmental life returned more or less to normal, at least for the time being. Congressional elections, which produced sizable gains for the Radicals and Democrats, were held on November 22, 1925, and the new Congress was called into session on March 1 of the following year. For a variety of reasons, including executive ineptitude, partisan divisions and bickering, and the maneuvering of the ambitious Carlos Ibáñez, relatively little was accomplished by the Figueroa administration, and the new president ultimately resigned in early 1927.

During this period, there was little fundamental change in Santiago's *junta de vecinos*. Although there was some shuffling of personnel, the majority of *vocales* remained in their positions. While subject to occasional fierce criticisms, more from without than from within the *junta*, Phillips remained in his post and there were no further threats by him or his colleagues to resign. There was some contention and sharp debate within the *junta*, but overall Phillips enjoyed solid majority support for his initiatives and actions. Adding to the general harmony was the fact that one of Phillips's most outspoken critics on the *junta*, Communist Manuel Hidalgo, was elected to the National Senate and left the local administration at the end of April 1926. Upon his departure, he apologized for his "occasionally lively and even violent language," saying he had never meant to offend any of his colleagues personally in presenting his often contrary points of view. His colleagues, including Phillips, assured him that no offense had been taken and encouraged him to look after the interests of the capital from his new post.[51] Conservative Carlos Echeverría Reyes replaced Hidalgo and was himself replaced at the end of September by a former *alcalde*, Conservative Luis Lira Lira. Along with Avendaño, Lira became the most vocal critic of Phillips and the majority within the *junta*.

For the most part, city officials continued to deal with the same issues as in the previous year. Problems involving public transportation persisted. At the beginning of the year, the regulation requiring all taxis to operate with meters went into effect. Over the next few months, complaints were heard from the public that the meters and fares were too often manipulated by unscrupulous drivers in an effort to cheat the unwary. The drivers, for their part, protested what they considered unduly low fare rates and the high cost of renting the meters. While the city was unable to fully satisfy either side, it did seem that by the end of the year the long-sought principle and practice of having all taxis equipped with meters had been achieved.

Relations between the city and the streetcar company followed a familiar pattern. Members of the *junta*, as well as the public and press in general, continued to accuse the company of failing to live up to its side of the bargain to improve service, particularly with respect to keeping the agreed-upon minimum number of cars in circulation. The company, in turn, continued to respond that it was meeting all its obligations and doing what it could to improve service as rapidly as possible. It also denied in particular a charge that it was not maintaining sufficient cars in circulation. An editorial in an August edition of *El Diario Ilustrado* lamented these apparently irreconcilable difficulties. Reflecting a burgeoning Conservative reaction against what were considered the abuses of foreign investors in Chile, the editorial criticized the inflexibility of the company in its dealings with the city and the public and its apparent concern with "making money and nothing else." The company, it charged, had done little to win over an increasingly hostile public, rejecting such measures as instituting a special 5 centavo student ticket or of providing a series of tickets at lower cost, as had been successfully done in Valparaíso. The paper also charged the company with failing to keep enough cars in operation, going on to say that many of the cars that did operate were "in a most deplorable condition." To counter continuing and growing complaints of poor and inadequate service at higher rates for both streetcars and electricity, the editorial urged the company to be "more flexible and more humane" so as to defuse the charged atmosphere of mutual antagonism between it and the public.[52]

In seeming response to such advice, the streetcar company went through a major reorganization at this time. A new subsidiary to administer the company's affairs only for the capital, the Compañía de Tracción y Alumbrado de Santiago (Santiago Traction and Lighting Company) was formed, with the express purpose of meeting the obligations of the 1925 contract. The company ordered new rolling stock and committed itself to substantial improvements in both streetcar and lighting service. Concerning the latter, it said it intended to soon make Santiago "the best lighted city in South America." The costs of these improvements were to be borne by the company itself through its own resources and through bonds that would be sold on the local market.[53]

These new commitments produced immediate results. At the end of August *El Mercurio* reported that the new and modern cars, especially constructed for Chile in the United States and possessing automatic brakes, heating, and comfortable seating, had arrived and would be in operation by the time of the Independence Day celebration in September.[54] By December, the same editorialist in *El Diario Ilustrado* who had so sharply attacked the company for its "inflexibility" in August enthusiastically praised it for what seemed a complete turnaround both in the quality of service and in its attitude toward the public. Extolling the virtues of "the splendid new cars that bring honor to the city," the writer commended the company for its attempts to establish better relations with the public through a "friendlier and gentler" treatment of its passengers. Even greater goodwill could be earned, he suggested, by such steps as allowing War of the Pacific veterans to ride free of charge and setting up discounted ticket sales for certain lines.[55]

Despite these improvements, not all was sweetness and light between the company and the *junta de vecinos*. Over the last months of the year, the two antagonists engaged in a running battle over city attempts to set limits on the number of standing passengers for both buses and streetcars, with the streetcar company generally ignoring these limits, claiming that their vehicles could more comfortably carry standing passengers than could buses (see Fig. 1). In late November, the company threatened to sue the municipality for one million pesos for what it alleged was a failure by the city to pay certain costs associated with the provision of electric service.[56]

The city's reluctance—and, in fact, its inability—to pay its lighting bill was part of a larger problem. In mid-year, complaints in the Senate from Manuel Hidalgo and others that the municipality was on the verge of bankruptcy had led the director of the national accounting office to conduct an investigation into the city's finances. He reported on August 8 that the city would end the year with a deficit of ten million pesos. While not questioning the personal honesty of the *junta de vecinos*, he strongly urged serious and rapid attention to the problem.[57] Phillips's response at the time was to claim that this estimate of the deficit was inflated and that the final figure would be closer to one and a half million pesos. At its session of October 29, the *junta* unanimously and quickly approved a budget of $27,285,000 pesos for 1927 (the peso was roughly eight to the dollar at that time), which projected a slight surplus.[58]

AS LOCAL OFFICIALS WRESTLED WITH THESE and other issues, important changes were taking place at the national level. On February 9, 1927, an in-

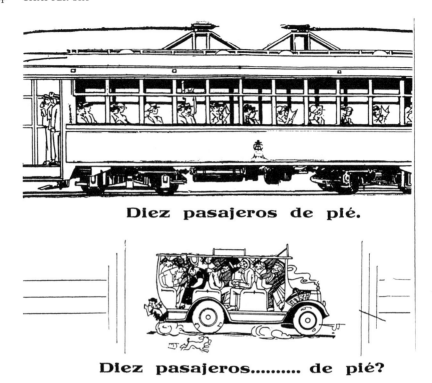

Diez pasajeros de pié.

Diez pasajeros.......... de pié?

FIG. 1. *Advertisement for the Santiago Streetcar Company showing the benefits of riding their vehicles, given new municipal regulations that no more than ten standing passengers ("Diez pasajeros de pié") would be allowed in either streetcars or buses.* SOURCE: El Mercurio, October 5, 1926, p. 15.

creasingly weak and ineffective President Figueroa dissolved his cabinet and named Carlos Ibáñez, who had been working behind the scenes for months to secure a solid base of military and civilian support, his minister of the interior, charging him with forming a new government. Now clearly the most powerful figure in the administration, Ibáñez selected a cabinet of his own allies and began a general housecleaning of the civil service and the judiciary. Imposing a variety of draconian measures, Ibáñez ordered some two hundred prominent politicians, ranging from Conservatives to Communists, and including Manuel Hidalgo, formerly of the Santiago *junta de vecinos*, deported or confined. On May 5, Figueroa succumbed to the inevitable and resigned the presidency. On May 23, in a special election, Ibáñez was chosen president with 98 percent of the vote. While his ascension to power ignored and trampled on many aspects of the democratic practices and procedures of which Chileans were so proud, there was little doubt that Ibáñez enjoyed a broad spectrum of popular support as he officially took office.[59]

As these events unfolded, the national government determined to cancel the municipal elections scheduled for April. In a message to all *intendentes* and governments in early March, Ibáñez, still minister of the interior at that time, had informed these officials that all municipalities and *juntas de vecinos* would be renovated as of May 1. In addition, the system of *juntas de vecinos* would be extended to all the cities in the nation. Accordingly, he had requested as much information as possible concerning their composition and performance over the previous two years. The information would be used to determine which local officials would be allowed to remain in office and which would be replaced. As Ibáñez put it, this moment offered "an exceptional opportunity to designate as members of future *juntas* men who, by their correctness, honesty, activity, preparation, and public spirit will provide a certain guarantee to participate in an honest and progressive municipal administration, in which they will invest municipal funds with economy, intelligence, and opportuneness."[60]

In light of these developments, Phillips made a strong case for his continuation as the city's chief executive. In an interview on April 1, he ticked off what he considered a substantial list of accomplishments, including improved lighting, paving, and sanitation. He admitted that traffic regulation, especially of buses, remained a major challenge, but pointed to the establishment, finally, of taxi meters in each city cab as a major achievement. He also took particular pride in what he considered largely successful efforts to lower the prices of foodstuffs through the creation of more city markets.[61] Supporting Phillips's case, if not explicitly, *El Mercurio*, in an April 15 editorial, expressed concern about the names of some of the "unknowns" that were being floated around as possible new members of the *junta*. The newspaper argued, with some exaggeration, that more had been achieved in two years of government by the present *junta* than in twenty years of the elected municipality.[62] Phillips's credentials were certainly enhanced when on April 23 he presided over the inauguration of a new garbage incinerator on Calle Mapocho between Bulnes and Cueto. Speaking in the presence of Ibáñez and other national figures, he described the new incinerator as the fulfillment of a promise made to the citizens of Santiago by him and the *junta* exactly one year earlier to see to completion the long-delayed project (albeit on a significantly smaller scale than originally envisioned). He then reviewed the improvements in lighting and paving, and the lower food prices, concluding with a request of the national government to approve a loan that would allow for the total paving of Santiago's streets in as short a time as possible. The tenor of his remarks indicated that he anticipated continuing to work with the national authorities on these and other projects for some time to come.[63]

By the end of April the national government had collected the necessary information and had received numerous nominations to fill the *juntas*. While the process was clearly controlled from the top, individual citizens were encouraged to contact the minister of the interior with comments and suggestions about likely candidates. On April 29 that minister sent another circular to all *intendentes* and governors explaining the rationale behind and the duties of the new *juntas*. These were to be nonpartisan bodies, dedicated to such matters as public health, sanitation, traffic regulation, control of gambling and the consumption of alcohol, lowering of the price of basic necessities, and fulfillment of social legislation. Unlike the municipalities of the past, the minister warned, the *juntas* should be less concerned with providing comforts and benefits for the well-to-do and more concerned with the needs of the masses. As he expressed it, "In general, local services ought to have a democratic tendency that causes the less fortunate to feel materially the support and shelter from the local authorities that they deserve."[64] The tone of this circular was reflective of the larger, populist message and orientation that the Ibáñez regime sought to convey.

In Santiago, the new *junta* took over, as scheduled, on May 1. It included Phillips, again as *alcalde* (replacing the label *intendente*), along with previous *vocales* Vicuña Subercaseaux, Corbalán Melgarejo, Zamudio Flores, and Manríquez. The four new members were Rafael Vives Vives, Victor Deformes, Luis Ugarte Valenzuela, and Bonifacio Veas. The first three were from well-known families and had downtown addresses. Veas, however, lived in the Población San Eugenio and seemed to be the sole member of the "less-fortunate" classes the *junta* was supposed to represent.[65]

Another administrative change affecting the capital had occurred two months earlier. On March 1, Alberto Mackenna, the longtime promoter of municipal reform, had stepped down after six years in office. He and others pointed to the establishment of the San Cristóbal Park, now equipped with a funicular train to the summit and a city-run zoo, as his major achievement, much in the way the construction of Santa Lucía Park had distinguished the administration of his illustrious ancestor, Benjamín Vicuña Mackenna.[66] His successor, former Santiago *vocal* Manuel Salas Rodríguez, promised to follow in Mackenna's footsteps.[67]

Both of these new administrations would enjoy a greater period of stability and prosperity, at least until 1930, than had been true of their immediate predecessors. The challenge for Santiago's new *junta de vecinos*, however, would continue to be to prove that it could accomplish more for the city than had the elected municipalities it had replaced.

7 Santiago and the Ibáñez Regime (1927-1931)

WHEN CARLOS IBÁÑEZ TOOK CONTROL in April 1927, the *New York Times* headlined its story "Fascism Vaults Ocean to Chile." Ibáñez, it claimed, "is now as much of a dictator as [Benito] Mussolini or [Miguel Primo] de Rivera."[1] While these observations might have been exaggerated, there is no doubt that for the next four years Ibáñez ruled Chile with the proverbial iron hand. Dominating a compliant Congress, he continued to harass, imprison, and force into exile his principal political opponents. Some of these, most notably former president Arturo Alessandri and former colleague Marmaduke Grove, plotted unsuccessfully to overthrow him by force. He kept organized labor relatively docile through a combination of carrots and sticks. He benefited from increased prosperity, at least until 1930, which allowed him to embark on an extensive and ambitious program of public works, many of which had direct consequences for Santiago. Despite occasional flashes of economic nationalism, he encouraged foreign investment, particularly from the United States. During his regime, the British-owned telephone company was sold to the International Telephone and Telegraph Company (IT&T) and, as we shall see, U.S. interests also bought out the streetcar and electric services in Santiago and elsewhere. To help pay for public improvements, Chile borrowed heavily from abroad, again principally from the United States, significantly increasing its overall indebtedness and vulnerability. When the consequences of the Great Depression hit Chile in 1930 with greater force than in almost any other country in Latin America, Ibáñez's political position deteriorated rapidly, resulting ultimately in his own resignation and exile at the end of July 1931.[2]

ONE OF IBÁÑEZ'S FIRST MEASURES had a direct impact on Santiago. During his initial days in office, he created a new national police force, combining the Army's Carabinero Regiment with local forces (up to that time, Santiago and Valparaíso had maintained their own police forces). The new force was called the Carabineros de Chile. While originally serving as an important prop for the authoritarian regime, the Carabineros evolved into a highly disciplined, well-trained, and well-regarded police unit, considered by many to be the finest in Latin America.[3]

Ibáñez appointed General Aníbal Parada, a close ally, as the first director of the Carabineros. One of Parada's first concerns was to try to bring some order to the capital's chronically chaotic traffic problem, responsibility for which was now in his unit's hands. In late May 1927 Parada personally took over the direction of traffic control in downtown Santiago, urging his charges not only to regulate vehicular movement but also to issue fines to those pedestrians who failed to observe the rules and regulations for street crossings, as well as encouraging pedestrians to keep to the right-hand side while moving along the city's sidewalks.[4] A few days later, Parada held a press conference to encourage public support for his efforts.[5] Soon thereafter, he divided Santiago into four zones for traffic control, hoping thereby to make regulation more orderly and effective.[6]

As the Carabineros expanded their authority over traffic, the local administration essentially surrendered any significant role with regard to regulation. At the *junta*'s session of June 14, Alcalde Phillips introduced a proposed decree that would have reduced the city's traffic office to a license bureau, reserving all other traffic control to the Carabineros. Various *vocales* questioned both the legality and the wisdom of such a decree, however, which would have even further eroded municipal autonomy and authority.[7] At the next session, on June 21, Phillips tried to reassure the doubters, observing that Parada had promised not to reduce the number of employees in the traffic office, as some had feared he would, or to make any other dramatic changes. The decree was then approved by a vote of 6 to 2, with *vocales* Corbalán and Veas abstaining.[8] As these deliberations proceeded, *El Mercurio* reported that Parada's efforts were beginning to have some effect, particularly with regard to pedestrian behavior, and that in meetings with bus and streetcar drivers he had warned that the Carabineros would soon be cracking down on any violations of the limits on the number of standing passengers.[9]

The debate over the role of the Carabineros reflected certain other tensions between the new national government and Santiago's *junta de vecinos*. In mid-June, Minister of the Interior Enrique Balmaceda Toro, after making several tours of inspection of the capital, sent an extensive note to Phillips criticizing, as he saw it, the sorry state of the city, especially with regard to housing and sanitation. In an equally detailed response, on June 13, Phillips defended his administration of the city, citing the progress that had been made and also listing the obstacles that had prevented more from being accomplished. Like so many of his predecessors, he traced the root of the city's problems to insufficient finances. The kind of progress and the modern municipal services that he desired were not possible without more revenue, he argued.[10]

Under some external pressure, Phillips also experienced difficulties within the *junta de vecinos*. From July through August a familiar scenario was repeated over what many *vocales* saw as a failure by the streetcar/electric company to abide by its contractual obligations to improve service and to lower electric rates. Some *vocales* accused Phillips of being less than aggressive in presenting the city's case in this matter. Ultimately, as often happened, the national government intervened and secured a verbal commitment from the company to respond to the city's demands and expectations.[11] The entire episode, however, did Phillips's standing with the *junta* and with national authorities little good.

Phillips's position was complicated further by the efforts of the Ibáñez government to improve local administration throughout the nation. On August 23 the minister of the interior issued a circular to all *intendentes* observing that the national authorities were aware that not all *juntas de vecinos* were "responding to the desires of public good" of the new regime, which "is not disposed to tolerate their placing obstacles in the way of the administrative regeneration that serves as the base of its program." Therefore, he encouraged the *intendentes* to immediately remove from the *juntas* under their jurisdiction any "*alcaldes* or *vocales* that do not demonstrate public spirit in the fulfillment of their duties."[12] Then, on August 29, the administration issued a decree that ordered all *juntas de vecinos* to reduce to the absolute minimum the number of municipal employees and to reduce substantially the salaries of those who were retained.[13] This measure paralleled similar efforts to streamline the federal bureaucracy. While there might not have been a direct connection to this decree, on the following day Phillips submitted his resignation as *alcalde*, citing the usual "personal reasons."[14] Once his resignation had been accepted, Phillips explained that he was fatigued after two and a half years as *alcalde* and needed time to rest. His decision, he asserted, had not resulted from any "spirit of protest or of resistance of any kind," but rather was a way to give the national authorities free rein to remodel the *junta de vecinos* as they saw fit. He did indicate, however, that over time he had found the local government to have less and less autonomy, which limited his and the *junta's* effectiveness.[15]

Problems within the *junta* itself did not seem to play much of a role in Phillips's decision. While various *vocales* had criticized his perceived lack of action on the streetcar/electric issue, the majority had supported him on most issues. *El Mercurio* praised Phillips as a hardworking and honest public official, crediting him with having improved the Alameda, initiated the transformation of the Plaza Italia, and stimulated the development of more city markets.[16]

There was more to the story, however. On August 29 the minister of the treasury had sent Phillips a reminder that the city owed the national government more than two million pesos as part of its obligation to repay a loan to build a new municipal slaughterhouse.[17] This was only one of a series of such problems involving Phillips's financial management. Throughout his tenure there had been charges leveled against him and his administration for allegedly misappropriating city funds, charges that had begun to accumulate with some weight in the office of the minister of the interior and that led ultimately to his resignation and departure from the country with his family soon thereafter.[18] While the charges against Phillips were never proved, they seemed to confirm that *juntas de vecinos*, like the elected municipalities before them, could be subject to internal divisions and external pressures, and that appointed *alcaldes*, like elected ones, could be compelled to resign with serious clouds of doubt over their heads.

*

THE IBÁÑEZ REGIME DID SOMETHING DIFFERENT when replacing Phillips. It appointed Provincial Intendente Manuel Salas Rodríguez, himself a former member of the *junta de vecinos*, to serve as *alcalde*, effectively placing him in both posts simultaneously. After meeting with the minister of the interior to accept the position, Salas announced that he would be accepting the resignations of the *junta* members, which had been submitted along with that of Phillips, and that he would be returning to the original number of four *vocales* on the junta.[19]

After meeting with and praising Phillips for his service to the city, Salas set immediately to work to implement the orders of the national government to reduce the numbers and salaries of municipal personnel. Even before the new *junta* held its first session, he toured city offices and recommended cutbacks that would save 300,000 pesos.[20] At the first session, the *alcalde* introduced more detailed plans for the reorganization of municipal departments, which included the pensioning of employees near retirement. All department heads were to submit within twenty-four hours their own plans for reorganization, along with detailed information on the base number of employees needed in each department and their salaries. The *junta* also agreed that Salas would meet with the minister of finance to discuss ways for the city to pay off its two-million-peso debt on the slaughterhouse loan.[21]

Streamlining the municipal bureaucracy and getting the city's financial house in order were the major preoccupations of the new *junta* for the rest of 1927. Throughout most of the following year, Salas and the *junta* continued to work well together. There was almost no open disagreement expressed and most sessions were marked by unanimity and the quick dispatch of items on the agenda. In February, for example, the *junta* unanimously approved a Salas proposal to float a four-and-a-half-million-peso internal loan to help pay for the Mercado de la Vega Central, using city property as collateral. This was the type of issue that in the past had produced considerable debate, but in this instance, there was virtually no discussion of the matter.[22]

Near mid-year, former provincial *intendente* Mackenna Subercaseaux offered unstinted praise for the combination of duties concentrated in one person that Salas represented. This system, he argued, fulfilled the vision of those who had been struggling for reform of municipal government since

1908. Under the current arrangement, he claimed, "that which in thirty years of sterile discussions had not been accomplished, despite the laudable activity of some *alcaldes*, has been achieved in two or three years. Garbage incinerators, the general lighting of the city, the transformation of the Alameda, ornamentation of the public gardens, the better and more efficient organization of municipal services, are the results that most immediately leap to public view and provide effective proof of the goodness [*bondad*] of the system."[23]

While the efficiency and unanimity of the new system may have been unprecedented, one of the major problems Salas and the *junta* faced was painfully familiar. In late February and early March, Salas sent two memoranda to the minister of the interior in which he relayed complaints from various sources that the streetcar/electric company was still failing to meet its contractual obligations.[24] After the usual extensive negotiations, involving the national government, local officials, and company representatives, the *junta de vecinos* of Santiago unanimously approved yet another new contract proposal on April 10. This proposal superseded all previous contracts, provided for a significant lowering of electric rates (with no change in streetcar fares), and for a company commitment to invest fifteen million pesos in new cars and the reconstruction and renovation of rails that had fallen into disrepair. The company, in return, would get a ninety-year extension of its concession, an end to the 2½ percent "contribution" of its revenues to the city (with the national government to compensate the municipality for this loss), and, perhaps most important from the company's point of view, a commitment by the city to regulate traffic in such a way that streets served by streetcars would not also be served by other forms of public transportation.[25] On April 24 Ibáñez approved the text of the new contract and sent it on to Congress. There, however, one month later, a Senate committee rejected the article that would have prevented other public transportation vehicles from traversing the same routes as the streetcars, an indication that the road to approval of this contract would not be a smooth one.[26]

As the Congress considered this new contract, a significant change in the ownership of the company occurred. During the first stages of negotiation of the new agreement, in March and April 1928, U.S. Ambassador William S. Culbertson reported that the difficulties between the company and the local and national government "leads me to think the time propitious for a study of this property, with a view to its eventual purchase, by American interests."[27] Whether this advice was relayed directly to interested parties is not clear. However, in October it was announced that the U.S.-based American Foreign Power Company (AFP), an affiliate of the Electric Bond and Share Company (itself a spinoff of General Electric) had begun arrangements to purchase the assets of the British-owned streetcar/electric company (then controlled by the Whitehall Electric Investment Company of London) for about fifteen million dollars.[28] This acquisition was part of an extensive effort by AFP to purchase electric power and streetcar systems throughout Latin America between 1925 and 1929.[29] Ambassador Culbertson reported that the news of the purchase was received with general satisfaction in Chile, with the attendant hope that streetcar service in Santiago would improve. He noted, too, however, that some expressed the fear that the takeover might increase the possibility of U.S. military intervention in Chile to protect its investors' property if threatened, as had been the case recently in Central America. While the ambassador considered such fears far-fetched, he also cautioned against gestures such as sending elements of the U.S. Navy to Chile anytime soon.[30] Although no such dramatic events did occur, the U.S.-owned company that now operated Santiago's streetcars and also provided electric service to the capital (and Valparaíso) would find its relationship with the traveling and consuming public and the local and national authorities no less troublesome than had its British and German predecessors.

AS THIS TRANSFER OF ASSETS WAS OCCURRING, another change took place in Santiago's junta de vecinos. Although many, like Mackenna, believed that Salas was performing well in his dual role, the Ibáñez administration determined in October that the twin responsibilities were too much for one man and asked Salas to resign as alcalde while remaining as provincial intendente. Named to replace him was Enrique Balmaceda Toro, who had been removed from his post as minister of the interior in May as part of an internal power struggle.[31]

Balmaceda was the most distinguished man to hold the post of Santiago's alcalde to that time. Son of the former president, he had first been elected to Congress as a national deputy in 1907 and had served in various cabinet positions under both Alessandri and Ibáñez.[32] Taking control of

the local administration on October 19, he promised to continue his predecessor's efforts and to give priority to modernizing the sanitation service,
addressing problems related to food quality and price, and giving special attention to providing athletic facilities and activities for children. In an interview, he professed that "his most ardent desires are to convert the city of
Santiago into a model among modern capitals."[33]

As was customary, Balmaceda began his term with a personal tour of inspection of various parts of the city and of city offices. One of his first visits
was to the city traffic office, where he asked officials there to come up with
a new overall plan of regulation, with particular attention to downtown
parking. He also ordered work to begin on modernizing various parks and
plazas. Like Salas, he operated with considerable freedom and the virtually
unquestioning support of the *junta de vecinos*, which remained the same and
in essence simply rubber-stamped his proposals, with little discussion or
disagreement. Such was the case when, at the end of December, the *junta*
unanimously approved yet another bond issue, this time in the amount of
eight million pesos, to pay for certain expropriations. Repeating a common
refrain, Balmaceda told the *junta* that while he and the public demanded
"that Santiago be transformed into a modern capital," the "ridiculous" lack
of revenues, especially when compared with other Latin American capitals,
made such a goal unrealizable without recourse to loans. He also reported
on a conversation he had had with U.S. president-elect Herbert Hoover, in
Santiago as part of a South American tour, who had "corroborated the good
will of North American capitalists to grant a [proposed] loan of fifteen million dollars for the transformation of Santiago."[34]

Balmaceda continued the steady pace of his activities over the next several months. Acting alone or with the *vocales'* approval, he instituted a decree
that provided some sick pay for municipal employees, oversaw the operation of new garbage trucks recently purchased by the city, signed a contract
to update the electrical wiring in the Teatro Municipal, closed down a theater where marathon dancing was performed, approved the construction of
several pergolas in various city parks, reviewed plans for the construction of
a new municipal slaughterhouse submitted by the same firm that recently
had completed such an establishment in Buenos Aires, and ordered that as
of June 11 all bus drivers and collectors would wear standard uniforms.[35]

From March through May the *junta* could hardly be called an obstacle to the *alcalde's* actions. It met on a regular basis and approved his actions unanimously and quickly. In late May, however, it fell victim to a further consolidation of power and reorganization of municipal government by Ibáñez. In response to a presidential demand, on May 27 the four *vocales* submitted their resignations to provincial *intendente* Salas Rodríguez, who accepted them the following day. A decree on May 29 then laid out the duties and responsibilities of the new government for Santiago, now to be called the *junta de alcaldes* and composed of a First and Second Alcalde but with no *vocales*. Balmaceda would continue, as First Alcalde, while Alberto Veliz, the director of public works and also in charge of street paving, would be named as Second Alcalde.[36] An editorial in the semi-official *La Nación* on June 5 compared this reorganization of Santiago's government to the city manager system in the United States, with the First Alcalde laying out the broad guidelines of administration and the Second Alcalde providing the necessary technical expertise and direction. The editorial expressed full confidence in the two men appointed as *alcaldes*. With Balmaceda already having shown "exceptional qualities of abnegation, probity, and rectitude as a civil servant" and Veliz with "a brilliant career as a municipal functionary," the future of the city would be in able and secure hands.[37] Whatever the quality of these two individuals, the removal of the *vocales* signaled an even greater concentration of power in the hands of the city executive and an even further erosion of whatever checks and balances or semblance of a broader popular representation had existed up to then.

The elimination of the *junta de vecinos* had little apparent impact on the way Balmaceda carried out his duties. In the next few months, he met with the streetcar company to work out the details of restricting its operations in certain downtown streets, submitted a plan for a new slaughterhouse to the national authorities, and named a committee to look into the possibility of the city constructing public housing for workers.

A national government publication that appeared in these months provided a strongly positive view of Balmaceda's accomplishments. A review of his administration contrasted the "progressive" current *alcalde*, "with his clear vision of what a modern city should be," with the "municipalities of the past, lost in sterile political combinations, [and] which showed little interest in resolving the pressing problems of the capital."[38] The official praise of Balmaceda obscured some reservations about him. In late August 1929, in preparation for congressional elections in March of the following year, Ibáñez reshuffled his cabinet so as to gain Liberal and Radical Party support. As part of this general maneuvering, Ibáñez requested Balmaceda's resignation, which was offered and accepted, and replaced him with a former army officer who was at that time the mayor of Nuñoa, Eliécer Parada Pacheco. El Mercurio lauded both men and urged the new alcalde "to continue the good work that had been undertaken with love and dedication by Enrique Balmaceda."[39] The U.S. embassy reported, however, that Ibáñez had replaced Balmaceda in part because of his "intellectual incapacity" and in part because Parada Pacheco "will be more sympathetic and reasonable to the interests of the American business firms which are now having difficulties with the Municipal Government in connection with the street railway and lighting concessions."[40]

LIKE MANY NEW ALCALDES, Parada Pacheco inherited an administration in serious financial difficulty. In an open letter published on September 18, he forecast an eight-million-peso deficit in the city budget by the end of the year.[41] To attack this problem, Parada announced that there would be no new initiatives for the rest of the year. He also combined certain city departments and, despite original assurances to the contrary, eliminated some city personnel. On October 17 he reported to the minister of the interior that he already had trimmed one million pesos from the budget.[42] A few days later, he requested permission from the national government to sell some of the municipal markets, including the Mercado Central, as a way to cut the deficit, a request that was ultimately denied.[43]

Continuing efforts to keep expenses under control, the junta de alcaldes approved what it considered to be one of the few "realistic" budgets of recent times in November. Expenditures for 1930 were set at 27,293,747 pesos, about two million pesos less than the budget for the preceding year.[44] Commenting a few days later, El Mercurio recognized the exigencies that had led to cuts in spending and a tight budget, but continued to lament the skimpy financial resources available to Santiago in comparison with other capitals. The newspaper encouraged local and national officials to continue to look for new sources of revenue that would allow Parada "to initiate those works that contribute to improve city life and embellish the capital of the country."[45] The timing could have been better. Although the full effects of the

Wall Street crash the previous month had yet to be felt in Chile, the subsequent repercussions would make it virtually impossible to develop enhanced revenue sources for much of anything over the next few years.

REGARDLESS OF WHO HELD the *alcalde* post in Santiago, the power of the national government over local affairs continued to grow in these years. In late 1928 the Ibáñez regime introduced and Congress approved three measures that dealt with municipal affairs in general, and with particular application for Santiago. One sought to end the rampant speculation in land and property that had accompanied rapid suburban development by requiring the extension of basic municipal services to such areas before construction could begin. This measure was accompanied by a directive from the minister of the interior to all *alcaldes* and *juntas* that would give priority to " '*barrios populares*' in the provision of sanitation services, paving, and lighting."[46] Another measure allowed Santiago to increase the tax on vacant lots and "inappropriate buildings" so as to increase revenues and encourage rapid and "proper" construction. The third measure was in response to an earthquake that had devastated the city of Talca in 1928. According to Law 4563, passed on January 30, 1929, the president of the republic was given the authority to regulate future construction throughout the country to assure that new buildings, to as great a degree as possible, could withstand seismic shocks.[47] As a result of this law, the government contracted Austrian city planner and urban specialist Karl Brunner to help rebuild the cities destroyed by the earthquake as well as to come up with an overall development plan for Santiago.[48]

During the Ibáñez years, many of the public works projects in Santiago were directed and financed primarily by the national government. One of the most prominent, for example, was the channeling of the Mapocho River by reinforcing its banks so that it would not periodically flood the city. In August 1929, as another example, the government earmarked ten million pesos for the construction of four downtown buildings to house various divisions of the Carabineros. To pay for these and other projects, the government borrowed heavily from abroad, about two billion pesos between 1927 and 1931. Included in this total was a fifteen-million-dollar consolidated municipal loan contracted in August 1929 with the Grace National Company, Brown Brothers, and E. H. Rollins and Sons. The loan, following European models, covered sixty-five Chilean municipalities, with 80 percent of the total proceeds earmarked for Santiago, Valparaíso, and nine other cities. The funds were to be used to construct and improve public buildings and for street paving, as well as to pay off past obligations. Also according to the agreement, the national government, through the ministers of finance and the interior, would exercise tight control and oversight over how the funds were spent.[49]

THROUGHOUT 1930 AND 1931 the national government continued to play a prominent role in Santiago's affairs. In early January 1930 Parada proudly announced that a promised "definitive agreement" with the streetcar/electric company had been reached. Working with a federal government commission appointed on April 27, 1928, as well as with representatives of the company, the municipality had hammered out a new contract, which, Parada argued, would greatly benefit the city. According to the terms of the new agreement, the company agreed to invest fifteen million pesos to improve existing service, purchase sixty new cars, bring to 555 the total number of cars in circulation, and lower electric rates overall. The city, for its part, would be required to pay off its debt to the company, calculated to be a little more than sixteen million pesos, for which a loan would have to be contracted. It was estimated that the new contract would save the city some 1,870,000 pesos per year.[50]

The *junta de alcaldes* approved the new agreement on January 7, 1930. Commenting on the negotiations involved, Parada praised the actions and attitudes of the company representatives, "who, with a more open spirit and a greater understanding of the city's realities and necessities [than past representatives], have tried to coordinate the interests they represent with those of the capital. Thanks, then, to that understanding, it has been possible to reestablish cordial relations between the company and the city, broken for such a long time."[51]

Conservative opinion seemed to favor the agreement. *El Diario Ilustrado* predicted that the public would receive the new accord "with pleasure."[52] *El Mercurio* was equally enthusiastic, saying, "It is evident that the city will be directly benefited by the accord, which has released an impression of optimism that is calming for the city." Like the *alcalde*, the newspaper lauded the efforts of the company's representatives in reaching a new agreement, but also gave great credit to "the diligence of Sr. Parada, who, from the time he assumed office, gave this matter his determined attention."[53]

These upbeat observations, as so often had been the case with this issue, proved to be slightly premature. Reading the fine print of the agreement, other publications offered a more critical assessment. While the original idea had been to develop a contract that would deal primarily with Santiago, the ultimate agreement granted AFP a virtual monopoly over electric and streetcar service throughout the country, with a ninety-nine-year, tax-free concession.[54] Questions about the contract were also raised when the members of the National Bureau of Electric Services resigned en masse to protest certain actions of the Bureau's director, Francisco Lobos. The members alleged that Lobos had failed to inform them of the contract negotiations and they also complained about not being sufficiently included in the discussions and negotiations for a similar contract that involved the Chilean Telephone Company, now owned by IT&T. Confronted with these objections, Ibáñez, who originally had agreed to the contract, decided not to approve it.[55]

In making his decision, Ibáñez may have had an eye on the upcoming congressional elections. A strong position in favor of Chilean interests in the face of what appeared to be an unfair advantage granted to a foreign enterprise would serve to strengthen his position and that of those associated with him, although in reality he had already assured tight control over all competing parties and had little to fear from the election results.[56]

At the time of Ibáñez's decision, company spokesmen expressed confidence that after careful and calm consideration the contract would be approved. Although it would take more than a year to accomplish, their confidence proved to be well placed. At the end of 1930 the Ibáñez administration would form another committee, composed of national, municipal, and company representatives, to hammer out a new agreement. After several months of hard work, Parada signed the new accord on behalf of the city of Santiago on March 10, 1931. Along with his signature, the *alcalde* also submitted to the vice-president of the company a check for $7,892,090 pesos to cover the city's debt for electrical service. The company, in turn, agreed to forgive an additional nineteen million pesos in city obligations, agreeing that the nineteen million pesos was equivalent to what the company owed the city as a result of its own contractual obligations.

Editorial opinion again was generally favorable. The new agreement was judged to be even more advantageous to the capital and the country than the previous one.[57] The contract did give the company a monopoly of service in the provinces of Santiago and Aconcagua, as well as a ninety-nine-year concession, but the rest of the country would now be opened up to competition. The company once again promised to increase investment and improve service as well as lower electric rates. It also agreed to pay certain taxes and return 10 percent of its profits to the city of Santiago. Streetcar fares remained at 10 and 20 centavos. The company also promised to use national resources and materials for power generation and facility construction to the greatest extent possible, and to provide employment for two to three thousand Chileans in its various development activities. In listing what he saw as among the main advantages to Santiago of the new contract, Parada claimed that it would "regularize legally the situation of the company and harmonize relations between it and the local authorities."[58] This sentiment was echoed by El Mercurio's headline: "The streetcar/electric company and the municipality renew their good relations," although the cynic might inquire as to just when those good relations had ever existed.[59]

Again, not all assessments were quite so positive. Thomas O'Brien has written that AFP put considerable pressure on Ibáñez to come up with a proposal that would "still put the company well on the road to establishing a monopoly in the field of electrical power generation." If not, the company threatened reprisals from the U.S. bankers upon whom the administration was so dependent. According to O'Brien, "The agreement remained a subject of deep-seated popular discontent over what was viewed as a surrender of national sovereignty."[60] U.S. Ambassador William Culbertson, writing in January 1931 about Ibáñez's attempts to get extraordinary powers from Congress to deal with the economic crisis, acknowledged that the agreement had the potential to offend nationalist sensitivities. U.S. companies in Chile, he reported, supported the granting of special powers, as they saw this as a way for the executive to resolve disputes with the government quickly and to their benefit. The ambassador cautioned these companies "to avoid even the appearance of having any part in this effort to give the President extraordinary powers."

> I pointed out the serious reaction against us which would follow if the enemies of the Government were to have reason to state the Ameri-

can interests were advocating extraordinary powers for the President in order to promote their own interests. Furthermore, it is probable that the President intends to use these extraordinary powers, if granted, for a settlement with the Electric Bond and Share Company with reference to the electric contract. Here again, the Government wishes to avoid discussions in Congress.[61]

Congress granted Ibáñez extraordinary powers on February 4, and the new agreement was signed, as we have seen, on March 10.[62] While the new contract seemed "to harmonize" relations by promising a "definitive" solution to the long-standing dispute between the city and the company that provided streetcar and electric service to the capital, it would turn out to be just one more chapter in an ongoing saga, with Chilean resistance to what many saw as the "abuses" of a foreign-owned monopoly continuing to be a central theme in the story.

PARADA'S ADMINISTRATION COINCIDED WITH some grandiose proposals for the physical transformation of Santiago. In early February 1930 Congress approved plans for the so-called Barrio Cívico, a massive complex of government buildings to be constructed around La Moneda on both sides of the Alameda. While this was to be basically a national government initiative, the municipal authorities were to cooperate with such matters as expropriating existing properties in the area to be cleared away to make room for the new buildings. In his summary of activities for 1930, Parada reported that the city attorney was already involved in several legal proceedings designed to compensate property owners for these expropriations.[63] The project itself, however, would be delayed by several years due to the economic crisis caused by the Great Depression.

Parada's term also overlapped with the visit of Karl Brunner. The *alcalde* met with the urban planner on various occasions to discuss his designs for the capital. In May 1930, for example, the *alcalde*, along with the provincial *intendente* and the minister of the interior, consulted with Brunner on his proposal to establish zones in the capital for the concentration of industrial activities.[64] On July 31, 1930, the *junta de alcaldes*, following a suggestion from Brunner to encourage the development of broad avenues as an integral part of Santiago's overall development plan, approved a project to broaden Calles Gálvez and Nataniel downtown.[65]

Earlier that year, on its own, the *junta de alcaldes* had recommended the expenditure of $4,342,800 pesos over five years to "isolate" Santa Lucía Park. This had been a long-standing proposal from the time of Vicuña's administration. It aimed to develop a series of streets around the park that would separate it completely from the surrounding commercial and residential buildings.[66]

There was little progress, however, on this or any other major project. Constrained by the economic crisis, Parada spent most of 1930 and 1931 economizing by cutting city personnel and keeping services to a minimum. Summarizing his activities in 1930, the *alcalde* observed that the budget for the year, at about twenty-seven million pesos, twelve million of which went to pay past debts, had been less than the year before, and that projections for 1931 were not more encouraging. The improvements he could point to included covering the San Miguel Canal and some modernization of sanitation equipment and the garbage incinerators. One accomplishment was literally cosmetic—the painting of various municipal buildings, including the Casa Consistorial. Problems associated with the deteriorating condition of the Parque Cousiño, the subject of some critical press commentary, Parada warned, would not be addressed in 1931 due to the "tight" budgetary situation. He also reported that considerable progress had nevertheless been made in street paving over the previous year, the funding for which had come from a special account.[67] In March 1931 *El Mercurio* praised the paving program, which since its inception in 1928 had extended both street and sidewalk paving to about half the city, an achievement that exceeded earlier expectations.[68]

Unable to carry out new initiatives, Parada did his best to assure that municipal services operated as normally and efficiently as possible. The sanitation service was again reorganized, to apparent good effect. The *alcalde* encouraged the city inspectors' office to exercise its functions with more vigor, and at the end of 1930 the office could report that some five hundred commercial establishments had been closed down for violating municipal ordinances.[69] Regulation of public transportation continued to receive attention. On August 29, 1930, Parada approved the operation of a new vehicle called the "*taxibús*," which was similar in some respects to the collective taxi, or "*colectivo*," that had appeared in Buenos Aires two years earlier.[70] This vehicle, a large automobile, could carry between seven and ten passengers over a fixed route for a fare of 2 pesos, considerably more than a bus or streetcar but less than the cost of a private taxi.[71] In January of the following year, the *alcaldes* approved new regulations for the *taxibús*, as well as for the ever-growing bus service. At its session of January 29, 1931, the *junta* approved a measure that would regularize sales of bus tickets, developing a uniform standard that called for the tickets to be provided on a small paper roll and numbered consecutively, a system that prevails to the present day.[72] On June 11, 1931, the *junta* introduced some modifications in the rules governing bus collectors and inspectors that had first been implemented in 1924. By that time, there were seven hundred buses officially operating in Santiago, with the greatest number of lines, sixty, serving the Alameda.[73] As the director of the city traffic office observed at the time, the bus service directly and indirectly provided employment and sustenance for about fifteen thousand Santiaguinos. In sharp contrast with the streetcar company, the buses were owned and operated primarily by Chileans and provided rapid and relatively inexpensive transportation to areas of the capital that the streetcar did not reach.[74]

During the first half of 1931, Parada did what he could to keep a financially strapped municipality functioning. He oversaw new regulations to control bicycle traffic, established new parking restrictions on downtown streets, changed certain street names, exempted the popular soccer team Colo Colo from some local taxes, sought to reinforce noise-abatement regulations, and decreed that chimney-sweeps would henceforth have to register with the city. None of these measures could be seen as particularly significant. Ultimately, of course, Parada's fate would rest with the man who had appointed him. On July 26, 1931, bowing to popular protest and pressure, Carlos Ibáñez resigned the presidency and left for exile in Argentina. Parada submitted his own resignation the next day.[75] While it might not have been clear at the time and would take several years to achieve, these events would mark the beginning of the end for municipal governments appointed by the national executive, be they *juntas de vecinos* or *juntas de alcaldes*.

1. Municipal Theater (Teatro Municipal), ca. 1900
SOURCE: Private collection

2. Central Station (Estación Central), ca. 1900
SOURCE: Private collection

3. Mapocho Station, ca. 1900
SOURCE: Private collection

4. The Alameda (*Avenida de las Delicias*), ca. 1900
SOURCE: Private collection

5. Entrance to Cerro Santa Lucía, ca. 1900
SOURCE: Private collection

6. *Museo de Bellas Artes, ca. 1910*
SOURCE: Private collection

7. *Private residences along the Alameda, ca. 1900*
SOURCE: Private collection

8. *Grandstand of the Club Hípico, ca.* 1900
SOURCE: Private collection

9. North side of the Plaza de Armas, ca. 1900

SOURCE: Courtesy of the Museo Histórico Nacional

10. *West side of the Plaza de Armas, ca. 1890, showing horse-drawn trolleys*
SOURCE: Courtesy of the Museo Histórico Nacional

11. Palacio Cousiño
SOURCE: Photograph by the author

12. Santiago City Hall (Casa Consistorial), with an
equestrian statue of Pedro de Valdivia in front
SOURCE: Photograph by the author

13. Main meeting room of the Municipality of Santiago
SOURCE: Photograph by the author

14. Plaza Argentina in front of the Central Station, ca. 1910
SOURCE: Courtesy of the Museo Histórico Nacional

15. Buildings of the Barrio Cívico
SOURCE: Photograph by the author

16. Plaza Italia, ca. 1950
SOURCE: Courtesy of the Museo Histórico Nacional

8 Santiago in 1930

THE NATIONAL CENSUS OF 1930 confirmed the continued population growth in and around Santiago over the previous ten years. The city itself had expanded from 427,658 inhabitants in 1920 to 542,432 in 1930, with the Department of Santiago growing from 606,429 to 839,565 and the province from 718,211 to 967,603.[1] While the city's growth was substantial, the growth of many of the neighboring *comunas* was even more dramatic. Continuing a pattern already evident by 1920, Providencia, Nuñoa, and Quinta Normal saw roughly a doubling of their populations, while the population of San Miguel almost tripled.[2] It was during this decade that Santiago's upper classes began to migrate from the central downtown area to the eastern suburbs, or "Barrio Alto," in a steady progression that in many ways continues to the present. Providencia, just to the east of the capital, in particular became a favored destination for many of the well-to-do. Attracted to what was then still something of a bucolic atmosphere, the new residents frequently constructed detached residences, which they called chalets, in a semi-Tudor style that incorporated front lawns and fences. They also favored attractive, tree-lined streets, like the Avenida Pedro de Valdivia.[3]

In the city of Santiago, women outnumbered men by a considerable margin, 300,067 to 242,365, while in the principal suburbs the ratio was closer to even. This may have reflected occupational patterns, since there were greater opportunities for employment for women, single and married, in industry and commerce and as domestic servants in the city as opposed to the suburbs. There were also substantially more widows (31,211) than widowers (6,508) in the capital, which also accounted for some of the difference. Nationwide, the country was pretty evenly divided between men (2,122,709) and women (2,164,736).[4]

Reflecting continuing advances in public education, the literacy rate in the capital remained high. According to the 1930 figures, an astounding 399,665 citizens over the age of eight were able to read and write, while only 32,831 were not. This produced a literacy rate of 92 percent, comparable to that of Buenos Aires and well above the average of 73 percent for the nation as a whole.[5]

The census again provided information on occupations, this time, however, only for the province as a whole. Unfortunately, these data were not sufficient to develop the kind of socioeconomic profile constructed for 1907 and 1920. The introduction to the census, however, contains information on national changes in some occupational categories over the decade, with particular implications for Santiago. An increase of almost 17,000 persons in public administration was recorded, for example, most of them located in and around the capital. By 1930, the national total in this category was 48,833 (40,327 men, 8,506 women) as compared with 31,897 (27,340 men, 4,557 women) in 1920, which represented substantial growth, despite the efforts of Ibáñez and others to trim the bureaucracy. The number of persons in the liberal professions, many of whom were also located in Santiago, also expanded in this period, although less markedly than those in administration: from 21,256 (9,986 men, 11,270 women) in 1920 to 27,465 (12,763 men, 14,702 women) in 1930.[6] While women, mostly schoolteachers, were well represented in this general category, their representation in the prestigious legal and medical professions was still slight. Of 1,498 lawyers (for some reason, the number of lawyers declined over the decade), for example, only 34 were women, and only 56 women were physicians as compared with 1,187 men.[7]

Mechanization had a clear impact on some categories. Again, while the figures were national, they had particular application for Santiago. The number of coachmen, for example, declined from 3,818 to 483 over the decade, while the number of *choferes*, or drivers of motorized vehicles, increased, from 4,600 to 10,029 (only 10 female *choferes* were listed). The number of machinists grew from 2,320 to 2,872 (2,845 males, 27 females); census-takers observed that this increase was probably even greater, given the large numbers of machines that had replaced manual laborers in the nation's factories. This dynamic was seen very clearly in the sharp decline in the number of telephone operators (*telefonistas*), from 1,037 in 1920 to 482 (399 women, 83 men) in 1930, as the system became more automated, particularly after IT&T's purchase of the telephone company in the late 1920s.[8]

A CONSIDERABLE AMOUNT OF CONSTRUCTION of public and private buildings in the center of Santiago continued throughout the 1920s. Two of the most notable structures, as previously mentioned, were the Club de la Unión at Alameda 1091 and the Biblioteca Nacional, a few blocks to the east at Alameda 651, both completed in 1925. During the decade the downtown area also saw the construction of the Hotel Mundial (1923), at the corner of Moneda and Bolsa; the Banco Central de Chile (1927) at Agustinas 1180; the Banco de Chile (1921–25) at Ahumada 251; and the Banco Sud Americana (1930) at Morandé 226, one of the first of Santiago's structures done in the art deco style.[9]

The commercial district, extending roughly from the Plaza de Armas south to the Alameda and north to Claras (now Mac Iver) also underwent important changes. Visiting Santiago in the 1920s, North American Frank G. Carpenter described the district in the following terms:

> There are many fine buildings; magnificent stores with the latest goods from abroad. The town is noted for elaborate window displays and its many arcades. The business blocks are large and the fact that they are not skyscrapers makes it possible to cut these covered passageways through them, roofing them over with glass. Often a block of several acres will be intersected by a number of arcades. Each is a favourite promenade, for the semi-transparent roof shuts out the heat of the sun and at the same time gives plenty of light. The stores in the arcades bring good rents.[10]

The intermingling of commercial blocks with galleries, arcades, and passageways remains a feature of Santiago's commercial district.

The lack of skyscrapers that Carpenter noted was true of some blocks downtown, but not of the entire area. While concerns about earthquakes placed some limitations on the heights of buildings, in the 1920s Santiago, like Buenos Aires and various other South American capitals, began to experience vertical as well as horizontal growth. The city's first skyscraper was the triangular-shaped, ten-story Ariztia Building, also the first to be constructed of reinforced concrete, built in 1921 and located, appropriately enough, on Calle Nueva York 52, just off the Alameda. At the time, the Ariztia Building "dominated all others."[11] By 1924, however, work was proceeding on the Errázuriz-Simpson office building nearby, a steel-and-concrete structure that included two subterranean floors, eleven main floors, and four tower floors. The new building was planned to be South America's tallest, at least at that time. One observer wrote: "All the ingenuity of architect and engineer is being brought to bear to rank this building with the great business edifices of the world. It will have all up-to-date accessories, there being three Otis Elevators, and central heating throughout, and the offices will be the finest in Chile." He also observed that "Nowhere in South America is a skyline changing more rapidly than in Santiago," and the "the rapid rise of the Errázuriz-Simpson structure [underscores] the confidence of Santiago's businessmen in the city."[12]

By the end of the decade, various other multistory buildings dotted the downtown area. These included the Díaz Building (1925) at Moneda 1000; the offices of La Nación newspaper (1930) at Agustinas 1269; and the ongoing construction at the Ministry of Finance Building at Teatinos 120, which would not be completed until 1933 and which would be the first major public building in Santiago built in the "rationalist" style influenced by Le Corbusier and others. While foreign influences were still prominent, most of Santiago's new buildings had been designed by Chilean architects.[13]

The changing skyline reflected the growing influence of New York City as a model for Santiago. Throughout the 1920s there were frequent articles in Chilean publications of that city's development, usually accompanied by photographs and sketches showing the modern and massive building taking place there. Not all Santiaguinos saw this as an unmixed blessing. A commentary in the March 1927 edition of Zig-Zag referred to a series of photographs showing the Chilean capital at night: "The skyscrapers imported from Yankilandia [sic] alienate Santiago from its traditions by trying to approximate it to the modern Babylons."[14] Writing in El Mercurio the following year, José Manuel Sánchez was even more critical. Adopting a tone reminiscent of Uruguay's José Enrique Rodó, who in his seminal essay "Ariel," written in 1900, had criticized the pragmatism and materialism of the United States as opposed to the idealism and romanticism of the Latin Americans, Sánchez described the skyscrapers of New York as an "exclusive product of the *yanqui* mentality" and "the intensive complexity of their material necessities." Skyscrapers, he argued, with their size and uniformity, rendered humans into "insects" and reflected a society dedicated to reducing everyone to the same "machine-made person, the same 'standard' man." "Our Latin American race," he continued, "needs to see the sun continuously . . . [and] is free and individualistic and does not want to see itself flattened by its own constructions." Skyscrapers, he concluded, were basically unnecessary in Santiago, where there was still plenty of room for horizontal development.[15] A somewhat more positive picture was provided two years later by another commentator in *Zig-Zag*, who described the appearance of skyscrapers in Santiago as "the triumph of new times, the advance of North America towards the extreme south of South America." While they might produce "ant-like" behavior, he also saw any attempt to halt their construction as in vain and urged architects and engineers to make them less monotonous and uniform.[16]

A report produced by the Austrian Karl Brunner addressed these issues as well. Reviewing the recent growth of multistory buildings in Santiago, and recognizing the inevitability that more would be built in the future, Brunner recommended that Chilean city planners learn from North American examples, where skyscraper construction often was chaotic and disorderly, and plan accordingly. Skyscrapers, he argued, should be built sparingly and only as part of a coherent plan of development. They should be integrated as much as possible with surrounding buildings and should not unduly block the circulation of air or access to sunlight. Aesthetically, he approved of the austere rational style of the Ministry of Finance and envisioned a time when "skyscrapers come to form part of the organic whole of the city and facilitate its orientation, much as previously did the towers of churches."[17] One can imagine what traditionalists must have thought of the comparison between skyscrapers and churches.

While the skyline was changing, other important changes were taking place on the ground. On the north side of the Alameda, in the block bounded by Bandera, Moneda, and Ahumada, two new streets, Nueva York and Bolsa, had been created as diagonals, at the junction of which was the Ariztia Building. The two streets served, to some degree, to disrupt the rigid gridiron pattern of the colonial city. Across the Alameda, a few blocks east,

yet another innovative street construction could be seen. In 1922 a building company had purchased property adjacent to the landmark San Francisco Church from the Franciscan order, with the aim of creating a "model"
residential neighborhood. The main distinguishing features of this small
and exclusive barrio were the two main intersecting streets, the Calle Londres and the Calle Paris, which were curved rather than straight or diagonal
(see Fig. 2). Following an overall design produced by the Austrian architect
Camilio Sitte, who opposed what he termed "cold modern architecture,"
subsequent Chilean architects would give each residence in this barrio a
particular style in an attempt to reproduce the atmosphere of a medieval
city with cobblestone streets but also with all the modern conveniences
and only minutes away from the bustling central downtown.[18] The experiment appeared to be a success. *Zig-Zag* estimated that the value of the land
for this development had increased from 700,000 pesos when it was first
purchased to around twenty million pesos by 1931.[19]

Farther along the Alameda to the east, at the edge of the capital's limits,
could be found one of the major public works projects of the period. In
1927 the city had held a competition for the renovation of the Plaza Italia, a
major connecting point of the capital. Following the acceptance of a proposal, work was begun under the administration of Alcalde Luis Phillips and
was completed under Intendente Salas Rodríguez. The project involved removing some existing structures, shifting certain streetcar lines, and clearing space for a main plaza that would display an equestrian statue of War of
the Pacific hero Manuel Baquedano at its center. The plaza served, then as it
does now, as the termination of the Alameda and the initiation point of
Avenida Providencia, which continues on to the east. The western entrance
to the Parque Forestal is just off the plaza, and to the north is Calle Pio
Noveno (Pius the Ninth), which connects the plaza to the Bellavista district
and the foot of the funicular that travels to the top of San Cristóbal. Extending to the south is the Avenida Vicuña Mackenna, the main thoroughfare
leading to the *comunas* of Nuñoa and Puente Alto. Also to the south is the
eight-story Turri Building, completed in 1929. Trees and tall buildings surrounding the new Plaza Italia, however, were kept to a minimum, so as to
enhance the plaza's most distinguishing feature, a magnificent view of both
San Cristóbal to the north and the cordillera of the Andes to the east.[20]

During these years, Santiago underwent many other transformations,

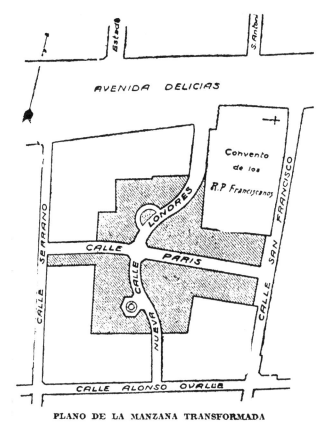

PLANO DE LA MANZANA TRANSFORMADA

FIG. 2. Sketch of the proposed "Barrio Londres" to be constructed
south of the Alameda and next to the San Francisco Church.
SOURCE: El Mercurio, June 1, 1922, p. 22.

both great and small. As early as 1921, the author Ricardo Donoso lamented
the disappearance of many of the old bookstores from the Calle Bandera,
which had been replaced by large commercial buildings. "With the disappearance of these bookstores," he lamented, "the first block of Bandera has
lost much of its charm."[21] By 1928, Zig-Zag described Bandera as being
full of "commercial brokers, hard-hearted cantina owners, and confidence
men (zorzales) . . . failed businessmen and bohemian artists." Bandera's extension to the south, along San Diego, was now a district of used bookstores
and secondhand shops (as it still is) and it became progressively seedier as

one moved southward.[22] In a review of city neighborhoods in 1931, *Zig-Zag* noted the continuing commercial nature of San Diego, where, with its great variety of shops and markets, shoppers could find some of the cheapest as well as some of the most expensive merchandise in the city. The areas on and around San Diego, combined with those on and around Avenida Manuel A. Matta, which it intersected to the south, also comprised some of the most densely populated districts in the city, and, according to *Zig-Zag*, these neighborhoods were among the most "popular" in terms of their social composition. The area bordering Matta, in particular, had grown dramatically in the previous years, largely due to the extension of street paving and lighting. While both districts lacked the large and imposing residential structures of other parts of the city, they were marked by constant animation and street life due to the abundant commercial activity, which set them in sharp contrast with the more staid barrios "where the hours seem to pass on tiptoe."[23]

Just to the west of San Diego was the area around the Palacio Cousiño. This district, which also was becoming increasingly populated, contained the Escuela Militar (Military School), the Arsenales de Guerra (Military Arsenal), and the racetrack of the Club Hípico, and still maintained much of its prestige. The Parque Cousiño, however, while it remained the center of the district, had deteriorated over the previous decade. In 1929 Alberto Mackenna Subercaseaux had gone so far as to call it "the ugliest park in the world."[24] *Zig-Zag* claimed that because of the municipality's failure to maintain and modernize the park, it had become a gathering place for the unemployed and the "less desirable" elements of the city. As a result, it was now "a somewhat sinister site, even during daylight hours."[25] *El Mercurio* described the area on and around Avenida Exposición, a few blocks to the west of the park, as one of the most dangerous in the city, and warned the unwary to avoid it due to the large number of criminals and petty thieves who frequented it.[26]

For *Zig-Zag*, the area around the Central Station had experienced fewer changes than most. "It is the only area," the magazine claimed, "that conserves, to a certain extent, the features of old Santiago." This was due, in large measure, to the tree-lined avenues of the Alameda and Ecuador, whose shade provided a kind of "provincial calm." Directly in front of the station was the Plaza Argentina, which served as a main connecting point for streetcars and buses, and which had undergone some transformation over the decade. As Zig-Zag described it, the district surrounding the station could be divided into two distinct areas. To the west, in the triangle formed by Avenida Ecuador and the Alameda, was a mixture of small homes and schools, that "despite its manifest lack of progress with respect to the rest of the city, maintains an appealing charm." On the eastern side, in the area around Matucana and Exposición, it was a different story. There could be found "merchants of all kinds, traffickers and others that life has marked with its worst stigmas, women of vice and misery. For that element, there are shady cafés, establishments where the music carries its waves of perversion, corners where the police are always on the watch."[27]

To the north of the Central Station lay the Quinta Normal Park and surrounding area. This district also had undergone significant growth and transformation over the previous decade, mostly for the better. The neighboring comuna of Quinta Normal, as mentioned, had doubled in population between 1920 and 1930, and the park of the same name continued to be a well-maintained site for cultural and social activities, not having suffered a decline similar to that of the Parque Cousiño. The Avenida Portales, leading into and bisecting the park, had been broadened and embellished into "one of the most beautiful arteries in Santiago, not so much for the buildings that surround it as for the gardens in the center, graced by charming fountains and large trees."[28] Much less attractive was the Avenida Matucana, the main north-south thoroughfare of the district, running roughly from the Mapocho along the eastern edge of the park to the Central Station. Bisecting this avenue was a rail line that over the years had caused numerous accidents, many of them fatal. Plans to place these tracks underground had been floated at both the local and national level. The Brunner report in 1932 mentioned that a project to remove the surface line and to place it underground a block to the west was being considered by the Ministry of Public Works.[29] In the meantime, the train crossings remained a prominent eyesore and hazard for this district.

There had also been considerable growth and progress north of the Mapocho. Zig-Zag identified the district along the Avenida Independencia as one whose development had been significantly stimulated by the extension of street paving and lighting. Anchored by the Faculty of Medicine of the University of Chile, the district was described as the most socially diverse in the capital, where one could find "merchants, workers of all kinds, students, and employees" reflecting an equally diverse mixture of "large factories, myriad industries, various businesses, movie theaters, workshops and laboratories, hospitals and churches, all grouped within a neighborhood of intense activity." Generally, the area lacked new and distinctive residential housing, much of the population living in rooming and boarding houses. An exception was the Avenida Francia off of Independencia, which was "formed by a group of chalets of imponderable grace, with gardens in front and with flower-laden balconies."[30]

Zig-Zag was equally enthusiastic about the expanding Bellavista area at the foot of San Cristóbal. As recently as 1928, residents of the area near the terminal of the new funicular had complained of the run-down, shabby, and unsanitary surroundings of the new main entrance to the city's newest park and its only zoo. One resident called the district a "forgotten corner" of Santiago, with a "filthy and anti-aesthetic appearance," despite the construction of some modern residences nearby.[31] By 1931, according to Zig-Zag, these defects had been completely remedied: "The streets of Pio IX, Siglo XX, Dominica, Circunvalación, Loreto and others of this sector are models of cleanliness, of new and progressive construction, where are combined elements of tranquility and progress, all of which daily increases the value of property in that sector. Few barrios of Santiago have better transportation services." The neighborhood, too, it was claimed, benefited from "a pure, healthy, and fresh air nourished by all the elements of abundant vegetation that the Cerro San Cristóbal possesses."[32] While the description might have been inflated, the Bellavista district by 1930 seemed clearly on its way to being one of the most interesting in the city, having acquired an artistic and Bohemian ambience that still prevails, one that was greatly enhanced when the famed Chilean poet Pablo Neruda built "La Chascona," one of his three houses in Chile, in Bellavista in the 1950s. Unfortunately, the "pure air" of which Zig-Zag wrote was, by the 1990s, only a distant memory.

Crossing back to the south of the Mapocho from Bellavista by way of the Pius IX Bridge led to the district surrounding the Parque Forestal. Unlike the Parque Cousiño, this park had been modernized and expanded, and was well maintained. In 1931 Zig-Zag called it the "preferred center of our elegant youth," who strolled through its gardens and sat on its benches throughout the day and well into the night, especially in the spring and summer. During the 1920s, there had been considerable residential construction along the south side of the park. These were costly structures, and included "residential skyscrapers, houses with elevated gardens, chalets and houses of various kinds, forming an ensemble in which buildings of three and four stories . . . provide comfort and well-being."[33]

There were many critics of the architectural eclecticism that characterized some of the new neighborhoods. Writing in late 1929, the commentator "Roxane" observed that in new barrios like those at the foot of San Cristóbal and around the Parque Forestal, too often, "each architect lets his fantasy run wild and next to a colonial construction they raise a skyscraper, a modern building, a Gothic one, in this way forming a variegated mélange of bad taste." What was needed, she argued, was "architectural harmony."[34] A year earlier, an English visitor who was interviewed by El Mercurio made much the same point. "Santiago," he said, "is a kind of Macedonia or confusion of capricious styles, among which no one tendency predominates to serve as a point of departure for a national architecture."[35]

Santiago certainly was not unique in this regard. Buenos Aires, for example, was subjected to much the same criticism, as the rapid construction and different styles of the early twentieth century came to (almost literally) overshadow and overwhelm colonial and nineteenth-century structures there. One of the purposes of plans like Brunner's, of course, was to give the city a more rational organization and a more coherent style. That was also the aim of Chilean architects and urban planners, such as Carlos Carvajal and others. In 1928 El Mercurio began publication of a special section entitled "La Ciudad Bella," or "The Beautiful City," which focused on the problems of Santiago's development. Carvajal was a frequent contributor, using the opportunity to introduce his plan for the overall transformation of the capital.[36] Another contributor, with his own plan to transform the capital, was Carlos Pinto Durán, a journalist and author. Pinto faulted "private building, which grows 'a la criolla' [in "typical Chilean fashion"], in the greatest disorder, without being subject to basic norms or effective control" as one of the city's greatest problems. "Each individual constructs his residence however he wants and with absolute liberty, without taking into account in any way the general well-being and progress of his neighborhood."[37] In addition to calling for greater control over individual construction projects in the future, Pinto, like Carvajal, strongly recommended the creation of new, broad avenues, as well as a main boulevard to encircle the city as a complement to the rail line that currently served that function.

WHATEVER THE CITY'S PROBLEMS and the plans, all seemed to agree that Santiago had undergone remarkable physical growth over the previous decade. Articles in El Mercurio in late 1928 and early 1929 described the capital as engaged in a "fever" of demolition and construction, to the point that those absent from the city for a few years found it almost unrecognizable upon their return.[38] The same "Roxane" who had criticized the lack of architectural harmony in some new neighborhoods, herself described the recent growth as a "building fever."[39] The Baedeker for 1930 said much the same thing:

> The city of Santiago is progressing and being rapidly modernized. In the last few years, building has been noticeably improved and is passing through a period of feverish activity of demolishing and rebuilding. Constructions are made on the European style, with separate apartments, lifts, central heating, and modern comfort. The city has an excellent street lighting system all over, being one of the better lighted cities. Good pavements are actively constructed and very soon will cover all its streets.[40]

Various other observers attested to this growth. Writing in the South Pacific Mail in 1929, one commentator argued that Chile itself had been "re-born in the last two years" and that, with paving, building, and beautification Santiago was on its way to being "a worthy capital."[41] Another visitor to the city, after an absence of several years, was particularly struck by the taller buildings, the increased bus traffic, and the greater wealth on display. "We noticed," he wrote, "that those who were content with taking afternoon tea at the 'Rio' at the cost of a peso, now patronize that palatial room of Gath and Chavéz which is three times as expensive." This, of course, was before the effects of the Great Depression undoubtedly led many Santiaguinos to return to less expensive venues. With all the changes, the visitor was also comforted by certain familiar sights:

> ... the feeling of stickiness that one associates with the Portal Fernández Concha, with its fruit stands, its cheese shops, bootblacks, perspir-

ing humanity and flies; the *empanada* [meat pie] vendor at Santa Lucía, the "olor de turco" that characterizes the Calle 21 de Mayo, the tawdry clothes signs in blue and red inks, the unchangeable type of the *futres* ("dandies") who line the pavement in calle Huérfanos ... the *tinterillos* (clerks, pettifoggers) of the calle Bandera; the perpetual swinging of the door at the Bar Santiago; ... the wonder that people still have the courage to visit one of the theatres without a tin of insect powder; and of course the beauty of the eastward view of the calle Agustinas, the sunsets and the exhilaration that one always experiences in Santiago.[42]

Foreign visitors continued to provide generally favorable commentary. Writing in *National Geographic Magazine* in September 1922, the travel author Harriet Chalmers Adams described her trip from the far north to the far south of Chile and offered several fine photographs of the capital's major sites and public buildings, in which she particularly extolled the "sublime panorama" offered from Santa Lucía at sunset.[43] A German visitor, one Dr. A. W. Ado Baezzler, writing in a Hamburg newspaper, also described Santiago in glowing terms, describing the charm and beauty of its young women (something Chileans and foreigners alike frequently referred to), the lively atmosphere around the Plaza de Armas, and the wide variety and abundance of the fruit available (something else frequently mentioned). Like many others, Baezzler had special praise for the constantly expanding Alameda, "the street of streets, the *paseo* of *paseos*, the avenue of avenues.... Where in the world is there another street like it?" For him, Santiago was "a burnished, brilliant city, full of life, fortunate."[44] Less poetic, but equally enthusiastic was the North American Frank G. Carpenter, who also praised the Alameda, the new National Library, and Santa Lucía, about which he said, "No city in the world has a public park to compare with it." Writing in 1927, Carpenter stated that over the previous few years the capital had grown "in beauty and modern improvements."[45]

A number of distinguished foreigners visited Santiago in these years, usually as part of a larger South American tour. England's Prince of Wales visited in 1925, in a continuation of his visit to Buenos Aires. His stop in Santiago was accompanied by considerable official fanfare and celebration and provided the stimulus for local and national officials to spruce up the capital and to accelerate ongoing improvements. As mentioned earlier, U.S. president-elect Herbert Hoover also visited Santiago, at the end of 1928, as did John Pershing, José Vasconcelos, and Santos Dumont earlier in the decade. Less heralded but also noted were the visits of U.S. authors Waldo Frank and Francis Parkinson Keyes, Spanish philosopher José Ortega y Gasset, and Germany's Count Keyserling. Perhaps making the greatest impact, however, was the St. Louis–born, Paris-based dancer and singer Josephine Baker, who performed before sold-out and enthusiastic audiences in several Santiago theaters in October and November of 1929. According to the journalist Daniel de la Vega, contrary to advance billing, Baker was not any more scandalously dressed (or undressed) than most stage dancers, nor did her songs extend beyond conventional limits. "On the other hand," he observed, "Josephine Baker, from the artistic point of view, presents some very interesting interpretations, and she is very deserving of the ardent ovations that every night land at her feet."[46] The staid El Mercurio also saw nothing particularly objectionable in her performance, or in the warm applause she received from the Santiago public.[47]

The number of theaters of the kind in which Baker performed continued to grow in the 1920s. The Baedeker of 1930 listed thirteen such venues, where musical, comedy, and serious dramatic presentations were shown, in the downtown area.[48] The number of hotels also continued to grow in these years, with the aforementioned Hotel Mundial at Bandera and Moneda joining the Hotel Crillón at Agustinas 1025 and the Hotel Savoy at Ahumada 165 as Santiago's elite, first-class downtown establishments.[49]

As in most large cities at this time, leisure time and opportunities for entertainment grew substantially. Radio broadcasting was initiated in these years, allowing popular music like the Argentine tango and North American jazz, among other genres, to reach ever-wider audiences. As was the case elsewhere, motion pictures became an increasingly popular form of entertainment. Reporting in 1924, an official in the U.S. consulate in Valparaíso described the "extraordinary" acceptance of movies in Chile. Hollywood productions were the most popular, but European films had also gained increasing acceptance. The consular official claimed that there were at least forty theaters in Santiago where movies were shown, some of them able to seat up to 3,000 persons. Generally, there were two showings per day, one at 6:30 p.m., called the "vermouth" showing, and another at 9:30 p.m. "On Sunday afternoon," he observed, "many of the more progressive theaters present a special juvenile program at reduced rates, in which slapstick comedy prevails."[50] Three years later, the U.S. ambassador reported on new national film censorship laws that prohibited children under fifteen and unmarried women from seeing certain films. He considered this noteworthy, "on account of the great number of American films shown in Chile."[51] Whatever the restrictions, Santiago audiences flocked to the cinemas in ever-growing numbers. An article in the May 6, 1929, edition of El Mercurio claimed that on most Sundays some 70,000 Santiaguinos attended the movies, producing 180,000 pesos in revenue.[52] Two months later, the same newspaper described a "typical" Santiago Sunday, asserting that in most barrios, during the afternoon and evening, most people were either at home dining with their families or at the movies. An accompanying drawing showed a banner stretched over a neighborhood street advertising the matinee of a film starring Charlie Chaplin, and a special nighttime performance of another that featured the Mexican actress Dolores del Rio. A caption explained that the street was deserted "because everyone is in a theater applauding Chaplin or Emil Jannings."[53]

As in Buenos Aires and elsewhere, European-style cabarets began to appear in Santiago in these years. Zig-Zag was particularly enthusiastic about "El Trocadero," which, like its Parisian namesake, offered fine food and music. A cut above the common cantinas and bars of the city, the magazine observed that " 'El Trocadero' has been, from the day of its opening, marked by the attendance of the most select class of our society, which enjoys gathering in this pleasant and luxurious cabaret, attracted by the good music and by the atmosphere of distinction which can be found in that elegant room." Establishments like this one, the article noted, offered the possibility of enlivening considerably the nightlife of the capital, which many considered still underdeveloped and provincial, by offering a stylish and sophisticated setting for high-class and wholesome entertainment.[54] Whether that was what most Santiaguinos, or even most foreign visitors, were looking for in terms of nightlife was another question altogether.

Horse racing continued to be an important ingredient of Santiago's social scene. Frank Carpenter described the Club Hípico as "one of the finest race tracks to be found anywhere."[55] The season began on the first Sunday in April and ended on the last Sunday in December, with part of the proceeds going to charities run by the Junta de Beneficencia. Races were also held at the Chile Hipodrome north of the Mapocho off Avenida Independencia, where ticket prices were lower and the audiences less distinguished than at the Club Hípico.[56]

In these years, Santiago's public athletic facilities continued to expand to keep up with population growth and popular demand. This was a matter that received attention from various municipal administrations. In addition, the number of private clubs also continued to grow. The *Baedeker* of 1930 highlighted the Estadio Policial, or Police Stadium, located on the north bank of the Mapocho at the northwest edge of the city. The facilities were open to the public for a fee and included two swimming pools, tennis and basketball courts, and a pistol-shooting range. During the milder months, the stadium hosted various swimming meets and soccer matches.[57] Soccer, of course, continued to grow in popularity, and in the late 1920s there was increased discussion in both local and national circles about the need to construct a large stadium in the capital for the major professional teams and to host major national and international matches.

Increasingly, Santiago's well-to-do spent much of the summer at the fashionable resort of Viña del Mar, just to the north of Valparaíso. Travel between the capital and the coast was made easier, faster, and less expensive with the inauguration of an electric rail line between the capital and Valparaíso in 1924. In May 1927 air service between these two cities was established, part of a general expansion of air transportation throughout the country. In 1929 Chile's first airline, the Línea Aeropostal Santiago-Arica (after 1932, LanChile, Línea Aérea Nacional) began operations, with the capital city as its base.[58] In July 1930 Zig-Zag reported that the city's new airport, Los Cerrillos, located about two kilometers southwest of the Club Hípico, was "the greatest current attraction in Santiago." There, especially on the weekends, gathered "a great quantity of persons of all social conditions" to enjoy a plane ride around the city for the price of only 30 pesos per passenger. It was also the site for competitions and demonstrations on the last Sunday of every month. "After these pleasant competitions," Zig-Zag concluded, "the members of the Club Aéreo de Chile meet in their Country Club, in happy and jovial comradeship, social gatherings that always have great brilliance and distinction."[59]

*

ACCORDING TO HISTORIAN ARMANDO DE RAMÓN, "The world-wide phenomenon of the so-called 'roaring 20s' also echoed in Santiago." Like many other large urban centers, the Chilean capital underwent a modernization that "left behind the styles that had dominated until the First World War. This upheaval brought with it the liberalization of customs, changes in fashion, in clothing, and in the way leisure time was spent . . . combined with a sense of prosperity."[60] But whatever the changes, general conditions in the city still gave critics plenty to chew on throughout the decade and, despite progress and improvements, many fundamental problems remained to be resolved.

As usual, the press was a frequent source of complaint about continuing problems. Commenting in 1923 on the favorable view of Santiago provided in the *National Geographic* by Harriet Chalmers Adams, a writer in the local *Chile Magazine* declared that under the "sublime panorama" offered by the capital lay an uglier reality of poor municipal services, inadequate housing, and general neglect.[61] Writing in *Zig-Zag* in 1926, a frequent contributor who used the pen name Mont-Calm compared Santiago unfavorably with other American and European cities. Under the headline "Santiago, the Uncomfortable City," he described in sarcastic terms the many filthy and abandoned streets, the uncollected garbage, the ever-present dust due to inadequate paving, the poor public transportation, the numerous street vendors, beggars, and vagrants, the frequent public drunkenness, and the incessant noise that characterized Chile's capital, hardly a flattering portrayal.[62] Another article in the same magazine claimed that Santiago's unplanned and chaotic growth had made it "the most irregular city in the country."[63]

By the end of the decade, as we have seen, some of these deficiencies had been addressed. Paving had been extended, garbage collection improved, and Brunner had been brought in to plan for more orderly growth. Nonetheless, while paving may have cut down on the quantity of dust, other pollutants, especially smoke from the growing number of factories and the exhausts of buses, taxis, and private automobiles, were contributing to the constantly deteriorating quality of Santiago's air. Writing in *El Mercurio* in 1929, an expert on the matter suggested that "to test the cleanliness of the air of the city one only need climb to the *terraza* of Santa Lucía or better yet that of San Cristóbal to observe that there is a faint, permanent cloud over the capital." This cloud would over time become less faint and even more permanent.[64]

Garbage disposal remained a serious problem. Even with the purchase of new trucks, new regulations for collection, and the opening of new incinerators, there were still frequent reports that many were using the Mapocho and its banks as a dump site. In September 1929 Intendente Salas Rodríguez met with the *alcaldes* of the neighboring *comunas* to crack down on the common practice of using vacant lots on the outskirts of the city to dispose of garbage. Salas and his counterparts in the *comunas* also aimed to control the men, women, and children who scavenged for food in these locales, in the process exposing themselves to possible disease that they could spread to others.[65] A July 1, 1930, article in El Mercurio praised the city's new garbage collection service, which was collecting more volume at less cost than was collected in Buenos Aires, but the paper also noted that the existing incinerators could only eliminate about one-third of all the garbage produced.[66]

The developments of the twenties also served to accentuate some of the persistent contrasts within the city. Frank Carpenter observed:

> The street scenes of Santiago are a combination of the old and the new. One still sees donkeys and mules carrying their panniers of vegetables and fruits from door to door. There are still horses close to the sidewalks hobbled by rope around their front legs, and the ox-cart still creaks its way through the town. At the same time there are automobiles and cabs everywhere, and huge motor trucks carrying heavy merchandise and building materials.[67]

Commenting favorably on the dress of well-to-do men and women in the downtown area, Carpenter also described Santiago as "a town of the very rich and the very poor," which echoed an observation made by many.[68]

The pattern of the city's growth reflected these disparities. An editorial in El Mercurio of May 5, 1930, once again noted the rapid development of the center and the eastern suburbs and the relative poverty of the barrios of the north, south, and west: "There is a vast belt of wretched *poblaciones*, with muddy streets in the winter and dusty ones in the summer, where rottenness and filth prevail." These areas generally lacked basic municipal services, and this lack had produced "a precarious situation that is not in accord with the most elemental urban necessities." Because these were often densely populated working-class districts located close to factories and workshops, the general lack of hygiene, the editorial commented, was a major contributing factor to the "frightful infant mortality that afflicts the population centers of Chile."[69]

One year earlier, El Mercurio had also lamented, as it had a decade before, the fact that these poorer districts left a bad impression with those travelers who arrived in Santiago by train. This was especially true for the entrance to the Mapocho Station, where most foreign visitors arrived. On the outskirts of the city, the traveler would encounter half-built, crude makeshift dwellings that had the look of a "gypsy camp." Passing by smoke-belching factories and garbage-strewn vacant lots, the visitor's experience could only be described as "sad, monotonous, and even insulting." The paper's reporter noted that two more-pleasant views were provided by the Police Stadium, bisected by the rail line, and a stand of trees near the station. Generally, however, the area immediately around the station left much to be desired. The river that gave the station its name was usually dirty and full of waste and the buildings along its banks were "fragile, jerry-built, and often falling apart."[70] In 1930 Zig-Zag wrote that the Mapocho near the station continued to be a major site for the city's garbage, providing an "unworthy spectacle" for those who first set eyes on Santiago.[71] On the way from the station to downtown, El Mercurio reported in the same year, was a large abandoned lot on Calle Morandé between San Pablo and General Mackenna that served as yet another garbage dump and public latrine.[72]

The development of adequate, affordable, and decent housing for Santiago's burgeoning population remained a persistent concern. In 1928 Carlos Carvajal estimated that there were 8,000 unsanitary residential buildings in Santiago, housing some 192,000 persons, or about 40 percent of all citizens, and that these contributed substantially to the continued appallingly high rate of infant mortality.[73] The conventillos were still the most common collective dwelling, despite efforts to eliminate them and public and private initiatives to construct low-cost housing. One source calculated that in 1930 there were 3,000 conventillos in Santiago, compared with 1,909 in 1910, in which 250,000 persons resided, compared with 72,076 twenty years earlier.[74] The Brunner plan underscored the "urgent necessity" of addressing this problem as a vital part of its overall scheme for the reorganization and rational future development of the capital.[75]

Journalists, city planners, and foreign visitors were not the only critics. Increasingly, Chile's fiction writers, especially its novelists, were examining the city and the social conditions within it, focusing in particular on the poor and the marginalized. To some extent, this was part of a larger "literature of national decline" that questioned the entire course and direction of the nation's history.[76] While authors like Alberto Blest Gana, with *Martín Rivas* (1862), and Luis Orrego Luco, with *Casa Grande* (1908), had set their classic novels in Santiago, they had dealt primarily with the city's upper classes. The generation of the 1920s focused instead on the lower classes and their environs. As Armando de Ramón put it, "The poor barrios of Santiago, full of *conventillos*, found their best historians among the novelists who appeared in the 1920s.... They recreated these poor and miserable neighborhoods and described them with poetic language."[77]

The best-known novel of the period was *El Roto* by Joaquín Edwards Bello, published in 1920. The title referred to the Chilean common man, but the main focus of the book was on the problem of prostitution. Very much like his Argentine contemporary Manuel Gálvez, Edwards saw prostitution as one of the many social ills besetting Santiago. Much of the action in the novel takes place in a brothel called La Gloria located on the Calle Borja just to the west of the Central Station. The story begins with a description of the surrounding neighborhood, one which may have been exaggerated for literary effect but which also smacks of realism and is not too different from the portrait of this neighborhood provided in the *Zig-Zag* article mentioned earlier. "Behind the Central Rail Station named the Alameda after that spacious avenue that is the pride of the Santiaguinos," Edwards begins, "has surged a sordid barrio, without municipal support. Its streets are dusty in the summer, muddy in winter; they are constantly covered with scraps, garbage, and putrid rats ... and with bodegas and cantinas [where] there is a constant movement of strangers, machinists, loaders, soldiers, and workers, who respond hungrily to vice, their senses excited by the view of this corner of licentiousness."[78] And while the barrio was the main locale for Edwards's novel, he saw the entire city as decadent and corrupting. Its many social problems, he argued, were visible to all but ignored by those in a position to do something about them. He intended his description of these conditions to serve as a warning to his readers about the consequences of allowing matters to fester and worsen, leading to an irrevocable chasm between the rich, "who live with all the material refinements of modern life," and the poor, "forced to live like beasts."[79]

BY 1930, SANTIAGO CLEARLY had made strides toward becoming the "modern" and "cultured" capital so many Chileans hoped it would be. But, as Edwards and others made equally clear, much remained to be done. Moreover, the challenges that would face the city and its leaders in the early 1930s, in the face of economic and political crisis, would be as formidable as any in Santiago's history. With challenges would come opportunities, especially opportunities to resume the dynamic physical growth that had marked much of the previous decade, as well as opportunities to reconsider and to reformulate the way the city was governed.

9 Turmoil and Transition (1931-1935)

THE RESIGNATION OF CARLOS IBÁÑEZ in July 1931 did little to resolve Chile's economic crisis or halt its ongoing political uncertainty. A series of caretaker governments tried to restore calm and order, overseeing a new presidential election in October. In that contest, Radical Juan Esteban Montero, backed by Conservatives, Liberals, and his own party, defeated the newly returned Arturo Alessandri by a two-to-one margin to gain the presidency. Inaugurated in December, he faced continued economic deterioration and numerous coup attempts and was himself forced to resign in June 1932 after barely six months in office. A combined military-civilian *junta*, with journalist and diplomat Carlos Dávila and the irrepressible Marmaduke Grove playing leading roles, presided over a short-lived "Socialist Republic of Chile," which, naturally, alarmed the civilian Right and Conservative elements within the military. No more successful than Montero in dealing with the economic crisis and various coup attempts, the "Socialist Republic" ended with a whimper in September.

The new provisional government under General Bartolomé Blanche scheduled yet another set of presidential elections for October 30. This time, Radicals, Democrats, and Liberals backed the candidacy of Arturo Alessandri, who won the election with 54 percent of the popular vote, easily defeating his Conservative, Liberal, and Communist rivals. Socialist Marmaduke Grove, however, came in a surprising second with 18 percent of the vote, indicating that not all Socialist sympathies had died with the ill-fated Republic. While Alessandri's victory, backed by a reconstituted Liberal

Alliance, seemed to promise a return to 1920, the contextual circumstances were quite different. Confronting the gravest economic crisis in Chile's history, Alessandri focused his energies on pulling the country out of the Depression, in the process moving steadily to the right on the political spectrum and gradually splintering the coalition that originally had backed him.[1]

AS ALWAYS, EVENTS AT THE LOCAL LEVEL in Santiago were influenced by these larger national developments. Following the resignation of Ibáñez and the Alcalde Parada of Santiago, the provisional government under Montero named Alfredo Santa María Sánchez, a distinguished attorney, law professor, and grandson of a former president, as the new chief executive of the capital. Assuming office on August 3, 1931, Santa María asked for "the support of all who want to work for the progress of the city" and promised to improve municipal services. He also promised to provide a more detailed program of action once he had familiarized himself with the overall resources and problems of the local administration.[2]

In the next few days, the national authorities determined to return to a broader municipal administration. On August 20 the new *junta de vecinos*, now including five *vocales*, met for the first time under Santa María's direction. Speaking for his fellow *vocales*, Lindor Pérez Gacitua proclaimed that the new administration would be committed to restoring democratic institutions that had been destroyed by the Ibáñez dictatorship. He promised that the new administration, claiming to have a more open and flexible attitude than its immediate predecessors, "would be inspired only by the interests of the city as a whole, seeing that its needs be duly attended. All problems of local importance, whatever their nature," Pérez asserted, "deserve our attention, and, for this, we shall gather ideas and suggestions from the community at large, and especially from the press, which reflects the true public opinion." Their time in office, he suggested, might be brief, since new representatives could now be chosen within a democratic framework.[3]

Part of this prediction proved accurate. The five new *vocales* served for only two months, but they were replaced not by democratically chosen successors but rather by a different group of appointed representatives. On October 1 a new *junta* assumed office. Santa María remained as *alcalde*, but none of the previous *vocales* were retained. Instead, they were replaced by nine new men. While biographical information is sparse, they included two Radicals,

Hernán Figueroa Anguita and Diego Fernández Ojeda; two Conservatives, former *regidor* Luis Lira Lira and José Alberto Echeverría; and lawyer and socialist Alberto Amo.[4] Simply by increasing the number of *vocales*, the national government had broadened the representative nature of the *junta*, perhaps not coincidentally, just a few days before the presidential election. Most of the new members had distinguished surnames and prestigious addresses.[5]

By the end of the month, the new *junta* had approved a budget for 1932. After consolidating some departments and making other adjustments, total expenditures for the following year were set at 27,890,906 pesos, with a separate budget of 9,718,000 pesos for paving.[6] These totals were similar to those of the previous several years, reflecting the continued fiscal constraints on the city despite a rapidly growing population and the pressing need to extend basic services. Given the realities of the economic crisis, there seemed little likelihood that these constraints would be lessened at any time in the near future.

Before and after the budget discussions, the *junta* sought to deal with the impact of the Depression on the capital. In a now familiar pattern, workers displaced from the collapsed nitrate industry of the North had flooded into the capital in search of shelter and support. Temporary quarters, or *albergues*, served as makeshift residences for thousands. Visiting two of these in late October, the social commentator Roxane described in some detail their grim conditions, suggesting that if all Santiaguinos were to visit such places they would soon recognize that "we are in a period of sorrow and not of banquets and social gatherings."[7] At about the same time, Vocal Alberto Amo complained of conditions in the Albergue Santa María, one of those described by Roxane, where residents were using the nearby Río Mapocho as a public latrine and garbage dump. He told his fellow *vocales* that it was "an urgent necessity to clean up this site and to assure that such practices be halted."[8]

As bad as the *albergues* were, some places were even worse. While the Parque Forestal remained for *Zig-Zag* the "preferred park of our distinguished young people," by early January 1932 the magazine also reported that in the shadow of its trees could be found sleeping every afternoon hundreds of the unemployed, and that the same was true for most of the other city parks.[9] Another article described how some five hundred of the unemployed had found shelter in the abandoned quarries of the Cerro Blanco to the north of

San Cristóbal and were living there in "filth, misery, and promiscuity."[10] Others had established temporary shelters, which with time gained some permanence, under the bridges of the Mapocho. Interviewed in 1933, "residents" of these shelters described a fruitless search for employment and being treated in general "like dogs."[11]

A sign of the desperation of many was the marked increase in beggars and in the number of street vendors. Writing in August 1931, Zig-Zag claimed that the city had never had so many street merchants, who had turned the capital into a vast open-air market where just about anything was bought and sold. The concentration of such activity around the Alameda in front of the Club de la Unión and the University of Chile, the magazine warned, was producing an environment comparable to a disorderly and unkempt suburban slum that demanded the attention of the local authorities.[12]

In response to these conditions, the junta, on November 14, agreed to establish soup kitchens for the unemployed in various parts of the city. At the same time, it began to discuss ways to regulate the numbers and activities of street vendors. Also, by the end of the year the national government began to close down some of the capital's albergues, relocating various of the residents to areas along the coast and to the south. While this was an action by the national government, the junta had several times expressed its concern with the situation in the albergues, especially the possibility that they might serve as breeding grounds for epidemic diseases, an ever-present threat in Santiago.[13]

As these and other issues were discussed in the junta, internal tensions soon appeared. While the expansion of the number of vocales had broadened the representative nature of the local administration, it had also opened up more possibilities for the kinds of disagreements and deadlocks that had characterized the elected councils of the past. Despite promises of cooperation, various issues produced fierce debates, especially those having to do with the retention or rehiring of city personnel that had been let go during Ibáñez's attempts to streamline the local administration. Moreover, before finally being approved, the initial vote to open soup kitchens for the unemployed had produced a tie.[14] In a sign of a how deep divisions had become, on December 6, 1931, El Mercurio reported that the minister of the interior had rejected the proffered resignations of the vocales and the alcalde, saying that the government maintained its confidence in Santa María.[15]

To resolve some of these tensions, the Montero government reconfig-ured the *junta de vecinos* in January 1932, reducing the number of *vocales* from nine to six. This reduction seemed to have the desired effect, and for the first few months of 1932 major disagreements seemed to be largely in the past. The new *junta* met regularly and, for the most part, with little apparent ran-cor addressed the city's most pressing needs. Among these was the escalat-ing price of basic foodstuffs. This matter was first discussed in the session of March 31, in which the *alcalde* and various *vocales* recommended setting price caps on essential items. Despite objections by the Director de Subsistencias (City Food Director), who argued that such efforts had failed elsewhere and were almost impossible to enforce, the *junta* named a committee to look into the matter of skyrocketing costs and excess profits on food due to the machinations of speculators and to come up with recommendations.[16] Soon thereafter, the *junta* agreed to set a maximum price on sugar. Over the next several weeks, in concert with the national administration, it also estab-lished price controls on such items as rice, cooking oil, coffee, tea, flour, pasta, and meats.[17]

Although there was considerable debate over these measures, there also was considerable agreement with the end result. This was not always the case, however. In mid-April, Socialist Vocal Alberto Amo brought serious charges of malfeasance involving the taking of bribes against various city officials, including the director of the Mercado Central, the head of the parks and gardens department, and the head of the local department of in-spection, Armando Silva Valenzuela. A discussion of these charges consumed several sessions and produced the kind of bitter partisan wrangling and im-passioned rhetoric that had been common in the pre-1924 municipalities. Amo argued that his charges were being swept under the rug by a majority on the *junta*, which, in reality, he claimed, reflected upon the national gov-ernment, which also was ruled by "an audacious and corrupt minority," heedless of the needs of the "humble and honest majority." The other *vocales*, for their part, attacked Amo in bitter and sarcastic terms for bringing what they considered unfounded charges against responsible and hard-working public servants. On April 14 the *junta* resolved, by a vote of 5 to 1, with Amo the lone dissenter, that the charges were "lacking [in] any serious founda-tion" and reiterated its full confidence in the employees so charged.[18]

When the *junta* met next, on May 3, Amo was no longer listed as a mem-ber, having been replaced by the former *vocal* Alfredo Urzúa Urzúa.[19] Even so, intense disagreements over personnel matters continued. All *vocales*, for example, participated in a heated exchange over the alleged irregularities and illegal activities of various city employees, notably those in the parks and gardens department, that had taken place during the Parada administration. After lively debate, the *junta* voted 4 to 1 to submit the matter to the criminal courts for further investigation.[20]

These were among this particular *junta's* final acts. The resignation of President Montero on June 4 brought yet another change to the local administration. On June 5, the new national authorities disbanded the *junta* and named former diplomat Joaquín Fernández Fernández as *alcalde*. He lasted only two weeks in that position, replaced by Armando Silva Valenzuela, who assumed office on June 18. As a young man, Silva had dedicated himself to public administration, having served as governor and *intendente* in several northern provinces in the 1920s before assuming the directorship of the capital's department of inspection in 1927.[21] His actions in that position, it will be recalled, had drawn the critical fire of the former *vocal* Alberto Amo only a few months earlier.

In taking office, Silva made a special effort to assure city employees and workers that so long as they carried out their duties honestly and efficiently their positions would be secure. He also said that his office door would be open to any who wanted to see him, and that "despite my new position, I have not ceased to belong to your ranks."[22] In this spirit, and reflecting the designs of the new administration, Silva served as *alcalde* without a *junta* of *vocales*, administering city affairs in consultation with two secretaries and the heads of the municipal departments. In yet another turn during this confusing period, Silva and the "Socialist Republic," along with the municipal bureaucracy, ran the city of Santiago, so that the city administration once again approximated the city manager system in the United States.

While Silva had the advantage of being able to operate unencumbered by *vocales*, he was not in office long enough to make much of a mark. His term ended with the fall of the Socialist Republic and the election of Alessandri. With these events, both the national scene and the local administration of Santiago returned to more familiar patterns.

ON NOVEMBER 8, FOLLOWING ALESSANDRI'S VICTORY, the interim government named a new *junta de vecinos* for Santiago. Selected as *alcalde* was Guillermo Labarca Hubertson, a former leader of the national student federation and a longtime Radical activist who had served as acting minister of the interior and, briefly, as minister of justice and public education in the first Alessandri administration. An educator by profession, he was perhaps best known as the author of an anthology of short stories published in 1905, *Al amor de la tierra*, that emphasized the virtues of rural life and of the *campesinos*, or common folk, who inhabited Chile's countryside.[23] When some in the press criticized Labarca's appointment as a case of replacing a professional administrator, Silva, with a politician, the conservative *El Diario Ilustrado* rose to his defense. Labarca, the daily argued, was a figure of distinction and experience who promised to run local affairs honestly and effectively. Why shouldn't Santiago be led by a politician, *El Diario* asked rhetorically, when such was the case for most major cities and indeed for the nation itself.[24]

Appointed with Labarca were nine *vocales*. Returning to the *junta* were the former *vocales* Arturo Besoaín, a physician and member of the Social Republican Party, Conservative José Alberto Echeverría, and Liberal Domingo Santa María. Joining them as new *vocales* were Liberals Gabriel Amunátegui and Pedro Préndez Saldías, both lawyers; Juan Urzúa, of the Unión Republicana; and José L. Quezada and Elias Torre Santa, affiliations and occupations unknown. Rounding out the nine was Galvarino Gallardo Nieto, a well-known member of the Radical Party, a graduate of the law school of the University of Chile, and, according to a biographical entry, one of the nation's leading authorities on criminal law.[25]

The new *junta* met for the first time on November 17. Labarca began by thanking the *vocales* for agreeing to serve with him and asked for their cooperation in helping him to administer the city in a way that would justify the confidence of the national government. Speaking for the *vocales*, Gallardo Nieto promised Labarca that "he could count always on the most enthusiastic and decided cooperation of the members of the *junta* in the productive labor of the administration in the city's interests."[26] And, as it happened, in this instance these pledges of cooperation frequently proved to be more than just the pious pronouncements they had so often been in the past. For the most part, Labarca and the *vocales* worked well together. Helping to unify their efforts over the next two years was a tendency to close ranks in various confrontations with the national government, usually over issues involving municipal autonomy.

As with all new city governments, Labarca's administration inherited certain ongoing problems. The most serious of these was the familiar one of the state of city finances. Labarca had inherited from Silva a budget for 1933 that projected 33,304,206 pesos in expenditures, an increase of several million over the budgets of the previous several years. Moreover, almost immediately upon assuming office, the new administration had been pressured to provide salary increases for city employees and workers. Near the end of December, day workers in the sanitation department had gone on strike, demanding higher wages, which had forced the *alcalde* and the *vocales* to find the funds to provide added pay for the strikers. Faced with what they considered unusual fiscal demands, and constrained by a budget crafted before they had taken office, the *junta* on December 28 petitioned the national government for a special law that would allow them to reconfigure the budget for the coming year, permitting them greater flexibility in meeting the city's financial needs.[27]

The executive branch agreed to the *junta*'s request and sent the proposal to Congress for the requisite legislative authority. The Congress, however, newly constituted following the national election, claimed that political considerations lay behind the request, that is, that the members of the *junta* wanted to manipulate the budget so as to punish opponents on the city payroll and reward supporters. Therefore, the Chamber of Deputies rejected the executive's proposal. Meeting on February 3, 1933, the *junta*, with Gallardo Nieto leading the way, strongly denied that politics had motivated their request, observing that representatives from all parties had supported it. The *vocales* then unanimously expressed their full confidence in Labarca and in acting *alcalde* Arturo Besoaín.[28] On the following day, *El Mercurio* reported that Alessandri had refused to accept the resignations of the *vocales* in protest of the congressional decision.[29] Momentarily quieted, the issue would continue to fester for several more months.

At the end of March, Alcalde Labarca sent a message to the minister of the interior requesting that full municipal autonomy be restored. Although there had been some loosening of the strict centralized controls imposed by the Ibáñez regime, he argued that the city still remained too constrained and limited by the authority of the national government. This was a particularly acute problem with regard to budgetary matters, especially since the city's request for modifications of the 1933 spending plan had been denied. That budget, he observed, "does not respond to the true expectations of revenues, nor can it be altered despite the fact that adjustment of some of its items is essential for budgetary success."[30]

Labarca's plea, at least for the moment, went unheeded. In the meantime, the national government named two more *vocales* to the *junta*, increasing the total to twelve.[31] Within the *junta*, in April and May considerable attention was given to plans to build a new slaughterhouse. After several sessions devoted primarily to this issue, the *junta* determined to build the new slaughterhouse with city funds so that it would remain under city control.[32] To finance this project, the *junta*, as was required, requested permission from the National Congress to float a loan to cover the costs. This request, however, coincided with a decision by the Chamber of Deputies to call for an external audit and for oversight of the city administration, in light of what appeared to be continuing fiscal problems and poor management of the city's finances. The *junta* reacted strongly, claiming that the proposal was an undue intervention in local affairs and threatening to resign en masse over the issue. Ultimately, the proposal was withdrawn, but Radical Vocal Gallardo Nieto did resign from the *junta* in protest, expressing his frustration with the actions of both the local and national governments in this matter.[33]

In the final months of 1933 there was some positive news for the municipality on the slaughterhouse issue. After considerable discussion and lobbying by both city officials and national deputies from Santiago, the Chamber of Deputies approved the city's proposal to build the facility on its own with a loan of sixteen million pesos and sent the measure on to the Senate. As often happened, however, just when it seemed that one controversial issue was on the verge of resolution, another arose to roil municipal waters. In late October, Labarca determined to crack down on the growing number of illegal gambling operations in the capital, ordering the local department of inspection to close any "games of chance" open to the public. This crackdown was soon extended to include one of the capital's most popular new attractions, the Canódromo, or dog-racing track, located on Avenida Balmaceda in the northwestern part of the city. Opened in 1932, the Canódromo featured greyhound racing over a 500-meter course, providing, as *Zig-Zag* described it, "a modern and original sporting event."[34] From Labarca's viewpoint, however, the sport was secondary to the gambling that accompanied it. According to his interpretation of the decree that had originally authorized operation of the Canódromo, the kind of pari-mutuel betting that was allowed at horse-racing tracks was not permitted for dog racing. Having received evidence of such betting, he ordered the closure of the Canódromo by decree on November 18.[35] Not surprisingly, the directors of the Canódromo had a different interpretation. They argued that the 1932 agreement did indeed allow for the same kind of betting as occurred at horse races. They also asserted that part of the proceeds from that gambling went to charity, especially for the care of sick and abandoned children. They implied that they were the victims of certain well-known but unnamed opponents, presumably those involved in horse racing who feared the competition, and that they were prepared to protest the *alcalde*'s actions and other efforts at preventing this "cultured spectacle" from being offered to the Santiago public.[36] The ensuing struggle between the owners and the city would prove almost as entertaining to the Santiago public as the races themselves.

THE FOLLOWING YEAR, 1934, saw a continuation of many of the same issues and problems that had confronted Labarca from the outset. Among the most prominent was the persistence of illegal gambling and the municipality's efforts to control it. Beginning in March and extending over several months, the *junta* debated various initiatives to assert their own authority in this arena. The *alcalde*'s decision to close the Canódromo, for example, had been overturned by the Supreme Court in January, and the dog track and attendant betting were back in operation. Despite municipal regulations to the contrary, "*chunchos*," a kind of slot machine, were omnipresent, as were reports that considerable illegal gaming was going on in several social clubs. An editorial in the April 15 edition of *El Diario Ilustrado* said that the newspaper had received hundreds of letters from its readers expressing their widespread "indignation over unconstrained gambling in Santiago," and asserting that much of this activity was controlled by a shadowy "foreign element." The paper severely criticized the local and national authorities for their failure to remedy this "deplorable" situation.[37]

The complaints seemed valid, and members of the *junta* sought to respond. At its session of March 5, Liberal Vocal Pedro Préndez Saldías introduced a resolution that would have virtually eliminated all gambling in the capital. Other *vocales*, however, argued that the matter was too complicated for such a sweeping measure and requested time for more careful study.[38] Two and a half weeks later, the *junta* considered both a majority report that more or less followed Préndez's motion, and a minority report from fellow Liberal Gabriel Amunátegui that more specifically targeted gambling at the Canódromo.[39] Two days later, the minister of the interior issued an official decree that stated that the concession for the Canódromo did not include authority to allow for pari-mutuel betting.[40] With the issue apparently resolved, it still took the junta almost two months of debate, disagreement, and delay before finally approving a new resolution on the matter on May 14. By a vote of 7 to 1, the resolution introduced by Social Republican Arturo Besoaín virtually outlawed all gambling in the capital.[41] At a subsequent session, the vocales unanimously approved another resolution that gave the alcalde the authority to personally visit various social and political clubs (among those mentioned were the Club de la Unión, the Club de Septiembre, the Club Social Republicano y Radical, and the Sociedad Unión Comercial) for the purpose of determining if illegal gambling were taking place in these establishments, and if so, to take the necessary measures to halt such activities.[42]

Whatever the intentions of these measures, they seemed to produce few immediate results. Gambling continued to flourish, and, for a while, the junta turned to other matters. However, on August 25, attention was once more focused on gambling when Alcalde Labarca again ordered the closure of the Canódromo for violation of the prohibition on pari-mutuel betting. Once again, too, the action of the local government was frustrated by higher authority. In this instance, the provincial intendente refused to order the police to shut down the dog track. This refusal, in turn, touched off a serious crisis, with reports surfacing that the entire junta would resign in protest and prompting urgent meetings between Labarca and the minister of the interior. On September 1, four vocales, three Radicals and one Conservative, did resign, and they were jointed soon thereafter by Social Republican Arturo Besoaín.[43] After consulting with their respective parties, however, the rest of the vocales determined to remain on the junta.[44] The national government accepted the proffered resignations and named three Radicals and one Conservative as replacements. They assumed office on September 14.[45] At the same time, there were some vocales who urged the municipality to take legal action to force the intendente to close the dog track, and a private citizen tried to bring suit to achieve the same result. These efforts got nowhere and the

Canódromo remained open for business, presumably with pari-mutuel betting as a continuing part of the attraction.

The resignation of five *vocales* over the Canódromo issue was the most notable of such incidents in 1934. But it was also reflective of frequent turnover in the composition of the *junta* throughout the year. In May, for example, the minister of the interior simultaneously accepted the resignation of one *vocal* and added four new ones to the *junta*.[46] Throughout this period, the national government sought to maintain a rough balance of parties and representatives that mirrored the balance that prevailed in Congress. By the end of 1934, accordingly, the *junta* included three Radicals, three Democrats, three Conservatives, and three Liberals, as well as two members of the Partido Social Republicano (Social Republican Party) and one member of the Unión Republicano (Republican Union), both of which were small, newly formed independent parties.[47] White-collar professionals predominated, with seven lawyers (two Liberals, two Radicals, two Conservatives, and one Social Republican), one physician (a Radical), one architect (a Liberal), one businessman (a Social Republican), and one public administrator (a Conservative). The three Democrats were exceptions, being mostly from humble backgrounds and with careers as part-time journalists, union organizers, and party functionaries. Several of the lawyers had been active in university student politics. Most had been born and raised in Santiago and their ages varied from their thirties to their fifties.[48]

OVER THE COURSE OF THE YEAR, there were some signs that national political developments were again having an impact at the local level. While Alessandri and his influential finance minister Gustavo Ross followed economic policies that were generally seen to favor upper-class business and agricultural interests, they received continuing support from the Conservatives and Liberals. The centrist Radicals, however, began to distance themselves from the administration, and in April its ministers left the government.[49] Increasingly, the Radicals looked to ally with the Left, whose prospects had been significantly bolstered by the election of Socialist Marmaduke Grove as senator from Santiago that same month. Although a direct correlation between these events and what happened in the *junta* could not always be discerned, and although it was not a hard-and-fast rule, on most roll-call votes the Radicals tended to vote as a bloc and usually on opposite sides from the Conservatives and Liberals. They did occasionally ally with the Democrats, who were often less cohesive in their voting.

Even though there was considerable turnover among the *vocales*, one constant was the presence of Labarca as *alcalde*. On the surface, at least, he seemed to enjoy the respect and confidence of both the *vocales* and the national administration. In 1934 he managed to deal successfully with a strike of municipal workers over wages; develop a budget that allowed for some slight spending increases and that was approved with relatively little dissent; pursue measures to control the price of food, especially meat; and do what he could to promote and protect municipal autonomy. At the end of the year, however, the *alcalde* became the target of growing criticism. Claiming to speak for a broad sector of public opinion, for example, the conservative *El Diario Ilustrado*, which originally had backed Labarca's appointment, now accused him of personal arrogance in refusing to take responsibility for the city's many problems and what it labeled a rapidly deteriorating situation overall. According to *El Diario*, the city government's failures included continued inadequate garbage disposal facilities, which had led to increased use of the Mapocho as a dump site; an insufficient response to yet another typhus outbreak; a general neglect of the municipal slaughterhouse and markets; and, worst of all from its point of view, an inability—or lack of concern—with controlling such vices as alcoholism, prostitution, and gambling.[50] The alleged indifference of the *alcalde*, an editorial concluded, "leaves us with a filthy capital, filled with garbage . . . and plagued with defects that make life unbearable."[51]

If the complaints were familiar, so too was the response. In an interview published in *El Mercurio*, Labarca claimed not to be bothered by the mounting press criticism and defended his actions to deal with the latest typhus epidemic, to control gambling and prostitution, and to remedy the problems of the slaughterhouse and markets. He admitted that there were certain deficiencies with regard to city services, especially sanitation and garbage disposal, but he strongly denied that these were due to any alleged "indifference" on his part. Instead, he asserted, "we return again to the eternal question: we cannot advance because we do not have the resources to do so. . . . The municipality has only meager revenues, the smallest in the world in terms of its size and population."[52]

Despite the criticisms and despite the fact that he headed an administration that was increasingly somewhat of a lame duck, Labarca managed to finish his term productively. Following a bruising internal fight over the appointment of a *junta* secretary, the *vocales* and *alcalde* had closed ranks to mark some significant achievements. During this period, the municipality gave its approval to the now completed Brunner plan, agreed to float a fifteen-million-peso loan for city improvements, earmarked funds to purchase the Cerro Blanco so that it could become a city park, continued efforts to control gambling, and worked out a temporary resolution to problems associated with the growing inadequacy of taxi meters.[53] But when the Congress finally gave its permission for the municipality to finance the construction of a new slaughterhouse, it did so under the condition that negotiations for the loan could only commence thirty days after the installation of a popularly elected municipality, thus denying Labarca the opportunity to move forward with an initiative for which he was primarily responsible.[54]

FROM THE TIME OF THE FALL OF IBÁÑEZ, the various *juntas de vecinos* of Santiago had realized that they constituted only a temporary expedient until elected municipalities could replace them. Ibáñez himself had issued a decree in May 1931 that paved the way for the formation of new electoral registries and municipal elections. The most dramatic features of this decree were its provisions to extend the vote to women over the age of twenty-five who were either property owners and/or professionals and who could read and write, as well as to foreign males who were legal residents. The implications of this measure were substantial. While the number of potential foreign voters in the capital was small, the inclusion of women could potentially double the electorate, and it seemed logical that the extension of suffrage at the local level would presage its adoption at the national level in the not-too-distant future.

The granting of women's suffrage was the result of a long-standing campaign in which upper-class women associated with the Catholic Church's social welfare efforts and the Conservative Party had taken the lead. The best-known proponent of women's right to vote was Adela Edwards de Salas, who had formed and led various charitable institutions, most notably Chile's Cruz Blanca, or "White Cross," which sought to shelter single mothers and young women caught up in prostitution. She, and others, had ar-

gued that the issues of greatest interest to women—such things as education, health care, and the integrity of the family—would only be fully dealt
with when women had an equal voice in political and governmental affairs
with men. Also prominent in this struggle was Amanda Labarca, the wife
of the *alcalde*, who as head of the Consejo Nacional de Mujeres (National
Council of Women), formed in 1919, had approached Alessandri to push
for women's suffrage in local elections. Like her husband a member of the
anti-clerical Radical Party, she had frequently spoken out against what she
considered the undue ecclesiastical influence within the Chilean women's
movement.[55]

Municipal elections had been scheduled on various occasions in 1931
and 1932, but due to the turmoil of the period, they had never taken place.
Soon after his presidential election, Alessandri made clear his desire to re-
institute municipal elections as soon as possible, and once the new Congress
was assembled he sent it a message urging the early consideration and passage of the necessary legislation. The Chamber of Deputies began consideration of such legislation on February 13, 1933. During the debate, which
lasted several weeks, representatives of various women's organizations filled
the galleries and lobbied hard for the inclusion of women's suffrage in the
final provisions. That issue dominated the discussion, with most speakers,
mainly Conservatives, strongly in favor. A prominent line of argument was
that suffrage had been granted to females in Europe, the United States, and
other Latin American countries and that Chile should not lag behind in this
regard. The strongest objections came from Rolando Merino Reyes of the
newly formed Socialist Party, who argued that extending the vote to women
was not a pressing "social necessity," that the campaign for its passage was
being promoted by a well-intentioned but self-interested minority, and that
it only dealt superficially with the real problems of women. The entire electoral process, he charged, was corrupt and venal and until it was cleansed,
he argued, the "stain" of such venality should not be spread to include females.[56] These and other arguments from the Left had little effect and on
March 9 the chamber, by ample margins and with little real disagreement,
approved the new municipal election and government law, which included
provisions for females and foreigners to vote.[57]

The Senate began to consider the Chamber's proposal on June 7. Over-
coming some objections from the Left, it approved the project in general on

June 22.[58] Working out the details in conference and among the senators themselves, however, proved more complicated. While there was general agreement on most of the provisions of the new law, there was considerable debate and conflict over the wording of the article that would extend the vote to women and foreigners. Some wanted to keep these rights restricted to professionals and property owners, while others wanted to have relatively unconstrained suffrage. Ultimately, after several months of consideration and haggling, the Senate in October approved the legislation, including Article 19, which gave literate women twenty-one years of age and over the right to vote in municipal elections as well as the same right to literate foreigners, male and female, who had resided in Chile for at least five consecutive years.[59]

President Alessandri signed the new law, No. 5357, on January 15, 1934. The registries were to be opened on May 15 of that year, and the first election was scheduled for April 7, 1935.[60] For Santiago, the law called for the election of fifteen *regidores* (replacing the *vocales*) to serve three-year terms. There had been some sentiment in Congress for an elected *alcalde*, but the capital's chief executive would remain appointed by the president of the republic. Clearly, the most important innovation was women's suffrage. In addition, women were now eligible to run for council positions themselves and, even conceivably, to be named as *alcaldes*. While, as we shall see, many continuities prevailed, local politics and government in Santiago would never be quite the same as a result of these changes.

10 Restoration of the Elected Municipality (1935)

THE MUNICIPAL ELECTIONS OF APRIL 7, 1935, marked the restoration of elected city governments in Santiago and in Chile generally after more than a decade of appointed administrations. The most notable feature of these contests was the participation for the first time in Chilean history of women as both voters and candidates. The contests also marked the continued restoration of party politics that had begun with the fall of the Ibáñez dictatorship. Returning to play important roles at both the national and local level were Conservatives, Liberals, Democrats, and Radicals. Joining the fray with increasing activism and enthusiasm were two parties on the left, the Communists and, especially, the Socialists. As had so often been the case in Chilean political history, the large number of parties necessitated coalition-building, especially for presidential elections. In these years, the movement of the Radicals to form an alliance with the Left continued. As usual, developments within the local government of Santiago both reflected and contributed to these dynamics.

PREPARATIONS FOR THE APRIL 7 ELECTIONS were slow and deliberate. Soon after Alessandri signed the enabling legislation, the minister of the interior had begun the process of inscribing the newly eligible foreigners and women into the electoral registry. This effort was not completed until the end of 1934. Once done, a definitive date was set for elections. Various observers expressed the hope that the inclusion of the formerly excluded groups, especially women, would change the tone and improve the quality of local government. An editorial in *El Mercurio* expressed the belief that the excessive partisanship that had afflicted previous elected municipalities, would be "neutralized with the intervention of women and foreigners, a political experiment that, fundamentally, is associated with the highest expectations."[1]

Whether these hopes would be realized remained to be seen. Early on, however, a spokesperson for the Acción Patriótica de las Mujeres de Chile, one of the groups that had been formed to mobilize women voters and support women candidates, made a stinging attack on Alcalde Labarca, demonstrating that women could be just as aggressive and as sarcastic as men when it came to political criticism. Writing in *El Diario Ilustrado*, a woman who identified herself only by the initials A. D. de I. took the *alcalde* and the *junta* to task for what she called secret negotiations to institute changes in the municipal management of city markets and the slaughterhouse that would be detrimental to consumers. She charged Labarca with acting in the manner of France's Sun King, substituting the king's famous phrase "L'Etat c'est moi" with "Santiago, soy yo."[2]

As the date for the elections approached, a dozen parties selected a total of ninety-three candidates to run for Santiago's fifteen *regidor* positions. These included the six parties previously mentioned, as well as the Social Republican Party, the Unión Republicana, and the Chilean Partido Nacista (written with a "c" to distinguish it from the German party of the same name). Organized in 1932 as the Movimiento Nacional Socialista (MNS, or National Socialist Movement), the Nacistas included a small but active core of mostly young male supporters who provided some of the major excitement of the campaign through occasional violent clashes with leftist organizations in the capital's streets in March and April.[3]

Most attention, however, focused on the female candidates. The first to announce her candidacy was the writer Luisa Zanelli of the Partido Liberal Femenino (Feminine Liberal Party). While concerned specifically with women's issues, she promised to also defend the interests of all the capital's citizens. She saw as top priorities the need to lower the cost of basic necessities, eliminate the 2 percent sales tax, create institutions to protect the family, and encourage the construction of housing for workers.[4] The two candidates of the Acción Nacional de Mujeres, Adela Edwards de Salas and Elena Doll de Díaz, emphasized the same issues. So, too, did Natalia Rubio Cuadra, representing the Acción Patriótica de Mujeres, a splinter group of the Acción Nacional. Seeking to ally with these candidates and to attract women's votes to his party, Conservative leader Horacio Walker Larraín, in a lengthy radio address (as elsewhere, the radio was becoming an increasingly important tool in Chilean political life) argued that within the program of his party could be found "the most solid defense of the stability of the family, of social peace, and of Christian morality."[5]

The election was important for a number of reasons. For one thing, it would provide something of a referendum on the Alessandri administration, now approaching its halfway point. For another, it would determine exactly how much influence women's suffrage might have on current and future political activity. Viewing this presence optimistically, if in somewhat traditional gendered terms, *Zig-Zag* suggested that women would enter the municipality "disposed to manage the city as they have managed their homes. For most, a city well swept, well lighted, and with its hygienic services in order will have the same agreeable aspect as a well-appointed house at tea time when the daughter nervously awaits the visit of her fiancé."[6] For *El Diario Ilustrado*, the election had special significance for Santiago as a showcase for the nation. Concerned with what it perceived to be a deterioration in the city's moral tone in recent years, it saw the election as one that would determine not only matters of comfort, ornamentation, and salubrity, "but also—and even more importantly—the health and life of its inhabitants, the betterment—or the perversion—of its inhabitants, the morality—or the immorality—of the environment in which children are formed and developed."[7] While nothing explicit was said, the message of this election-day editorial argued strongly in favor of the women candidates for office.

The election itself proceeded smoothly. Separate polling places were established for women to cast their ballots, a practice that continues to the present day. Women were in charge of these polling places and by all accounts handled their newfound responsibilities with skill and enthusiasm. In Santiago, the Acción Nacional de Mujeres listed central locations in each of the capital's ten main voting districts (*comunas*) where women voters could go for information. It also urged women to vote early and to mark their ballots carefully. All reports indicated that the contest was remarkably free of the fraud and bribery which usually accompanied Chilean elections. A feminist interviewed by *Zig-Zag* attributed "the tranquility of the electoral act to the presence of women," an assertion that would be difficult to prove, in that men voted separately in areas presumably removed from such influences.[8]

Whatever the reasons for the "tranquility" of the contest, the results were clear—a major triumph for the parties of the right. Nationwide, Conservatives and Liberals took 47.2 percent of the total vote and candidates of the right captured about two-thirds of the seats up for grabs. The big losers were the divided Radicals, who gained only 18.5 percent of the total. Also doing poorly were the Communists, who gained only three seats, and somewhat more surprisingly, the Nacistas, who were expected to do well but who only won one seat. While the irreverent humor magazine *Topaze* claimed that no one except the candidates themselves and the Acción Nacional de Mujeres had taken the election seriously, turnout was high, at better than 86 percent. It should be noted, however, that voting was obligatory and those who failed to cast ballots were subject to a 100-peso fine. It should also be noted that nationwide only 35.6 percent of all eligible males and only 9 percent of all eligible females were actually registered to vote.[9]

The Conservatives benefited most directly, gaining almost half of the women's vote nationwide. Moreover, of the twenty-five female candidates elected to Chile's municipalities in 1935, sixteen were either from the Conservative Party or affiliated with the Acción Nacional de Mujeres. In Santiago, Adela Edwards de Salas was the capital's leading vote-getter with 5,417 tallies. While trailing far behind in number of votes, Rubio and Doll de Díaz were also elected as the first women to serve as Santiago *regidoras*. According to one careful analysis, while the candidates themselves were of the upper class, they drew most of their support from the middle and lower classes, especially "from women who were associated as employees, clients, and/or members of the social beneficence and union-like organizations that they led."[10]

The conservative press was predictably enthusiastic about these results. *El Mercurio* proclaimed, "Taking her first political steps, the Chilean woman has inclined toward the side of forces that desire progress within a climate of social peace."[11] *El Diario Ilustrado* saw things in virtually the same terms, claiming that the female voter "has placed, in general, her vote at the service of order, social peace, and political honesty and has shown respect for the conscience of the country and democratic institutions."[12] Reporting to the State Department, a U.S. embassy counselor saw the results as providing approval and support for the Alessandri administration and observed that they indicated "a trend which must be gratifying to Finance Minister [Gustavo] Ross whose presidential ambitions are an open secret."[13] Ross, or any other Conservative candidate, however, would not be able to count, in a national election, on the female votes that had given the Right the edge in the municipal contests.

The Left, of course, was much less enthusiastic about the outcome of the election and the role women had played in it. Socialist and Radical publications attacked the Catholic Church for what they alleged was undue influence over female voters and claimed that a disproportionate number of nuns had been mobilized to account for the triumph of the Right. Interviewed soon after the election, Radical Party president Pedro Aguirre Cerda stated that while his party still favored women's suffrage, it now favored postponing its extension to national elections, while a group of Radical women went on record as opposing such an extension altogether.[14]

WHILE THE ELECTION OF THREE WOMEN as *regidoras* was the most dramatic result of the April 7 contest in Santiago, it was not its only noteworthy feature. Joining the three Conservative females were four male representatives of the party. They included two former *vocales* from past *juntas de vecinos*, Germán Domínguez, a high-ranking official in the national Caja de Crédito Hipotecario (Mortgage Credit Office), and attorney José Alberto Echeverría. The two new Conservatives were Jorge Richard Barnard, a lawyer who, like Domínguez, had been associated with various Catholic social welfare organizations, and Gustavo Monckeberg Bravo, a well-known architect. In a pre-election interview, Monckeberg had stated his agreement with Brunner's plan for the transformation of Santiago and had promised, if he were elected, to focus on questions of adequate city planning so as to assure the regularity of building heights and the creation of broad public avenues, both areas in which he believed the capital lagged behind comparable cities.[15] Also returning to the council was Liberal Ricardo González Cortés, like Monckeberg, an architect. Joining him was fellow Liberal Jorge Horeau Eldredge, a longtime party activist who had held various positions in public administration.

The seven Conservatives (counting the three women) and two Liberals gave the Right a clear majority on the new council. The Center and the Left were in the minority. While the Radicals had done poorly overall, they did manage to elect Angel Faivovich R., an agronomist of some national and international distinction. Returning to the municipality after a lengthy absence and a stint as a national deputy from Santiago was Rogelio Ugarte, who had run as an Independent but who still had connections with the Radicals. Another returnee was Juan Urzúa Madrid of the Unión Republicana, who had been a *vocal* on the most recent *junta de vecinos*.

Also competing in the April 7 elections had been the Block de Izquierda (Block of the Left). Foreshadowing future alignments, it was a coalition of the Radical Socialist, Democratic, Socialist of Chile, and Communist parties, although the Communists had also run a separate list of candidates. While overall the Block had done less well in Santiago than expected, it had shown some strength among middle- and lower-class voters that boded well for the future.[16] Three members of this coalition were elected to the council in 1935. Representing the Democrats was Arturo Muñoz Gamboa, yet another former *vocal* who had served in the most recent *junta de vecinos*. Two Socialists were also chosen, both serving on the council for the first time. César Godoy Urrutia was a schoolteacher whose political activism had forced him into exile in Argentina, Uruguay, and Europe in the late 1920s and early 1930s. Returning to Chile after the fall of Ibáñez, he had participated in the Socialist Republic and in the formation of the new Socialist Party under Marmaduke Grove. The other Socialist, Ricardo A. Latcham, was a well-traveled and well-known writer and professor of literature, who, like Godoy, had been active in the Socialist Republic and in the founding of the new party, where he had been in charge of developing ties with similar parties and groups in other countries.[17]

The new council, then, was marked by diversity. White-collar, male professionals dominated, but there were also a number of representatives with different occupations, backgrounds, and interests. Six of the fifteen had served in previous municipalities, but most were newcomers. A substantial range of parties was represented, although this fact was not particularly different from previous administrations. What was unusual, of course, and what most set off this council from all its predecessors was the addition of three women to its ranks.

ONCE THE COMPOSITION OF THE COUNCIL had been set, the Alessandri administration moved to change the executive. Two weeks after the elections it named Absalón Valencia Zavala to replace Labarca as *alcalde*. A lawyer and long-time Liberal Party luminary, Valencia had served in both houses of Congress and as national minister of public works in 1914–15, and again briefly in 1922–23.[18] El Mercurio greeted the appointment positively, calling the job Valencia had assumed one of the "most important" in the country and replete with challenges that it was confident the new *alcalde* could successfully meet.[19] In an interview with *Zig-Zag* a few days after his appointment, Valencia stressed the importance of contracting a loan to construct a new slaughterhouse, proceeding with improvements to the Vega Municipal and Mercado Central, encouraging the development of the capital along the lines of the "excellent" Brunner plan, and doing what he could to rid the streets of vagabonds and beggars. In these and other efforts he asked for the cooperation of all, and he stated his most profound desire for "the absolute banishment of politics from the tasks of the municipality."[20] Of all the challenges he faced, this, as he undoubtedly knew and if history was any guide, would be the most difficult of all.

While Valencia indeed faced formidable challenges, he also assumed office at a relatively propitious time and with some advantages. So far as the council was concerned, at the beginning at least, he could count on a solid majority of Conservatives and Liberals to support his initiatives. Theoretically, too, he would benefit from the initial enthusiasm generated by the restoration of a democratically elected city council. While not as directly conversant with Santiago's government and problems as some of his predecessors, Valencia was a seasoned politician and administrator who seemed to enjoy the full support and confidence of the national administration. Perhaps most importantly, by mid-1935 Chile seemed to be recovering from the worst effects of the Depression and was returning to some kind of economic normalcy and even growth. One of the measures that had been enacted in 1933 to deal with the crises—the suspension of taxes on construction projects that were to be completed by 1935—had stimulated a building boom in Santiago, especially in 1934. While some worried that much of the construction under this program had proceeded in a haphazard and often unaesthetic manner, it had provided employment for thousands and had done much to reduce the worst effects of the crisis for many working-class families. Between 1929 and 1934, the *Boletín Municipal de la República* reported, some 337 million pesos had been invested in construction in Santiago, the results of which had changed the city's appearance dramatically. "The center of Santiago," the *Boletín* wrote, "is full of new buildings that should be finished by the winter. Also, in residential neighborhoods construction is proceeding rapidly." It was also noted, however, that very little activity had taken place in the construction of housing for workers.[21]

VALENCIA OFFICIALLY ASSUMED OFFICE on April 26. The newly elected *regidores* would not be installed until June 9. In the interim, Valencia presided over the appointed municipality. After several weeks of relative inactivity, the new municipality was officially installed on June 9. As was customary, a spokesperson for each of the parties made a brief speech. Also as was customary, each pledged to work with the *alcalde* for the good of the city. Representing the three women *regidoras* was Elena Doll de Díaz. She assured her male colleagues:

> The feminist movement does not imply a struggle of the sexes or the supplanting of men by women. This movement consists of the union of all women who, feeling themselves sisters and understanding their mutual necessities, anguishes, or desires, work to achieve a greater well-being, a greater social justice, a worthy recognition of the rights and of the participation that correspond to them in all the activities of collective life.... Our program deals with the interests that touch us most closely: to procure healthy and comfortable housing; to provide sufficient nourishment through *ferias libres* and abundant supplies of the items of basic necessity; to stimulate popular education with courses on domestic economy and family industries. An object of special attention for us will be all that refers to the protection of minors; making sure that the laws concerning public performances, publications, and centers of entertainment be observed; trying at the same time to maintain public entertainments and moral spectacles [*espectáculos*] in all neighborhoods. Nevertheless, we shall not forget problems of general interest and offer our most decided cooperation in their resolution.[22]

Also making their debut at this session were the *regidores* of the Socialist Party. While Socialists had served in the municipality before, Godoy and Latcham were the first representatives of the new party that had been created in 1932–33 and that henceforth would play a significant role in Chilean national life.[23] Speaking for both of them, Latcham described his party as representative of the workers and professionals of Santiago and promised to struggle on their behalf for real social justice. Sounding a familiar Socialist theme, he argued that Santiago was actually two cities, "one of luxury, of art, of beauty, which is shown to foreign visitors, and another that is sordid, tragic, and full of misery and misfortune." To close this gap, he urged the new municipality to focus on providing the basic necessities for the masses—food, housing, and education. Then, in reference to the words of Doll, he pointed to what he considered an irony in her emphasis upon teaching "domestic economy to a people who do not have enough to eat." Conservative Jorge Richard Barnard came to Doll's defense, arguing that Latcham had twisted her meaning to make a political point. The matter was not pursued, but the brief exchange foreshadowed future clashes and disagreements among the newcomers on the council. They would continue as a significant leitmotif of the new municipality.[24]

A certain spirit of optimism and expectation accompanied the installation of the new municipality. The resumption of democratic practices and the inclusion of previously excluded sectors of society in the process seemed to promise an administration that might be significantly different from those of the past. And initially it did appear that this might be the case. The first few sessions saw the municipality address a number of items without undue division or partisanship. These included proposals to improve working-class housing, stricter enforcement of building heights around the Barrio Cívico, and renewed attention to regulations concerning *conventillos*. In these early sessions, Doll and Edwards were fairly active, whereas Rubio maintained a low profile. The first recorded roll call of the new municipality occurred during the session of June 24. It involved the relatively minor matter of the female owner of a *conventillo* who was requesting the postponement of a deadline for required repairs. In this case, the three women voted with the two Socialists, one Liberal, one Democrat, one Conservative, and the *regidor* of the Unión Republicana to reject the request. Voting in favor were two Conservatives and one Radical, with one Conservative abstaining.[25] This particular vote proved no predictor of future alignments. Afterward, Edwards criticized what she considered inadequate enforcement of the regulations that prohibited the operation of cantinas within two hundred meters of schools and churches, as well as deficiencies in the city-run school breakfast program. Her criticisms prompted a response from *alcalde* Valencia in defense of the administration's efforts in this regard.[26]

As the *regidores* began to take hold of their duties, the *alcalde* maintained an energetic pace of activity. He made regular visits to various parts of the city, met with the *alcaldes* of neighboring *comunas* to discuss common metropolitan problems, and initiated high-profile surprise inspections of numerous bakeries throughout the capital. These inspections frequently uncovered violations of the rules that prohibited night work as well as those that regulated hygienic conditions. In addition to trying to improve the quality of bread in the capital, both the *regidores* and the *alcalde* renewed efforts to crack down on gambling. The *regidores*, for example, once again authorized the *alcalde* to close down those locales where "*chuncho*" machines were being operated. Then, on July 22, the provincial *intendente* announced that he would be sending in the police to close the Canódromo, pursuant to the original municipal request in this regard and a July 11 decision by the Court of Appeals to reject the dog-track owners' argument that the municipal measure was illegal.[27] Anticipating the *intendente*'s action, the owners closed the Canódromo on their own and planned to take their case to the Supreme Court. Valencia hailed the *intendente*'s action (or threat thereof) and reaffirmed his and the municipality's commitment to enforce the accord that "prohibited all games of chance wherever they might occur."[28]

As these events unfolded, the female *regidores* continued to make their presence felt. Edwards's first major intervention took place on July 29, when she delivered a lengthy exposition on the subject of prostitution. She began by recalling that she had first become involved with what she called this "gravest" of problems through her work with the Cruz Blanca, and then went on to argue that the current system of regulated prostitution was not working. Drawing on foreign examples, she highlighted the many failures of regulatory systems elsewhere and concluded that it was folly to think such regulations would operate any more effectively in Chile. She also discounted the argument that sexual abstinence was somehow bad for one's health, labeling it a "medieval superstition." "None of us know," she said, "of an illness or symptom of physical weakness that we can attribute to having lived a moral and self-disciplined life." The only solution to "this most terrible of plagues that threatens the destruction of the strong Chilean race" was, first, to totally abolish the white slave trade that forced young women into a life of vice and, then, to eliminate prostitution altogether. Edwards also recognized that the fundamental conditions that forced or led young women, mostly of the lower classes, to become prostitutes—low wages, the breakup of the family, alcoholism, crowded living conditions—also needed to be addressed for a successful resolution of the problem. To this end, she moved for the creation of a special committee to study measures that would end prostitution and combat and control social diseases. Finally, she argued that the problem of prostitution, the resolution of which she called crucial for "the future progress of the nation," was of special interest to women, and had been an important factor in her own decision to enter the political arena. But it was important to men, too, whose support she sought: "Without men who are sound in body and soul, there is no possibility of stability or national prosperity."[29]

A few days after this presentation, the *alcalde* announced a 25 percent salary increase for city workers and employees, to become effective on January 1, 1936.[30] This decision, coming at a time of continued budget deficits, reflected the growing political influence of city employees and workers. In December 1935 the national government had officially recognized the Asociación de Empleados Municipales de Santiago (Association of Municipal Employees of Santiago), which had been created to promote the interests of the city's white-collar employees. The organization was similar to other groups that had been formed in the 1920s and 1930s to represent middle-class interests.[31] Six months later, in reaction to what they considered the Labarca administration's harsh repression of a 1934 strike for higher wages that had led to scores of dismissals, Santiago's city workers had formed their own union (the Unión de Obreros Municipales, or Union of Municipal Workers). Among its goals were fair salaries, decent housing, just treatment by supervisors, city-provided work clothes and equipment, job security, a shorter workday, and the rehiring of those colleagues who had been dismissed because of previous strike activity. The union's secretary-general noted that several of the new *regidores* as well as the *alcalde* had "shown interest in our problems," and he specifically remarked on "the decided support" of the Socialist *regidores*. Godoy, in particular, at the first session of the new municipality, had pushed for the rehiring of the dismissed workers, an action that had produced some positive results. His colleague Latcham also promised his party's continued attention to the needs of the city's blue-collar laborers.[32]

*

THE SOCIALISTS WERE ALSO PROMINENT in the debate over what was described as the most important issue to come before the municipality in its first months. At its session of August 14, Conservative Regidor Jorge Richard Barnard introduced a motion to suspend the closing of the Canódromo for thirty days while the owners' appeal made its way to the Supreme Court. He claimed that the city's closure of the track had thrown several hundred people out of work and that it was unfair that they had lost their jobs while the legality of the municipality's measure had yet to be fully determined. Various *regidores* objected to this reasoning, arguing that the kind of gambling associated with the Canódromo was a serious social ill that had to be combated vigorously. Socialist Latcham particularly lamented what he saw as the connection between gambling and politics and alluded to the undue influence being exercised in the debate by the respective interests of dog and horse racing. Others made the same point. According to *El Mercurio*, the decisive voice in this discussion was that of Juan Urzúa Madrid of the Unión Republicana, who, among his other arguments, suggested that the owners of the Canódromo had the economic resources to invest in a more productive enterprise than dog racing, such as a badly needed factory that might better serve the national interest and provide steady employment. In the end, even Richard joined the other *regidores* in defeating his own motion by a vote of 9 to 2, with four abstentions (the only votes in favor were those of Conservative Echeverría and Liberal Jorge Horeau Eldredge). After the session was over, two *carabineros* had to escort Urzúa from City Hall to his automobile to protect him from the many Canódromo employees who had gathered at the municipal building to observe the proceedings, and who aggressively manifested their objections to the final result.[33]

Having, for the moment, resolved the Canódromo question, the *regidores* then returned to Edwards's proposal on prostitution. At an extraordinary session on August 16 called specifically to address this matter, Edwards elaborated on the major points of her argument. The other principal speaker, Socialist Ricardo Latcham, agreed in general with Edwards about the importance and complexity of the issue and also favored the goal of eventual abolition of white slavery and prostitution. He also appreciated, as did Edwards, that prostitution was one result of the abysmal social conditions of Chile's poorer classes. However, he went further than his female colleague when he argued that these conditions were the result of the capitalist system, or, in his words, the "regime" that prevailed in Chile. The problem, which he also suggested had important links to various governments and the upper class, could not really be resolved until there was "a vast economic offensive to raise the people's standard of living." So long as the "regime" persisted, he concluded, prostitution might be lessened but never fully suppressed.[34]

At the following session, Regidor Doll took strong exception to what she considered had been the excessively partisan and polemical tenor of Latcham's remarks. Instead of seriously addressing the important issue of prostitution in a constructive manner, she charged, Latcham had used the occasion to express his own "doctrinal propaganda." Moreover, by running over his allotted time (something he had been allowed to do by a unanimous vote), he had prevented a final consideration of Edwards's proposal. Finally, he had employed phrases that "wounded my own religious and moral sentiments." These comments, in turn, produced a strong reaction from Latcham and Godoy, leading the *alcalde* to intercede and to ask Doll to retract her statements so as to avoid a more impassioned debate. Out of deference to the *alcalde*, she agreed to do so. Latcham then tried to assure Doll that he had not intended his remarks as she had interpreted them and "had never meant, at any time, to offend the morality or the religious beliefs of anyone."[35]

Following this episode, the council functioned rather smoothly over the next few months. It stood firm against pressures to reopen the Canódromo and continued to press its anti-gambling efforts. On September 16, following a renewed plea by Edwards for both the majority and the minority to cooperate, the council finally approved her proposal on prostitution, naming a committee that included the three female *regidores*, Conservative Richard, Independent Ugarte, Socialist Latcham, two city officials, and six physicians to study measures that would lead to its total abolition.[36]

DESPITE THESE AGREEMENTS, partisan political tensions, especially involving the two Socialist *regidores*, were never far from the surface and often exploded during council meetings. After a nasty debate over Valencia's budget proposal for the following year, for example, the lead editorial in El Mercurio, on November 27, bemoaned the partisan wrangling that was dividing the municipality. It had been hoped that the new municipality would be different from those of the past, but to date that had not been the case, according to the daily, and the current administration had to be declared "a relative failure." The editorial chastised both the majority for lacking leadership and cohesion and the minority for being obstructionist and narrowly doctrinaire. Too many *regidores* on both sides, it charged, seemed more interested in rewarding their political supporters with patronage and city jobs than with basic administrative duties, a familiar complaint. The one bright spot, the editorial concluded, was the behavior of the female *regidores*, "who have shown a superior and much stricter understanding of their duties than have their [male] colleagues."[37]

Despite efforts by some *regidores* to argue that these criticisms were overblown, there continued to be plenty of evidence of rifts and realignments within the council. As a sign of these, *El Mercurio* reported on Christmas Eve that several *regidores* had formed a new coalition that pledged to cooperate with the *alcalde* for the good of the city. It included the two Liberals Horeau and González, Democrat Muñoz, Radical Faivovich, Independent Ugarte, and Urzúa of the Unión Republicana. The three female *regidores* were said not to have joined this alliance. Distancing themselves a bit from the Conservatives, they "would continue supporting any project that could be identified with the ends they sought." Not included were the four Conservatives and the two Socialists, who were most unlikely to form any alliance of their own. If these arrangements held, then, there would be no real cohesive majority and the council would be divided into at least four separate blocs.[38]

WHILE THE NEWLY ELECTED MUNICIPALITY struggled through its first months in office, a new controversy emerged over the operations of the U.S.-owned electric/streetcar company. Although most of the major developments involved the national government, these had important implications for Santiago and significant repercussions on the local level as well.

When the Depression hit, the company, like the country, had been severely affected. According to one source, the foreign exchange earnings of the AFP had fallen by 90 percent in Chile over a three-year period beginning in 1930, the largest rate of loss for any of the company's Latin American operations.[39] To make up for these losses, at least partially, the company had raised electricity rates, primarily through surcharges, which produced predictable howls of protest from already beleaguered consumers. Alessandri had tried to mollify all sides by allowing for certain increases. Nonetheless, criticism of the company, especially from consumer groups and the Socialist Party, had intensified. In 1933, in light of the higher rates in effect, the Chamber of Deputies had urged the executive to revise the agreement that had been signed between the company and Ibáñez in 1931.[40] While this measure had produced no action, it reflected a renewed public discontent with the company.

With these events in the background, in July 1935 Alessandri's controversial financial minister, Gustavo Ross, ordered an investigation into the company's operations. Over the next few months, it was revealed that the company had engaged in illegal foreign exchange transactions, which led the government to bring suit against it for damages and to order the arrest of its directors. Ultimately, by the end of the year, in what had become a major cause célèbre, an agreement was worked out between Ross, representing the government, and Curtis Calder, the president of the AFP. According to its terms, the government would drop its charges and claims against the company, and would even provide it with $2.5 million in foreign exchange, in return for a restructuring that would place a Chilean president as well as a Chilean majority on the local board of directors. The company agreed to improve its service as well as make payments to the government that would eventually allow it to purchase the franchise.[41]

The whole affair aroused considerable public interest and anger against the company. And as these events unfolded the municipality sought to respond to them. In September, Regidores Faivovich, Ugarte, and Urzúa criticized the company for its failure to improve streetcar service. They alleged, especially, that the company had failed to extend existing lines into new neighborhoods and, sounding a familiar refrain, that it had ignored municipal regulations concerning its activities.[42] At the council session of December 2, Socialist Godoy urged the municipality to press the national government to come to an agreement that would be of benefit to the city, especially at a time of "fortunate weakness for the Company." The *regidores* then agreed to a motion by Conservative Echeverría to devote an entire extraordinary session to this matter.[43]

That session was held on December 11. Conservative Monckeberg, serving as acting *alcalde*, led off the discussion. After a review of his actions on the matter, he introduced the following resolution for consideration: "The municipality agrees fully with the note and accompanying memorandum presented to the president of the republic by Acting Alcalde Gustavo

Monckeberg [referring to a previous communication of the city with the company] and to commission the [regular] *alcalde* to try to obtain from the national government the fulfillment of the aspirations contained in this document." Monckeberg announced that Regidores Doll, Rubio, Richard, and Horeau had co-authored the resolution and that Regidores Domínguez, González, Munoz, and Urzúa had also indicated their support.

While the Socialist *regidores* did not object to the resolution, on which they claimed not to have been consulted, they did not believe it went far enough or would be particularly effective. Godoy predicted that it would end up like most such documents, gathering dust in some government archive. Along with Latcham, he pointed to what he considered the many flaws in the new agreement being discussed (some of this discussion being public, but some also private), certain provisions of which, he argued, would significantly weaken municipal regulation of streetcar service. Going farther in their rhetoric and analysis than most *regidores* seemed willing to do, the Socialists saw the proposed new contract as yet another example of the damaging effects of imperialism in Chile. In Latcham's words, this was "the principal cause of our problems, in which, unhappily, the American Foreign Power Company plays the principal role." In this instance, he alleged, the AFP had been aided and abetted by its main domestic agent in Chile, Finance Minister Ross. Moreover, he warned, the *regidores* and the public should not be fooled by the apparent promise of nationalization of these services, which, under present conditions, would be no more than "a change of names, the same dogs with different collars."[44]

While the Socialists' words and reasoning might have been exaggerated, some of the flaws they saw in the contract proved to be on target. As Thomas O'Brien has pointed out, even with subsequent congressional modifications the new contract in essence would have kept company control in U.S. hands, which would have allowed the company to manipulate the new financial arrangements to its own advantage. In O'Brien's words, "Ross' AFP scheme did little to address popular demands for the nationalization and socialization of major foreign-owned industries."[45] Although the municipality held an open town meeting (*cabildo abierto*) on December 22, in which numerous *regidores* participated, to present the city's point of view on the Ross-Calder agreement, in the last analysis these and other efforts had little effect on the final formulation of the contract.[46]

*

BY THE END OF 1935 THE JURY WAS still very much out on the new municipality. The hope that the restoration of democratically elected *regidores* and the inclusion of women and foreigners in the electoral process would somehow produce greater harmony, unity of purpose, and efficiency in local administration, a somewhat unrealistic hope to begin with, seemed far from being realized. As always, the Santiago city council provided a microcosm of the partisan divisions, alignments, and realignments occurring in Chile more generally. One difference, at least as compared with the National Congress, was the role of the three female representatives on the municipality. While they might not have acted in quite the superior fashion to their male colleagues, as *El Mercurio* claimed, the three newcomers, especially Doll and Edwards, had clearly begun to make their mark on the council and to prove themselves active and effective participants—as well as able politicians—in an institution in which females had never before been represented. This was no small accomplishment. The remainder of the city council's term would reveal whether this would continue to be the case and if the patterns established in these first months would prevail into the future.

11 Political Realignment, Polarization, and the Popular Front (1936-1938)

THE NEXT TWO AND A HALF YEARS in Chile saw an intensification of political realignments and polarization at both the national and local level. The most important development was the creation in mid-1936 of the Chilean Popular Front, composed of the Communist, Socialist, and Radical Parties. Seeking to mobilize the working classes as a main bastion of electoral support, the parties of the front tested their strength in the 1937 congressional elections and prepared to back a single candidate, Radical Pedro Aguirre Cerda, in the presidential contest of 1938. On the right, the Conservatives and Liberals, joined by the now greatly diminished and increasingly opportunistic Democrats, rallied behind the presidential candidacy of Finance Minister Gustavo Ross.[1] As usual, developments at the level of local government in Santiago mirrored these larger national trends.

AT THE BEGINNING OF 1936, the National Congress considered and ultimately approved the Ross-Calder agreement. As this was taking place, the municipality of Santiago focused most of its attention on ways to deal with the ever-present problem of the high cost of food. The main focus of this effort in the council's early sessions were attempts to control the activities of intermediaries (*consignatarios*) in the Vega Municipal, a group blamed for artificially inflating prices and earning enormous profits as a result. Various *regidores* supported a motion to have the *alcalde* investigate these practices and do what he could to bring them to a halt.[2]

At the end of January 1936, national events intruded into the municipality's deliberations. In a brief session on January 29, Socialist Godoy announced that fellow Socialist Regidor Ricardo Latcham had been arrested in the southern city of Concepción for allegedly making "injurious" remarks about the president of the republic and other state officials. In a statement issued the day before, the Block of the Left had denied that Latcham had made any personal references about individuals in the government and demanded that he be released.[3] Godoy, recognizing that *regidores* had no immunity from arrest, nonetheless called on his colleagues to cancel the day's session as a sign of solidarity with Latcham. Speaking for the Conservatives, Jorge Richard Barnard "very much lamented what has happened" but said he and his colleagues did not have sufficient information on which to act. Liberal Horeau, Democrat Muñoz, and Radical Faivovich, however, expressed their support for the motion and the session was terminated as a sign of protest over the government's action.[4]

Latcham's detention was connected to his support for an impending strike by the nation's railroad workers. Frustrated by the rejection of their demands for a wage increase, they had walked off their jobs on February 2. In response, Alessandri took the occasion to crack down generally on the labor movement and the Left. He ordered the army to replace the striking workers and to get the railroads running again, dissolved the Congress, and declared a three-month state of siege that suspended constitutional guarantees. He also closed down the left-wing press and ordered the arrest and/or exile of labor leaders as well as principal figures in the Communist and Socialist Parties. Forced to depart the country for several months as a result were the two Socialist *regidores*, Latcham and Godoy.[5]

These events played an important role in propelling the Popular Front to the fore. Aside from the removal of the two Socialists, however, the government's actions had little direct impact on the municipality of Santiago. Throughout February and March, except for the usual breaks for summer vacation, most of the *regidores* met on a regular basis, continuing to concentrate primarily on efforts to control the price of food. Their cause got a boost from Alessandri, when he urged local authorities to do what they could to end the kind of speculation that drove up costs.[6] The *alcalde*, in early February, ordered the city's food director to establish *puestos reguladores* (regulating posts) in municipal markets, creating a kind of free zone where goods could be sold directly to the public.[7] However, efforts initiated primarily by Radical Faivovich to eliminate the *consignatarios* from the municipal markets ran into resistance, both from the affected parties and from the provincial *intendente*. After several weeks spent addressing this matter, it ultimately proved for naught.

There were few dramatic developments within the council until May 4, when the two Socialist *regidores* returned from exile. Their return, to put it mildly, greatly enlivened subsequent sessions. On May 18, for example, Latcham accused Doll of owning a *conventillo* that was maintained in the same unsanitary condition for which she herself had criticized so many others. Doll admitted to owning the property in question, but strongly denied that it was improperly maintained. At the same session, Godoy reported that Conservative Richard was the owner of the "Moulin Rouge" cabaret at San Antonio 361, an establishment that also was reported to house prostitution and to serve liquor illegally. Richard denied being the owner, but did admit to "intervening in its administration," a distinction that Latcham said smacked of "Jesuitical" reasoning.[8] A week later, the debate continued, with Richard accusing the Socialists of "impudent and cowardly attacks against him." He pledged to continue to fight against "revolutionary communist doctrines" and to defend "the prestige and honor" of any *regidor* subjected to similar attacks.[9] Nothing was resolved with these exchanges, but they were clear reflections of the continuing partisan divisions, especially between Left and Right, on the council.

AN OPPORTUNITY TO BRIGHTEN this generally gloomy picture seemed to present itself on June 8. Citing poor health, Valencia presented his resignation as *alcalde*. Previously, in reviewing his first year in office, Valencia had listed the various decrees he had issued and the measures that had been enacted during his administration. These included the creation of a municipal statistical office and various efforts to deal with the prices and provisioning of foodstuffs.[10] The list of accomplishments was a rather slim one, however, and while it would be unfair to blame the *alcalde* alone for this mediocre record, there was always the hope that new leadership might provide the municipality with renewed dynamism to more successfully confront the capital's continuing problems.

The national government immediately named Augusto Vicuña Subercaseaux as the new *alcalde*. Like his predecessor, Vicuña was a former Liberal Democrat who now held a high-ranking position in the Liberal Party. He was no stranger to local administration or to the problems of governing Santiago, having first been elected as a *regidor* in 1909 and later appointed to the *junta de vecinos* in 1924. He had also served as a national deputy from Santiago on several occasions between 1912 and 1930, had been prominent in the Junta de Reforma Municipal, and had written and commented frequently on issues related to the city and its administration. Vicuña was a lawyer, having received his degree from the University of Chile in 1905, not the first lawyer to serve as *alcalde*. And like many in the second Alessandri administration, he had been forced into exile during the Ibáñez regime.[11] Commenting favorably on the appointment, El Mercurio described Vicuña as having "the same qualities and virtues" as his predecessor and promising to bring the luster of an already distinguished career to this new office.[12]

Wasting no time, Vicuña took over on June 10. He pledged to continue efforts to provide more and cheaper food and, to that end, to encourage the creation of more of the so-called "popular" restaurants that had begun to appear in the capital. But he also highlighted what he saw as the main problem for local government, and his main concern, namely, the lack of financial resources due to "insufficient" revenues. Like many of his predecessors, he made the comparison with Buenos Aires to prove his point. Seeking ways to relieve some of Santiago's financial burdens and to increase its revenues would be at the top of his list of priorities.[13]

FOLLOWING HIS OWN AGENDA, Vicuña met with Alessandri on June 27, handing over to the president a plan to increase municipal revenues. Alessandri expressed his support and promised to send a message to Congress in this regard.[14] A few days later, on July 3, the *alcalde* sent a note to the president of the Senate, which was considering legislation that had already been approved by the Chamber of Deputies to virtually eliminate any role for local government in supplying water to the capital. Vicuña protested the

Chamber's actions and urged the Senate to reconsider the legislation with the city's role and interests in mind.[15]

As the new *alcalde* wrestled with these issues, politics intruded. In late June and early July, the minority members of the council refused to attend the group's scheduled sessions, including one slated to discuss the water issue. This, combined with some illnesses among the majority members, denied a quorum and brought municipal business, at least so far as the *regidores* were concerned, to a standstill. Some speculated that the behavior of the three members of the minority who were involved—Faivovich, Ugarte, and Urzúa—was deliberately calculated to embarrass Vicuña and weaken his effectiveness.[16] Vicuña himself publicly expressed puzzlement over the *regidores'* behavior and urged them to resume their duties. *El Mercurio* editorialized that this clear sign of the return of "*politiquería*," or petty politics, to the council might make one long for a return to the *junta de vecinos*.[17] Finally, on July 13, the minority returned to City Hall and regular council sessions resumed. Speaking in rather vague terms for the dissidents, Faivovich claimed that the protest stemmed from certain high-handed and arbitrary actions by the majority. Whatever the accuracy of these charges, the crisis of the moment seemed resolved. Divisions, however, remained. A roll call vote in this session on the price to be paid for a municipal expropriation found the two Liberals and four Conservatives on one side, Faivovich, Rubio, and the two Socialists on the other.[18]

Over the next few months, the gulf between the two Socialists and the *alcalde* continued to grow. At the beginning of December, for example, Godoy and Latcham pressed the *alcalde* to pressure IT&T into providing more extensive information about the company operations before he signed a new contract with them. The implication was that the telephone company's behavior was not much different from that of the electric/streetcar company, and that it also enjoyed protection from highly placed government officials. While not a direct criticism of Vicuña, the tenor of Godoy and Latcham's remarks implied that the *alcalde* was not doing enough to prevent Santiaguinos from suffering the depredations of yet another foreign-owned monopoly.[19] At the session of December 17, Godoy refused to consider the telephone contract, in light of the fact that the *alcalde* had failed to provide the information earlier requested. His motion to postpone consideration of the matter received unanimous support. Then, confronting Vicuña on a relatively minor matter involving the payment of a repair bill, Godoy engaged the *alcalde* in a shouting match, trading insults with him. The confrontation led Godoy to abandon the chamber, bringing an end to the session for lack of a quorum.[20]

The fireworks continued at the council's next session. On December 21, the *regidores* were set to consider a proposal co-authored by Socialist Godoy, Liberal Horeau, and Radical Faivovich that would give municipal personnel a substantial bonus at the end of the year. Speaking for the majority, Conservative Richard argued that the dire fiscal straits of the municipality made such an expenditure unwise. Vicuña joined in with a similar observation, proclaiming that while he recognized the desirability of the bonus and hoped to work out some compromise in that regard, the budget for the following year was already faced with a revenue shortfall of two million pesos. He then asked to be excused from the chamber to attend to an unspecified pressing matter. His request produced a blistering exchange between the *alcalde* and Conservatives Domínguez and Echeverría on the one side and the two Socialists on the other. Godoy and Latcham accused the *alcalde* of behaving in an autocratic manner, treating them and the other *regidores* much like "*inquilinos*" (tenants) on his own estate, and of having squandered sixty thousand pesos of city funds to visit Buenos Aires earlier in the year while ignoring the economic plight of the personnel in his own administration. Vicuña and his defenders, in turn, charged the Socialists with a total lack of respect for the nation's institutions and of resorting to slanderous demagoguery for their own political purposes. Finally, after the discussion had degenerated into a wild and confusing melee of charges and countercharges, the *alcalde* adjourned the meeting and announced that the public galleries would be closed for a week. This was a reference to the numerous municipal employees who were in attendance as interested parties in this debate and who, he asserted, had helped to "promote the disorders" into which the council had descended.[21]

Soon after the meeting, *El Mercurio* interviewed an unnamed observer to get his impression of these events. According to his interpretation, which seemed valid, the whole issue had its roots in partisan maneuvering for advantage in the national congressional elections slated for March of the following year. The 500 municipal employees and 2,500 city workers formed a substantial voting bloc for the parties competing in Santiago, and offering them a year-end bonus was "an easy way to whet the appetite of this group with city funds," and hence win their electoral support.[22]

It seems likely that Vicuña had these considerations in mind when he met the next day with Finance Minister Gustavo Ross to discuss municipal finances. Ross expressed his support for Vicuña's plan to increase revenues through the implementation of a measure to charge a fee for the required municipal seal on all legal, commercial, and industrial transactions that occurred within the city limits, and he observed that Santiago needed a budget twice the amount of its current one if it were to provide adequate services and keep up with growing demands. These sympathies were undoubtedly colored by Ross's own presidential ambitions and his awareness of the potential voting bloc made up of what could be a grateful group of city employees and workers.[23] Seemingly reassured by his meeting with Ross, Vicuña indicated his willingness to go along with the bonuses at the next council session, which took place on December 24. There was some debate about the amount of the bonuses and the formula for determining them. The key vote was 7 to 3 in favor for Horeau's proposal that the bonuses should be in the amount of 50 percent of one month's salary but not to exceed 1,000 pesos. In favor were the two Liberals, the two Socialists, Democrat Muñoz, Radical Faivovich, and Rubio, of the Asociación Nacional de Mujeres de Chile. Opposed were Conservatives Richard and Monckeberg and the Unión Republicana's Urzúa.[24]

The resolution of this matter notwithstanding, it was obvious by the end of 1936 that Vicuña had not accomplished much more than his predecessor. He had managed to highlight the city's financial plight and had extracted some promises from the national administration that help was on its way. But he had been unable to craft a new budget for 1937 and was forced to extend the 1936 budget to serve for the following year. Little seemed to have been done with regard to long-standing problems with the slaughterhouse, what many saw as inadequate and inefficient public transportation, the continued problematic relationship with foreign companies that provided many basic services, and the still abysmal situation of many neighborhoods. So long as he continued to enjoy the confidence of the national authorities, however, Vicuña could count on another year and a half in which to make a more indelible mark on Santiago's development.

*

THE NEW YEAR BEGAN RATHER WELL for Vicuña. He managed to avoid a potential dispute with the bus drivers' association by postponing once more, for six months, a requirement that all were to wear standard uniforms. The *regidores* approved the establishment of a basic fare for all taxis, thereby alleviating some of the complaints from passengers who were charged different rates by different drivers for the same ride. Moreover, the city attorney's office definitively rejected a request that they be allowed to reopen for business by the owners of the Canódromo. Along with Regidor Rogelio Ugarte, the *alcalde* promised efforts to improve conditions along Avenida Matta and urged the provincial *intendente* to help him find funds to address deficiencies in other poor neighborhoods.

Vicuña's difficulties with the Socialists persisted, however. At the council session of April 5, 1937, presided over by Monckeberg, Godoy lambasted the *alcalde* for his absences when important matters were on the agenda, calling his behavior laughable (*una chacota*). "Never, in my judgment—and you can review the history of the municipality—have we had an *alcalde* who is more inept and less qualified, morally, to continue to be in charge of the city's destiny." Latcham chimed in with a call to the Conservatives and the female *regidoras* to join with the Socialists in a common effort to provide a "more responsible" administration for the city than the one that currently presided.[25]

Fortunately for the *alcalde*, he would not have to endure such comments for long. In the March congressional elections, Latcham and Godoy, along with Radical Faivovich, had been elected national deputies from Santiago and all three would be forced to abandon their council seats to assume their congressional positions in May.[26] According to the rules of the new municipal law, the three departing *regidores* could not be replaced until the next local elections, scheduled for April of the following year. As a consequence, seven of the remaining *regidores* agreed to form a multiparty group that would constitute a quorum (the term majority was not employed) for future sessions. The group was composed of the three female *regidoras*, Juan Urzúa Madrid of the Unión Republicana, Conservatives Jorge Richard Barnard and Gustavo Monckeberg Bravo, and Liberal Ricardo González Cortés. In a so-called "pact of honor," they committed themselves to nine principal points of action, the first being "to obtain in the briefest time possible the initiation of the work of reconstruction for the city slaughterhouse." They also pledged to focus on renovations of the municipal markets, to earmark funds for the construction of workers' housing, to achieve as soon as possible the "isolation" of Santa Lucía, to not create additional bureaucratic positions in local government, and to regularly attend all council sessions.[27]

These developments appeared to be good news for Vicuña. Gone from the council were three of his sharpest critics, and their departure had severely depleted the minority faction on the council. The group had perhaps not provided the insurmountable obstacles of which the conservative press often complained, but they had certainly not made Vicuña's life easy. The new coalition and their "pact of honor" seemed to offer the promise of greater collaboration on a common agenda. Vicuña also received assurances, in a personal visit from Regidor Germán Domínguez, that, contrary to what was rumored, the Conservatives did not want him, a Liberal, removed in favor of one of their own, and he pledged his and his party's full cooperation.[28]

The first sessions of what might be called the "new" council also seemed to proceed smoothly for Vicuña. On May 31 the *regidores* approved with little debate the *alcalde*'s proposal to purchase the Cerro Blanco for 100,000 pesos and transform it into a public park. After more discussion, and true to the promise of the "pact of honor," they also approved a new resolution from Urzúa that authorized the *alcalde* to raise the funds and accept bids for a new slaughterhouse.[29] There were, however, some danger signs for the *alcalde* as well. At a session on June 14, during a discussion of regulation for *conventillos*, Doll implied that the city had not done enough to address the inadequate provision of municipal services for outlying neighborhoods, which, in her words, remained "without paving, without sewers, without water and electricity, in miserable conditions." She urged the *alcalde* to order the city's department of public works to develop a municipal plan to construct low-cost housing for the working classes, implying at the same time that the administration had been insufficiently concerned about this problem.[30]

Frustration with the administration became even more apparent early the next month. At its session of July 5 the *regidores* unanimously approved a resolution introduced by the three women council members, Conservatives Echeverría and Domínguez and Democrat Muñoz, to name one of their number as a "special advisor" to the *alcalde*, "to collaborate with him in the realization of all the projects approved by the council." The city attorney, in attendance, gave his opinion that this proposal was probably illegal. In response, Doll claimed that the legal aspects of the issue were less important to her than letting the *alcalde* and the public know that the *regidores* were unhappy about how they were depicted by the press as "inept, weak, and useless" since the various measures they proposed usually produced no executive follow-up. "For these reasons," she concluded, "in our desperation . . . we believe that there remains no alternative but to advise the *alcalde*, with one of our own, who will represent the council and make the *alcalde* do what he does not want to do. This is clearly what we desire. It is not a legal question. The *alcalde* will know how to deal with our representative."[31]

Interviewed the next day, a stung and surprised Vicuña strongly objected to the resolution. If he accepted the suggested advisor, he argued, the power and prestige of local administration would be diminished even more, leading the way, he warned, repeating an earlier threat, to a restoration of the *junta de vecinos*.[32] El Mercurio agreed with the *alcalde*. In a sharply worded editorial, it labeled the *regidores'* resolution "the most pernicious invasion of the *alcalde's* powers and which, if realized, would mean the beginning of the total dissolution of his authority." Contrary to the spirit of the "pact of honor" signed only a few weeks earlier, the newspaper concluded, this maneuver seemed to smack of the petty politics which its signers had promised to eschew.[33] In an open letter two days later, Doll took strong exception to this interpretation. She argued that "the press and the *alcalde* himself have given this matter a belligerent character that did not exist in either the spirit or the letter of this resolution." In response to a suggestion that the authors of the proposal should have consulted with Vicuña beforehand, thereby avoiding any confrontation, Doll observed that "the public is not generally aware of the fact that the *alcalde* attends very few sessions and lives totally disconnected from the *regidores*." She then asked rhetorically, "How long should we have waited for the *alcalde* to have consulted with us?"[34]

Vicuña was very much present at the session of July 8. He began, perhaps with not a little sarcasm, by thanking the *regidores* for their offer to collaborate with him through an advisor. But he repeated his objections to the proposal as limiting to his authority and illegal. Doll was the first to respond, claiming that it was never her intention, nor that of the other *regidores*, to infringe on the *alcalde's* prerogatives, but rather "to aid" him in the fulfillment of a number of projects that remained pending. Vicuña, in turn, defended his administration, falling back on the familiar argument that he had inherited a municipality in fiscal crisis and that he had done what he could within those constraints. He admitted that there had been no real progress on the new slaughterhouse, but he tried to place blame for that on the resistance of the Socialists to efforts to raise a loan for that purpose. Doll recognized the *alcalde*'s good intentions, but added, "We desired a bit more activity." Other *regidores* chimed in to assure Vicuña that the idea of an advisor had enjoyed broad support and had not been politically motivated. In any event, the *regidores* then voted to move on to other business and the resolution to name an advisor was abandoned.[35]

RELATIONS BETWEEN THE COUNCIL and the *alcalde* seemed to improve somewhat in late 1937 and early 1938. At any rate, there were no overtly hostile confrontations. Within the council itself, divisions continued, as evidenced by many split votes, usually with the *regidores* who had signed the "pact of honor" on one side and those who had not, notably Ugarte and Urzúa, what was left of the old minority, on the other. On some issues, as was often the case, there was considerable unity. One such issue involved a request by the streetcar company to raise its fares to 30 centavos for first class and 20 centavos for second class. According to the new Chilean president of the company, Ernesto Barros Jarpa (also a close friend of Finance Minister Ross), this "modest" increase was necessary to provide salary increases, improve rolling stock, and extend lines.[36] These arguments did not sway the *regidores*, who on August 9 unanimously rejected the request. In recording his vote, Ugarte accused the company "of always avoiding the stipulations of the contracts it signs." Given its profits, he argued, the company could easily provide benefits to its personnel and improve services without the necessity of higher fares.[37]

Much of the council's time in the first months of 1938 was taken up once more with questions related to public transportation, which had become an increasingly complex and difficult matter for the municipality. All three major modes of public transport—taxis, buses, and streetcars—seemed to be constantly demanding fare increases and complaining about what they considered excessive and unjust regulations. While competition among the three provided the public with alternatives, it also produced conflicts, congestion, and confusion as they fought for the same passengers over many of the same routes. In response, it had been suggested that a coordinating body should be created, as had been established in Buenos Aires in 1936, to bring some order out of the growing chaos. In a lengthy discussion of the matter in the council, however, Urzúa pointed out that the creation of the Transport Corporation in Buenos Aires had been to the decided benefit of the British-owned streetcar company and to the decided detriment of the bus owners, an example and a result that should serve as a warning to Santiago.[38] Finally, after struggling with the issue for several months, the *regidores* threw up their hands in despair and passed the whole matter on to the national government.[39]

AS USUAL, MUNICIPAL ELECTIONS, IN APRIL 1938, were seen as an important prelude to the presidential contest later in the year. All parties campaigned aggressively to make their mark in Santiago. Once again, female candidates were prominent. Generally, the assessment of their participation in local government up to that time was favorable, even if it was still described by some in traditional stereotypical terms. Writing in the *Boletín Municipal de la República* in April, for example, one commentator argued that women, by nature, were "without doubt incompatible with politics." It was that very characteristic, however, that made them most suitable to serve on city councils, which, in theory, "should have nothing to do with politics." Referring favorably to their activity in the Municipality of Santiago, the writer saw the *regidoras* as representatives who took their seats not out of "vanity" or "exhibitionism," but rather "to develop a program and to give life to ideas full of humanism and well-being."[40]

In all, the various competing parties put up a total of forty-four aspirants for the fifteen slots on the city council. This was about half the total who had run in 1935, but it included sixteen women, seven more than previously. The best-known and now most seasoned of the female candidates was Elena Doll de Díaz. Like most other candidates who increasingly used radio as a campaign tool, Doll went to the airwaves to broadcast an appeal to the women of Chile to support her and the other females who were running in the upcoming election. The women running for office, she proclaimed, were prepared to deal with solutions to problems of particular concern to the working classes, such as alcoholism and poor housing.[41] Her candidacy received the strong backing of her colleague, Adela Edwards de Salas, who, for health reasons, was not running in this contest. In an open letter of support, Edwards recalled how she had embarked on her duties in 1935 with the belief that "good will and a good spirit" would be sufficient to carry the day but that she had quickly realized that "the realities of politics," as well as the limits of municipal authority, presented substantial obstacles to getting things done. Despite these obstacles, she argued, Doll "was disposed to realize feminine ideals at the cost of whatever sacrifice and in part, at least, had realized some of these." She called on her readers to review the records of the council meetings and to see for themselves "the enormous influence she has exercised in these debates." She then listed the rather impressive list of measures that bore her colleague's stamp and called on all women voters to cast their ballots for her.[42] Implicit in her remarks was the contention that Doll had learned to deal with "the realities of politics" as well as, if not better than, most of her male peers.

The election itself went smoothly, generally repeating the pattern of three years earlier. Nationwide, there was a substantial increase in the total vote, from 327,711 in 1935 to 485,006 three years later, with most of the increase coming from male voters (264,598 versus 410,247) as opposed to female voters (63,113 versus 74,759).[43] Turnout in the capital was respectable, with about 70,000 of 90,000 registered voters participating.[44] Nationwide, the Right, and especially the Conservative Party, increased its strength, building on a good showing in the 1937 congressional elections. The Left, however, did well in the northern mining area and in the larger cities, including Santiago, where Socialist Humberto Godoy Camus was the leading vote-getter. Overall, the Conservatives and the Liberals continued to get the lion's share of the women's vote, 39 percent and 18 percent of the total, respectively, with the Radicals gaining slightly, from 7,912 votes from women in 1935 to 10,348 in 1938, or about 14 percent of the total.[45]

In Santiago, the Popular Front edged the Conservatives seven seats to six. Elected as *regidores* of the Left were three Socialists, Humberto Godoy Camus, Astolfo Tapia Moore, and René Frías Ojeda; three Radicals, Juan Urzúa Madrid, Rogelio Ugarte, and Jorge Rivera Vicuña; and one Communist, Isidoro Godoy Bravo, the first member of this party to serve on the council. Urzúa had switched his affiliation from the Unión Republicana to the Radicals, and longtime Radical Rogelio Ugarte had returned to the fold after having been officially an Independent for some time. On the right, there were four Conservatives—Jorge Richard Barnard, Germán Domínguez, Sergio Larraín, and Rafael A. Gumucio Vives, and two females, Elena Doll de Díaz of the Acción Nacional de Mujeres and Amelia Díaz Lira de Díaz of the Acción Patriótica de Mujeres. Two men elected were unaffiliated with either bloc and could conceivably tip the balance either way. They were Arturo Natho Davidson of the Democratic Party and Mauricio Mena Mena of the Chilean Nazi Party. Natho was also listed as belonging to the Unión Socialista, an organization made up primarily of dissidents from the Socialist Party that had been formed to support the presidential aspirations of the former dictator Carlos Ibáñez, who had returned to Chile as part of a general amnesty in 1937. The real wild card, in many senses of the term, was Mena, an aristocratic lawyer and one of the founders of the *nacistas*. He was a close collaborator of the movement's *"jefe,"* Jorge González von Marees, who had been elected to the Chamber of Deputies in 1937. In May 1938, in a move that may have been as much political calculation as ideological, González broke with European fascism and began to move to the left in support of the Popular Front. If Mena were to follow the same course, that shift would have significant implications for the lineup on the new council.[46]

Five of the fifteen *regidores* selected in 1938—Domínguez, Richard, Doll, Urzúa, and Ugarte—had been reelected for a second term. These results meant that the new council would be made up primarily of *regidores* serving for the first time, with most holding their first elected office. Nonetheless, most of them had been quite active within their own parties and other political organizations. Conservative Rafael Gumucio Vives, for example, who received his law degree from the Catholic University in 1936, had been president of the Conservative party youth branch in Santiago and had held other party posts as well. Fellow Conservative Sergio Larraín had received his degree in architecture from the Catholic University after study abroad in Paris. He was also a member of the Club de la Unión. Democrat (or Unión Socialista) Arturo Natho Davidson also had studied abroad and had received his law degree from the University of Chile in 1929. Radical Jorge Rivera Vicuña was awarded his law degree from the University of Chile in 1933. He had served as president of the Centro de la Juventud Radical (Radical Youth Center) prior to his election. Socialist René Frías Ojeda studied law at the University of Chile, although his biographical entry does not list him as having received his degree. He was, however, president of the National Student Federation (FECh) (which may explain why he had not graduated), a member of the "revolutionary committee" of June 4, 1932, and a founder of the Socialist Party. His Socialist colleague, Astolfo Tapia, had a similar career, having studied law and pedagogy but with no record of having received a degree. He, too, had been a director of the FECh, as well as head of the international division of the Socialist Party. Once again, white-collar professionals, especially lawyers or those who at least had studied law, continued to be prominent on the council.[47]

A LITTLE MORE THAN A MONTH AFTER the municipal elections, on May 7, Vicuña submitted his "undeclinable" resignation as *alcalde*. The national government quickly accepted it. Thanking President Alessandri for the confidence shown in him over the previous two years, Vicuña cited "personal" reasons involving the need to travel abroad as having prompting his decision.[48] An editorial in *El Mercurio* the following day praised Vicuña for having consistently highlighted the need for enhanced municipal revenues and for having overseen an "honest, austere, and exemplary administration." When it came to listing concrete achievements, however, even this laudatory piece could only mention the acquisition of the Cerro Blanco and some initial progress in "isolating" Santa Lucía and building a new slaughterhouse, a not particularly "exemplary" balance after two years in office.[49]

As had been the case two years earlier when Valencia had resigned, the Alessandri administration wasted little time in naming a successor. In this instance, the choice was Onofre Lillo Astorquiza, a well-known member of the Liberal Party. The selection followed Alessandri's custom of choosing members of that party, like Valencia and Vicuña, for the *alcalde* position, a custom probably dictated by the needs of satisfying the governing coalition that supported him. Lillo was also close to the former finance minister Ross. Indeed, he had been forced to resign from the Conservative presidential candidate's campaign committee to assume his new position. It may well have been that Alessandri and Ross calculated, in naming Lillo, that they would have a trusted ally presiding over the new municipality, one who would provide an advantage to Ross as the presidential election neared. If so, given the strength of the Popular Front on the council, as well as the well-known anti-Ross sentiments of the *nacista* Mena, it turned out to be a serious miscalculation.

After an extensive conversation with Vicuña, Lillo assumed office on May

12. He immediately extended an olive branch to the new council, scheduled to be sworn in three days later. Echoing the promises of so many of his predecessors, he pledged to conduct an administration free of "partisan action and political hate," one devoted solely to the interests of the city. "My position in the administration of the capital of the republic," he concluded, "will be one of peace and harmony, not of battle."[50]

It did not take long for these pious hopes to be dashed. At the inaugural session of the new council, on May 14, the Popular Front *regidores* made known their intention to resist the naming of Lillo as *alcalde*. Regidor Astolfo Tapia, speaking for the Socialists, noted that Lillo, a Liberal, belonged to a party that had failed to elect a single *regidor* to the council in the recent election. He also charged that Lillo lacked the necessary qualifications and experience to serve in the post, and that his "nomination follows a general plan on the part of the reactionary forces to occupy the most important strategic [administrative] positions so as to try to impose at all cost the triumph of the anti-popular presidential candidacy of Señor Gustavo Ross, given that Señor Onofre Lillo has been a director of the campaign in support of that candidacy." Accordingly, he concluded, "it is incumbent on the representatives of the Popular Front to struggle with all their energy for the fulfillment of their program, both within and outside the Municipality of Santiago, without arriving at any compromises of any kind with Señor Lillo."[51]

The following day, the Front's *regidores* went a step further. At that session, Radical Urzúa introduced a resolution calling upon Lillo to resign and be replaced by "another who represents the prevailing current in the municipality." He urged that a *cabildo abierto* be held to discuss this matter. In his own defense, Lillo argued that he had been legally appointed to his position and that he had done nothing to merit removal. Conservative Gumucio and others also rose to his defense, but to little avail. A motion to consider the Urzúa resolution without sending it to committee was approved 9 to 3, with two abstentions. In favor were the seven *regidores* of the Popular Front plus Natho and Mena. Opposed were Amelia Díaz de Díaz and Conservatives Richard and Domínguez. New Conservatives Gumucio and Larraín abstained.[52]

After this vote, the municipal government descended into an apparently intractable stalemate that lasted for several months. The *regidores* of the Popular Front followed a dual strategy of either refusing to attend council sessions, thereby denying a quorum, or, when they did, engaging in a kind of contentious "guerrilla warfare" against the *alcalde*. For his part, Lillo remained firm, bolstered by a decision from the provincial *intendente*, who refused to allow the *cabildo abierto* called for in Urzúa's resolution to be convened. Lillo was also bolstered by a lengthy meeting with the minister of the interior in which he received renewed assurance of national government confidence in his continued presence as *alcalde*. Lillo frequently met with the *regidores* of the minority to discuss ways that they could work together, and in late June and early July, in their company, he made some high-profile visits to various neglected neighborhoods, including the area southeast of the Central Station, suggesting that the *regidores* of the left might abandon their intransigent position and begin to work with him to resolve some of the problems his visits had revealed.[53]

This suggestion produced few initial results. The pattern of sessions either being cancelled due to the lack of a quorum or of meetings dissipating into chaotic disagreement continued through July. However, on August 1, after three failed attempts to hold a session, the *regidores* of the Popular Front finally returned to the Casa Consistorial to provide the necessary quorum. Tapia, again speaking for the Front, explained that their continued objection to Lillo's serving as *alcalde* did not mean that they were unwilling to fulfill their responsibilities as *regidores*. In the event, they had returned to the council to deal with an issue of particular concern, namely "to cast our votes, within legal norms, so that our comrades, the city workers, can be paid their family supplements."

The system of supplements had been instituted in 1935. It allowed both municipal employees and workers to receive extra amounts in their monthly paychecks based on the number of children they had—under the age of eighteen for employees, and sixteen for workers, provided that the children were not earning a separate income. By the time of the August 1 meeting, it was incumbent on the council to vote for the funding of this supplement, and the *regidores* of the left could ill afford to alienate an important constituency by letting the date slip due to their intransigence. Nor could the other parties be seen to lack enthusiasm in support of the supplement. Accordingly, there occurred a rare, unanimous vote in favor of a motion from Socialist Frías to earmark 150,359 pesos from the current budget to pay for the family supplements of city workers for the month of July.

A proposal from Lillo to fund the supplement from off-budget sources, however, was defeated 7 to 6, with the Popular Front, Natho, and Mena opposed, the four Conservatives and the two *regidoras* in favor. Perhaps as a sign that they were sensitive to the political advantages to the *alcalde* of his visits to the poorer neighborhoods of the city, and to his calls for collaboration to meet the neighborhoods' needs, in this same session the Left majority joined with the minority to approve an expenditure of 5,000 pesos for the construction of drainage ditches in the southeastern part of the capital.[54]

THE RETURN OF THE POPULAR FRONT *regidores* at the beginning of August signaled the resumption of regular council sessions and a return, more or less, to normal. Over the next few weeks, most meetings produced general unanimity on a number of issues. One of these issues involved the question of streetcar service and fares, an item that always seemed to produce some consensus, no matter how fierce the partisan divisions within the municipality. On August 2, President Alessandri had sent to Congress a proposal to have the national government take over from the municipalities control over the management and regulation of public transportation. This, of course, was in line with a request made earlier by the previous municipality of Santiago. The new council, however, had second thoughts. With the Popular Front *regidores* arguing that Alessandri's action was merely a ruse to allow the streetcar company to raise its fares, the council rescinded their earlier request of April 19 and asked for the return of all the material related to public transportation problems that had been forwarded to the national government at the time. The council then called for the creation of a new committee to pursue further study of the matter. The only dissenting vote came from Doll, who agreed with the principle of retaining municipal control over public transportation but who objected to the wording of the resolution.[55]

The resumption of council business and occasional unanimity on certain matters did not mean that the breach between Lillo and the majority was healed. Typical of the strained relationship was an episode that occurred at the council meeting of August 24, when Lillo got into a very heated exchange with Nacista Mena over the *alcalde*'s authority to name *regidores* to help organize the city's upcoming Independence Day celebration on September 16. At one point, Mena accused Lillo of "trampling" over the council and acting like a "despot," prompting the *alcalde* to deny him the right to speak. At that point, Mena rose from his seat and advanced toward Lillo, demanding that "he repeat some of his concepts, which he [Mena] deemed offensive." In response, Lillo summoned two *carabineros* to restrain the agitated *regidor*. Once order had been restored, Socialist Tapia, in the name of the Popular Front, protested the actions and attitude of the *alcalde*. For his part, Gumucio, a Conservative but also a member of the Falange Nacional (National Falange), an organization created in 1936 from the Juventud Conservador (Conservative Youth) and one which frequently competed and clashed with the Nacistas (and eventually would evolve into the Christian Democratic Party), criticized the actions of Mena as "damaging to the reputation of the municipality." Only in Chile, it seemed, could a member of the local Nazi Party be defended by the Left and criticized by the Right. At any rate, after some further exchanges, the Conservatives left the chamber and the session concluded.[56]

AS SPECTACULAR AS THESE CONFRONTATIONS within the municipality sometimes were, they were only a sideshow to the main event. Most eyes were focused on the presidential campaign, and in early September there was an important turning point in that contest. On the fifth of that month, following a large rally for Carlos Ibáñez in Santiago, a group of *nacistas* attempted a coup by occupying the main building of the University of Chile in downtown Santiago as well as the Caja de Seguro Obligatario, a government office building near La Moneda. A combined force of *carabineros* and military units soon retook the buildings and in the aftermath shot and killed sixty-one young rebels. Whether Alessandri directly ordered the massacre is not clear, but as a result, Ibáñez withdrew his candidacy, urging his followers to support the Popular Front. Given Aguirre Cerda's ultimate narrow win over Ross, this support was decisive in the final outcome. While the election itself, held on October 25, was close nationwide, Aguirre carried the province of Santiago by more than 13,000 votes, 64,297 to 50,998, and bested Ross comfortably in the capital, winning nine of the ten *comunas* and doing particularly well, by two-to-one margins, in working-class areas like Estación, Canadilla, and Recoleta.[57] At the local level, although Lillo doggedly refused to resign in the face of Popular Front pressure to do so, the election of Aguirre meant that his days in office were clearly numbered.

Because of the closeness of the election, the weeks following it until congressional confirmation of the results were tense and involved considerable maneuvering on all sides. Ultimately, the forces of the right, including the military, capitulated and Aguirre's victory was accepted and confirmed. In the meantime, the Santiago city council continued to meet and, while Lillo officially remained *alcalde*, Rogelio Ugarte presided over most meetings. At its session of October 31, with Mena, who had been detained for his part in the events of September 5, back in the fold, the council, by a vote of 8 to 4, approved a motion to invite Aguirre to City Hall for a special ceremony to pay homage to his election. The opposition, with Doll joining three Conservatives to vote against the proposal, argued that the invitation was inappropriate in light of the fact that Aguirre's victory had not yet been officially confirmed, but the votes of the Popular Front, joined by Mena, prevailed.[58] Although nothing was said explicitly, it seems likely that the invitation had been calculated by the Front's *regidores* to bestow some legitimacy on Aguirre's election at a time when that was still in doubt.

The unprecedented appearance by the president-elect took place on November 11. Following a full day of ceremonies and speeches throughout the capital, Aguirre, accompanied by Socialist Senator Marmaduke Grove, arrived at City Hall around 7 p.m. He made his way through a large crowd that had gathered in the Plaza de Armas to greet him and to hear his speech over loudspeakers that had been especially set up for the occasion. From the plaza, he passed through a City Hall crammed with well-wishers and supporters and took his seat in the council chamber to hear various *regidores* from his coalition offer their praise and cooperation. Among them was Mauricio Mena, who asserted that his party had always struggled against the "crude materialism" of the traditional Right and that Aguirre's triumph over the candidate of those forces represented "a ray of optimism" for a better future. In his own address, frequently interrupted by applause, Aguirre thanked the *regidores* for their remarks, made sure to mention and identify the leading figures of each party of the coalition that supported him and who were present, and, perhaps to reassure the Right, denied that the Front, as some had charged, was committed to provoking class struggle in Chile. Listing the many evident social and economic problems of the country, he claimed that "the Popular Front ... has no other purpose, no other sentiment, no other goal than to try to bring happiness [*hacer la felicidad*] to all in the republic, whatever might be the difficulties that present themselves." Municipalities, he emphasized, had a special role to play in this process, by supporting the new government with policies of "equity, cooperation, and social justice." What local government should not do, he warned, was to expand the bureaucracy simply as a way to reward political clients. Although this line drew applause, whether the audience of *regidores* to which it was addressed and, indeed, whether the president-elect himself, who had a lot of supporters to satisfy, would heed this admonition remained very much an open question.[59]

12 An Alcaldesa of the Popular Front (1938-1940)

FINALLY INAUGURATED AS PRESIDENT on December 24, 1938, Pedro Aguirre Cerda, as John Reese Stevenson wrote, "stepped into no political bed of roses."[1] On the one hand, he faced a suspicious and hostile Right, which controlled both houses of Congress and was prepared to resist any executive measure they believed smacked of "extremism." There was also Carlos Ibáñez, who in some ways had handed Aguirre the presidency and whose own ambitions and unpredictability made him a constant threat. On the other hand, the new president had to satisfy a diverse coalition of supporters, who ranged from the Far Left to the Far Right, all of whom had their own agendas, all of whom could make a legitimate claim to having been crucial to his victory, and all of whom expected rewards, especially positions within the government. In addition, his election, based on a progressive program and promises of betterment for the deprived majority of Chileans, much like Alessandri's in 1920, had raised expectations among many that this administration would be more attentive to their needs than had been its predecessor.

Within this constellation of challenges, naming a new *alcalde* for Santiago was not the most prominent, but neither was it insignificant. On December 28, the new administration named Radical Rogelio Ugarte, who had been presiding over most council sessions during the previous two months, as substitute *alcalde* until a definitive choice could be made. This decision was well received by Conservatives and others, and on January 2, 1939, *regidores* of the Right and the Left paid homage to Ugarte by recommending him for the permanent appointment.[2]

There was little doubt that Ugarte was well regarded and well qualified. Having served in the municipality, both as *regidor* and as *alcalde*, off and on over four decades, few had had as much experience or engagement with local affairs for so long a period. Many, apparently including Ugarte himself, fully expected Aguirre to nominate a fellow Radical for the local executive position. They were, however, in for a surprise.

On January 4, 1939, the new president named Graciela Contreras de Schnake as the first Socialist and first female *alcalde* (now *alcaldesa*) of Santiago. Appointing the wife of the Socialist Party's secretary general, Oscar Schnake, to this post was clearly part of Aguirre's strategy of rewarding the leftist partners of his coalition. In addition to this nomination, Aguirre also named three Socialists to his cabinet; the brother of Marmaduke Grove, Eduardo, as mayor of Viña del Mar; and a Communist as mayor of Valparaíso.[3] The appointment of Contreras may also have been calculated to appeal to female voters, as a follow-through on the president's campaign commitment "to support the rights of women and to elevate their social, economic, and political position."[4] As it happened, the Radical Party did significantly increase its share of the women's vote over the course of Aguirre's administration.[5]

Reactions varied. The magazine *Hoy*, directed in part by Carlos Dávila of the Socialist Republic and generally sympathetic to the Left, expressed its hope that the *alcaldesa* would embark on a program as "progressive" as the one that had been promised by the brief tenure of Rogelio Ugarte.[6] The Radical *La Hora*, whose party had received the lion's share of the posts in the new government and who probably would have preferred the continuation of Ugarte as *alcalde*, featured the naming of Contreras prominently but without initial comment. It did, however, run a lengthy interview with her on January 7.[7] *El Mercurio* also had relatively little to say, although it did run an opinion piece on January 8 that fit Contreras's appointment into the larger context of advances for women in Europe and the United States, but that also warned that no mayor of Santiago, male or female, would have much success unless municipal finances were significantly bolstered.[8] *Topaze*, of course, had its own interpretation. In its edition of January 6, it carried a cartoon caricature of Oscar Schnake escorting his wife to the door of City Hall, with the caption reading, in part, "Charity begins at home."[9] Another cartoon on January 13 (see Fig. 3) showed Graciela Contreras with her arms akimbo and one foot on a prostrate Rogelio Ugarte, who exclaimed, "And still there are those who say they are the weaker sex!"[10]

The most openly skeptical newspaper was El Diario Ilustrado. In an editorial on January 8, it noted that while it had not endorsed Rogelio Ugarte for the position of alcalde, as had some Conservatives, it had hoped that the new alcalde would be someone experienced in municipal affairs and that the choice would be free of political considerations. Instead, the president had chosen a neophyte for this most important of posts, "one that is most delicate and full of responsibilities." Moreover, the political considerations could not be clearer, meaning that the alcaldesa's actions "are going to be viewed with fear and mistrust."[11]

Partisan considerations aside, there was some validity in these concerns. Contreras was inexperienced, untested, and, as the first female to assume the capital's executive office, under considerable pressure to perform. There were also reports that she herself had been reluctant to accept the nomination and that members of her own party were upset that they had not been consulted or allowed to vote on her appointment.[12] Moreover, it was abundantly clear to all that she owed her position not to her own merits but to the fact that she was married to an important and now, thanks to the victory of the Popular Front, influential politician.

In the face of these difficulties, Contreras would prove herself more politically astute and nimble than many had predicted. Even before her nomination had become official, she gave a series of interviews, unprecedented in the number and range of publications in which they appeared, in which she detailed her agenda and her qualifications for her position. On January 1, for example, Zig-Zag published its conversation with her, in which she promised to work in close collaboration with the national government of the Popular Front and to focus in particular on matters involving women and children. She also pledged to work to lower the cost of food by cracking down on "unscrupulous speculators who seek to gain through the stomachs of consumers"; to encourage the development of low-cost housing "within the reach of families with scarce resources"; and to improve

ROGELIO UGARTE. — ¡Y todavía hay quien diga
que son del sexo débil!

FIG. 3. *Graciela Contreras over a prostrate Rogelio Ugarte, who decries
that "And still there are those who say they are the weaker sex."*
SOURCE: *Topaze*, January 10, 1939.

basic municipal services in preparation for the four-hundredth anniversary
celebration of the founding of Santiago, slated for February 1941.[13]

In an interview published in the *Boletín Municipal* on January 5, Contreras
sought to turn her marriage to her political advantage. As the wife and close
companion of her activist husband since 1923, Contreras pointed out that
she had experienced with him his leadership role in the founding of the
Socialist Party, where he had been secretary general since 1933, and had
suffered with him through exile and clandestine struggle in Chile.[14] Like her
husband, Contreras was a member of the Socialist Militia. Members of the
militia, dressed in their uniforms consisting of gray shirts, red ties, and
peaked campaign hats, drilled in military formation and served as a potential counterweight to any possible coup attempts by the Right or even the

Army.[15] In addition to being an important political partner to her husband, she had been secretary of the Acción de Mujeres Socialistas (AMS, or Socialist Women's Action), which was recognized in 1937 by the party as its female confederation. Contreras had also been active in the Movimiento pro Emancipación de la Mujer Chilena (MEMCh, or Movement for the Emancipation of Chilean Women), created in 1935, as well as the Popular Front election campaign.[16] She had also helped to found a library and a school, to be inaugurated on March 15, dedicated to practical homemaking activities, and she had helped to create Humanidad, the official publication of the AMS. In other words, while she lacked a background in elected office and in municipal affairs per se, she was not without political and organizational experience, both in collaboration with and independently from her husband.[17]

Contreras took office on January 9. Her first weeks were not much different from those of her male predecessors. She took time to visit various neighborhoods and various municipally run institutions, like the slaughterhouse and the markets, to acquaint herself personally with prevailing conditions. On January 13 she met with representatives of the Conservative wing of the council, as a way to get to know them and to hear their points of view, and on the same day she requested the city treasurer to prepare a full report on the state of municipal finances. Also on that day, she sent a note to the national minister of health, in which she suggested new ways to control and discourage prostitution. No action had been taken on earlier proposals in this regard, and Contreras promised to give this matter renewed attention and priority.[18]

Her first major initiative was the creation of ferias libres in various parts of the city. While others in the past had encouraged the creation of markets where farmers could sell goods directly to consumers, it was Contreras who gave the initiative an impetus and importance that up to that time it had lacked. On January 23, by decree, the alcaldesa named a committee of city officials to draw up plans for the ferias libres, with the idea that they would be open two days a week in six central locations. In an interview a few days later, she promised that municipal inspectors would undertake "a strict vigilance" of these proposed markets to assure good-quality food at reasonable prices and without the infamous "middle-men" taking their cut of the profits.[19] The first of the ferias, located on the north sidewalk of Avenida Matta between San Diego and Arturo Prat, opened for business at 7 a.m. on

February 19 and proved enough of a success that others soon followed.[20] Largely due to the new *alcaldesa*'s initiative and commitment, these *ferias* became prominent features of the Santiago landscape, although they were not always universally praised or without controversy.

Contreras established the *ferias libres* by decree. After several failed attempts to assemble a quorum, the *regidores* of the city council met for a bare three minutes on January 25 to officially oversee the swearing in of the new mayor. They then abruptly adjourned after approving a donation of 100,000 pesos to aid the victims of one of Chile's most devastating earthquakes, which had hit the southern and central regions on the previous day, leaving thousands dead and tens of thousands homeless.[21]

The early adjournment indicated that the political ground under the new *alcaldesa* was itself a bit shaky. At first glance, it would seem that she held one obvious advantages over Onofre Lillo Astorquiza, her immediate predecessor. Contreras could govern the city in conformity with rather than opposed to the Popular Front majority. Her position seemed even stronger when the generally conservative Elena Doll de Díaz decided to take a year-long "sabbatical" to travel in Europe. As it happened, however, at least initially, this advantage was more apparent than real. From the outset, Contreras had trouble getting the council to hold regular meetings. At one of its rare sessions, on February 6, some *regidores* suggested that the council not meet again until the end of March since, they alleged, there was no particularly pressing business to consider.[22] While this may or may not have been the case, other dynamics were at play. At the next scheduled session, on February 10, the Conservatives and Mena appeared, but the Radicals and Socialists did not, thereby denying a quorum. According to *El Mercurio*, the parties of the Popular Front were prepared to place obstacles in the *alcaldesa*'s path because she was planning to name a committee to review the status of municipal personnel to determine their qualifications for employment, with an eye to a significant reorganization of the bureaucracy. This, of course, would have implications for the patronage the Socialists and Radicals hoped to dispense. There were also rumors that Contreras intended to resign as a result of this opposition. These reached the ears of Aguirre, who reaffirmed his full confidence in her.[23] *Topaze* offered another explanation, suggesting that the male *regidores* of the Left were uncomfortable with a female mayor and wanted to "remasculinize" the municipality. The humor magazine singled out Socialist Astolfo Tapia as the leader of the Left's boycott and the *regidor* who himself aspired to replace Contreras as *alcalde*.[24]

As usual, *Topaze* may have been close to the mark. There were still many men on the Left who were uncomfortable with the enhanced political role of women and with feminism in general, and this dispute with Contreras may have reflected this discomfort.[25] However, there was also a lot of behind-the-scenes maneuvering within and between the parties involved, all of it taking place within the complex structure of the Popular Front, that makes determining the motives behind particular actions difficult to ascertain. In this instance, interparty struggles probably had more of an influence than questions of gender.

Contreras tried to allay some of the concerns of the Popular Front majority when the council finally met again, on February 22. With eight members present, including six from the Popular Front (but not the Radicals), she presented a detailed exposition of her plans for the city. She began by observing that Santiago was at an auspicious moment since, "for the first time in this term there exists an exact harmony of doctrine between the majority of the Corporation and the Alcalde." She also recognized the historical significance of her own appointment as the first female mayor of the capital and called upon all the *regidores* for their assistance to make the experiment a successful one. But she also pointedly promised that in case of "doctrinal divergence" within the council, her orientation would be alongside "the program of social advance that constitutes the essence of the Chilean Popular Front." She then laid out her program, which was basically a more detailed rendition of the issues and problems she had emphasized in earlier interviews and which, like the high cost of food, she already had begun to address. Among the first items she discussed, however, was the sensitive issue of how to deal with city personnel, especially those who had been contracted for special duties, which seemed to be at the nub of the dispute with the Radicals and Socialists. Detailing her plans in this regard, she declared, "My action will always be inspired by the goal of administrative betterment, for whose end I shall not vacillate in adopting all the measures the circumstances suggest are advantageous." In other words, political considerations would not play a role.[26]

The session of February 22 was also the first "regular" meeting of the council over which Contreras presided. Despite the political maneuvering that was going on behind the scenes, there was little out of the ordinary to distinguish this meeting from countless others under male *alcaldes*. In the only roll call, the *regidores* of the Popular Front, including Mena, voted 6 to 2 in favor a resolution from Communist Isidoro Godoy to provide extra pay for the thirty-five city workers who had finally been rehired after having been dismissed as a result of strike actions in 1934. The two negative votes came from Conservative Richard and Falangist Gumucio. There was also general agreement to provide bonuses to workers in several departments for extra work performed and to hold future meetings only once a week, on Monday evenings.[27]

Despite the "normality" of this session and the *alcaldesa*'s gestures of re-assurance, the political jockeying and turmoil continued throughout the month of March. By the end of the month, it was reported that due to con-tinued resistance from Radicals and Socialists, Contreras was prepared to re-sign. Rumors also circulated that she would be replaced by a Radical, per-haps a female.[28] On March 30, however, *El Mercurio* reported that in a secret session, the Socialist Party leaders who had called for her to step down had reversed themselves and now agreed that Contreras should stay in office. The reason given was the favorable reaction her initiatives to cut food costs and to deal with juvenile vagrancy had received. Most importantly, Aguirre had once again reaffirmed his confidence in the *alcaldesa* "as representative of the Left and of Chilean women" and was disinclined to accept her resignation.[29]

Beginning in April, with Contreras finally secure in her post, the San-tiago city council began meeting on a generally regular basis. Issues con-cerning public transportation came to dominate the discussion over the next few months. The complaints and the concerns were familiar. Streetcar service was still seen as antiquated and inadequate, with overcrowded cars, deteriorating rolling stock, and surly personnel. Even the streetcar workers themselves complained that the company's failure to modernize and expand the number of vehicles in operation had produced dangerous conditions and accidents for which they were blamed. In a petition to the *alcaldesa*, they called for the nationalization of electric service and the municipalization of the streetcars.[30] Moreover, bus service, while expanding and improving, also left much to be desired. Although new, smaller, and faster "microbuses" had been introduced to provide greater speed and flexibility, they were also more expensive to ride and carried fewer passengers than did the regular buses. City officials called for more buses of all types to be put into operation, while bus owners countered that such an expansion could only be accomplished by charging higher fares, which produced the usual standoff with the municipality.

Within the city council, debate over these matters dragged on through May, June, and July. Ultimately, a majority of *regidores*, with the *alcaldesa's* backing, recommended the creation of a national transport corporation as the best way to resolve the problems with the buses, leaving the streetcar issue for later resolution. The sessions to discuss this proposal were often contentious and found *regidores* not only sparring verbally with one another but also occasionally with representatives of the bus owners' associations who packed the City Hall galleries to register their displeasure with the transport corporation plan. A final vote on the matter was scheduled for the July 26 session of the council. At one point during that session, frustrated by what she called "a lack of culture and respect" from the audience, the *alcaldesa* had called for a brief recess when Regidor Mauricio Mena engaged in an exchange of insults with one of the audience. This led to a more serious exchange of punches that left Mena with a bloody nose. His antagonist then fled, along with the rest of the crowd, as the galleries were cleared. Expressing their solidarity with Mena, his colleagues then "energetically protested this attack," although it appeared that it was the *regidor* himself who had thrown the first punch. The measure was then approved by a slim 6 to 5 margin, with the *regidores* of the Popular Front in favor and Conservatives opposed, after which Mena thanked his colleagues for their support and the meeting adjourned. If nothing else, the incident, not totally unprecedented in the annals of council meetings, showed the depth of the passions aroused over this issue.[31]

THROUGHOUT THE DISCUSSIONS OF public transportation and other issues, Contreras was an active and engaged *alcaldesa*. While there undoubtedly remained more than a few skeptics and critics, she seemed to be firmly in command of her office and unafraid to take a straightforward stance on controversial issues. She presided over most council meetings with what appeared to be confidence and even-handedness. Whether because the Popular Front controlled the majority, because of deference to her gender, or for other causes, Contreras received much less criticism from the *regidores*, at least openly, than was usually the case, and especially when compared with her immediate predecessors. In September, however, both the pace and intensity of criticism of the *alcaldesa* began to pick up. While the criticism was not strictly personal, it did go to the heart of her proudest achievement, the establishment of the *ferias libres*. On September 8, Contreras issued a decree that laid out new regulations for the operation of the *ferias*. While the regulations allowed for some intermediaries to participate in the sale of certain products, they were intended mainly to tighten municipal supervision over who was allowed to operate in the *ferias* and to assure a certain quality control of the items sold. To this end, all sellers would be required to present their goods clearly marked as to price and quality, to treat the public in a fair and honest manner, and to maintain both personal cleanliness and the proper appearance of their vehicles and equipment.[32]

At the council session of September 25, with Contreras presiding, Conservative Domínguez complained that the *regidores* had not been consulted prior to the issuing of these new regulations. Moreover, he asserted, in general the *ferias* had not reduced prices and were often in a hygienic state that left much to be desired (something, of course, which the new regulations were designed to address). Radical Jorge Rivera agreed with Domínguez. While he generally supported the *alcaldesa*'s initiative, he claimed that, too often, the *ferias* did "not meet the necessities of the city or conform with the aesthetics of a capital such as ours." Rivera recalled that he frequently passed by these sites and had viewed scenes that were "almost Dantesque," with people sleeping on the streets and covered with rags in preparation for the next day's sales, and with the products lacking the needed sanitary conditions to assure their quality. Mena, for his part, argued that the *ferias* had lowered costs and that, at the moment, they were the best alternative available in light of the fact that the municipality lacked the funds to build more permanent markets. Ultimately, the council agreed to a motion from Socialist Astolfo Tapia to send the matter to committee for further study.[33]

During this debate, Contreras strongly defended the *ferias*, in particular, and her administration, in general. In an interview published soon thereafter, when asked if she was considering resigning in the face of mounting attacks on the *ferias* and other matters, Contreras recognized that "many people want me to leave," but she claimed that she had developed "considerable affection" (*mucho cariño*) for the job and felt "in my element" and would not leave her post until asked to do so by Aguirre, who up to that point, still retained his confidence in her. Part of her problem, she said, came from "a lack of cooperation from some sectors" and from "certain *regidores*" who "wanted all the city department heads to be of their particular party."[34] This was an apparent reference to the ongoing struggle among the component parts of the Popular Front, especially the Radicals and the Socialists, to staff both the national and local bureaucracy with their own partisans.[35]

Various other political developments at the international and national level implied possible repercussions for Contreras. In September, Hitler and Stalin signed their non-aggression pact, loosening but not breaking the Communist Party's links with the Popular Front. As there was only one Communist *regidor*, Isidoro Godoy, this development would probably have little impact on the Santiago city council. Of potentially greater significance was the decision by the Socialist Party in September to replace the relatively little-known party figures named to the three minor cabinet slots they had been originally allotted with three major leaders, as a way to strengthen their position within the Popular Front government. These included Contreras's husband, Oscar Schnake Vergara, who abandoned his senate seat and the secretary-generalship of the party to become minister of development. The party also agreed to disband the Socialist militias and curtail other more militant mobilization efforts. One result of these maneuvers was a further exacerbation of the divisions between the "accommodationist" wing of the party and the younger and more idealistic "noncomformist" members led by former *regidor* Cesar Godoy Urrutia, who would eventually split from the Socialists to form the Socialist Workers' Party in mid-1940. For their part, at this stage, Aguirre and the Radicals were prepared to make their own "accommodations" to keep the Socialists within the Popular Front coalition and to try to prevent the schism that ultimately occurred.[36]

THE LIMITS ON RADICAL ACCOMMODATION to the Socialists at the local level, however, became clear at the council session of November 27. The issue of contention was once again the *ferias libres*. The committee named to look into the matter had produced a majority and minority report. The majority, led by Socialist Astolfo Tapia, proposed creating new and permanent neighborhood markets and, in the meantime, maintaining the *ferias* as they were but under increased supervision. Tapia argued that the *ferias* were worthwhile because they had been shown to offer food at lower prices than either private groceries or the stalls of the established markets. Speaking for the minority, who would have preferred to shut down the *ferias* altogether but who had suggested weekend closings as a compromise, Radical Jorge Rivera argued that protecting the interests of the three hundred or so small merchants of the established municipal markets who were being adversely affected by the competition from the *ferias libres* should be a paramount concern. To these *comerciantes*, he claimed, who had made many sacrifices to serve the city and the public, and who now faced "economic asphyxiation" because of the competition from the *ferias libres*, the city "owed a debt of honor." Mena, however, a consistent supporter of the *ferias*, suggested that Rivera's interests were less in "honor" than in partisan advantage, in that the *comerciantes* were largely backers of his Radical Party. After others on both sides of the issue chimed in, the *regidores* voted 6 to 5 to approve the majority report. This vote showed an important fissure in the Popular Front coalition. In favor were the three Socialists, Radical Ugarte, Mena of the ALP, and Elena Doll de Díaz, only recently returned from her lengthy trip to Europe. Opposed were Conservative Domínguez along with Radicals Rivera, Poblete, and Urzúa, and Communist Isidoro Godoy.[37]

While this vote concluded the session, it did not quell passions over this issue. Indeed, just the opposite ensued. Seeking to apply pressure on the *regidores* of the majority, a large group of *comerciantes* who had crowded the council galleries and the area outside of City Hall to listen to the debate, now protested the result. While accounts differed, it was clear that the hostile crowd of *comerciantes* had followed Socialist Regidores Tapia and Godoy to the party's headquarters on Calle Morandé to express their displeasure. When the crowd had refused to disperse, the *comerciantes* claimed, Tapia had appeared at the balcony of the party building and fired five shots into the air in an attempt to disperse them without having to call in the *carabineros* to intercede. The next day, however, Tapia sent a note to the press denying that he had fired any shots.[38] At its next session, all the *regidores* joined in solidarity with Tapia and Godoy to condemn the attacks on their persons by the hostile crowd of *comerciantes*.[39]

Overshadowed in the furor over the *ferias libres* was the return of Elena Doll de Díaz to the council. Three years after leaving office, in an interview with the *New York Times*, Contreras would recall how at first the male *regidores* had refused to accept her but that she had ultimately won them over to her side. Contreras would note, however, that throughout her time in office, "she had the complete cooperation of two women Council members who, like the men, had been elected by popular vote."[40] This recollection was something of a distortion. One of the two elected women, Amelia Díaz de Díaz, had died in May 1939 and so had attended very few council sessions, while the other, Regidora Doll, had been in Europe until the end of 1939. In an interview of her own, soon after her return, Doll stated that while she was still unaffiliated with any party, she sympathized with certain socialist principles and found the Scandinavian brand of social democracy particularly appealing. When asked what she thought of Contreras, Doll claimed to have heard many good things about her. But, she added, "personally I can only criticize one thing about her: she is too political." While she had supported Ross in the presidential election of 1938, Doll noted, she had hoped the Popular Front government would change some of the things she had found "deplorable" about the second Alessandri administration. So far, Doll concluded, not much had changed, however.[41]

It would be difficult to describe Doll's first significant intervention in the council debates, on December 4, as an example of "complete cooperation" with the *alcaldesa*. Contreras, in preparation for the four-hundredth anniversary celebration, had introduced a rather controversial project that called for selling off the city block that was occupied by the venerable Mercado Central and constructing in its place a new City Hall, an idea apparently first introduced by Rogelio Ugarte. Doll, making clear that she did not mean "to wound anybody, no *regidor*, much less the Señora Alcaldesa," nonetheless expressed her strong skepticism about the soundness of the project. As she saw it, the state of municipal finances continued to be perilous and spending money on projects like this one could only deepen public disagreement with and distrust of the local government. Others joined in to make many of the same points, and the conversation soon evolved into an argument over the achievements and failures of the local administration under Contreras, with Socialist Regidor Tapia defending her and Mena arguing that, given the Popular Front majority, more could have been accomplished. During this discussion, Doll observed that much of what Tapia lauded as Popular Front achievements had actually been initiated during Conservative administrations. In the end, no decision was reached on Contreras's proposal for a new City Hall at this session.[42]

On December 22, the *Boletín Municipal* published Contreras's review of her first year in office. Heading her own list of major achievements was the establishment of the *ferias libres*, followed by the creation of a special fund to provide credit to small farmers who served the metropolitan area. She also listed several items that aimed to improve the lot of city employees and workers who had called her attention to their plight early on in her administration. These included special housing constructed for them and, for city workers, a two-peso-a-day pay raise. The creation of housing and shelter for university students, especially female students, measures to deal with juvenile vagrancy, attention to abandoned children, and initiatives to confront the issue of prostitution were also detailed. The *alcaldesa* underlined the problem of transportation as "surely the most difficult" she had faced in her term, but held out hope that the suggested transportation corporation, if approved, would provide a "rapid and efficient" solution.[43]

The *Boletín* also reprinted an editorial from *La Nación* that reviewed the *alcaldesa*'s first year as well. Beginning by noting that she had assumed office in an environment of "hostile indifference from some and ironic skepticism from many others," the piece went on to say that her performance had dealt a "rude blow" to "*criollo* prejudices" against the idea of a woman in the *alcalde*'s seat. After the first few months of "sterile political maneuvering, even her adversaries have had to recognize the productive labor realized by the first *alcaldesa* of Santiago."[44]

This favorable opinion notwithstanding, there was serious trouble for Contreras on the immediate horizon. On the evening of the same day her review of the year appeared, the Radical Assembly of Santiago met to discuss her administration. They were treated to a blistering attack by Alfredo Larraín Neil, a longtime party activist and official and until recently head of the city revenue department. He claimed that under Contreras the municipality was currently suffering "a political, economic, and moral crisis." The Popular Front coalition within the council, he observed, was now divided among and even within its component parts, while the administration as a whole was in a state of "disorganization" due primarily to the *alcaldesa* spending funds on dubious projects without bringing in sufficient revenues to cover the costs. He pointed particularly to what he alleged were hundreds of thousands of pesos expended on publications to promote Contreras's achievements and the hiring of unnecessary personnel in the city paving office, presumably to satisfy a partisan clientele.[45] This last point would soon assume larger significance.

Larraín might well have been following a personal agenda in these remarks. However, it had been clear for some time that whatever the "accommodationist" tactics of the national administration, there were growing tensions, as revealed in the recent debate over the *ferias libres*, between Radicals and Socialists at the local level. At its next meeting, on December 30, after others joined the discussions initiated by Larraín, the Radical assembly instructed its *regidores* on the council, in the name of the party, to call for a thorough investigation of the charges made against the *alcaldesa* and to bring these to the attention of the provincial *intendente*, the minister of the interior, and the president of the republic.[46]

A serious confrontation between Radicals and Socialists at the beginning of the new year found Contreras caught in the middle and added substantially to the pressures on her. On January 3, 1940, Arturo Lermanda Molina arrived at the city paving office to take over as its director. An engineer who had received his degree from the University of Chile in 1925, he had exercised his profession in a number of capacities before appointment to this post.[47] There seemed little doubt as to his professional qualifications for the job or about the legality of his appointment. According to a reorganization of this office several years earlier, the municipality was in charge of naming all the personnel in the department except for the director, who, as in this case, was to be named by the president of the republic. The dispute arose not over Lermanda's qualifications or legal right to be director, but rather over his political affiliation as a member of the Radical Party. Most of the personnel in the office were Socialists, who, claiming that they and their party had not been consulted as they should have been on this appointment, protested and resisted Lermanda's assumption of office. Leading the resistance was the acting director, Carlos Charlín Ojeda, a former military officer and Socialist militant who had been active in the formation of the party, who had been in city employ since 1934, and who had been named to his current post by Contreras.[48]

According to *El Mercurio*'s account, the clash began in the early afternoon when Lermanda arrived to take over. Finding Charlín in the director's office, Lermanda ordered him to leave, which, after an exchange of words, he did. Soon thereafter, however, a group of workers and Charlín returned to the director's office, demanded that Lermanda leave, and began a forced occupation. Refusing to quit the office, Lermanda called on the *carabineros* to clear his office and the building of the protestors. When this was done, the *carabineros* withdrew, whereupon the protestors reoccupied the building. According to one account, accompanying the Socialist militants were some ex-*nacistas*, now called "*vanguardistas*." At this point, Socialist Party leaders intervened and prevailed upon the occupiers to abandon the building, which then restored some calm to the situation.[49] After two days of intense negotiations involving Radical and Socialist leaders and local and national officials, Lermanda was reconfirmed in his position, with Charlín remaining as subdirector.[50]

Throughout these events, Contreras was an active participant in negotiating a resolution. She appeared to handle the matter with some skill, trying to calm both sides and seeking to interpret the matter as a minor misunderstanding rather than a more serious disagreement among contending parties. The Conservative press, however, explicitly placed much of the blame for the fracas directly on her shoulders. *El Diario Ilustrado*, for example, argued that the entire episode underscored the lack of "order and discipline" in local administration and besmirched the "authority and dignity" of the president of the republic since it was workers in city employ who had refused to accept his nomination of Lermanda.[51] The recently created *La Crítica*, organ of the Socialist Party, on the other hand, strongly defended the actions of the *alcaldesa* and accused the Conservatives of exaggerating and distorting what had happened so as to serve their own partisan interests.[52] The Radical Assembly, however, saw the incident as seriously harmful to the integrity of the Popular Front, and in an extraordinary meeting on January 5 voted to petition Aguirre to ask for Contreras's resignation.[53] *Topaze*, with its usual insight, suggested that the Radical Assembly had acted not so much out of a principled concern with the integrity of the governing coalition as with guaranteeing their control over municipal patronage. In the magazine's humorous recreation of the January 5 meeting, they had the head of the assembly addressing his fellow "*correlipresupuestarios*," which can be roughly translated as "those who wanted to take advantage of budgetary spoils."[54]

The city council, with Contreras presiding, spent most of its January 8 session discussing these events. Radical Jorge Rivera initiated the debate by asserting that the Right had sought to take advantage of this episode but that the integrity of the Popular Front remained intact. Nonetheless, he sharply criticized the *alcaldesa* for not acting more aggressively to deal with the crisis. Doll added her voice to the criticism, chastising Contreras for having placed Charlín, whose qualifications she questioned, in a position "whose duties are exceedingly delicate." Others chimed in, and despite Rivera's disclaimer, some of the exchanges clearly revealed the underlying tension between the two main component parties of the Popular Front.[55]

Mounting criticism of Contreras's handling of the paving office crisis produced renewed rumors that she was about to resign. In an interview published in the magazine *Vea* on the day the council met to discuss the issue, she repeated her assertion that the office takeover had been blown out of proportion, that no real "mutiny" had occurred, as *Vea* and other publications had implied, and that upon hearing of the disturbance she had met immediately with the minister of the interior and the provincial *intendente* to come to a resolution of the crisis, thereby countering Rivera's allegation that she had been slow to act.[56] She repeated these main points in an interview in *Ercilla* that appeared a few days later. When questioned about the action of the local Radical Assembly in asking the president to demand her resignation, she observed that the assembly did not represent the main directive body of the Radical Party and that so long as she continued to enjoy Aguirre's confidence she had no intention of resigning. She did admit, however, that her first year in office had been one of "struggle, of obstacles, of a persistent campaign of calumnies," and she expressed the hope that the next year would be better.[57]

THE NEXT FEW MONTHS OF LOCAL GOVERNMENT and politics, at least on the surface, were relatively uneventful. The divisions between Radicals and Socialists seemed momentarily healed, as the *regidores* from both parties voted together on most issues that came before the council in January and February. There was also unanimity in rejecting a plan from one Salvador Castro to undertake the transformation of Santa Lucía park, and in requesting a special subsidy from the national government for the celebration of the four-hundredth anniversary of the founding of the city.[58] The council also approved, with little debate and disagreement, new regulations governing street stalls and kiosks and street sales in general.[59]

These developments notwithstanding, El Mercurio found much to criticize in the city's administration in these months. An editorial on February 19, for example, blamed the municipal authorities for failing to resolve continuing problems involving public transportation, "the permanent impasse over construction of a new slaughterhouse, the 'shame of Santiago,' " inadequate local services of street cleaning and garbage collection, and, adding to this list of "local torments," the general neglect of city parks and gardens.[60] Not surprisingly, the Socialist La Crítica had a more positive view of the city administration. At the same time as El Mercurio published its critical editorials, the Socialist daily made it a point to highlight what it considered the major accomplishments of the alcaldesa. The edition of February 28, for example, included an article praising the municipally run boarding school for young girls that had been created by Contreras, just as a year previously the paper had commented favorably on a hostel for bootblacks that she had established. Despite the enormous demands of her job, the same article claimed, "Señora Graciela Contreras de Schnake has time for all. Blessed with an exquisite sensitivity, there is no human suffering that does not move and trouble her."[61]

These laudatory comments, however, were not sufficient to prevent the alcaldesa from submitting her resignation on March 1. In her letter to Aguirre, she once again expressed her appreciation for the boldness of his action in naming her as head of Santiago's government and the constant confidence in her he had provided. She spoke with pride of having served the city and its people, but also noted that throughout her tenure, both "within and without the municipality, I was the object of unjust and slanderous attacks." Her presence as alcaldesa, too, "has awakened the envy of elements that have sought to take advantage of it of which you are well aware." Not only have these elements "sought to destroy the reputation of a humble woman," but they have also tried to use criticism of the alcaldesa to undermine the position of "my husband, the current minister of development." In light of these facts, and to remove herself as an obstacle to the effectiveness of the Popular Front government, she concluded, she was offering her resignation.[62]

There was undoubtedly more behind this action than this official letter reveals. Reporting on the resignation, Ercilla suggested that it had resulted from a combination of "incomprehension and conservatism" and "a constant struggle with her enemies and members of her own Socialist Party."[63] The Conservatives certainly were not sorry to see her go. *El Diario Ilustrado* welcomed the resignation and said that Contreras's year in office had justified their initial skepticism about her appointment. Lacking credentials and experience, the daily alleged, the *alcaldesa* had spent too much time obeying the dictates of her party to find city jobs for Socialist partisans and not enough on her main duties. With partisan exaggeration of its own, *El Diario's* lead editorial on the resignation claimed that "never in any administration has there been greater disorder in municipal services," and "of the great needs of the city, she had no concern."[64] In the council meeting of March 18, when discussion turned to the naming of a new *alcalde*, Conservative *regidores* Richard and Larraín urged the president to name a well-qualified and seasoned successor, with the latter arguing that over the previous year the *regidores* of the Popular Front had shown too much deference to Contreras, which had led to "errors committed everyday."[65] While refraining from criticizing Contreras directly, *El Mercurio* called on Aguirre to appoint a capable, experienced, and nonpartisan figure to the post. In addition, while making no explicit reference to the recent experiment, they used the word "*hombre*" to describe any future *alcalde*.[66]

At least one member of the *alcaldesa's* own party did not shy from making abundantly manifest his own disappointment with and disapproval of certain aspects of her performance. At the city council meeting of March 18, Socialist Regidor Frías sharply criticized Contreras for three recent actions. First, despite an earlier unanimous vote in opposition, a vote in which Frías himself had played a leading role, the *alcaldesa* had proceeded to name Salvador Castro as the new administrator of Santa Lucía Park. Second, on March 1, the same day she announced her resignation, she had signed 110 decrees allowing for the special distribution of funds totaling more than 1,700,000 pesos without consulting the council. Third, and most seriously, there were reports that in a meeting with Juan Tonkin of the electric/streetcar company, she had signed an agreement to allow a fare increase to 60 centavos on first class, 20 centavos on second class, and to maintain some cars at "popular" prices. He suggested that the *alcaldesa* had been subjected to certain pressures and had been "the victim of imperialist machinations" in this regard, but that neither the Socialist Party nor the Popular Front could countenance such an increased burden on the working classes.[67]

In an interview a few days later, Tonkin admitted that he had discussed these arrangements with Contreras. He argued that in light of the extensions and improvements in service the higher fares would allow, he found it "difficult to conceive of a proposition more advantageous for the city," but neither did he say anything about any agreement having been signed.[68] Following Frías's presentation, Radical Regidor Jorge Rivera assured his colleagues that the new *alcalde* would resolve these questions and stated "categorically" that "no member of the government, neither a Radical nor a Socialist, has placed his [or her] signature on any kind of agreement, public or private, that refers to a fare increase." These assurances notwithstanding, the *regidores* approved a resolution introduced by Mena that asked Contreras, who was still officially in office although not presiding over council meetings, to supply them with information on and explanations of the special decrees that had been issued on March 1, as well as on the matter of the alleged streetcar fare increases.[69]

Almost three weeks after Contreras submitted her resignation, Aguirre still had not accepted it. The discussion in the council on March 18 prompted her, the following day, to send a new communication to the president, insisting that he accept her original request. His delay in deciding, she argued, had allowed "enemies of the latest hour (*última hora*) to take advantage of this time . . . to pursue their own interests, cooperating with this suicidal labor to produce instability, not only in the harmony of the city but also within the Popular Front government itself." She claimed that these actions were prompted by a "small group of men who seek to pervert my labor, guided only by egoism and base passions." She assured the president that "the calumnies flowing in the press and most recently in the municipality are totally false."[70] Two days later, Aguirre finally accepted the resignation and named Rogelio Ugarte as acting *alcalde*.[71]

AGUIRRE'S DELAY IN ACCEPTING Contreras's resignation may have been calculated to minimize the political damage. Her abandonment of the office before her term expired, while certainly far from unprecedented, was a clear indication that the bold step of naming a woman to lead Santiago's government had not turned out as well as originally hoped. The president had supported the *alcaldesa* through thick and thin, as she herself consistently mentioned, and it would probably have done him and the Popular Front little good with women voters to accept the resignation immediately, even though it seemed that the die was firmly cast as of March 1. At the national level, Aguirre had faced a cabinet crisis in February that had led him to replace four "progressive" Radicals with more moderate members of that party, leading to some dissatisfaction from the left wing of the Popular Front coalition. U.S. embassy counselor Wesley Frost interpreted these actions as indicating that the president was "adopting a firmer attitude and ... steering away from extremists." He included Contreras's resignation as part of this trend, which may or may not have been the case.[72] Her husband, Oscar Schnake Vergara, remained in the cabinet as minister of development and continued as a prominent figure of the "accommodationist" group. Strongly anti-communist, he also became the leader of the movement to establish closer relations with the United States and, along with his wife, visited that country in late 1940 and early 1941. In April, as mentioned, the dissidents within Schnake's Socialist Party, including Deputy César Godoy Urrutia and others, were expelled and formed the rival Socialist Workers' Party. These developments, in turn, seemed to play an important role in the opposition to the *alcaldesa* from within the ranks of her own party. Regidor Rene Frías Ojeda, for example, who had criticized her so severely at the March 18 council meeting, was reelected to the municipality as a candidate of the dissident socialist faction the following year.

Ercilla published a lengthy interview with Contreras on March 20. In it she reiterated her appreciation of Aguirre for his steadfast support, but admitted that the opposition from within her own party, "for reasons I do not know," had caused her pain. She also explained that she had appointed Salvador Castro as administrator of Santa Lucía because he had plans for the transformation of that park in preparation for the four-hundredth anniversary celebration that would not place an undue burden on municipal funds. Recognizing that there was still much left to do to prepare the city properly for that celebration, she reviewed all that she had been able to accomplish and concluded, "I am satisfied with my efforts."[73] In her later interview with the *New York Times*, in 1943, she repeated her satisfaction with the *ferias libres*, which had not only become established institutions in Santiago but also had spread to other parts of Chile. While she had not been able to do as much to directly improve the lot of women in Santiago as she had hoped, she believed that her time in office "gave them a lot of confidence" that a female could handle these duties effectively and responsibly.[74]

*

A FINAL ASSESSMENT OF CONTRERAS'S STEWARDSHIP of Santiago presents a mixed picture. She assumed office with certain advantages. Most importantly, President Aguirre had been courageous enough to appoint her, and, at least publicly, he remained behind her throughout. It helped immensely, of course, that her husband was an important figure in one of the main component parties of the Popular Front coalition, a figure that the president needed on his side to make his government work. The *alcaldesa* also benefited from the fact that the Popular Front was a majority within the city council. Her gender, too, might have been an advantage in that her male colleagues might have been more reluctant to criticize her openly as compared with a male executive, thereby blemishing their own "gentlemanly" reputations.

There were disadvantages as well. Her husband's position, without which she never would have been appointed, meant she had to exert considerable effort to establish her own independent stance and qualifications for the job, as well as fend off those opponents who sought to attack him through her. In addition, the Popular Front majority was often more apparent than real, as the coalition at the local level suffered some of the same internal strains and tensions as at the national level. Finally, whatever the special deference she might have enjoyed, she still had to overcome, as she often mentioned, deeply ingrained skepticism that a woman could function effectively as *alcalde*. It is never easy to be a pioneer.

Given these circumstances, Contreras's list of accomplishments is certainly respectable if not spectacular. She had done more than some of her male predecessors within a comparable period of time and less than some others. Judging such matters is complicated and difficult because contexts and conditions differ from one local administration to the next. What does seem clear, however, is that Contreras had proved that there was no inherent reason that a woman could not serve effectively as *alcalde*, just as Elena Doll de Díaz and others had shown the same as elected members of Santiago's city council.

13 Santiago in the Early 1940s

THE STORY OF SANTIAGO'S LOCAL administration in the early 1940s followed familiar patterns. In April 1940, trying to keep his fractious coalition together, Aguirre named Socialist Rafael Pacheco Sty to replace Contreras as *alcalde*. (Again, many expected Rogelio Ugarte to receive the nod.) Pacheco was a relatively unknown quantity, having held minor governmental positions until he was named *intendente* of the southern province of Linares in 1939, where he helped direct reconstruction efforts after the disastrous earthquake of that year. In an interview soon after being named *alcalde*, he admitted that he had never served in a municipal post before, but he emphasized that he had spent most of his life in Santiago and was intimately aware of its many problems, especially those involving public transportation and the cost of food.[1]

Pacheco's administration trod a well-worn path. Beginning with the usual good intentions and promises of cooperation from the *regidores*, the new *alcalde* soon became handicapped and frustrated by partisan bickering and standoffs between Left and Right within the council. By the end of the year, the Socialist *La Crítica* blamed the *alcalde*'s difficulties on the defections of three former members of the majority that had originally supported him, Nacista Mena, Dissident Socialist Frías, and former Radical Urzúa, who had been expelled from his party. These men, *La Crítica* claimed, had formed a tacit alliance (*conturbenio*) with the Right to block any worthwhile initiatives the *alcalde* might propose.[2] Throughout these months, too, the council was often unable to form a quorum, a reflection of its continuing internal struggles.

242

By the beginning of 1941, the list of Pacheco's achievements was a meager one. Reviewing his first year in office, he mentioned the purchase of new sanitation equipment, the establishment of new municipal bakeries and laundries, the repair and cleaning up of various *conventillos*, and improvements to public buildings. He also had managed to get a majority of the council to agree to his scheme to create a "meat corporation" (*corporación de carnes*), which was a proposal to work jointly with the national government to finally build a new city slaughterhouse. A majority had also agreed to purchase the Palacio Cousiño as a city museum. The four-hundredth anniversary celebration in February also had gone reasonably well, although much of that success was due to the efforts of the national government.[3]

One of the items mentioned in this review was particularly contentious. It involved reorganizing the municipal bureaucracy and raising the pay and providing end-of-the-year bonuses for city personnel. Critics observed that while the municipal employees and workers might be deserving recipients, the bonuses were difficult to justify while the city continued to accumulate ever larger deficits and when *alcaldes*, as did Pacheco, claimed that they were hamstrung in providing services and making greater municipal improvements due to fiscal constraints. Generally, the *regidores* of the Center and Left supported expenditures on bonuses and salaries, while those of the Right, notably Doll, opposed them.[4]

As was often the case, increased pay for city personnel was a particularly salient issue prior to elections. All parties wanted to court the potential votes of this constituency, especially in light of the national congressional elections in March 1941 and the municipal elections the following month. In the March contests, the Popular Front had achieved a major victory, gaining control of both houses of Congress. Elected to the Chamber of Deputies were *regidores* Jorge Rivera Vicuña (Radical), Astolfo Tapia Moore (Socialist), and Germán Domínguez (Conservative).[5] The municipal elections produced similar results, with the Left gaining nationwide and the Right losing a substantial number of seats overall. In Santiago, the candidates of the now renovated Popular Front (Radicals, Dissident Socialists, and Democrats) won seven seats, and the Socialists, officially no longer part of the Front, gained two, providing a potential majority for the Left, with four Conservatives in the minority.[6]

Turnout was again low, at about 45 percent, and the women's vote was again significant. Nationwide, 80,744 females cast their ballots, about 6,000 more than in 1938. While almost half of these votes went to Conservatives and Liberals, the parties of the original Popular Front achieved notable gains, especially the Radicals, who took only about 14 percent of the women's vote in 1938 but who captured better than 24 percent three years later. The efforts of Aguirre to reach out to women voters undoubtedly played a role in this shift. In addition to naming and standing by Contreras as *alcaldesa* of Santiago, in January 1941 he had introduced legislation to extend suffrage to women in all elections, and in March had named Señorita Olga Boettcher, a Radical of German descent, as the governor of La Unión Province, the first female appointed to such a position.[7] Despite these developments, for the first time since 1935 not a single woman of the seven who entered the contest won election to Santiago's city council. Elena Doll de Díaz ran at the top of the list put forth by the Asociación Nacional de Mujeres, which also backed some Conservative male candidates, but she failed to win re-election. Graciela Contreras de Schnake, who ran on the Socialist ticket, received almost the same number of votes as Doll but also failed in her election bid.[8] No one seemed to interpret these results as a broader rejection of women's participation in local administration. Rather, they seemed to reflect the consequences of fewer female candidates and the more complicated and shifting dynamics of coalition-building and realignments that preceded the elections. Indeed, in 1944 Doll again won election to the council, as did Carmen Lazo, a young female activist of the Socialist Party.

During the period just prior to the installation of the new council, an event unfolded that had significant implications for the local authorities. In late April and early May, both bus drivers and streetcar personnel threatened to go on strike. The bus drivers were protesting the failure of owners to adhere to an agreement that had been negotiated by the provincial *intendente* in January as the result of a previous strike to raise their wages. The streetcar workers hoped to force the national or local administration to intervene on their behalf to achieve the same kinds of salary increases and other improvements that the bus drivers had received. The bus drivers struck on May 1, but after direct intervention by the *intendente* and Minister of Interior Arturo Olavarría Bravo, service was resumed on May 3, with owners, drivers, and collectors all agreeing to abide by the *intendente*'s original arbitration decision.[9]

The streetcar issue proved more intractable. For several months, Pacheco and the council had been considering the possibility of municipalization of the service but had been unable to come to any definitive decision. At the end of April, faced with the twin strike threats, Pacheco consulted with company directors and the minister of the interior. He then recommended that the *regidores* allow fare increases for both buses and streetcars in return for better service and to fund the requested salary increases. The case for a bus fare increase became less pressing with the resolution of that dispute on May 3. Pacheco's plan for a streetcar fare increase (40 percent of the cars to charge 20 centavos, and 60 percent to charge 60 centavos, with a special student fare of 20 centavos), however, remained pending. Despite extensive discussion over three separate meetings on April 30, May 5, and May 6, the council was unable to come to a decision on this proposal. Some members, especially those on the Left, remained resolutely opposed to any fare increase whatsoever, whereas others argued that the matter should be postponed until the new council assumed office later in May.[10]

The lack of council action had a clear impact on ensuing developments. Meeting on the same day as the council, May 6, the Sindicato de Maquinistas y Cobradores de la Compañía de Tracción de Santiago (Union of Conductors and Collectors of the Santiago Streetcar Company), along with the inspectors' and employees' association, were notified by their colleague and recently elected *regidor*, Socialist Wenceslao Morales, that the council had failed to act on the fare increase proposal. The streetcar employees immediately and unanimously voted to strike the following day, being careful to say that their action was not necessarily aimed at supporting higher fares or intruding on contractual arrangements between the company and the municipality, but rather it was aimed mainly at improving the quality of the company's rolling stock and its overall service, as well as achieving higher wages. It was estimated that the walkout would involve some six thousand workers and employees.[11]

On the following day, Minister of the Interior Olavarría intervened in dramatic fashion. Faced with the possibility that the bus owners and drivers would now take the opportunity to renew their strike, thus effectively bringing to a halt almost all public transportation in the capital, the minister ordered the immediate detention not only of the leaders of the bus and streetcar unions but also of the directors of both the bus owners' union and the streetcar company, implying a collusion between management and labor to force higher fares. At the same time, in an unprecedented move, he ordered elements of the army and the *carabineros* to themselves operate the streetcars and buses, something they appeared to manage with considerable success.

For the short term, these actions had the desired effect. After two days of negotiation, those who had been detained were released and normal service resumed, with the understanding that the national government would investigate whether or not the streetcar company could afford to pay higher wages and improve service without a fare increase. In the meantime, the provincial *intendente* had named engineer Miguel Vergara Imas as general director of the streetcar company until these matters could be resolved.[12] As it happened, Vergara would continue to manage the streetcars until the company finally sold them to the national government in 1945. At the same time, Olavarría sought a more lasting and comprehensive solution to public transportation problems in general. Accordingly, he sent to Congress a proposal that would authorize the president of the republic to resolve the pending questions regarding public transportation within 120 days, based on a complete study of the finances of the streetcar and bus companies. In the event that suitable arrangements with those companies could not be arrived at, the president would be authorized to expropriate the companies' assets and equipment. While this matter was under consideration, no fare changes were to be allowed.[13]

Judging the matter to be of some urgency, the Chamber of Deputies met in extraordinary session on May 10 to consider Olavarría's proposal. According to the minister's recollection, much of the urgency was due to the fact that "the Municipality of Santiago had failed completely in its efforts to solve the problem."[14] In his own report to Congress, the minister recognized that his proposal represented a "transitory" violation of the principle of municipal autonomy, "a beautiful achievement (*conquista*) of yesteryear," but that the current circumstances demanded such action. While not all the deputies agreed, and some accused the minister of using his proposal to camouflage an attempt to raise fares, they voted 35 to 12 in favor of a modified version that gave the president 120 days to come up with a transportation plan, subject to congressional approval.[15] The Senate added its unanimous approval on May 14. Although it would take several more years, the proposal ultimately led to the establishment of a national transportation corporation to manage streetcars and buses in Santiago and elsewhere.

In most quarters the minister's swift action was met with favor. La Crítica, for example, praised Olavarría's decisive behavior in dealing with the strike.[16] The streetcar workers themselves hailed the outcome as a "triumph of organization and discipline" and saw it as a measure that would lead to higher wages.[17] The Socialist newspaper, La Opinión, congratulated the legislators for approving the proposal, calling it "a law that honors the Congress for its high patriotic sentiments." It also praised the efforts of the minister, who was "a political adversary" but whose actions in this instance sought "to defend the collective interest, devoid of awkward vanity or intending to impose his own opinions."[18]

The city council of Santiago was less enthusiastic. Meeting on May 8, it considered a number of resolutions that would have condemned the minister's proposal as an infringement on municipal authority and asked the president to withdraw it from Congress. Adamant in their criticism of Olavarría were fellow Radicals Jorge Rivera Vicuña and Santiago Poblete, reflecting, apparently, some interparty dissent.[19] Equally critical were Nacista Mena, Dissident Socialist Frías, and Communist Godoy. Among other things, they denied that the council had been slow to act on the proposal to raise fares, which had only been introduced ten days earlier, and they asserted that the national government's decision to take the matter out of their hands was unfair and precipitate. Socialist Humberto Godoy, however, defended the government's action, arguing that the federal authorities had more resources to deal effectively with the issue than did the municipality. While not exactly endorsing the minister's move, Conservative Richard asserted that the politically divided and partisan council was incapable of resolving any matter of a "technical" nature, leaving no recourse but for the national government to take over. After the usual heated exchanges and finger-pointing, with Doll taking both sides to the verbal woodshed, the council voted 5 to 4 in favor of the Rivera-Poblete motion asking the president to withdraw Olavarría's proposal.[20]

With congressional approval of the measure on May 10, the point soon became moot. As in so many instances involving public transportation, the action of the Congress underscored the municipality's inability to deal with the streetcar company on its own and its increasing marginalization from the debate and the decision-making process. In the council's discussion of May 8, some valid points had been made. Partisan considerations and divisions undoubtedly hindered effective action, and were complicated by the natural reluctance of any party or official to be associated with recommending a fare increase, no matter how necessary or justified. It seemed clear, too, that given the complexity of the problem and the fact that public transportation increasingly involved various jurisdictions within Santiago, a solution had to be found at a level higher than the city administration. Moreover, if some state takeover of the system was to be part of the solution, it seemed unlikely that the city of Santiago, with its limited resources and continuing budget deficits, could act alone to expropriate and manage the streetcars and buses.

THE NEW CITY COUNCIL ASSEMBLED for its first meeting on May 18. It included several *regidores* who had been reelected, among them Rogelio Ugarte and Juan Urzúa Madrid, former Radicals now identified as Independents, and Radical Santiago Poblete and Dissident Socialist René Frías Ojeda, both running on the Popular Front list. Also returning, after a three-year hiatus, was the former *vocal* of the *junta de vecinos* and *regidor* Arturo Muñoz Gamboa of the Democratic Party and the renovated Popular Front.

The four Conservatives chosen to the council were all newcomers. They included Ricardo Fox Balmaceda, who had studied law and worked on the national food council; Carlos Flores Vicuña, a lawyer and diplomat who had held various party positions and was a member of the Club de la Unión; Francisco León Gaete, a professor of history; and Mario Valdés Morandé, a lawyer educated at the Catholic University.[21] The two new Radicals were Desiderio Bravo Ortíz, a lawyer, former student leader, and longtime party activist; and Héctor Pacheco Pizarro, a dentist who had organized the dental department of the city's public health office.[22] The two new Socialist *regidores* were from more humble backgrounds. Leopoldo Sánchez Vásquez, originally of the Democratic Party, was a furniture maker, labor organizer, and among the founders of the Socialist Party.[23] His colleague, Wenceslao Morales Ibáñez, was a streetcar worker who publicly thanked their organization for its impact on his election victory.[24] While no specific biographical information is available, it seems likely that the one Communist elected, Moisés Ríos, came from a similarly humble background.[25] Enrique Phillips, the lone Liberal Party representative, was a dentist and professor as well as a former member of the party's youth branch.

If there had been any expectations that the new council would operate in a more cooperative, harmonious, and nonpartisan manner than its predecessor, these were soon dashed. Early meetings were taken up with wrangling between the Left and Right in an effort to form a majority, with neither side prevailing. While a putative majority of the Center and Left was ultimately formed, it did not prove to be one on which the *alcalde* could consistently count. In early July, for example, he had to fight off an attempt led by Radical Santiago Poblete to close down the *ferias libres*, a measure which a majority approved but which Pacheco, with the support of Minister of the Interior Olavarría, refused to enforce.[26] In August, *regidores* of both the Left and Right accused Pacheco of financial mismanagement and of ignoring the basic administrative problems of the city.[27] Finally, on October 9, a majority of *regidores* voted to abandon the *alcalde's* proposed *corporación de carnes*, which was proceeding slowly through Congress, in favor of a plan more directly under municipal control.[28]

Socialist defenders of the *alcalde* saw the decision on the meat corporation as further evidence of a continuing "sinister alliance" at work. On the new council, members of this "sinister alliance" included, they alleged, Independent Urzúa, Dissident Socialist Frías, and Communist Ríos, along with, on occasion, the three Radicals.[29] While Pacheco himself did not publicly agree with this analysis, preferring to characterize the decision on the meat corporation as an honest difference of opinion, being rebuffed on this matter appeared to be the final straw. Two days after the council decision, Pacheco turned his office over to the first *regidor*, Radical Héctor Pacheco Pizarro, and took an extended leave of absence that lasted, except for a brief interlude, until his resignation as *alcalde* in early December.[30] These events coincided with and probably, to some extent, were connected to the decision on November 10 by Aguirre, who was suffering from tuberculosis, to turn over the reins of office to the minister of the interior. Aguirre died on November 25, and with his death, for all practical purposes, the original Popular Front came to an end.[31]

By most accounts, Pacheco Pizarro seemed to do an able job as acting *alcalde*. He appeared to enjoy the support of the majority of the *regidores* and to want to continue as *alcalde* on a permanent basis. Larger political concerns, however, intruded. Following Aguirre's death, the interim administration had slated new presidential elections for February 1, 1942. Trying to attract Socialist support for Radical candidate Juan Antonio Ríos, the national government had named Juan Vidal Oltra, a founding member of the Socialist Party, to replace Pacheco Sty as the new *alcalde*.[32]

Without criticizing the Vidal appointment directly, El Mercurio bemoaned the role that political maneuvering had played in his selection as *alcalde*. In these matters, it concluded, the voices of a few party activists carried more weight than those of "great and respectable nuclei of inhabitants, who also are citizens with the right to be heard, even when they do not rally around doctrinal banners or agitate in partisan assemblies."[33] This lament was by now numbingly familiar. No real progress could be made on major city problems, El Mercurio and others argued, so long as partisan considerations lay behind practically every appointment and decision involving municipal government. And frustration with the existing system was certainly understandable. Municipal finances and services remained inadequate, and despite a flurry of activity over the previous year or so, no real resolution of such long-standing matters as the coordination and control of public transportation or the construction of a new *matadero* had been achieved. These complaints notwithstanding, there also seemed little enthusiasm for a return to the allegedly more efficient *juntas de vecinos* or to an elected *alcalde*, or even for one chosen from within the ranks of the *regidores*. Indeed, even if one of the previous systems had been adopted, partisan political considerations would still have played a role. Whatever their disappointments, the hope remained that the democratic restoration and the reforms of the 1930s would ultimately produce the results and benefits that so many of Santiago's citizens envisioned and desired.

DESPITE POLITICAL TURMOIL AND ECONOMIC CRISES, Santiago continued to grow rapidly throughout the 1930s into the early 1940s and beyond. The national census of 1940 counted 1,261,717 persons in the Province of Santiago, up from 967,603 in 1930, with 1,100,725 in the Department of Santiago, up from 836,928 in 1930. The *comuna* of Santiago grew respectably in population from 542,432 to 639,546 in this period, but the outlying *comunas* grew even more dramatically. Some, like Nuñoa and San Miguel, had once more nearly doubled their number of inhabitants.[34] The *comuna* of Santiago continued to have markedly more females (352,759) than males (286,787), as did the Department of Santiago (451,044 males, 541,132 females).[35] Overall, by 1940, Greater Santiago had 21 percent of the nation's population.[36]

Much of this growth was related to industrial expansion. By 1930, Santiago could boast 28 percent of the nation's industry (and by 1980 it would have 56 percent).[37] It was in the 1930s that one of Chile's most notable industrialists, Juan Yarur Lolas, established Chile's largest and most modern cotton mill in Santiago, providing the base for the family's substantial fortune. Early in the decade, tens of thousands of unemployed workers from the mining regions of the North, along with numerous others from the impoverished South, had migrated to the capital, as they had throughout the 1920s, in search of jobs in the growing industrial sector.[38]

Data from the 1940 census show the dominance of the Province of Santiago in terms of its share of particular groups. These included 43 percent of those who worked in manufacturing, 39 percent of those in commerce, 42 percent of those in hotel and personal services, 38 percent of those in public service, and 39 percent of those in domestic service. Gender differences were also pronounced, with few females in construction and building (367 of 22,497) and transportation and communication (1,489 of 22,280), but with significant numbers in manufacturing (39,768 of 128,255) and hotel and personal services (12,420 of 25,096), and a respectable proportion in commerce (14,587 of 64,031) and public services (28,299 of 84,183). Females were most prominent in the domestic service sector, with 54,848 of the total 58,337.[39]

Table 4 provides a more detailed analysis of the social structure of Greater Santiago, gleaned from data on several hundred occupations for 1945. Overall, the proportions of the working class, middle class, and upper class remained about as they were earlier. As before, the numbers also reveal some interesting information about the status of women in Santiago. Reflecting the information on general categories for 1940 noted above, 40,797 female domestic servants accounted for the large number of women in the menial and unskilled category. The largest single group in this category, however, were *jornaleros* (day-laborers), with 42,765 men and 11,939 women.

TABLE 4. *Social Structure of Greater Santiago*
by Occupational Category and Gender, 1945

	Male	Female	Total	%
Working class				
Unskilled and menial	45,670	59,623	105,293	27.2
Semiskilled service	28,882	31,579	60,461	15.6
Rural semiskilled	2,216	172	2,388	0.6
Skilled	66,120	12,492	78,612	20.3
Middle class				
Rural skilled	584	59	643	—
Low non-manual	42,279	12,766	55,045	14.2
Middle unspecified non-manual	25,449	7,311	32,760	8.5
Upper class				
High non-manual	4,836	4,168	9,004	2.3
Low professional	6,669	2,641	9,310	2.4
High professional	8,164	4,750	12,914	3.3
Miscellaneous	14,118	6,405	20,523	5.3
Total	244,987	141,966	386,953	

SOURCE: Chile, Dirección de Estadística y Censos, *Chile: XI censo de población* (1940), 399–409.

Women also predominated among *lavanderos* (laundry workers), with 6,528 to only 111 males in this category. In the unskilled category, women were most prominent as *cocineros* (cooks), with 6,699 as opposed to 477 males; and all the 11,476 *costureras* (seamstresses) and 7,417 *modistas* (dressmakers) were women.

Males dominated the skilled worker category, especially among those involved in construction. There were relatively few women in the middle-class occupational categories, although they were 7,275 of 32,505 *comerciantes*, and 9,684 of the 35,255 *oficinistas* (clerks). At the upper levels, their numbers were still relatively small among white-collar professionals, with only 100 lawyers out of 1,504, 21 architects out of 575, and 143 physicians out of 1,499. They were, however, 168 of 644 dentists. They also dominated some of the professions listed in categories eight through ten, including 425 of 616 pharmacists, 2,358 of 2,593 nurses, and 4,329 of 6,123 teachers. Women were also well represented among those who identified themselves as artists of various types, including 7 female cinema artists, 31 of 66 radio artists, and 44 of 102 theater artists. Less glamorously, they also totally dominated such occupations as manicurist (105) and prostitute (310). In sum, while women had made some advances at the higher levels, they still were a relatively small minority among the most prestigious professions.

BUILDING IN SANTIAGO HAD CONTINUED APACE. Visiting the capital in August 1931, the French writer André Siegfried had commented unfavorably on the dozen or so skyscrapers that "now break the harmonious outline of the low-built city." Arguing that they "serve no useful purpose," he had also questioned whether they ever would be completed, given the economic crisis at that time.[40] In fact, as previously mentioned, thanks to government tax policy, Santiago experienced something of a building boom in the 1930s. The most prominent project was the construction of the Barrio Cívico, intended to house government ministries in uniform eight-story, square, concrete-veneered structures. The project, which began in 1932 and was completed in 1938, was one of the few projects in the Brunner plan to be fully realized. Reactions to the buildings have varied over time. Visiting Santiago as part of a larger tour of Latin American cities in the early 1940s, the U.S. urban planner Francis Violich called the Barrio Cívico "the finest grouping of public buildings to be found in Latin America, in that it achieves dignity without monumentality."[41] Simon Collier and William Sater, however, describe the complex, perhaps more accurately, as composed of "uninspiring gray slabs that still surround the Moneda."[42] Whatever its merits or flaws, the Barrio Cívico was part of a major transformation of the downtown area along the Alameda and contributed to the further expansion of nearby streets and plazas, especially to the south.[43]

Another important building of the period, completed in 1934, was the Hotel Carrera at Teatinos 160. Facing the Plaza Constitución on the north side of the Alameda, it was built in a "functional" style and featured, on its second floor, decorations by Luis Meléndez done in black crystal and depicting native themes. Upon its opening, it became Santiago's most luxurious and most expensive hotel. According to The South American Handbook of 1941, the hotel had a total of 300 beds, and rates for rooms ranged from 60 to 140 pesos a night, as compared with its closest competitor, the Hotel Crillón at Agustinas 1025, which had 128 beds ranging from 50 to 80 pesos per night.[44] To the northeast, just across the Pius IX bridge, the new law school of the University of Chile, with its dramatic curved facade and large glass windows, had been completed in 1938. In that same year, work was also finished on the national soccer stadium in nearby Nuñoa. Another major public works project, completed in late 1940, was the railroad tunnel connecting the Estación Yungay with the Estación Central, moving underground the surface line that had run down Avenida Matucana and which had caused so many accidents and complaints.

As usual, there were mixed reactions to the construction over these years. El Mercurio, for example, looked with favor on some of the modern constructions going up around the Parque Forestal, especially some of the apartment buildings done in the then popular art deco style. In an editorial in 1935, it lauded the many up-to-date features of the new residential and commercial structures that were changing the city's skyline, complete with elevators, central heating, garbage incinerators, "and a thousand more details that make these buildings pleasant and agreeable." The same editorial noted, however, that much of the new construction was limited to a radius of about six blocks out from the Plaza de Armas and that vast sectors of the city, especially to the north and south, were not receiving the same attention and benefits.[45] Three years later, another editorial made much the same point, describing the southwestern neighborhoods as having "tragic characteristics" and the densely populated Recoleta and Independencia districts north of the Mapocho as generally abandoned and neglected by public officials and private entrepreneurs alike.[46]

Articles in Zig-Zag reflected similar ambiguities. One contributor, for example, lamented the fact that "old Santiago is disappearing," overwhelmed by the "blind and enslaving tide of cruel time."[47] Another described Santiago as a "complex of urban problems," among which was "the formation of neighborhoods that were developed without any method, without any municipal control, without any vision of the future." This same author underscored the influence of a disciple of Le Corbusier on the rationalist architectural style that had come to characterize much of the new building in Santiago in the 1930s and 1940s, as had been the case in Buenos Aires.[48] Also as in Buenos Aires, Santiago by the early 1940s was what another observer called a "tumult" of architectural styles, where one often found modern, concrete, multistory buildings towering over adobe colonial residences "lightly covered with powder over their facades to hide their years."[49] On the other hand, new building regulations in the 1930s had served to produce some harmony and uniformity in certain areas of the downtown commercial district. Various blocks along San Antonio, Mac Iver, Bandera, Morandé, and Teatinos, for example, saw the construction of new buildings of more or less the same style and height, the results of which are still very evident.[50]

As in most cities, the continued rapid growth of Santiago created new problems while many of the old ones remained or were exacerbated. There were numerous complaints, for example, of overcrowding in the downtown area, making it difficult for pedestrians to progress along sidewalks and streets, a problem aggravated by the inadequate and overburdened public transportation system. Moreover, as more people moved farther from the center where they worked, the increased use of private automobiles for commuting added to the problems of congestion and parking. The growth in the number of taller buildings in the center also meant less light and air circulating, underscoring the relative lack of open, green spaces in the capital's center. Moreover, while progress had been made on many fronts in preparation for the four-hundredth anniversary celebration in early 1941, the main entrances to the city still left much to be desired, especially in terms of the impression they made on first-time visitors. The entrance into Mapocho Station by train remained a journey through run-down neighborhoods and past abandoned buildings along a river bank that housed many vagrants in makeshift structures. The poorly planned plaza in front of the station often put recent arrivals at risk of life and limb as they made their way through confusing traffic patterns to the nearest streetcar or bus stop. The ride from the airport at Los Cerrillos to the downtown obliged the visitor to travel through streets lined with "rustic dwellings and miserable shacks" and to pass through "really ugly neighborhoods."[51]

Perhaps the most notable and persistent problem was the need to provide adequate housing for a burgeoning population. There were a number of private and public initiatives in this regard. In the late 1930s, for example, construction had begun on a revitalized area just south of the Plaza Italia and east of the Avenida Vicuña Mackenna, with residences in a wide range of prices.[52] At the same time, plans were announced to construct "a beautiful residential neighborhood" in Bellavista, north of the Mapocho, on the site of a former orphanage.[53] In addition, the national government, through the Caja de Habitación Popular (Popular Housing Fund), created in 1936, stimulated the construction of some public-housing projects to supplement those created earlier. Francis Violich called the nation's effort in this regard "the most effective and the best administered program in Latin America." He was favorably impressed by several of these, including the Población Pedro Montt, close to the Yarur cotton mill, and the Población Vivaceta, the largest in Santiago. Vivaceta housed six hundred families, who paid rents that ranged from 170 pesos (the peso was at 31 to the dollar) to 300 pesos a month.[54] Nationwide, between 1938 and 1941, the Caja had constructed 3,650 houses for 25,450 inhabitants. While this was a notable effort for a chronically underfunded agency, it still represented only the barest beginnings of an attack on one of the nation's and the capital's most glaring deficiencies.[55]

In Santiago, conventillos continued to house tens of thousands. In 1937, as part of a larger study, the city's statistical office had located 194 conventillos in a triangular twenty-nine-block area enclosed by Avenidas Bulnes, Independencia, and Borgoño, just north of Mapocho Station. According to the survey, overcrowding meant that two or three persons in each room shared one bed, and services were such that in many conventillos running water was available for only three hours a day. These conditions, the office concluded, were widespread throughout the city.[56] A few years later, Violich reported that the city's statistical office estimated that almost half of Santiago's population lived in conventillos.[57] And despite municipal regulations and attempts to improve these residences that dated from the beginning of the century, little progress had been made.

SANTIAGO CONTINUED TO HOST A VARIETY of foreign visitors in these years. Among them were various distinguished personalities from the United States. These included Yale historian Samuel F. Bemis, who lectured on the Monroe Doctrine in 1938; Nelson Rockefeller, who visited in 1942 in his capacity as director of the State Department's Office of the Coordinator of Inter-American Affairs; and Vice-President Henry Wallace, the highest-ranking U.S. official to visit Chile up to that time, whose stay in March 1943 received extensive press coverage. Receiving as much if not more attention were several Hollywood figures, including the actors Clark Gable, Errol Flynn, Lew Ayres, and Douglas Fairbanks, as well as the director Walt Disney. Although Fairbanks came as a "special ambassador" of the Good Neighbor Policy, all these visits were intended to promote Hollywood's growing dominance of the Latin American cinema scene, with Chile being no exception. Part of the "fever of construction" in downtown Santiago in these years included several modern movie theaters, which, with their "capricious facades," served to break some of the architectural uniformity of the period.[58] Visiting in the 1940s, the journalist Carleton Beals highlighted the Real Cinema at Compañía 1040 across from the City Hotel as one of the "fashionable" and "elegant" movie houses in the capital, and one where the relatively few but high-quality Chilean films could be viewed.[59] *The South American Handbook* for 1941 listed the Real, the Central, the Cervantes, the Santa Lucía (all of which were still in operation in the year 2000) "and many others" among the theatres and cinemas of Santiago.[60]

In addition to the visits of important individuals, in 1941 large groups of foreigners visited Chile to attend such special events as the four-hundredth anniversary celebration in February, the Second Inter-American Congress of Municipalities in September, and a eucharistic congress at the end of the year. One of those in attendance at the Municipal Congress was Buenos Aires parks director Carlos Thays, who expressed his pleasure with the advances that had been made in developing San Cristóbal, whose potential he had recognized in an earlier visit. Nonetheless, he also did not hesitate to make recommendations for further improvements there and in some of the other city parks and avenues.[61]

Most foreign visitors continued to have very favorable views of Chile's capital. U.S. author Waldo Frank described Santiago as "a lovely town . . . [where] the near heights of the Andes, liquid green beneath the sky, pour a cool radiance upon the city. . . . The river [Mapocho] flashes like a quickened glacier between haughty houses which strive to be unaware of the Andean invasion."[62] Another positive impression was provided by Peruvian Aprista Luis Alberto Sánchez, who spent more than a decade in Chile. He later fondly recalled the bohemian life of Santiago, commenting favorably on the atmosphere to be found in cafés, bars, and parks. He remarked, in particular, on the "Posada del Corregidor," a restaurant-café located in one of the city's oldest buildings, a two-story colonial structure at Esmeralda 732 on the small plaza of the same name near the corner of Mac Iver. There, he said, wine and *sangría*, among other drinks, were always "abundant."[63] Another longtime foreign resident, Claude Bowers, the U.S. ambassador from 1939 to 1953, called the Posada "the one unique restaurant of Santiago . . . , which only the more adventurous in search of color are apt to visit today."[64]

There were others who remarked on what they considered the active social life in Santiago. Writing for the *New York Times* in an article set to coincide with the four-hundredth anniversary celebration, Lyn Smith observed that, "because Chileans like to 'eat, drink, and be merry,' despite hard times, Santiago boasts a gay night life and luxurious clubs such as the Club Hípico, with the snow-capped Cordillera forming the background for racetracks, gardens and lagoons, and the Golf Club Los Leones, Prince of Wales Country Club and Stade Francais."[65] A little later, the U.S. travel writer Erna Fergusson described the period between tea-time (*once*) and dinner at around 9 p.m. as when Santiago's streets "are at their giddiest." She was particularly enthusiastic about Chilean cuisine: "Dinner is a joy, for Chile dines on the best of everything. Crustaceans from Robinson Crusoe's isle, tender oysters and small lobsters of a delicacy unequaled, crabs and shrimps; Chile's special conger eel, *congrio*, and dozens of other fish. Even opulent Buenos Aires advertises Chile's seafood as the rarest treat. Fowl and meat are good, but fish and shellfish are superlative. And served with just the right white wine— dry and smooth and nutty—every Chilean dinner is a banquet."[66]

As with most foreign visitors, Beals and Fergusson found the Plaza de Armas still to be "the city's heart." On the south side of the plaza, as Beals wrote, could be found, "under the arches . . . numerous curb drinking and eating stands that give these parts of the plaza something of the appearance of a busy Eastern bazaar. Here at *once* . . . the passageway is jam packed with clerks and shoppers taking their afternoon repast standing up."[67] Describing the same area, Fergusson added that "for those who lunch more elegantly there is the remarkable Chez Henri, where everything is of the best, exquisitely served, and as immaculate as few of Santiago's eating-places are."[68] In the year 2000, the south side of the plaza still contained much of the character that Beals and Fergusson had noted, and Chez Henri was still open for business, although perhaps somewhat less "remarkable" than it had been in the 1940s.

Both Fergusson and Beals provided vivid portraits of the Vega Municipal, north of the downtown area and the Mapocho, as a place where bargaining was practically a competitive sport.

Fergusson had little to say about the area south of the Alameda. Beals, however, characterized it as "filled with typical middle-class dwellings." He also described Avenidas Prat and San Diego, main north-south thorough-fares, as bustling with commercial activity, much as had earlier accounts of this neighborhood. "Here," he said, "are knockdown household goods, low-cost clothing, cheap furniture, junk shops, secondhand book stores, poor wine taverns, cubbyhole restaurants, ratty old hotels, sometimes a frowzy female in the doorway."[69]

The Alameda itself continued as the city's main east-west axis. Parts of it had been modified in these years, especially around the Barrio Cívico. Several observers noted, however, that the major change to the Alameda was the marked decline in the number of Santiaguinos who used it for casual strolling, largely due to the significant increase in vehicular traffic. Stephen Clissold asserted that by the late 1940s "the motor traffic which fills the Alameda with its fumes and its raucous anarchy has killed the habit of the *paseo*. No one walks today in the Alameda for pleasure." This was a condition, one might add, which became even more pronounced as the decades progressed.[70]

Most observers continued to remark favorably on the capital's parks and gardens. Santa Lucía and the Parque Forestal, which was gradually being extended in a strip of new parks eastward along the southern bank of the Mapocho, were often singled out for praise. Beals called the Forestal "one of the notable public recreation gardens of the world [and] . . . in spite of being so near the center of the city . . . an unusually quiet retreat."[71] Clissold wrote, however, that "this park [Forestal] changes in aspect according to the hour of the day or night, like the successive scenes on a stage." Although a haven for students, nursemaids and children, and hand-holding couples in the daylight, "at the dead of night, it is a beat for prostitutes and a dormitory for tramps."[72]

Descriptions of the Parque Cousiño were mixed. Beals claimed that Cousiño Park was "the chief playground for the whole city, frequented by all classes," while Bowers wrote that "the once favored Cousiño Park now seems to be dreaming of more gaudy days."[73] The Chilean author Benjamín Subercaseaux agreed with Bowers that the Parque Cousiño had lost much of its previous luster, due in part, he argued, to the demands placed on it by making it the centerpiece of the centennial celebrations of 1910 and the subsequent neglect, something that from time to time preoccupied the municipality. Moreover, he added, "today, no park can be aristocratic, because the 'nice people' of Santiago have lost their taste for strolls. They live distressedly in a slothful moroseness which is one symbol of their decadence."[74] Perhaps more to the point, the "aristocracy" was increasingly moving eastward into Providencia, Los Leones, Las Condes, and beyond, thereby making Cousiño Park for them much less centrally located than it once had been.

Most foreign observers who published their impressions of Santiago continued to comment on the contrasts between rich and poor in the capital. Beals, as could be expected of one with his leftist sympathies, wrote of the many *conventillos* and other slumlike dwellings in various parts of the city. "La Chimba," for example, "north of the Mapocho River, except for fine residences and apartments along its banks, is mostly a factory and workmen's section and contains the worst remaining slums." The same could be said, he wrote, for the rest of the area along Avenida Independencia to the Hippodrome, as well as that northwest of the Quinta Normal.[75] One of the most compelling pictures of these contrasts was provided by Clissold, who described a settlement of some five thousand souls who lived on the banks of the Mapocho near the aristocratic district of El Golf, a place "whose very wretchedness and unfitness for buildings is the best guarantee that the squatters will not be evicted." Many of these squatters, who formerly had found refuge under the bridges that spanned the Mapocho, made their living by providing the sand "to make cement for houses in which they can never aspire to live.... [For them,] life is a constant struggle against want and shortages which one would expect to find only in the war-devastated lands of Europe."[76]

Chilean novelists also continued to portray these contrasts. Joaquín Edwards Bello, who had so effectively written about the capital's lower classes in *El Roto*, provided an equally telling portrait of the city's upper classes enjoying the "high life" of Santiago in his *La chica del Crillón*, published in the 1930s. Continuing along the lines of *El Roto*, Alberto Romero wrote evocatively of life in Santiago's slums in *La viuda del conventillo*, published in 1930. A similar treatment was provided by Nicomedes Guzmán in his *La sangre y la esperanza*, published in 1943, which described the trials and tribulations of a working-class family living in a *conventillo* near the Central Station. This fictional story was set within a realistic framework of union organization and strike activity as well as detailed depictions of the city's poorer districts.[77]

EACH OBSERVER, FOREIGN OR CHILEAN, had a different overall assessment of the nation's capital city. Clissold had the most negative view. In contrast to Frank, he described Santiago as "a large but unlovely city," where "one can search in vain through the monotonous maze of its streets for a touch of the picturesque" and "there is little beauty or originality to be found, almost no building of historical interest for the earnest sightseer to seek out." Moreover, he wrote, "it is aesthetically and architecturally undistinguished . . . noisy and incredibly dusty." Referring to what many observed as the Santiaguinos' and Chileans' phlegmatic manner, he also commented that "there is bustle and hurry in the streets, but no sense of gay vivacity." Moreover, in contrast with Buenos Aires, "there are no spacious open-air cafés where you can drop in to rest from the hubbub and yet still keep the feel of the pulsing life of the street."[78]

Bowers was less critical, but believed that in its rush to modernize, Santiago was, in his words, a "city that snubs the past." "Today," he wrote, "it seems a strangely modern city, and, unlike Lima, which preserves and exploits its colonial treasures, Santiago, with a truly Yankee disregard for yesterday and living intensely for today, has wiped out most of the monuments of the past, and where a colorful colonial residence once stood, an apartment or office building has been raised." The downtown section, "with its high office buildings of concrete reinforced with steel . . . resembles that of any large city in the United States."[79] For Bowers, the real charm of Santiago could be found more in its parks and unique residential neighborhoods than in its downtown core.

For Subercaseaux, who undoubtedly knew Santiago best, the capital was "a strange city, profoundly original." He, too, remarked on how dusty it was, and added that because of its particular design it "lacks the comfort of intimacy." Despite "its apparent simplicity," he continued, Santiago "is a chaos of sensations and variegated vistas. . . . A contradictory city par excellence, it has a difficult personality which generally discourages those endeavoring to pin it down and makes them give up their task." The key to understanding Santiago, he argued, was to conceive of it as an agglomeration of discrete neighborhoods rather than a coherent metropolis, where "each neighborhood is a small village and its inhabitants seem to forget that they belong collectively to a larger group." "This local life of the neighborhood," he concluded, "explains many things which we cannot understand at first: for example, the lack of a community life in a great city; its sad, deserted aspect at night; finally, its lack of love and collective amusement."[80]

Beals, who knew Latin America well, had a more positive view than most. "The people of Santiago," he wrote, "especially in these later years, have taken great pride in their unique metropolis and seem determined not only to have it match the grandeur of nature but to make it correspond to all the requirements of modernity, to wipe out all slums and unsightliness and make it one of the world's most beautiful metropolises. Always a handsome city, it promises to become, in the not distant future, one of the real showplaces of the Americas, with the mighty snow mountains towering in the background, visible down every boulevard, through every break in the buildings. By nature, Santiago is dramatic and spectacular; the setting is grandiose."[81]

This vision of Santiago as a city that matches its natural surroundings is one that has driven local and national officials from the time of its founding to the dawn of the twenty-first century. While many would argue that this vision has yet to be realized, the fact that Beals considered it within reach by the 1940s is a testimony to the many efforts expended in that direction up to that time, efforts in which the local government, with all its flaws, helped play a major role.

Conclusion

BOTH BUENOS AIRES AND SANTIAGO grew dramatically in the first four decades of the twentieth century. Unlike Buenos Aires, foreign immigration played a relatively minor role in Santiago's growth, which was driven primarily by internal migration. Both cities began the twentieth century with what James R. Scobie labeled a "commercial-bureaucratic" character, but over time, industrial concentration and expansion in and around the respective capitals, especially in the 1930s and into the 1940s, did much to change these cities and served as an important magnet for internal migration to the metropolitan area. Among the most important changes were the emergence to prominence of new social-economic groups, especially the urban middle and working classes. Developments in these decades reinforced the primacy of both capitals, producing resistance and resentment from other cities and regions in both countries with regard to the inequitable concentration of power and resources that these main urban centers attracted.

As with most large cities, Santiago and Buenos Aires faced similar problems and challenges. These included the need to provide basic services—lighting and electrification, sewers and sanitation, drinkable water, paved streets, garbage collection—and to regulate citizens' behavior and the pattern and pace of growth, as well as many aspects of the physical construction of the city. In both capitals, too, the contrast between rich and poor and the services they received was striking, although perhaps more pronounced in Santiago than in Buenos Aires.[1] Many commented on what appeared to be and often was an inequitable distribution of resources and attention within the respective capitals that favored the well-to-do and the downtown area and neglected the poorer sections, often on the outskirts and fringes, although often, too, not that far from the city's heart.

In both cities, an ever-growing group of homegrown architects and city planners tried to address the problems of urban growth. Both capitals, too, contracted foreign experts to provide advice and to draw up overall plans for urban development. For the most part, in both cases, these elaborate and ambitious designs remained just that, although there were occasional results, such as the Barrio Cívico in Santiago and various avenues, parks, and neighborhoods in Buenos Aires.

Foreign models and inspirations were important in both capitals. Santiago's leaders often looked to Buenos Aires with admiration and not a little envy, and developments there were frequently monitored and referred to as the Chilean capital struggled with similar problems and issues, ranging from the form and composition of local government to how to deal with complex public transportation issues. Santiago's leaders also looked to other South American capitals, such as to Montevideo for the construction of garbage incinerators and to Lima for the establishment of "popular" restaurants, but Buenos Aires, at least for this period, seemed the most influential example to emulate. The reverse, however, was not true. The leaders of Argentina's capital made scant mention of Santiago and continued to look to Europe and the United States for metropolitan centers by which to measure Buenos Aires.

In these decades, both capitals experienced significant growth in their surrounding suburbs. While not the direct responsibility of the local administration, this growth had obvious implications for these authorities when it came to such matters as extending basic services outward and when it came to trying to regulate and coordinate various forms of transportation, which increasingly crossed jurisdictional lines on a daily basis. Structurally, Santiago had an advantage in this regard in that the provincial *intendente* had a certain administrative authority over both the capital and its surrounding *comunas*, while in Buenos Aires the federal district was under one set of officials and the surrounding suburbs under the authority of separate provincial authorities. Despite this advantage, beginning in the 1920s, it became increasingly the practice for the *alcaldes* of Santiago and its immediate surrounding suburbs to meet on a fairly regular basis to discuss and try to deal with common problems. In both cases, the need to address matters with the entire metropolitan region in mind became more and more evident as the greatest population growth increasingly occurred outside the immediate boundaries of the respective capitals.

Municipal politics and government played important roles in both cities. In both, they reflected and contributed to larger national developments. In both, politicians wrestled with many similar issues, including the city's relationship with a foreign-owned streetcar company and the need to regulate and control other means of public transportation. While the details differed, in both cases city officials were able to keep fares for these services from increasing, or at least increasing at the rate the owners desired. In both, the struggle with the streetcar company, in particular, saw the early emergence of economic nationalism directed against the operations of a powerful foreign enterprise, a sentiment that ultimately led to state acquisition of the streetcar systems in both capitals.

There were other issues common to both. How to control and regulate—and eventually eliminate—*conventillos* was a joint concern, with the problem more widespread and persistent in Santiago than in Buenos Aires. Problems related to the availability, price, and distribution of food and other basic necessities was another shared preoccupation, although more frequent and of more concern in Santiago than in Buenos Aires, the capital city of one of the world's leading agricultural producers. Issues of public health, especially the prevalence of alcoholism, recurring epidemic diseases, and high rates of infant mortality, while shared to some extent, also seemed more pronounced and more serious in Santiago than in Buenos Aires. In this, as in other areas, Buenos Aires had an advantage of which Santiago's leaders often complained, it being the capital of a wealthier nation and with more financial resources at its command to deal with these kinds of problems than did its western neighbor.

In terms of the form and function of local politics and government, both capitals were fundamentally similar. Both were governed by elected city councils, in the case of Buenos Aires by a Consejo Deliberante (Deliberative Council) and for Santiago the Municipalidad (Municipality), although there was a brief interruption of this form of governance in Buenos Aires in the early 1930s and a longer hiatus in Santiago with the *juntas de vecinos* and *juntas de alcaldes* between 1924 and 1935. Both councils were presided over by local executives, *alcaldes* in the case of Santiago and *intendentes* in the case of Buenos Aires, who corresponded to the mayors of European and North American cities.

Within this basically similar framework, however, there were some notable differences. At the beginning of the twentieth century, Buenos Aires was governed by a city council of twenty-two elected councilmen, chosen for four-year terms, with half elected every two years, and a presidentially appointed *intendente*, confirmed by the National Senate for a three-year term that could be renewed. A reform that became effective in 1918 increased the council to thirty members but retained the appointed *intendente*. That reform also extended the vote to foreigners and significantly increased the size of the electorate. While turnout in local contests was generally lower than for national elections, as was the case in Santiago, it was still respectable, at about 65 percent in the 1920s and 75 percent in the 1930s.

For Santiago, the story was more complicated. After the municipal autonomy law of 1891, the municipality was expanded from twenty-five to thirty *regidores*, with *alcaldes* elected by and from their ranks. Reforms some two decades later reduced the council to thirteen members and also reduced the size of the electorate, although *alcaldes* were still chosen in the same fashion. During the *juntas de vecinos* and, briefly, the *juntas de alcaldes*, of the 1924–35 period, the number of council members fluctuated from two to thirteen, and all were appointed by the national government. As a result of the reforms that went into effect in 1935, the elected municipality was restored, with fifteen *regidores* elected, as they had been in the past, for three-year terms. In addition, after 1935, as in Buenos Aires, the *alcalde* was appointed by the president of the republic. But, unlike Buenos Aires, women were given the vote, and women were also eligible to be elected to and serve on the city council. Extending the vote to women had been considered in Buenos Aires and actively promoted by Argentina's Socialist Party but was not realized until the late 1940s. The role of women, as voters, *regidoras*, and as *alcaldesa*, is one of the most striking differences between the experiences of the two capitals.

In both cities, a wide range of political parties representing a wide range of interests and constituencies competed actively and energetically for positions on the respective city councils. Several of these parties reflected and represented the changing social and economic forces and groups in their respective cities. The Radicals in both cities were the principal advocates of the emerging middle classes, while the Socialists (and in Santiago, the Democrats as well, at least earlier on) spoke for the urban working classes. In general terms, Radicals and Conservatives in both cases were prominent throughout the period under consideration, with consistent and significant participation in almost every council. From time to time, too, representatives of the Far Left and the Far Right won council seats in both cities. In Buenos Aires, however, Argentina's Socialist Party played a more consistently important role and had a larger representation on the city council than its various counterparts, Democrats and Socialists, in Santiago. On the other hand, there was no Socialist *intendente* in Buenos Aires during this period, as was the case with Santiago's *alcaldesa* and the subsequent *alcalde* in the late 1930s and early 1940s. Whatever these differences, party competition, often complex, lively, and aggressive, and especially competition to reward supporters with city jobs, was a common ingredient in the local governments of both capitals.

The overall political context clearly had a significant impact on the similarities and differences noted. In Argentina, electoral reform in 1912 spelled the end of a long period of conservative oligarchical dominance and the beginning of a democratic experiment that commenced with the election of Radical Hipólito Yrigoyen as president in 1916. That experiment was seriously interrupted but not totally derailed by a military coup in 1930 that overthrew Yrigoyen (who was reelected overwhelmingly in 1928) and initiated a conservative restoration wherein elections were held but considerable fraud and coercion prevailed. During what was called Argentina's "infamous decade" of the 1930s, while the Buenos Aires city council did not exactly cover itself in glory in a scandal-ridden period, it did help to sustain and strengthen some of the democratic momentum at the local level that had been stalled and weakened at the national level.

In Chile, the period of reform between 1910 and 1915 and the first election of Arturo Alessandri in 1920 can be seen to offer some parallels with developments in Argentina. Military intervention in 1924 and 1925 and the Ibáñez regime, however, offer strong contrasts, although they perhaps foreshadowed some of the events in Argentina in the 1930s, as well as the populist regime of Juan Perón in the 1940s and 1950s. The second Alessandri administration (1932–38) was, like its counterpart in Argentina for the same years under Agustín P. Justo, conservative and primarily concerned with re-covering from the effects of the Depression. While working to promote industrial development and greater economic independence, both of these regimes made some concessions to foreign interests that provoked strong nationalist responses. In the case of Alessandri, the Ross-Calder agreement of 1935 stands out, whereas in Argentina Justo negotiated the infamous Roca-Runciman pact of 1933 that seemed to underscore and deepen that na-tion's dependence on Great Britain as well as encouraging the develop-ment of a transport corporation and a new electric power contract in 1936 that also seemed to favor foreign interests. Generally, however, the second Alessandri administration was more democratic than Justo's and initiated the changes in municipal elections and governance that took effect in 1935. The victory of the Popular Front in 1938 had no equivalent in Argentina, and this development, of course, allowed Pedro Aguirre Cerda in 1939 to ap-point the first *alcaldesa* and Socialist to lead Santiago.

With regard to the social class backgrounds of city council members in both capitals, the patterns seem similar. Most *regidores* of the Conserva-tive and Liberal Parties of Chile were from the upper class and were usu-ally university-educated professionals, with lawyers predominating. The Radicals also had *regidores* from well-to-do families and a fair number of university-trained professionals, again with lawyers prominent, but as in Argentina, over time, more of that party were from the emerging middle class and with a wider range of occupational backgrounds. Quite a few, too, were veterans of student political battles. Democratic and Socialist *regidores* included both middle-class professionals as well as some from working-class backgrounds, with the Socialists also numbering some former student ac-tivists within their ranks. In both cases, a significant number of those elected to the city government eventually moved up the ladder to positions in the National Congress.

As in Buenos Aires, appointed *intendentes* in Santiago were generally from the upper class and usually had considerable administrative experience and occasional distinction prior to taking office. Even during the period of the *juntas de vecinos*, however, Santiago's *alcaldes* rarely had an easy time of it, fre-quently coming into conflict with members of either *juntas* or councils and often forced to resign well before their terms were due to expire. Such conflicts were certainly not absent in Buenos Aires, but frequent executive turnover was less common. During the years from 1891 to 1924 in Santiago, when *regidores* elected *alcaldes* from their own ranks, executives suffered from some of the inherent constraints and structural weaknesses previously described. During the period of the *juntas de vecinos*, between 1924 and 1927, *alcaldes* often succumbed to the shifting changes in national power and to the internal maneuvering of the Ibáñez regime thereafter. From the mid-1930s to the early 1940s, *alcaldes* often had to deal with fluid and uncertain majorities within the council, which ultimately weakened their overall position and led to stalemate and resignation. The greater prominence of coalition politics in Chile as opposed to Argentina also played a part in the greater turnover and instability of *alcaldes* there.

Another common feature of the history of local politics and government in both Buenos Aires and Santiago in these decades was the frequent occurrence of scandals of one kind or another. Generally, these seem to have been more serious and of a grander scale in the Argentine capital than in the Chilean case, especially those of 1936 involving the renegotiation of the electric power contract. In 1941, a scandal involving bribes from bus owners to council members led the national government to dissolve the municipal government of Buenos Aires altogether. There were no such developments in Chile, perhaps again because the overall national context was different. Whether large or small, these scandals did little to enhance the reputation and image of local government in either capital. According to various press reports, the general public in both Buenos Aires and Santiago often viewed the municipal administration as corrupt, inefficient, and increasingly irrelevant as the respective national governments absorbed more and more of the city councils' duties and increasingly limited their authority.

The poor image of local government prompted various efforts at reform. For the most part, these failed to produce the results the reformers envisioned and often deepened the disillusionment with democratically elected local administrations. In the case of Santiago, some argued that the city's greatest progress had occurred under the appointed *juntas de alcaldes* and *juntas de vecinos*. However, even these institutions were not free of partisan division and occasional scandal. While it is true that Santiago enjoyed one of its most dynamic periods of growth in the latter part of the 1920s under the *juntas*, there, as elsewhere, the boom in urban growth turned to bust with the Great Depression and the subsequent political turmoil of the early

1930s. Not to discount the importance of local leadership, this experience suggests that overall conditions of political stability and healthy economic growth are clearly vital factors in the expansion and modernization of any large city. When these conditions are favorable, the city flourishes and local officials bask in the credit, and when they are not, the reverse is true. The local government, too, is only one factor in the equation. If the private sector is unable or unwilling to contribute its share, then urban expansion and improvement suffers, regardless of the form of local administration. In sum, the historical record for the period under study does not lead inescapably to the conclusion that more can be accomplished under an authoritarian local administration than under one that is more popularly chosen.

At the time this book was written, the choice between an appointed as opposed to an elected local government for Santiago seemed, at least for the moment, moot. For most of the twentieth century, the capital's chief executives were appointed by the president of the republic, sometimes serving with an elected council and sometimes not. Beginning in the 1990s, however, and reflecting a trend that could be found in Buenos Aires, Mexico City, and elsewhere, reforms were instituted to make the selection of both the city council and the *alcalde* more democratic.[2] One of the arguments against the election of the *alcalde* had been that it would be difficult for a mayor of the national capital, with its special relationship to the national government, to accomplish much if he or she were a member of a party in opposition to the president. In the past, *alcaldes* were either of the governing party or of the governing coalition. Even that, of course, did not guarantee success.[3] Nonetheless, it at least strengthened the odds of productive collaboration. The trend toward elected mayors has produced the results that skeptics feared. In the late 1990s, in both Buenos Aires and Mexico City, the movement from appointed to elected chief executives produced in the former Fernando de la Rúa and in the latter Cuauhtémoc Cárdenas, both belonging to parties in opposition to those in power. The same disjuncture currently prevails in Santiago, with Conservative Joaquín Lavín serving as the elected *alcalde*, while the man who barely defeated him for the presidency, Socialist Ricardo Lagos, serves as president. Just how this new dynamic will play out remains to be seen.

In conclusion, while there was much in the history of the local governments of Santiago and Buenos Aires to justify a popular image of an often fractious and ineffective municipal administration, that image should not be allowed to overshadow the sincere and serious efforts of many at the level of local government to try to direct urban growth in a humane, rational, and progressive manner, efforts that have been ongoing throughout the twentieth century and into the twenty-first. Whatever their many flaws and weaknesses, these various administrations were not entirely bereft of good intentions and not entirely lacking in accomplishments. If nothing else, they provided an experience in and a certain continuity for democratic institutions and practices that emerged with renewed vigor in both nations in the 1980s and 1990s. A study of their respective histories also offers examples both to be emulated and to be avoided as future governments in both capitals continue to wrestle with the many and complex challenges of governing their nations' most important cities.

Notes

CHAPTER ONE

1. For a description of Chile's "crazy geography," see Subercaseaux, *Chile*.

2. Scobie, "The Growth of Cities," 165.

3. For a general review of Santiago's growth that stresses the role of architects, both foreign and domestic, in the city's development, see Bannen Lanta, *Santiago de Chile*. This collaborative effort also includes a very good selection of photographs and maps.

4. As of the year 2000, the Central Station was still in operation for some commuter trains and a greatly reduced southern service, no longer extending, as it once did, to Puerto Montt. There is no longer a rail connection to Valparaíso, although there has been talk of restoring it, and none to Argentina by way of Los Andes to Mendoza, once one of the world's most spectacular rail journeys. The Mapocho Station from which these trains left has been converted into a cultural center.

5. For a review of these developments, see Gross, Ramón, and Vial, *Imágen ambiental de Santiago*; and Ramón, *Santiago de Chile*, 181–235.

6. The province of Santiago, including the city, had a population of 549,719 in 1907 (Mamalakis, *Historical Statistics of Chile*, 391).

7. Two important works on the Chilean agricultural sector and its problems are Bauer, *Chilean Rural Society from the Spanish Conquest to 1930*; and McBride, *Chile*.

8. A good description of the industrial growth in and around Santiago in this period is provided in DeShazo, *Urban Workers and Labor Unions in Chile*, 10–22. For the role of industrialization in the demographic growth of Santiago throughout much of the twentieth century, see Geisse, *Economía y política de la concentración urbana en Chile*.

9. Solberg, *Immigration and Nationalism*, 35.

10. República de Chile, *Censo de 1907*, 427. For more on the Jewish community, see Elkin, *The Jews of Latin America*, 35–36, 59–60. Information on the Arab community is pro-

vided in an article on the adverse reaction to it in Rebolledo Hernández, "La 'turco-fobia.' "

11. Solberg, *Immigration and Nationalism*, 37. Most of the remaining foreign-born were Bolivians and Peruvians located primarily in the northern part of the country.

12. Ibid., 52.

13. Ibid., 60.

14. Chile, Comisión Central del Censo, *Censo de 1907*, 430–31.

15. Solberg, *Immigration and Nationalism*, 63.

16. Arturo Alessandri was twice president of the republic (1920–25; 1932–38), and his son, Jorge, served as chief executive from 1958 to 1964. Eduardo Frei was president from 1964 to 1970, and his son, Eduardo, Jr., was also president from 1994 to 2000.

17. For information on Chuaqui, see Solberg, *Immigration and Nationalism*, 47; and Vial Correa, *Historia de Chile*, vol. 1, bk. 2, 734–41. For Yarur, see Winn, *Weavers of Revolution*, 13–21.

18. Walter, *Politics and Urban Growth in Buenos Aires*, 12.

19. Chile, Comisión Central del Censo, *Censo de 1907*, 430.

20. Walter, *Politics and Urban Growth in Buenos Aires*, 8.

21. Chile, Comisión Central del Censo, *Censo de 1907*, 423.

22. These occupations were organized along lines suggested by Szuchman and Sofer, "The State of Occupational Stratification Studies in Argentina."

23. DeShazo, *Urban Workers and Labor Unions in Chile*, 18.

24. Chile, Comisión Central del Censo, *Censo de 1907*, 429. The national figure is from Mamalakis, *Historical Statistics of Chile*, 142.

25. Vial Correa, *Historia de Chile*, vol. 1, bk. 2, 690.

26. DeShazo, *Urban Workers and Labor Unions in Chile*, 5–6.

27. Santiago (Chile), *Boletín de actas i documentos de la ilustre Municipalidad de Santiago, 1900*, pp. 111–28. These are the minutes of the meetings of Santiago's city government. Hereafter, they will be identified as BMS with date and page numbers.

28. DeShazo, *Urban Workers and Labor Unions in Chile*, 57–58.

29. Ramón, "Estudio de una periferia urbana," 267–70.

30. Ibid., 270–74; Vial Correa, *Historia de Chile*, vol. 1, bk. 2, 698–701.

31. Ramón, "Estudio de una periferia urbana," 264.

32. Ibid.

33. Gross, Ramón, and Vial, *Imágen ambiental de Santiago*, 20.

34. DeShazo, *Urban Workers and Labor Unions in Chile*, 56.

35. Vial Correa, *Historia de Chile*, vol. 1, bk. 2, 626.

36. For a study that underscores the interlocking nature of Chilean elite families and their diversified holdings and interests, see Zeitlin and Ratcliff, *Landlords and Capitalists*.

37. Ossandón Vicuña, *Guía de Santiago*, 104. The Palacio is still open to the public and still hosts foreign visitors.

38. Scarpaci, "Chile," 123.

39. Gross, Ramón, and Vial, *Imágen ambiental de Santiago*, 46.

40. Vial Correa, *Historia de Chile*, vol. 1, bk. 2, 661–62.

41. Ruhl, "Santiago," 139.

42. Vial Correa, *Historia de Chile*, vol. 1, bk. 2, 663.

43. DeShazo, *Urban Workers and Labor Unions in Chile*, 62.

44. Vial Correa calls this "social resentment" between the upper and middle classes "one of the most important factors of our contemporary history" (Vial Correa, *Historia de Chile*, vol. 1, bk. 2, 707). The pioneering analysis of the role of the "middle sectors" in Latin America, including Chile, is Johnson, *Political Change in Latin America*, 66–93. For more on the middle classes, see Vega, "La clase media en Chile"; and Viviani Contreras, *Sociología chilena*, 58–67.

45. "General Conditions," [Ambassador William] Collier to the Secretary of State, in U.S. Department of State, *Records of the Department of State Relating to Internal Affairs of Chile* [Record Group 59], June 5, 1925 (file number 825.00/416). Hereafter, this record group will be cited as USNA with date and file number.

46. See DeShazo, *Urban Workers and Labor Unions in Chile*, 56–64.

47. Chile, Dirección General del Trabajo, *Boletín de la Oficina del Trabajo* (1911): 117–36.

48. See DeShazo, *Urban Workers and Labor Unions in Chile*, 88–128. Other studies of the Chilean labor movement include Angell, *Politics and the Labor Movement in Chile*; and Bergquist, *Labor in Latin America*, 20–80.

49. As quoted in Gross, Ramón, and Vial, *Imágen ambiental de Santiago*, 47.

50. Maitland, *Chile, Its Land and People*, 165.

51. Ibid.   52. Elliot, *Chile*, 279.

53. Maitland, *Chile, Its Land and People*, 165.   54. Elliot, *Chile*, 280–81.

55. Bingham, *Across South America*, 181.   56. Koebel, *Modern Chile*, 64.

57. Mansfield, *Progressive Chile*, 239.   58. Ossandón Vicuña, *Guía de Santiago*, 49.

59. Gross, Ramón, and Vial, *Imágen ambiental de Santiago*, 66.

60. Sociedad Editora Internacional, *Baedeker de la República de Chile*, 305.

61. Ramón, *Santiago de Chile*, 196.

62. Gross, Ramón, and Vial, *Imágen ambiental de Santiago*, 208–10.

63. Ruhl, "Santiago," 142.

64. For an entertaining description of Santiago at the time of the centennial, see Calderón, *Cuando Chile cumplió 100 años*.

65. Ruhl, "Santiago," 141.

66. Bingham, *Across South America*, 189.

67. Bryce, *South America*, 217.

68. As quoted in Gross, Ramón, and Vial, *Imágen ambiental de Santiago*, 28.

69. As quoted in ibid., 30.

70. This anonymous visitor did find Santa Lucía attractive and the wine excellent—but the food ordinary (V. Donoso R., "Veinticuatro horas en Santiago: Anotaciones traducidas de la carta de un turista yankee," *La Semana*, March 12, 1911, 331–33).

71. Mansfield, *Progressive Chile*, 241.

72. See, e.g., Hahner, *Poverty and Politics*; Johns, *The City of Mexico in the Age of Díaz*; Pineo and Baer, *Cities of Hope*; and Scobie, *Buenos Aires*.

73. For Chile's predominance on the Pacific Coast at the turn of the century, see Burr, *By Reason or Force*.

74. As quoted in Ramón, *Santiago de Chile*, 204.

75. DeShazo, *Urban Workers and Labor Unions in Chile*, 70.

76. Vial Correa, *Historia de Chile*, vol. 1, bk. 2, 462.

77. DeShazo, *Urban Workers and Labor Unions in Chile*, 66–67.

78. Collier and Sater, *A History of Chile*, 176–77.

79. BMS, March 15, 1901, pp. 441–42. The most thorough study of this issue is Góngora Escobedo, *La prostitución en Santiago*.

80. As quoted in Ramón, "Estudio de una periferia urbana," 262.

81. Mamalakis, *Historical Statistics of Chile*, 25.

82. DeShazo, *Urban Workers and Labor Unions in Chile*, 72.

83. Ibid., 73.

84. According to the national labor office survey of 1910, of the 71,060 persons employed in industrial activities nationally, 16,480 were women and 5,549 were children (Chile, Dirección General del Trabajo, *Boletín de la Oficina del Trabajo* [1911]: 113). The matter of child labor has not been much studied in Chile. A recent effort focusing on the glass industry is Rojas Flores, *Los niños cristaleros*.

CHAPTER TWO

1. The best single source in English for these events is Blakemore, *British Nitrates and Chilean Politics*.

2. For a good review of this period, see Heise González, *Historia de Chile*.

3. For a summary of these developments, see Valenzuela, *Political Brokers in Chile*, 183–92. See also León Echaíz, *Historia de Santiago*, 2:153–55.

4. León Echaíz, *Historia de Santiago*, 2:193.

5. Ibid.

6. For a review of the parties at this time, see Collier and Sater, *A History of Chile*, 188–201;

and Vial Correa, *Historia de Chile*, vol. 1, bk. 2, 574–85. The general literature on Chilean political parties is extensive. A pioneering study in English is Gil, *The Political System of Chile*. A more recent study that examines the fluctuating party alignments and positions on various issues is Scully, *Rethinking the Center*. See also Remmer, *Party Competition in Argentina and Chile*.

7. Heise González, *Historia de Chile*, 92.

8. El Ferrocarril, October 8, 1891, p. 1.

9. El Ferrocarril, October 11, 1891, p. 1. Lack of access to credit forced many workers to rely on the goodwill of store owners to allow them to run up accounts or on pawnshops, which were often exploitative (DeShazo, *Urban Workers and Labor Unions in Chile*, 83–84).

10. The Liberals chose their municipal candidates on October 12. The Conservatives, perhaps confident of victory, selected theirs on October 16, only two days before the election (El Ferrocarril, October 13, 1891, p. 1; October 17, 1891, p. 1).

11. El Ferrocarril, October 17, 1891, p. 1.   12. El Ferrocarril, October 17, 1891, p. 1.

13. El Ferrocarril, October 18, 1891, p. 3.   14. El Ferrocarril, October 10, 1891, p. 3.

15. BMS, November 10, 1891, pp. 130–31. Affiliations were determined by candidate lists in various editions of El Ferrocarril for October 1891.

16. BMS, March 8–11, 1894, pp. 88–93.

17. The strong comeback showing of the Liberal Democrats and, to a lesser extent, the Radicals, at the local level was a reflection of their overall campaign efforts in 1894, when they worked with greater enthusiasm and discipline than the more lethargic Conservatives and Liberals (Collier and Sater, *A History of Chile*, 189; Heise González, *Historia de Chile*, 106–11).

18. El Ferrocarril, March 9, 1897, p. 1.   19. BMS, May 6, 1894, pp. 20–23.

20. El Ferrocarril, March 13, 1894, p. 3.   21. BMS, December 17, 1909, pp. 366–70.

22. BMS, April 26, 1910, pp. 100–105.   23. BMS, May 2, 1910, pp. 117–21.

24. BMS, July 15, 1910, pp. 193–208.   25. BMS, July 18, 1910, pp. 211–22.

26. BMS, July 20, 1910, pp. 224–26.   27. BMS, June 28, 1895, p. 360.

28. In favor were seven Liberal Democrats, six Liberals, two Radicals, and one Democrat, while four Conservatives voted against the measure (BMS, October 25, 1895, p. 457).

29. Góngora Escobedo, *La prostitución en Santiago*, 194. See also Vial Correa, *Historia de Chile*, vol. 1, bk. 2, 514–18.

30. BMS, July 8, 1901, pp. 18–19.

31. The regulations were printed in BMS, October 16, 1901, pp. 18–19.

32. Ramón, *Santiago de Chile*, 188.

33. BMS, June 22, 1894, pp. 105–6.

34. BMS, June 27, 1894, pp. 112–13.

35. F. Díaz Ossa, "Tranvías," Zig-Zag, January 28, 1944, 21. For a description of the introduction of the electric streetcar into the cities of the United States, see Jackson, Crabgrass Frontier, 103–15.

36. F. Díaz Ossa, "Tranvías," Zig-Zag, January 28, 1944, 21.

37. El Ferrocarril, December 17, 1896, p. 1.

38. La Tarde, April 17, 1897, p. 2.

39. El Ferrocarril, April 22, 1897, p. 1.

40. Appendix to BMS, April 22, 1897, pp. 259–75.

41. BMS, April 23, 1902, pp. 197–206.

42. The regulations were approved on April 25 and printed in BMS, June 3, 1902, pp.
   707–14.

43. BMS, August 31, 1903, pp. 179–85.

44. BMS, September 7, 1905, pp. 107–8.

45. BMS, September 13, 1905, pp. 110–21.

46. F. Díaz Ossa, "Tranvías," Zig-Zag, January 28, 1944, 23.

47. BMS, January 19, 1910, pp. 58–60; January 20, 1910, pp. 64–69.

48. Sociedad Editora Internacional, Baedeker de la República de Chile, 1910, 282–283.

49. El Mercurio, March 1, 1909, p. 7.

50. El Mercurio, March 6, 1909, p. 1.

51. Luz y Progreso, May 1908, pp. 1–2.

52. El Santiaguino, December 3, 1908, pp. 1–2.

53. Empresa Periodística "Chile," Diccionario biográfico de Chile, 1936, 685.

54. El Santiaguino, December 20, 1908, p. 3.   55. El Santiaguino, January 5, 1909, pp. 1–2.

56. El Santiaguino, March 6, 1909, p. 4.   57. El Santiaguino, January 21, 1909, p. 2.

58. El Santiaguino, January 15, 1909, p. 1.   59. El Santiaguino, January 26, 1909, p. 2.

60. Empresa Periodística "Chile," Diccionario biográfico de Chile, 1936, 647.

61. El Santiaguino, January 29, 1909, p. 2.

62. El Santiaguino, February 20, 1909, p. 2.

63. El Santiaguino, January 22, 1909, p. 3.

64. For a discussion of the social background of Chilean legislators at the national level,
   see Remmer, Party Competition in Argentina and Chile, 124–35.

65. El Ferrocarril, March 7, 1900, p. 1. Also cited in Valenzuela, Political Brokers in Chile, 194.

66. El Ferrocarril, March 9, 1900, p. 1.

67. BMS, May 25, 1900, pp. 448–49.

68. El Mercurio, March 6, 1902, p. 4. Commenting on the same contest, El Ferrocarril noted
   "the considerable increase of electoral venality" (March 9, 1903, p. 1).

69. El Mercurio, March 8, 1906, p. 5.

70. El Mercurio, February 17, 1903, p. 3.

71. BMS, December 17, 1909, pp. 366–70.

72. An article in a Santiago publication on the "colossal" development of Buenos Aires over the past few years, for example, pointed out that the Argentine capital had a budget of over 31 million pesos in 1910, roughly ten times that of Chile's capital (Ricardo Larraín Bravo, "El colosal desarrollo de Buenos Aires," *La Semana*, November 20, 1910, pp. 164–71).

73. Ochagavía Hurtado, *Dos causas de la ineficacia de nuestro sistema comunal*. The other basic reason for municipal inefficiency, according to this author, was "the lack of men with the necessary honesty and preparation to fill municipal positions," but this he also related to the lack of adequate finances, which made municipal careers unattractive for such men (3–4).

74. Valenzuela, *Political Brokers in Chile*, 198–200.

CHAPTER THREE

1. El Mercurio, July 9, 1908, p. 1.

2. Valenzuela, *Political Brokers in Chile*, 211.

3. One of the first to highlight this aspect of municipal reform in the United States was Hays, "The Politics of Reform in Municipal Government in the Progressive Era."

4. "La reforma municipal," *La Semana*, January 16, 1911, p. 8.

5. El Mercurio, June 16, 1911, p. 7.

6. El Mercurio, June 18, 1911, p. 5.

7. "Ese pobre alcalde!" *Pica-Pica*, June 1911, p. 11.

8. "Reforma Municipal," *La Semana*, May 21, 1911, p. 12.

9. El Mercurio, June 14, 1911, p. 13.

10. El Mercurio, December 25, 1911, pp. 3, 5. An excerpt from Mackenna Subercaseaux's address and more on the meeting can be found in Valenzuela, *Political Brokers in Chile*, 211–12.

11. El Mercurio, December 20, 1911, p. 20.   12. El Mercurio, January 10, 1912, p. 14.

13. El Mercurio, January 28, 1912, p. 18.   14. *El Mercurio*, February 1, 1912, p. 13.

15. El Mercurio, February 29, 1912, p. 3.

16. These included Independent Liberal Carlos Ureta, who had been serving as *alcalde* after the scandal broke; Radicals Guillermo Figueroa, Plácido Briones, Viterbo Osorio, and Arturo Braga Castillo; and Conservative Juan Antonio Venegas (El Mercurio, March 5, 1912, p. 15).

17. El Mercurio, March 6, 1912, p. 3.   18. USNA, March 16, 1912 (825.00/98).

19. *South Pacific Mail*, February 7, 1912, p. 5.   20. *La Ilustración Popular*, November 5, 1912.

21. El Mercurio, March 10, 1913, p. 14.   22. El Mercurio, March 20, 1913, p. 14.

23. El Mercurio, April 1, 1913, p. 3.   24. El Mercurio, March 31, 193, p. 14.

25. A lawyer, born in 1853, Valdés Vergara had helped found Santiago's law academy and

the Club del Progreso. He had fought with the forces that opposed Balmaceda, and afterward, like several men involved in city government, had been associated with the local fire brigade. He also, as mentioned, had been a prominent member of the Junta de Reforma Municipal (Figueroa, *Diccionario histórico, biográfico y bibliográfico de Chile,* 5:976).

26. *El Mercurio,* July 23, 1914, p. 3.

27. Heise González, *Historia de Chile,* 145–46.

28. Vial Correa, *Historia de Chile,* vol. 1, bk. 2, 592–94.

29. *El Mercurio,* July 23, 1914, p. 3.

30. Valenzuela, *Political Brokers in Chile,* 213–14.

31. For reform and its results in Buenos Aires, see Walter, *Politics and Urban Growth in Buenos Aires,* ch. 3.

32. *El Mercurio,* July 13, 1914, p. 18; July 14, 1914, p. 16.

33. Collier and Sater, *A History of Chile,* 169–70. See also Monteón, *Chile in the Nitrate Era,* 111–12.

34. *South Pacific Mail,* August 20, 1914, p. 5.

35. *South Pacific Mail,* August 27, 1914, p. 5.

36. *El Diario Ilustrado,* December 29, 1914, p. 3.

37. *El Mercurio,* January 1, 1915, p. 25.

38. *El Mercurio,* January 3, 1915, p. 17.

39. *El Mercurio,* January 7, 1915, p. 11.

40. *El Mercurio,* January 13, 1915, p. 10.

41. *El Mercurio,* January 14, 1915, p. 12.

42. *South Pacific Mail,* February 25, 1915, p. 7.

43. *El Mercurio,* February 1, 1915, p. 11.

44. *El Mercurio,* January 22, 1915, p. 11.

45. *El Mercurio,* January 22, 1915, p. 11.

46. *El Mercurio,* March 17, 1915, p. 12.

47. Heise González, *Historia de Chile,* 154.

48. *El Mercurio* reported that 286 voters attended the assembly, with the leading vote-getter, Horacio Manríquez, receiving 163 tallies (*El Mercurio,* March 17, 1915, p. 11).

49. *El Mercurio,* March 24, 1915, p. 10.

50. The *regidores* elected on April 11, in order of votes received, were: Washington Bannen, Alfredo Bonilla Rojas, and Horacio Manríquez, all Radicals; Alfredo Urzúa Urzúa, an Independent Liberal; Guillermo Tagle Carter, Liberal Democrat; Juan B. Martínez, Democrat; Eduardo Almarza, Independent National; Aquiles Talavera, Independent Conservative; Rafael Lorca P., Independent Liberal Democrat; Vicente Adrian, Democrat; Guillermo Aguirre Luco, National; Luis Lira Lira, Conservative; and Robinson Gaete, National (*El Mercurio,* April 12, 1915, p. 12).

51. *El Mercurio,* April 13, 1915, p. 3.

52. *El Mercurio,* May 4, 1915, p. 13.

53. Bannen's father, Pedro P., also a lawyer, had served in the national Congress as a deputy and as a senator. One source credits him with being among the first to rec-

ognize the potential of San Cristóbal hill as a future park (Parker, *Chileans of To-Day*, 287–88).

54. *El Mercurio*, October 26, 1915, p. 13; October 27, 1915, p. 12.

55. *El Mercurio*, November 3, 1916, p. 12.

56. *South Pacific Mail*, March 29, 1917, p. 8.

57. *El Mercurio*, March 28, 1917, p. 3.

58. The successful candidates, with their party affiliations and total votes, were: Enrique Phillips, Independent (19,090); Rafael Gaete, National (16,108); Aquiles Talavera, Conservative (15,591); Viterbo Osorio, Independent (15,591); Eduardo del Campo, Conservative (13,732); Eduardo Almarza, National (13,627); Rogelio Ugarte, Radical (12,323); Eduardo Larraín, Conservative (12,149); Nicasio Retamales, Democrat (11,428); José D. Gajardo, Radical (10,185); Horacio Manríquez, Radical (10,136); Diego Escanilla, Democrat (10,080); and Pedro Marín, Liberal Democrat (9,902) (Santiago [Chile], *Gaceta Municipal*, April 16, 1918, p. 3).

59. Details on the strike and the city's role are from *El Mercurio*, April 19–May 2, 1918; and *South Pacific Mail*, April 25, 1918, p. 5. For more on labor activity in general during this period, see DeShazo, *Urban Workers and Labor Unions in Chile*, 146–78.

60. *El Mercurio*, May 6, 1918, p. 15.

61. Ugarte, *Mi labor como alcalde y como regidor*, 20.

62. *El Mercurio*, August 2, 1918, p. 17.

63. Municipalid de Santiago, *Gaceta Municipal*, September 6, 1918, pp. 3–7. Phillips was something of a loose cannon. A retired army officer, he became active in veterans' organizations, including the Liga Patriótica Militar (Patriotic Military League), serving as director and president. This organization had allied itself with the larger, nationalist Liga Patrótica (Patriotic League) in 1911. Running as an independent committed to cleaning up municipal government, he was, as noted, the leading vote-getter in the election for *regidores* in 1918. More on the organizations with which he was affiliated can be found in McGee Deutsch, *Las Derechas*, 19–21. Biographical information on Phillips is from Figueroa, *Diccionario histórico, biográfico y bibliográfico de Chile*, 5:508–9.

64. *El Mercurio*, August 24, 1918, p. 16.

65. Municipalid de Santiago, *Gaceta Municipal*, September 3, 1918, p. 16.

66. *El Mercurio*, April 22, 1919, p. 16.   67. *El Mercurio*, June 14, 1919, p. 18.

68. *El Mercurio*, June 25, 1919, p. 19.   69. *El Mercurio*, June 26, 1919, p. 22.

70. *El Mercurio*, June 27, 1919, p. 19; *South Pacific Mail*, June 26, 1919, p. 17.

71. *El Mercurio*, July 28, 1919, p. 18.

72. Ugarte, *Mi labor como alcalde y como regidor*, 10.

73. *El Mercurio*, August 14, 1919, p. 19.

74. *El Mercurio*, December 27, 1919; *South Pacific Mail*, January 8, 1920, p. 8.

75. In a blistering attack on Manríquez, fellow Radical *regidor* José D. Gajardo accused his colleague of having "a furious desire to be alcalde" (*El Mercurio*, February 16, 1920, p. 16).

76. *El Mercurio*, March 5, 1920, p. 16.

77. For a careful analysis of the 1920 presidential election, see Millar Carvacho, *La elección presidencial de 1920.*

78. *El Mercurio*, August 21, 1920, p. 18.

79. Figueroa, *Diccionario histórico, biográfico y bibliográfico de Chile*, 5:190–91.

80. *El Mercurio*, October 10, 1920, p. 25.

CHAPTER FOUR

1. Chile, Comisión Central del Censo, *Resultados del X censo ... de 1930*, 1:42.

2. Chile, Dirección General de Estadística, *Censo de 1920*, 282, 294.

3. Ibid., 319.

4. Mamalakis, *Historical Statistics of Chile*, 142.

5. E.g., Albes, "Santiago, Chile's Charming Capital," 168. For more on the status of women, especially women of the working class, in Santiago during this period, see Hutchison, *Labors Appropriate to Their Sex.*

6. Chile, Dirección General de Estadística, *Censo de 1920*, 465–67.

7. Millar Carvacho, *La elección presidencial de 1920*, 179–89.

8. For more on the evolution of the student movement, see Bonilla and Glazer, *Student Politics in Chile*, 21–75.

9. DeShazo's figures (*Urban Workers and Labor Unions in Chile*, 16) show a slight decline in the number of industrial establishments in Santiago, from 1,172 in 1910 to 1,147 in 1925. However, he warns, this may have been due to under-reporting on official surveys by owners anxious to avoid taxation.

10. Collier and Sater, *A History of Chile*, 159–60.

11. Albes, "Santiago, Chile's Charming Capital," 172.

12. *La Industria Nacional*, July 1918; DeShazo, *Urban Workers and Labor Unions in Chile*, 22.

13. *La Patria Israelita*, May 15, 1920. For more on the Jewish community in Chile, see Elkin, *The Jews of Latin America*, 59–60.

14. *South Pacific Mail*, May 24, 1917, p. 16.

15. Phillips's comments can be found in *El Mercurio*, October 14, 1919, p. 18.

16. Gross, Ramón, and Vial, *Imágen ambiental de Santiago*, 22.

17. *El Mercurio*, August 10, 1917, p. 3. Valdés Valdés's articles on Santiago's transformation were published prominently on page 3 of each edition of *El Mercurio* from August 5 through August 10, 1917. For information on Valdés Valdés, see Figueroa, *Diccionario histórico, biográfico y bibliográfico de Chile*, 5:969–73; and Parker, *Chileans of To-Day*, 71–72.

18. Bannen Lanata, *Santiago de Chile*, 101–3.

19. *El Mercurio*, August 30, 1915, p. 11.

20. Biographical information on Carvajal is from Empresa Periodistica "Chile," *Diccionario biográfico de Chile, 1936*, 153.

21. *El Mercurio*, December 3, 1919, p. 22; December 17, 1919, p. 17.

22. *El Mercurio*, March 18, 1920, p. 7.

23. *South Pacific Mail*, July 8, 1920, p. 5.

24. Albes, "Santiago, Chile's Charming Capital," 156.

25. Ibid., 172.

26. *El Mercurio*, November 9, 1915, p. 3.   27. *El Mercurio*, February 18, 1916, p. 13.

28. *El Mercurio*, February 1, 1917, p. 9.   29. *El Mercurio*, October 3, 1918, p. 17.

30. *El Mercurio*, June 26, 1918, p. 16.

31. USNA, September 17, 1920 (825.00/173).

32. *El Mercurio*, April 4, 1921, p. 9.

33. *El Mercurio*, August 3, 1920, p. 3.

34. USNA, September 17, 1920 (825.00/173).

35. This was a development that received some attention in the United States; see *New York Times*, December 26, 1920, pp. 1, 7.

36. *New York Times*, January 15, 1921, p. 24; USNA, January 21, 1921 (825.00/187).

37. *New York Times*, December 26, 1920, pp. 1, 7; USNA, December 24, 1920 (825.00/185).

38. As reported by the U.S. Embassy (USNA, January 21, 1921 [825.00/187]).

39. *El Mercurio*, September 23, 1920, p. 17.

CHAPTER FIVE

1. There is considerable, and often contentious, literature on the Alessandri adminis- tration. The most detailed treatment is Alexander, *Arturo Alessandri*. A strongly critical account is Donoso, *Alessandri*. Of interest are Alessandri's own memoirs: *Recuerdos de Gobierno*.

2. *El Mercurio*, March 8, 1921, p. 12.

3. Claudio Vidal, "El problema municipal," *La Industria Nacional*, March 1921, 5.

4. *El Mercurio*, March 21, 1921, p. 13.

5. *El Mercurio*, April 1, 1921, p. 16.

6. *El Mercurio*, April 11, 1921, p. 3.

7. Results from *El Mercurio*, March 8, 1921, p. 12; April 11, 1921, p. 3.

8. The winning candidates (with their votes) were: Nicasio Retamales, Democrat (10,443); Viterbo Osorio, Radical (10,268); Bernardo Quiroga, Democrat (9,972); Arturo Ramírez, Liberal Democrat (9,972); Pedro León Ugalde, Radical (9,247); Ro-

gelio Ugarte, Independent Radical (8,891); Luis Cariola, Conservative (8,862); Diego Escanilla, Democrat (8,742); Gustavo Walker, Conservative (8,491); Eusebio Silva Espic, National (8,418); Arturo Besoaín, Radical (8,021) (*El Mercurio*, April 11, 1921, p. 3).

9. *El Mercurio*, May 1, 1921, p. 21.

10. *El Mercurio*, May 9, 1921, p. 14.

11. Figueroa, *Diccionario histórico, biográfico y bibliográfico de Chile*, 2:354–55.

12. *El Mercurio*, December 8, 1921, p. 16.

13. *El Mercurio*, December 16, 1921, p. 14.

14. Tocornal had been born in Santiago in 1865, graduated from the law school of the University of Chile, and enjoyed a distinguished legal and political career. A cabinet minister in various administrations and president of the Senate under Sanfuentes, he was also on the board of several banks and the owner of several large estates near the capital (Parker, *Chileans of To-Day*, 207–8).

15. USNA, October 11, 1921 (825.00/207).

16. Coverage of these developments was provided by *El Mercurio* and the *South Pacific Mail* (April 1921–May 1922).

17. *El Mercurio*, May 10, 1922, p. 22.

18. *El Mercurio*, October 3, 1922, p. 19.

19. *El Mercurio*, October 14, 1922, p. 21.

20. *El Mercurio*, November 30, 1922, p. 23.

21. *El Mercurio*, November 30, 1922, p. 23.

22. *El Mercurio*, December 17, 1922, p. 35.

23. *El Mercurio*, December 15, 1922, p. 21.

24. *El Mercurio*, December 17, 1922, p. 35.

25. *El Mercurio*, December 22, 1922, p. 5.

26. *El Mercurio*, December 28, 1922, p. 25.

27. *El Mercurio*, December 27, 1922, p. 3.

28. *El Mercurio*, December 13, 1922, p. 5.

29. *El Mercurio*, April 4, 1923, p. 19.

30. *El Mercurio*, March 3, 1923, p. 3.

31. *El Mercurio*, March 14, 1923, p. 16.

32. *El Mercurio*, March 15, 1923, p. 20.

33. *El Mercurio*, March 17, 1923, p. 18.

34. *El Mercurio*, March 18, 1923, p. 29.

35. For more on this matter in Buenos Aires, see García Heras, *Transportes, negocios y política*.

36. *El Mercurio*, November 9, 1921, p. 13; June 7, 1922, p. 21.

37. *El Mercurio*, February 20, 1923, p. 15.

38. *El Mercurio*, November 6, 1922, p. 1.

39. *El Mercurio*, April 10, 1923, p. 18.

40. *El Mercurio*, November 16, 1923, p. 7.

41. *El Mercurio*, November 17, 1923, p. 18.

42. *El Mercurio*, November 23, 1923, p. 3.

43. *El Diario Ilustrado*, March 26, 1924, p. 11.

44. *El Mercurio*, March 29, 1924, p. 13.

45. *El Mercurio*, April 11, 1924, p. 12.

46. One paid advertisement, for example, claimed that "The initiatives of Don Rogelio Ugarte in favor of metropolitan progress are varied and transcendental" (*El Diario Ilustrado*, April 7, 1923, p. 9).

47. *El Mercurio*, March 23, 1924, p. 3. Ugarte had laid out his plans for municipal reform in a series of articles published as *Por el progreso de Santiago: Proyecto de reforma de la ley de municipalidades y razones en que se fundamenta*.

48. El Mercurio, March 5, 1924, p. 9.

49. The winning candidates (with their votes) were as follows: Rogelio Ugarte, Independent (13,103); Rafael Gaete, National (12,376); Rafael Vives, Independent (10,551); Carlos Cariola, Conservative (10,117); Adolfo Guzmán, Conservative (9,672); Ricardo Guerrero, Democrat (9,329); Domingo A. Garfías, Radical (9,322); Gonzálo Echenique, Conservative (9,272); Calixto Martínez, Conservative (9,268); Julio E. Ramírez, Democrat (9,264); Enrique Ramírez, Liberal Union (9,184); Humberto Mardones, Radical (9,063); and Viterbo Osorio, Radical (8,832) (El Mercurio, April 16, 1924, p. 15).

50. El Mercurio, May 6, 1924, p. 19.

51. El Mercurio, May 29, 1924, p. 20.

52. El Mercurio, July 1, 1924, p. 21.

53. El Mercurio, July 26, 1924, p. 15.

54. Zig-Zag, May 31, 1924.

55. El Mercurio, May 22, 1924, p. 3.

56. El Mercurio, June 17, 1924, p. 20.

57. El Mercurio, August 6, 1924, p. 18.

58. For more details on developments at the national level, see Nunn, Chilean Politics, 47–70.

59. El Diario Ilustrado, September 18, 1924, p. 11; September 19, 1924, pp. 3, 5.

60. El Mercurio, September 8, 1924, p. 11.

61. USNA, September 22, 1924 (825.00/293).

62. El Mercurio, September 22, 1924, p. 3.

CHAPTER SIX

1. For more on these events, see Collier and Sater, A History of Chile, 211–15; and Nunn, Chilean Politics, 70–133.

2. Biographical information on Aldunate and Vicuña Subercaseaux is from Empresa Periodística "Chile," Diccionario biográfico de Chile, 1936, 21 and 685, respectively. For Santa María Sánchez, see Empresa Periodística "Chile," Diccionario biográfico de Chile, 1946–1947, 995. Their addresses (and telephone numbers) were published in Santiago (Chile), Boletín municipal de la ciudad de Santiago, February 12, 1925 (hereafter cited as BMCS).

3. USNA, September 30, 1924 (825.00/316).

4. BMCS, February 11, 1925, p. 2.

5. El Mercurio, September 27, 1924, p. 3.

6. Zig-Zag, October 11, 1924.

7. El Mercurio, October 12, 1924, p. 15.

8. BMCS, February 23, 1924; El Mercurio, November 13, 1924, p. 19.

9. El Diario Ilustrado, October 8, 1924, p. 11.

10. El Mercurio, October 8, 1924, p. 5.

11. El Mercurio, October 15, 1924, p. 17.

12. El Diario Ilustrado, October 31, 1924, p. 14.

13. El Mercurio, November 20, 1924, p. 20.

14. BMCS, February 21, 1925, pp. 6–7.

15. Góngora Escobedo, La prostitución en Santiago, 232–38.

16. El Mercurio, November 29, 1924, p. 7.

17. El Mercurio, December 2, 1924, pp. 11, 18.

18. El Mercurio, December 3, 1924, p. 5.   19. El Mercurio, December 6, 1924, p. 17.

20. El Mercurio, December 18, 1924, p. 9.   21. El Mercurio, January 8, 1925, p. 21.

22. El Mercurio, February 6, 1925, p. 12.   23. El Mercurio, February 13, 1925, p. 7.

24. El Mercurio, February 19, 1925, p. 3.   25. El Mercurio, February 20, 1925, p. 11.

26. El Mercurio, February 21, 1925, p. 7.   27. El Mercurio, February 22, 1925, p. 13.

28. Empresa Periodística "Chile," Diccionario biográfico de Chile, 1936, 523; and Figueroa, Diccionario histórico, biográfico y bibliográfico de Chile, 5:509–10. El Mercurio (February 25, 1925, p. 3) described Phillips as "a man of proven civic spirit, selfless, intelligent and in various spheres has showed his interest in the progress of the capital."

29. Biographical information is from Figueroa, Diccionario histórico, biográfico y bibliográfico de Chile, 2:39–40 (for Avalos); 2:41–42 (Avendaño); 2:93 (Balmaceda Toro); and 2:463–66 (Hidalgo). The home and office addresses for the members of the junta were listed in BMCS, March 10, 1925.

30. El Mercurio, March 1, 1925, p. 29.

31. USNA, February 16, 1925 (825.00/402).

32. The details of the rent protest are provided in DeShazo, Urban Workers and Labor Unions in Chile, 223–26.

33. El Mercurio, March 29, 1925, p. 37.

34. BMCS, May 11, 1925, pp. 2–5; El Mercurio, May 6, 1925, p. 17.

35. BMCS, May 16, 1925, pp. 1–3.

36. BMCS, May 19, 1925, pp. 1–7; El Mercurio, May 9, 1925, p. 14.

37. Rivas Vicuña was a former secretary of the municipality, a successful businessman specializing in art sales, and a member of both the national Chamber of Commerce and the Club de la Unión (Empresa Periodistica "Chile," Diccionario biográfico de Chile, 1936, 563).

38. BMCS, May 19, 1925, pp. 1–7.

39. El Mercurio, May 10, 1925, p. 29.

40. USNA, May 12, 1925 (825.00/413).

41. The budget surplus was reported in El Mercurio, December 19, 1925, p. 8.

42. El Mercurio, August 8, 1925, p. 8.

43. El Diario Ilustrado, September 16, 1925, p. 17.

44. USNA, September 25, 1925 (825.15/5).

45. El Diario Ilustrado, September 25, 1925, p. 1; El Mercurio, September 25, 1925, p. 3. The U.S. ambassador, reporting on these developments, stated that Salas was trying to centralize his own authority on social welfare matters in preparation for a presidential bid and in so doing had come into conflict not only with Phillips and the mu-

nicipality but also with John Long, the North American advisor who was drafting a new sanitary code (USNA, September 29, 1925 [825.00/446]).

46. El Mercurio, November 11, 1925, p. 3.

47. El Mercurio, December 31, 1925, p. 1.

48. El Diario Ilustrado, October 29, 1925, p. 17.

49. USNA, October 27, 1925 (825.00/455).

50. El Diario Ilustrado, September 24, 1925, p. 3.

51. BMCS, May 19, 1926, p. 2.

52. El Diario Ilustrado, August 6, 1926, p. 3. For more on the development of conservative economic nationalism in these years, particularly as it was directed against U.S. firms, see O'Brien, The Revolutionary Mission, 183–84.

53. USNA, September 4, 1926 (825.00/472).

54. El Mercurio, August 28, 1926, p. 1.

55. El Diario Ilustrado, December 4, 1926, p. 3.

56. El Mercurio, November 19, 1926, p. 9.

57. BMCS, November 8, 1926, p. 1.

58. BMCS, October 29, 1926, p. 1.

59. Nunn, Chilean Politics, 117–33.

60. El Mercurio, March 10, 1927, p. 12.

61. BMCS, April 1, 1927, pp. 1–4.

62. El Mercurio, April 15, 1927, p. 3.

63. El Mercurio, April 24, 1927, p. 35; El Diario Ilustrado, April 23, 1927, p. 9.

64. El Mercurio, April 30, 1927, p. 8.

65. BMCS, May 11, 1927, p. 1.

66. El Mercurio, March 1, 1927, p. 3.

67. El Mercurio, March 1, 1927, p. 9. See also Zig-Zag, March 5, 1927.

CHAPTER SEVEN

1. New York Times, April 11, 1927, p. 4.

2. For more on the Ibáñez regime, see Collier and Sater, A History of Chile, 214–22; and Nunn, Chilean Politics, 134–68. A generally sympathetic view is provided in Wurth Rojas, Ibáñez. A more critical perspective can be found in the recollections of Radical politician Arturo Olavarría Bravo (Chile entre dos Alessandri, 1:192–296). Another detailed account of this period is provided in Charlín Ojeda, Del avión rojo a la república socialista. A study of Ibáñez's relationship with the labor movement is Rojas Flores, La dictadura de Ibáñez y los sindicatos.

3. Collier and Sater, A History of Chile, 217. See also Hudson, Chile, 326–29.

4. El Mercurio, May 29, 1927, p. 35.

5. El Mercurio, June 1, 1927, p. 9.

6. El Mercurio, June 8, 1927, p. 12.

7. BMCS, June 22, 1927, pp. 1–3; El Mercurio, June 14, 1927, p. 5.

8. BMCS, July 4, 1927, pp. 1–3; El Mercurio, June 22, 1927, p. 3.

9. El Mercurio, June 16, 1927, p. 19.   10. El Mercurio, June 14, 1927, p. 20.

11. El Mercurio, August 28, 1927, p. 11.   12. El Mercurio, August 24, 1927, p. 5.

13. El Mercurio, August 30, 1927, p. 11.   14. El Mercurio, August 31, 1927, p. 5.

15. El Mercurio, September 1, 1927, p. 12.   16. El Mercurio, September 1, 1927, p. 3.

17. El Mercurio, August 30, 1927, p. 3.

18. Figueroa, Diccionario histórico, biográfico y bibliográfico de Chile, 5:509–10.

19. BMCS, September 15, 1927, p. 1; El Mercurio, September 2, 1927, p. 5.

20. El Mercurio, September 4, 1927, p. 1; September 6, 1927, p. 5.

21. BMCS, September 15, 1927, p. 2; El Mercurio, September 7, 1927, p. 5.

22. BMCS, February 14, 1928, p. 1; El Mercurio, February 9, 1928, p. 10.

23. El Mercurio, May 9, 1928, p. 3.

24. BMCS, March 1, 1928, p. 1; BMCS, March 8, 1928, p. 1; El Mercurio, February 29, 1928, p. 8; El Mercurio, March 6, 1928, p. 3.

25. BMCS, April 16, 1928, p. 1; El Mercurio, April 11, 1928, p. 5.

26. El Mercurio, May 26, 1928, p. 9.

27. USNA, April 6, 1928 (no file number).

28. New York Times, October 10, 1928, p. 37.

29. For more on the AFP, see Robinson, "American & Foreign Power Company in Latin America," 18–37; and Wilkins, The Maturing of Multinational Enterprise, 131–34.

30. USNA, November 1, 1928 (no file number).

31. Nunn, Chilean Politics, 147. Nunn mistakenly dates Balmaceda Toro's appointment as alcalde as May 8. According to U.S. Ambassador Culbertson, the appointment of Balmaceda Toro was "to be in line with the present policy of the Government to minimize past [political] differences" (USNA, November 1, 1928 [no file number]).

32. Fuentes and Cortés, Diccionario político de Chile, 49–50.

33. El Mercurio, October 20, 1928, p. 15.

34. BMCS, May 28, 1929, p. 5.

35. El Mercurio, March 15–May 16, 1929.

36. BMCS, June 3, 1929, p. 3; BMCS, June 4, 1929, p. 3; El Mercurio, May 28, 1929, p. 18; El Mercurio, May 29, 1929, p. 15; El Mercurio, May 30, 1929, 3, 21.

37. As reproduced in BMCS, June 6, 1929, p. 3.

38. Chile, Gaceta de Chile (July 1929).

39. El Mercurio, August 24, 1929, p. 3.

40. USNA, October 20, 1929 (no file number).

41. El Mercurio, September 18, 1929, p. 14.

42. El Mercurio, October 18, 1929, p. 13.

43. El Mercurio, October 21, 1929, p. 3.

44. BMCS, November 25, 1929, 1–2; El Mercurio, November 16, 1929, p. 13.

45. El Mercurio, November 19, 1929, p. 3.   46. El Mercurio, February 23, 1929, p. 5.

47. Chile, *Gaceta de Chile* (January 1930).   48. Ramón, *Santiago de Chile*, 265.

49. *New York Times*, August 29, 1929, p. 31; August 21, 1929, p. 39.

50. BMCS, January 20, 1930, 3–6; El Mercurio, January 8, 1930, p. 14.

51. BMCS, January 20, 1930, p. 5.

52. El Diario Ilustrado, January 9, 1930, p. 3.

53. El Mercurio, January 9, 1930, p. 3.

54. *New York Times*, February 11, 1930, p. 19; O'Brien, *The Revolutionary Mission*, 185.

55. *New York Times*, February 12, 1930, p. 48.

56. Nunn, *Chilean Politics*, 156–57.

57. An editorial on the contract from El Diario Ilustrado was reprinted in BMCS, March 14, 1931, p. 7. See also El Mercurio, March 12, 1931, p. 3.

58. BMCS, March 12, 1931, p. 8.

59. El Mercurio, March 11, 1931, p. 15.

60. O'Brien, *The Revolutionary Mission*, 185.

61. USNA, January 24, 1931 (825.00/625).

62. For more on national developments at this time, see Nunn, *Chilean Politics*, 155–61.

63. BMCS, February 24, 1931, p. 4.

64. El Mercurio, May 15, 1930, p. 16.

65. BMCS, August 20, 1930, p. 1; El Mercurio, August 1, 1930, p. 9. Brunner's plans are laid out in detail in Brunner, *Santiago de Chile*.

66. BMCS, April 21, 1930, p. 1; El Mercurio, April 11, 1930, p. 17; El Mercurio, April 12, 1930, p. 3.

67. BMCS, February 24, 1930, 3–10.

68. El Mercurio, March 16, 1931, p. 7.

69. BMCS, February 24, 1931, p. 4.

70. For more on the "colectivo" in Buenos Aires, see Walter, *Politics and Urban Growth in Buenos Aires*, 136–38.

71. This *taxibús* seems to be the origin of the collective taxis that operate in Santiago today. The current version is a smaller black and yellow vehicle with its routes posted on a white rooftop sign. It can carry four passengers (not always comfortably) and charges fares that vary according to distance and that are competitive with buses but generally much lower than for regular taxis.

72. BMCS, February 3, 1931, pp. 2–3.   73. BMCS, June 30, 1931, pp. 7–8.

74. BMCS, April 25, 1931, pp. 11–12.   75. El Mercurio, July 29, 1931, p. 1.

CHAPTER EIGHT

1. Chile, Comisión Central del Censo, *Resultados del X censo . . . de 1930*, 1:167.

2. Between 1920 and 1930, Providencia grew from 23,130 to 42,414, Nuñoa from

26,756 to 43,287, Quinta Normal from 19,711 to 40,448, and San Miguel from 13,234 to 35,923 (ibid., vol. 1, p. 42).

3. Bannen Lanata, *Santiago de Chile*, 73–74; Ramón, *Santiago de Chile*, 252–53.

4. Figures for Santiago are from Chile, Comisión Central del Censo, *Resultados del X censo … de 1930*, 2:63; for the nation, see ibid., 2:7.

5. Ibid., 2:337; Mamalakis, *Historical Statistics of Chile*, 142–43.

6. Chile, Comisión Central del Censo, *Resultados del X censo … de 1930*, 1:viii.

7. Ibid., 1:xvii.

8. Ibid.

9. Ossandón Vicuña, *Guía de Santiago*, 77–81.

10. Carpenter, *The Tail of the Hemisphere*, 39–40.

11. "Santiago en la actualidad," *Chile Magazine*, September 1921, 80–81.

12. *South Pacific Mail*, September 4, 1924, p. 1.

13. Ossandón Vicuña, *Guía de Santiago*, 70–99.

14. *Zig-Zag*, March 12, 1927. 15. *El Mercurio*, July 29, 1928, p. 13.

16. *Zig-Zag*, July 17, 1930. 17. Brunner, *Santiago de Chile*, 75.

18. Ossandón Vicuña, *Guía de Santiago*, 68. 19. *Zig-Zag*, May 23, 1931.

20. *El Mercurio*, November 4, 1928, p. 15; Tornero, *Baedeker de Chile*, 221.

21. Ricardo Donoso, "Las librerías de antaño," *Chile Magazine*, November 1921, 221.

22. *Zig-Zag*, September 8, 1928. 23. *Zig-Zag*, May 16, 1931.

24. *El Mercurio*, July 2, 1929, p. 3. 25. *Zig-Zag*, April 4, 1931.

26. *El Mercurio*, April 20, 1930, p. 37. 27. *Zig-Zag*, January 14, 1931.

28. *Zig-Zag*, March 7, 1931. 29. Brunner, *Santiago de Chile*, 45.

30. *Zig-Zag*, February 7, 1931. 31. *El Mercurio*, July 29, 1931, p. 13.

32. *Zig-Zag*, April 11, 1931. 33. *Zig-Zag*, February 28, 1931.

34. *Zig-Zag*, November 23, 1929. 35. *El Mercurio*, October 21, 1928, p. 15.

36. *El Mercurio*, September 23, 1928, p. 13. 37. *El Mercurio*, September 30, 1928, p. 15.

38. *El Mercurio*, November 21, 1928, p. 1; January 3, 1929, p. 3.

39. *Zig-Zag*, November 23, 1929. 40. Tornero, *Baedeker de Chile*, 214–15.

41. *South Pacific Mail*, August 1, 1929, p. 21. 42. *South Pacific Mail*, October 2, 1929, p. 38.

43. Adams, "A Longitudinal Journey through Chile," 242.

44. As reprinted in translation in *El Mercurio*, July 26, 1927, p. 3.

45. Carpenter, *The Tail of the Hemisphere*, 37.

46. *Zig-Zag*, October 19, 1929. 47. *El Mercurio*, October 19, 1929, p. 11.

48. Tornero, *Baedeker de Chile*, 258. 49. Ibid., 253.

50. USNA, December 12, 1924 (825.406/19).

51. USNA, December 12, 1927 (no file number).

52. *El Mercurio*, May 6, 1929, p. 20. 53. *El Mercurio*, July 21, 1929, p. 33.

54. *Zig-Zag*, July 28, 1928. 55. Carpenter, *The Tail of the Hemisphere*, 42.

56. Tornero, *Baedeker de Chile*, 250–51.

57. Ibid., 251.

58. Collier and Sater, *A History of Chile*, 217.

59. *Zig-Zag*, July 5, 1930.

60. Bannen Lanata, *Santiago de Chile*, 68.

61. *Chile Magazine*, January 1923.

62. *Zig-Zag*, June 5, 1926.

63. *Zig-Zag*, March 13, 1926.

64. *El Mercurio*, May 12, 1929, p. 9.

65. *El Mercurio*, September 6, 1929, p. 12.

66. *El Mercurio*, July 1, 1930, p. 11.

67. Carpenter, *The Tail of the Hemisphere*, 40.

68. Ibid., 41–42.

69. *El Mercurio*, May 5, 1930, p. 3.

70. *El Mercurio*, February 24, 1929, p. 9.

71. *Zig-Zag*, April 11, 1931.

72. *El Mercurio*, February 1, 1930, p. 12.

73. *El Mercurio*, April 27, 1929, p. 3.

74. Bannen Lanata, *Santiago de Chile*, 118.

75. Brunner, *Santiago de Chile*, 15.

76. Collier and Sater, *A History of Chile*, 183–86.

77. Ramón, *Santiago de Chile*, 230.

78. Edwards Bello, *El Roto*, 9–14.

79. Ibid., 266. For more on Edwards Bello and other novelists of the period who set their stories in Santiago, see Morand, *Visión de Santiago en la novela chilena*, 85–111.

CHAPTER NINE

1. Collier and Sater, *A History of Chile*, 221–26.

2. BMCS, August 1931 (special edition), 1–3; *El Mercurio*, August 4, 1931, p. 7.

3. *El Mercurio*, August 4, 1931, p. 7.

4. Figueroa Anguita was a lawyer in his early thirties and a member of the Club de la Unión (Empresa Periódistica "Chile," *Diccionario biográfico de Chile, 1936*, 274).

5. The nine *vocales* were Luis Lira Lira, Fernando de la Cruz Rojas, Alberto Amo, José Alberto Echeverría, Hernán Figueroa Arquita, Juan Gaete Cuadra, Guillermo Somerville Briceño, Alfredo Urzúa Urzúa, and Diego Fernández Ojeda (BMCS, October 20, 1931, p. 1).

6. BMCS, November 3, 1931, p. 6.

7. *El Mercurio*, October 22, 1931, p. 3.

8. BMCS, November 3, 1931, p. 3.

9. *Zig-Zag*, January 2, 1932.

10. *Zig-Zag*, May 7, 1932.

11. *Zig-Zag*, July 7, 1933.

12. *Zig-Zag*, August 8, 1931.

13. These concerns, for example, were detailed in a note from the *alcalde* to the minister of the interior sent in late October (BMCS, November 4, 1931, pp. 2–3).

14. BMCS, December 30, 1931, 5–6.

15. *El Mercurio*, December 6, 1931, p. 21.

16. BMCS, May 13, 1932, 1–3.

17. BMCS, May 14, 1932, 2–7.

18. BMCS, May 17, 1932, 4–15.

19. Also gone from the *junta* in these months were Fernando de la Cruz Rojas and Juan Gaete Cuadra. Added on were Radical Ebrispide Letelier and physician Paulino Díaz.

20. BMCS, May 23, 1932, pp. 2–9.

21. Empresa Periodística "Chile," *Diccionario biográfico de Chile, 1936*, 617–18.

22. BMCS, June 21, 1932, p. 1.

23. Empresa Periodística "Chile," *Diccionario biográfico de Chile, 1936*, 391–92.

24. *El Diario Ilustrado*, November 11, 1932, p. 3.

25. Empresa Periodística "Chile," *Diccionario biográfico de Chile, 1936*, 296.

26. BMCS, November 30, 1932, pp. 4–5.   27. BMCS, January 11, 1933, pp. 2–3.

28. BMCS, February 22, 1933, pp. 1–5.   29. *El Mercurio*, February 4, 1933, p. 11.

30. *El Mercurio*, April 1, 1933, p. 9.

31. The two new members were Radical Ernesto Correa Fontecilla and Conservative Germán Domínguez Echenique.

32. BMCS, April 17, 1933, pp. 1–5.

33. These developments can be found in BMCS, June–September, 1933.

34. *Zig-Zag*, October 1933.

35. *El Mercurio*, November 19, 1933, p. 29.   36. *El Mercurio*, November 19, 1933, p. 33.

37. *El Diario Ilustrado*, April 15, 1934, p. 3.   38. BMCS, April 4, 1924, pp. 983–86.

39. BMCS, April 25, 1934, pp. 1228–29; *El Mercurio*, March 22, 1924, p. 21.

40. *El Mercurio*, March 24, 1934, p. 15.   41. BMCS, July 10, 1934, pp. 2149–55.

42. BMCS, June 14, 1934, pp. 1825–26.   43. *El Mercurio*, September 2, 1934, p. 31.

44. BMCS, October 3, 1934, p. 3108.   45. *El Mercurio*, September 25, 1934, p. 13.

46. *El Mercurio*, May 23, 1934, p. 13.

47. In the 1932 congressional elections, the Social Republicans had gained only a bit more than 2 percent of the total vote in electing four national deputies. Independent groups overall, however, had won a respectable 15.3 percent nationwide (Urzúa Valenzuela, *Historia política de Chile y su evolución electoral*, 482–85).

48. The members of the *junta* at the end of 1934, with their party affiliations and occupations, were as follows: Gabriel Amunátegui Jordan (Liberal, lawyer); Ricardo González Cortés (Liberal, architect); Pedro Préndez Saldías (Liberal, lawyer); José Alberto Echeverría (Conservative, lawyer); Alberto Morere Petit (Conservative, public administration); Pedro Undurraga Fernández (Conservative, lawyer); Armando Alvárez González (Radical, lawyer); Alfredo Gunberg Smith (Radical, physician); Eduardo Guevara Guevara (Radical, lawyer); Carlos Parra Melo (Democrat, union organizer); Luis Rubio Celis (Democrat, party functionary); Osvaldo García Burr (Social Republican, lawyer); Víctor Maldonado Cueva (Social Republican, businessman); and Juan Urzúa Madrid (Republican Union, journalist and labor organizer). Biographical information is from a special edition of the BMCS, June 8, 1935, pp. 5765–5802.

49. For more on these developments, see Stevenson, *The Chilean Popular Front*, 61–63; and Urzúa Valenzuela, *Historia política de Chile y su evolución electoral*, 489–92.

50. *El Diario Ilustrado*, November 21, 1934, p. 3.

51. *El Diario Ilustrado*, November 24, 1934, p. 3.

52. *El Mercurio*, November 26, 1934, p. 3.

53. These and other measures were reviewed in a full-page interview with Labarca in *El Mercurio* (April 4, 1935, p. 25). The interview was also reprinted in *Boletín municipal de la República* (April 1935): 17–23.

54. *El Mercurio*, February 12, 1935, p. 7.

55. For more on Edwards de Salas and Labarca, as well as the antecedents to the granting of the municipal vote to women, see Maza Valenzuela, "Catholicism, Anticlericalism, and the Quest for Women's Suffrage in Chile," 1–27. See also Lavrin, *Women, Feminism, and Social Change in Argentina, Chile, and Uruguay*, 286–320.

56. Chile, Congreso Nacional, Cámara de Diputados, *Boletín de las sesiones ordinarias* (February 14, 1933): 735–40.

57. Chile, Congreso Nacional, Cámara de Diputados, *Boletín de las sesiones ordinarias* (March 9, 1933): 1372–86.

58. Chile, Congreso Nacional, Cámara de Senadores, *Boletín de las sesiones ordinarias* (June 22, 1933): 435–49.

59. *El Mercurio*, October 18, 1933, p. 13. The complete text of the law can be found as reprinted in *Boletín municipal de la República* (January 1934): 26–37.

60. Newhall, "Woman Suffrage in the Americas," 424–28.

CHAPTER TEN

1. *El Mercurio*, December 11, 1934, p. 3; *Boletín municipal de la República* (October 1934): 20–21.

2. *El Diario Ilustrado*, December 15, 1934, p. 3.

3. For more on the MNS, see McGee Deutsch, *Las Derechas*, 143–92.

4. *Zig-Zag*, January 15, 1935.

5. *El Mercurio*, April 6, 1935, p. 17.

6. *Zig-Zag*, April 5, 1935.

7. *El Diario Ilustrado*, April 7, 1935, p. 15.

8. *Zig-Zag*, April 12, 1935.

9. Election information is from *El Mercurio*, April 7, 1935, p. 25; *El Mercurio*, April 8, 1935, pp. 1, 15; and Maza Valenzuela, "Las mujeres chilenas y la ciudadanía electoral," 29–36. The observations of *Topaze* are from its edition of April 3, 1935.

10. Maza Valenzuela, "Las mujeres chilenas y la ciudadanía electoral," 34.

11. *El Mercurio*, April 8, 1935, p. 3.

12. *El Diario Ilustrado*, April 9, 1935, p. 3.

13. USNA, April 10, 1935 (825.00/879).

14. Maza Valenzuela, "Las mujeres chilenas y la ciudadanía electoral," 34–36.

15. *Zig-Zag*, April 5, 1935.

16. Maza Valenzuela, "Las mujeres chilenas y la ciudadanía electoral," 36.

17. Biographical information is from BMCS, June 8, 1935, pp. 5785–5802.

18. Biographical information is from BMCS, April 25, 1935, pp. 5273–74; and Empresa Periodística "Chile," Diccionario biográfico de Chile, 1936, 663.

19. El Mercurio, April 25, 1935, p. 3.

20. Zig-Zag, May 3, 1935.

21. Boletín Municipal de la República (February 1935): 13–14. See also Ellsworth, Chile, 25–32.

22. BMCS, June 25, 1935, p. 6004.

23. For more on the Socialist party, see Drake, Socialism and Populism in Chile; and Jobet, El partido socialista de Chile.

24. BMCS, June 25, 1935, pp. 6004–6005.   25. BMCS, July 5, 1935, p. 6107.

26. BMCS, July 5, 1935, p. 6110.   27. El Mercurio, July 23, 1935, p. 11.

28. El Mercurio, July 24, 1935, p. 13. Tongue-in-cheek, Topaze (August 22, 1935) suggested that Valencia Zavala's pleasure at the closing of the Canódromo was not totally devoid of self-interest, observing that he was an owner and breeder of race horses and a member of the Club Hípico of Santiago, the organization that most keenly felt the competition of the dog track. While perhaps not too much should be made of it, the banquet to honor his appointment as alcalde had been held at that very same club.

29. El Mercurio, July 31, 1935, p. 17.

30. El Mercurio, August 9, 1935, p. 15.

31. Boletín Municipal de la República (January 1935): 26.

32. El Obrero Municipal, October 18, 1935, pp. 1–2.

33. BMCS, September 14, 1935, pp. 6567–71; El Mercurio, August 15, 1935, p. 27.

34. BMCS, September 16, 1935, pp. 6588–94.

35. BMCS, September 17, 1935, p. 6627.

36. BMCS, November 15, 1935, pp. 7191–93.

37. El Mercurio, November 27, 1935, p. 3.

38. El Mercurio, December 24, 1935, p. 28.

39. Robinson, "American & Foreign Power Company in Latin America," 55–56.

40. Chile, Congreso Nacional, Cámara de Diputados, Boletín de las sesiones ordinarias (May 8, 1933): 2550–60; (May 15, 1933): 2742–59.

41. O'Brien, The Revolutionary Mission, 198–99. For Ross's role, see Fermandois, Abismo y cimiento, 159–62.

42. El Mercurio, September 10, 1935, p. 15.

43. BMCS, February 22, 1936, p. 616.   44. BMCS, March 13, 1936, p. 792.

45. O'Brien, The Revolutionary Mission, 200.   46. El Mercurio, December 23, 1935, p. 15.

CHAPTER ELEVEN

1. For more on the Popular Front and the Conservative response, see Collier and Sater, A History of Chile, 232–33; and Stevenson, The Chilean Popular Front, 57–75.

2. BMCS, April 8, 1936, p. 1054 (session of January 20). It should be noted that the *Boletín* at this time often appeared several months after the session upon which it reported.

3. *La Opinión*, January 29, 1936, p. 1.

4. *El Mercurio*, January 30, 1936, p. 9.

5. Stevenson, *The Chilean Popular Front*, 64.

6. Collier and Sater, *A History of Chile*, 230–31; *El Mercurio*, February 12, 1936, p. 3.

7. *El Mercurio*, February 8, 1936, p. 3.

8. BMCS, July 13, 1936 (session of May 18), pp. 2098–2113.

9. BMCS, June 8, 1935, p. 5790.

10. *El Mercurio*, April 23, 1936, p. 3.

11. BMCS, June 10, 1936, p. 1747; Empresa Periodística "Chile," *Diccionario biográfico de Chile, 1936*, 685.

12. *El Mercurio*, June 9, 1936, p. 3.

13. *El Mercurio*, June 11, 1936, p. 21.

14. *El Mercurio*, June 28, 1936, p. 25.

15. *El Mercurio*, July 4, 1936, p. 15.

16. *El Mercurio*, July 7, 1936, p. 22.

17. *El Mercurio*, July 9, 1936, p. 3.

18. BMCS, September 10, 1936 (session of July 13), pp. 2661–66.

19. BMCS, April 21, 1937 (session of December 3, 1936), pp. 1147–51.

20. BMCS, April 27, 1937 (session of December 17, 1936), pp. 1240–1347.

21. BMCS, May 3, 1937 (session of December 21, 1936), pp. 1395–1403.

22. *El Mercurio*, December 22, 1936, p. 25.

23. *El Mercurio*, December 23, 1936, p. 24.

24. BMCS, May 7, 1937 (session of April 5), pp. 2727–39.

25. BMCS, September 10, 1937 (session of April 5), pp. 2727–39.

26. Latcham, Godoy Urrutía, and Faivovich had run on the same list of the Partido Radical, underscoring the growing cooperation of Radicals and Socialists in the Popular Front coalition. Rogelio Ugarte was a candidate on the same list, but failed to be elected and remained on the council. Other former council members who were elected as deputies included Liberal Gregorio Amunátegui Jordan and Radical Humberto Mardones, while Nicasio Retamales Leiva of the Democrats and Osvaldo García Burr of the Partido Socialista Republicano failed to win seats (*El Mercurio*, March 7, 1937, p. 21; May 14, 1937, p. 17).

27. *El Mercurio*, May 25, 1937, p. 3.

28. *El Mercurio*, June 5, 1937, p. 17.

29. *El Mercurio*, June 1, 1937, p. 11.

30. BMCS, December 28, 1937, p. 3949.

31. BMCS, March 2, 1938 (session of July 5, 1937), pp. 540–42.

32. *El Mercurio*, July 7, 1937, p. 15.

33. *El Mercurio*, July 7, 1937, p. 3.

34. *El Mercurio*, July 9, 1937, p. 3.

35. BMCS, March 11, 1938 (session of July 8, 1937), pp. 628–34.

36. El Mercurio, August 6, 1937, p. 15. On Barros Jarpa's connection with Ross, see O'Brien, The Revolutionary Mission, 200.

37. BMCS, April 26, 1938 (session of August 9, 1937), pp. 1324–38.

38. BMCS, February 8, 1938, pp. 1609–16.

39. BMCS, April 19, 1938, pp. 1609–16.

40. Roberto López Meneses, "La mujer en las funciones edilicias," Boletín Municipal de la República (April 1938): 7–8.

41. El Mercurio, March 25, 1938, p. 13.

42. El Mercurio, March 29, 1938, p. 13.

43. Maza Valenzuela, "Catholicism, Anticlericalism, and the Quest for Women's Suffrage in Chile," 32, 37.

44. El Mercurio, April 4, 1938, p. 21.

45. Maza Valenzuela, "Catholicism, Anticlericalism, and the Quest for Women's Suffrage in Chile," 32–38.

46. For more on these developments, see McGee Deutsch, Las Derechas, 183–85.

47. Biographical information is from Empresa Periodística "Chile," Diccionario biográfico de Chile, 1936; and Empresa Periodística "Chile," Diccionario biográfico de Chile, 1946–1947.

48. El Mercurio, May 8, 1938, p. 40.   49. El Mercurio, May 9, 1938, p. 3.

50. El Mercurio, May 13, 1938, p. 3.   51. BMCS, May 15, 1938, p. 1885.

52. BMCS, May 16, 1938, p. 1886.   53. El Mercurio, June 27–July 4, 1938.

54. BMCS, August 1, 1938, pp. 3893–3904.

55. BMCS, October 28, 1938 (session of August 3), pp. 3950–51.

56. BMCS, November 5, 1938 (session of August 24), pp. 4115–17; McGee Deutsch, Las Derechas, 180–83.

57. El Mercurio, October 30, 1938, p. 31; Urzúa Valenzuela, Historia política de Chile y su evolución electoral, 500. The one comuna that did support Ross was Santa Lucía, also including the Parque Forestal and part of the downtown core. For more on working-class backing for Aguirre Cerda, see Drake, Socialism and Populism in Chile, 204–5.

58. BMCS, November 23, 1938 (session of October 31), pp. 4343–54.

59. BMCS, November 28, 1938 (session of November 11), pp. 4396–4440; El Mercurio, November 12, 1938, p. 23.

CHAPTER TWELVE

1. Stevenson, The Chilean Popular Front, 94.

2. BMCS, February 1, 1939 (session of January 2), pp. 224–26.

3. For more on Aguirre Cerda's strategy, see Drake, Socialism and Populism in Chile, 210–11.

4. This point was made in Ercilla (January 6, 1939, p. 6).

5. Maza Valenzuela, "Catholicism, Anticlericalism, and the Quest for Women's Suffrage in Chile," 38–39.

6. Hoy, January 5, 1939, p. 4.

7. La Hora, January 7, 1939, p. 1.

8. El Mercurio, January 8, 1939, p. 5.

9. Topaze, January 6, 1939.

10. Topaze, January 13, 1939.

11. El Diario Ilustrado, January 8, 1939, p. 7.

12. Ercilla, January 6, 1939, p. 6.

13. Zig-Zag, January 1, 1939.

14. For more on Oscar Schnake's role within the Socialist party, see Jobet, El partido socialista de Chile, 1:104–12.

15. The U.S. embassy reported "rumors that Aguirre secretly countenanced its [the Socialist Militia's] development with a view to having its support in case General Ibáñez should attempt to utilize the army against him" (USNA, February 4, 1939 [825.00/1,122], 1–2). A photograph in the June 9, 1939, edition of Zig-Zag shows the Schnakes together in uniform at a public demonstration to commemorate the June 4 anniversary of the founding of the Socialist Republic.

16. For more on these organizations, see Rosemblatt, Gendered Compromises, 98–100.

17. BMCS, January 5, 1939, pp. 25–26. See also Ercilla, December 30, 1938, p. 11, for more on Contreras de Schnake's background.

18. El Mercurio, January 14, 1939, p. 17.

19. Ercilla, January 27, 1939, p. 8.

20. El Mercurio, February 19, 1939, p. 21; February 24, 1939, p. 20.

21. BMCS, March 2, 1939 (session of January 25), pp. 430–31.

22. El Mercurio, February 7, 1939, p. 16.

23. El Mercurio, February 11, 1939, p. 3.

24. Topaze, February 17, 1939.

25. For more on the Left and feminism at this time, see Rosemblatt, Gendered Compromises, 98–104.

26. BMCS, March 2, 1939 (session of February 22), pp. 423–30.

27. BMCS, March 21, 1939 (session of February 22), pp. 558–63.

28. El Mercurio, March 28, 1939, p. 3; March 29, 1939, pp. 3, 18.

29. El Mercurio, March 30, 1939, p. 17.

30. El Despertar Tranviario, May 1, 1939, p. 2.

31. BMCS, August 18, 1939 (session of July 26), pp. 1774–82.

32. El Mercurio, September 9, 1939, p. 23; September 12, 1939, p. 16.

33. BMCS, October 9, 1939 (session of September 25), pp. 2204–2207.

34. Ercilla, October 4, 1939, p. 9.

35. For more, see Drake, Socialism and Populism in Chile, 226–27, 238–41.

36. Ibid., 238–43.

37. BMCS, December 18, 1939 (session of November 27), pp. 2757–67.

38. El Mercurio, November 29, 1939, p. 19.

39. BMCS, January 2, 1940 (session of December 4, 1939), p. 5.

40. *New York Times*, January 30, 1943, p. 12.

41. *Ercilla*, November 22, 1939, p. 11.

42. BMCS, January 2, 1940, pp. 6–13.

43. BMCS, December 22, 1939, pp. 2796–99.

44. BMCS, December 22, 1939, p. 2795.

45. *El Mercurio*, December 23, 1939, p. 15.

46. *El Mercurio*, December 31, 1939, p. 28.

47. Empresa Periodística "Chile," *Diccionario biográfico de Chile, 1946–1947*, 622.

48. Ibid., 288; *Ercilla*, January 10, 1940, p. 11.

49. *El Mercurio*, January 4, 1940, p. 9.   50. *El Mercurio*, January 6, 1940, p. 9.

51. *El Diario Ilustrado*, January 5, 1940, p. 3.   52. *La Crítica*, January 4, 1940, p. 1.

53. *El Mercurio*, January 6, 1940, p. 9.   54. *Topaze*, January 13, 1940.

55. BMCS, January 22, 1940 (session of January 8), pp. 196–207.

56. *Vea*, January 8, 1940, p. 8.

57. *Ercilla*, January 10, 1940, p. 8.

58. For rejection of the Castro proposal, see BMCS, February 10, 1940 (session of January 15), pp. 435–39; and for approval of the subsidy request, see BMCS, March 11, 1940 (session of February 12), p. 680.

59. BMCS, April 2, 1940, pp. 789–91.   60. *El Mercurio*, February 19, 1940, p. 3.

61. *La Crítica*, February 28, 1940, p. 1.   62. *El Mercurio*, March 2, 1940, p. 7.

63. *Ercilla*, March 6, 1940, p. 1.

64. *El Diario Ilustrado*, March 4, 1940, p. 13.

65. BMCS, April 9, 1940 (session of March 18), p. 832.

66. *El Mercurio*, March 21, 1940, p. 3; March 22, 1940, p. 3.

67. BMCS, April 9, 1940 (session of March 18), pp. 827–32.

68. *El Mercurio*, March 27, 1940, p. 17.   69. *El Mercurio*, March 27, 1940, p. 17.

70. *El Mercurio*, March 20, 1940, p. 16.   71. *El Mercurio*, March 22, 1940, p. 3.

72. USNA, March 6, 1940 (825.00/1,204), p. 3.

73. *Ercilla*, March 20, 1940, p. 10.

74. *New York Times*, January 30, 1943, p. 12.

CHAPTER THIRTEEN

1. *Ercilla*, April 10, 1940, p. 6.

2. *La Crítica*, October 29, 1940, p. 1.

3. BMCS, April 9, 1941, pp. 733–44.

4. The bonuses were approved during budgetary discussions in December (BMCS, Jan-

uary 10, 1941 [session of December 10, 1940], pp. 92–97; January 15, 1941 [session of December 17, 1940], p. 133).

5. Chile, Congreso Nacional, Cámara de Diputados, *Boletín de las sesiones ordinarias* (May 15, 1941).

6. *El Mercurio*, April 15, 1941, p. 16.

7. Maza Valenzuela, "Catholicism, Anticlericalism, and the Quest for Women's Suffrage in Chile," 37–39; USNA, April 10, 1941 (825.00/1,331), p. 2.

8. *El Mercurio*, April 15, 1941, p. 16.

9. *El Mercurio*, May 4, 1941, p. 33; *La Crítica*, May 4, 1941, p. 5.

10. BMCS, May 26, 1941 (session of May 6), pp. 976–87.

11. *El Mercurio*, May 7, 1941, p. 13.

12. *El Mercurio*, May 10, 1941, p. 13; May 11, 1941, p. 31.

13. *El Mercurio*, May 13, 1941, p. 14; Olavarría Bravo, *Chile entre dos Alessandri*, 1:502.

14. Olavarría Bravo, *Chile entre dos Alessandri*, 1:502.

15. Chile, Congreso Nacional, Cámara de Diputados, *Boletín de las sesiones ordinarias* (May 10, 1941):3607–51.

16. *La Crítica*, May 10, 1941, pp. 3, 9.

17. *El Despertar Tranviario*, May 1941, p. 1.

18. *La Opinión*, May 15, 1941, p. 3.

19. For more, see Olavarría Bravo, *Chile entre dos Alessandri*, 1:491–500.

20. BMCS, May 27, 1941 (session of May 8), pp. 994–1002.

21. Information is from Empresa Periodística "Chile," *Diccionario biográfico de Chile, 1946–1947*, 272 (for Cox Balmaceda), 391 (Flores Vicuña), 620 (León Gaete), and 1126 (Valdés Morandé).

22. *Ercilla*, March 26, 1941, p. 5.

23. *Ercilla*, April 2, 1941, p. 5; *La Crítica*, April 6, 1941, p. 1.

24. *El Despertar Tranviario*, May 1, 1941, p. 3.

25. For more on the socioeconomic backgrounds of Socialists and Communists in general, see Drake, *Socialism and Populism in Chile*, 247–52.

26. BMCS, July 31, 1941 (session of July 1), pp. 1514–20; *La Crítica*, July 10, 1941, p. 7; Olavarría Bravo, *Chile entre dos Alessandri*, 1:545.

27. BMCS, September 22, 1941 (session of August 12), pp. 1886–94.

28. Ten *regidores* voted in favor, with only the two Socialists opposed and with Conservative León Gaete abstaining for procedural reasons (BMCS, October 27, 1941 [session of October 9], pp. 2222–28).

29. E.g., *La Crítica*, October 10, 1941, p. 1.   30. *El Mercurio*, December 4, 1941, p. 26.

31. Stevenson, *The Chilean Popular Front*, 117.   32. *El Mercurio*, December 4, 1941, p. 26.

33. *El Mercurio*, December 4, 1941, p. 3.

34. Chile, Dirección de Estadística y Censos, Chile: XI censo de población (1940), 2. For more on the dramatic expansion of the surrounding comunas and demographic stagnation and even decline of the comuna of Santiago between 1940 and 1970, see de Ramón, Santiago de Chile, 243–45.

35. Chile, Dirección de Estadística y Censos, Chile: XI censo de población (1940), 85–87.

36. Schteingart and Torres, "Procesos sociales y estructuración metropolitana en América Latina," 742.

37. Ramón, Santiago de Chile, 259.

38. For more on industrial growth and migration in general, see Geisse, Economía y política de la concentración urbana en Chile, 157–96.

39. Chile, Dirección de Estadística y Censos, Chile: XI censo de población (1940), 75.

40. Siegfried, Impressions of South America, 65–66.

41. Violich, Cities of Latin America, 122.

42. Collier and Sater, A History of Chile, 230.

43. Ramón, Santiago de Chile, 265–66.

44. Davies, The South American Handbook, 1941, 271. The Hotel Carrera was still in operation in the year 2000, but the Crillón was not.

45. El Mercurio, March 9, 1935, p. 3.

46. El Mercurio, February 21, 1938, p. 3.

47. Zig-Zag, January 12, 1941, p. 4.

48. Zig-Zag, March 6, 1941, pp. 9–10.

49. Zig-Zag, August 15, 1940, p. 15.

50. Ramón, Santiago de Chile, 269–70.

51. El Mercurio, April 1, 1940, p. 3; Zig-Zag, January 19, 1941, p. 6.

52. El Mercurio, February 15, 1937, p. 17.

53. El Mercurio, February 15, 1937, p. 22.

54. Violich, Cities of Latin America, 138.

55. Ellsworth, Chile, 104–5.

56. El Mercurio, March 3, 1937, p. 15.

57. Violich, Cities of Latin America, 71.

58. Ramón, Santiago de Chile, 269–70.

59. Beals, The Long Land, 7.

60. The South American Handbook, 1941, 271.

61. El Mercurio, September 26, 1941, p. 15.

62. Frank, América Hispana, 138–39.

63. Sánchez, Visto y vivido en Chile, 134–36.

64. Bowers, Chile through Embassy Windows, 54. The Posada is no longer a restaurant, but the original building has been renovated and restored and is still a Santiago landmark.

65. New York Times, January 26, 1941, sec. 10, p. 1.

66. Fergusson, Chile, 124.

67. Beals, The Long Land, 57.

68. Fergusson, Chile, 124.

69. Beals, The Long Land, 62.

70. Clissold, Chilean Scrap-Book, 96–97.

71. Beals, The Long Land, 44.

72. Clissold, Chilean Scrap-Book, 104.

73. Beals, The Long Land, 62; and Bowers, Chile through Embassy Windows, 49.

74. Subercaseaux, Chile, p. 80.

75. Beals, The Long Land, 61.

76. Clissold, Chilean Scrap-Book, 94–95.

77. For additional information, see Morand, *Visión de Santiago en la novela chilena*, 115–57.

78. Clissold, *Chilean Scrap-Book*, 89–90.

79. Bowers, *Chile through Embassy Windows*, 45, 54.

80. Subercaseaux, *Chile*, 63–83.

81. Beals, *The Long Land*, 67.

CONCLUSION

1. Writing in the early 1990s, Pamela Constable and Arturo Valenzuela underscored the continuing sharp social-economic divisions visible in Santiago, observing: "Above the Plaza Italia . . . lie the glittering new malls and suburbs of affluent Santiago. Below the plaza, as residents say, lies the other city: A vast grid of crumbling colonial facades that stretches south and west to gritty working-class districts" (Constable and Valenzuela, *A Nation of Enemies*, 222).

2. For more on these developments, see Oppenheim, *Politics in Chile*, 200–203.

3. A recent example of the tensions that can exist between *alcaldes* and national governments of the same party was revealed in a cover story in the news magazine *Ercilla* that appeared in July 1994. Interviewing the then "dynamic" *alcalde* of Santiago, Christian Democrat Jaime Ravinet de la Fuente, the story underscored the disagreements that existed between the local leader and the national administration controlled by his own party, particularly disagreements with the minister of transportation over how best to relieve traffic congestion in the capital. As the reporter noted, "The [current] discord between the national government and the chief executive of the Illustrious Municipality of Santiago is not the first and surely will not be the last" (Patricia Fernández G., "Ravinet a ministro Irueta," *Ercilla*, July 1–7, 1994, pp. 12–15).

Bibliography

GOVERNMENT PUBLICATIONS

Boletín Municipal de la República. Santiago de Chile, 1932–38.

Chile. Gaceta de Chile. Santiago, 1929–30.

Chile. Comisión Central del Censo. Censo de la República de Chile, levantado el 28 de noviembre de 1907. Santiago: Sociedad "Imprenta y Litografía Universo," 1908.

———. Comisión Central del Censo. Resultados del X censo de la población efectuado el 27 de noviembre de 1930 y estadísticas comparativas con censos anteriores. Santiago: Imprenta Universo, 1931–35.

Chile. Congreso Nacional. Cámara de Diputados. Boletín de las sesiones ordinarias. Santiago, 1933–1941.

———. Congreso Nacional. Cámara de Senadores. Boletín de las sesiones ordinarias. Santiago, 1933.

Chile. Dirección de Estadística y Censos. Chile: XI censo de población (1940): Recopilación de cifras publicadas por la Dirección de Estadística y Censos. Robert McCaa, comp. Santiago: Centro Latinoamericana de Demografía, [1976].

———. Dirección General de Estadística. Censo de la población de la República de Chile, levantado el 15 de diciembre de 1920. Santiago: Sociedad Imprenta y Litografía Universo, 1925.

———. Dirección General del Trabajo. Boletín de la Oficina del Trabajo. Santiago, 1911–.

Santiago (Chile). Boletín de actas i documentos de la ilustre Municipalidad de Santiago. Santiago, 1891–1910.

———. Boletín municipal de la ciudad de Santiago. Santiago, 1925–42.

———. Gaceta Municipal. Santiago, 1918–1919.

U.S. Department of State. Records of the Department of State Relating to Internal Affairs of Chile,

1910–29. Washington, DC: National Archives, National Archives and Records Service, General Services Administration, 1968.

———. Records of the Department of State Relating to Internal Affairs of Chile, *1930–44.* Record Group 59. National Archives Building, College Park, MD.

MAGAZINES AND NEWSPAPERS

Chile Magazine (Santiago), 1921

La Crítica (Santiago), 1940–1942

El Despertar Tranviario: Organo Oficial de los Obreros Tranviarios de Santiago (Santiago), 1939–1940

El Diario Ilustrado (Santiago), 1914–1942

Ercilla (Santiago), 1939–1942

El Ferrocarril (Santiago), 1891–1906

La Hora (Santiago), 1935–1942

Hoy (Santiago), 1939–1940

La Ilustración Popular (Santiago), 1912

La Industria Nacional (Santiago), 1918–1921

Luz y Progreso (Santiago), 1908

Magazine del Autobús (Santiago), 1936

El Mercurio (Santiago), 1900–1942

New York Times, 1910–1942

El Obrero Municipal: Organo de la Unión de Obreros Municipales (Santiago), 1935–1940

El Obrero Tranviario (Santiago), 1932–1933

La Opinión (Santiago), 1936–1942

La Patria Israelita: Periódico Semanal: Organo de la Federación Sionista de Chile (Santiago), 1920

Pica-Pica (Santiago), 1911

Revista Chilena (Santiago), 1917

El Santiaguino (Santiago), 1908–1909

La Semana (Santiago), 1911

South Pacific Mail (Valparaiso), 1912–1942

La Tarde (Santiago), 1897

Topaze (Santiago), 1935–1942

Vea (Santiago), 1939–1942

Zig-Zag (Santiago), 1920–1945

BOOKS AND ARTICLES

Adams, Harriet Chalmers. "A Longitudinal Journey through Chile." *National Geographic Magazine* 42, no. 3 (September 1922): 219–55.

Agar Corbinos, Lorenzo. "El comportamiento urbano de los migrantes arabes en Chile." *Revista EURE* (Santiago) 9, no. 27 (1983): 73–84.

Albes, Edward. "Santiago, Chile's Charming Capital." *Bulletin of the Pan American Union* 66, no. 2 (February 1918): 141–72.

Alessandri, Arturo. *Recuerdos de gobierno: Administración, 1920–1925.* Vol. 1. Santiago: Editorial Universitaria, 1952.

Alexander, Robert J. *Arturo Alessandri: A Biography.* 2 vols. New Brunswick, NJ: Rutgers University Press, 1977.

Angell, Alan. *Politics and the Labour Movement in Chile.* London: Oxford University Press, for the Royal Institute of International Affairs, 1972.

Aránguiz Donoso, Horacio, Richardo Coudyoudonjian Bergamil, and Juan Eduardo Vargas Cariola. "La vida política chilena, 1915–1916." *Historia* (Santiago) 7 (1968): 15–87.

Bannen Lanata, Pedro, ed. *Santiago de Chile: Quince escritos y cien imágenes.* Santiago: Ediciones ARQ, Escuela de Arquitectura, Pontificia Universidad Católica de Chile, 1995.

Bauer, Arnold. *Chilean Rural Society from the Spanish Conquest to 1930.* Cambridge: Cambridge University Press, 1975.

Beals, Carleton. *The Long Land: Chile.* New York: Coward-McCann, 1949.

Bergquist, Charles. *Labor in Latin America: Comparative Essays on Chile, Argentina, Venezuela, and Colombia.* Stanford, CA: Stanford University Press, 1986.

Bingham, Hiram. *Across South America.* Boston: Houghton Mifflin, 1911.

Blakemore, Harold. *British Nitrates and Chilean Politics, 1886–1896: Balmaceda and North.* London: Athlone Press, for the Institute of Latin American Studies, 1974.

Bonilla, Frank, and Myron Glazer. *Student Politics in Chile.* New York: Basic Books, 1970.

Bowers, Claude G. *Chile through Embassy Windows: 1939–1953.* New York: Simon and Schuster, 1958.

Bravo Lira, Bernardino. "Santiago de Chile: Una capital con cinco siglos de historia." *Boletín de la Academia Chilena de la Historia* 57, no. 101 (1990): 403–52.

Brunner, Karl H. *Santiago de Chile: Su estado actual y futura formación.* Santiago: Imprenta "La Tracción," 1932.

Bryce, James. *South America: Observations and Impressions.* New York: Macmillan, 1913.

Burr, Robert N. *By Reason or Force: Chile and the Balancing of Power in South America, 1830–1905.* Berkeley: University of California Press, 1967.

Calderón, Alfonso. *Cuando Chile cumplió 100 años.* Santiago: Editora Nacional Quimantú, 1973.

Carpenter, Frank G. *The Tail of the Hemisphere: Chile and Argentina.* Garden City, NJ: Doubleday, Page, 1927.

Charlín Ojeda, Carlos. *Del avión rojo a la república socialista.* Santiago: Quimantú, 1972.

Cleaves, Peter S. *Developmental Processes in Chilean Local Government.* Berkeley: Institute of International Studies, University of California, 1969.

Clissold, Stephen. *Chilean Scrap-Book.* New York: Praeger, 1952.

Collier, Ruth Berins, and David Collier. *Shaping the Political Arena: Critical Junctures, the Labor Movement, and Regime Dynamics in Latin America.* Princeton, NJ: Princeton University Press, 1991.

Collier, Simon, and William F. Sater. *A History of Chile, 1808–1994.* Cambridge: Cambridge University Press, 1996.

Constable, Pamela, and Arturo Valenzuela. *A Nation of Enemies: Chile under Pinochet.* New York: W. W. Norton, 1993.

Davies, Howell, ed. *The South American Handbook, 1941.* London, 1940.

DeShazo, Peter. *Urban Workers and Labor Unions in Chile, 1902–1927.* Madison: University of Wisconsin Press, 1983.

Donoso, Ricardo. *Alessandri: Agitador y demoledor; cincuenta años de historia política de Chile.* 2 vols. Mexico City: Fondo de Cultura Económica, 1952.

Drake, Paul W. *The Money Doctor in the Andes: The Kemmerer Mission, 1923–33.* Durham, NC: Duke University Press, 1989.

———. *Socialism and Populism in Chile, 1932–1952.* Urbana: University of Illinois Press, 1978.

Edwards Bello, Joaquín. *La chica del Crillón.* Santiago: Zig-Zag, 1935.

———. *El Roto.* Santiago: Chile Nascimento, 1927.

Elkin, Judith Laikin. *The Jews of Latin America.* Rev. ed. New York: Holmes and Meier, 1998.

Elliot, G. F. Scott. *Chile: Its History and Development, Natural Features, Products, Commerce, and Present Conditions.* London: T. F. Unwin, 1920.

Ellsworth, P. T. *Chile: An Economy in Transition.* New York: Macmillan, 1945.

Fergusson, Erna. *Chile.* New York: A. A. Knopf, 1943.

Fermandois, Joaquín. *Abismo y cimiento: Gustavo Ross y las relaciones entre Chile y los Estados Unidos, 1932–38.* Santiago: Ediciones Universidad Católica de Chile, 1997.

Fernández C., Juan F. *Pedro Aguirre Cerda y el Frente Popular Chileno.* Santiago: Ediciones Ercilla, 1938.

Fernández G., Patricia. "Ravinet a ministro Urureta." *Ercilla* (Santiago), July 1–7, 1994, 12–15.

Frank, Waldo. *América Hispana: South of Us; The Characters of the Countries and the People of Central and South America.* New York: Garden City Publishing Company, 1940.

García Heras, Raúl. *Transportes, negocios y política: La Compañía Anglo Argentino de Tranvías, 1876–1981.* Buenos Aires: Editorial Sudamericana, 1994.

Geisse, Guillermo. *Economía y política de la concentración urbana en Chile.* Mexico City: Colegio de México, 1983.

Gil, Federico. *The Political System of Chile.* Boston: Houghton Mifflin, 1966.

Góngora Escobedo, Alvaro. *La prostitución en Santiago: Visión de las elites.* Santiago: Dirección de Bibliotecas, Archivos y Museos, 1994.

Gross, Patricio, Armando de Ramón, and Enrique Vial. "Un acercamiento a los planes de transformación de Santiago de Chile (1875–1985)." In *Nuevas perspectivas en los estudios sobre la historia urbana latinoamericana,* compiled by Jorge E. Hardoy and Richard P. Morse, 305–25. Buenos Aires: Grupo Editor Latinoamericano, 1989.

————. *Imágen ambiental de Santiago, 1880–1930.* Santiago: Ediciones Universidad Católica de Chile, 1984.

Guzmán, Nicomedes. *La sangre y la esperanza.* 4th ed. Santiago: Editorial Nascimiento, 1952.

Hahner, June E. *Poverty and Politics: The Urban Poor in Brazil, 1870–1920.* Albuquerque: University of New Mexico Press, 1986.

Hays, Samuel P. "The Politics of Reform in Municipal Government in the Progressive Era." *Pacific Northwest Quarterly* 55 (October 1964): 157–63.

Heise González, Julio. *Historia de Chile: El período parlamentario, 1861–1925.* Santiago: Editorial Andrés Bello, 1982.

Hudson, Rex A., ed. *Chile: A Country Study.* 3rd ed. Washington, DC: Government Printing Office, 1994.

Hutchinson, Elizabeth Quay. *Labors Appropriate to Their Sex: Gender, Labor, and Politics in Urban Chile, 1900–1930.* Durham, NC: Duke University Press, 2001.

Instituto de Economía, Universidad de Chile. *La población del Gran Santiago.* Santiago, 1959.

Jackson, Kenneth T. *Crabgrass Frontier: The Suburbanization of the United States.* New York: Oxford University Press, 1985.

Jobet, Julio César. *El partido socialista de Chile.* Vol. 1. Santiago: Ediciones Prensa Latinoamericana, 1971.

Johns, Michael. *The City of Mexico in the Age of Díaz.* Austin: University of Texas Press, 1997.

Johnson, John J. *Political Change in Latin America: The Emergence of the Middle Sectors.* Stanford, CA: Stanford University Press, 1958.

Koebel, W. H. *Modern Chile.* London: G. Bell & Sons, 1913.

Lavrin, Asunción. *Women, Feminism, and Social Change in Argentina, Chile, and Uruguay, 1890–1940.* Lincoln: University of Nebraska Press, 1995.

León Echaíz, René. *Historia de Santiago.* 2 vols. Santiago: Imprenta Ricardo Neupert, 1975.

Maitland, Francis J. G. *Chile, Its Land and People: The History, Natural Features, and Industrial Resources of a Great South American Republic.* London: F. Griffiths, 1914.

Mamalakis, Markos J. *Historical Statistics of Chile: Demography and Labor Force.* Vol 2. Westport, CT: Greenwood Press, 1980.

Mansfield, Robert E. *Progressive Chile*. New York: Neale Publishing Co., 1913.

Maza Valenzuela, Erika. "Catholicism, Anti-Clericalism, and the Quest for Women's Suffrage in Chile." Working Paper no. 214, Kellog Institute, University of Notre Dame, December 1995.

———. "Las mujeres chilenas y la ciudadanía electoral: De la exclusión al voto municipal, 1884–1934." Paper presented at the Twentieth International Congress of the Latin American Studies Association, Guadalajara, Mexico, April 1997.

McBride, George M. *Chile: Land and Society*. New York: Octagon Books, 1971.

McGee Deutsch, Sandra. *Las Derechas: The Extreme Right in Argentina, Brazil, and Chile, 1890–1939*. Stanford, CA: Stanford University Press, 1999.

Millar Carvacho, René. *La elección presidencial de 1920: Tendencias y prácticas políticas en el Chile parlamentario*. Santiago: Editorial Universitaria, 1981.

Monteón, Michael. *Chile in the Nitrate Era: The Evolution of Economic Dependence, 1880–1930*. Madison: University of Wisconsin Press, 1982.

Morand, Carlos. *Visión de Santiago en la novela chilena*. Santiago: Ediciones Aconcagua, Colección Bello, 1977.

Newhall, Beatrice. "Woman Suffrage in the Americas." *Bulletin of the Pan American Union* 70 (January–December 1936): 424–28.

Nunn, Frederick M. *Chilean Politics, 1920–1931: The Honorable Mission of the Armed Forces*. Albuquerque: University of New Mexico Press, 1970.

O'Brien, Thomas F. *The Revolutionary Mission: American Enterprise in Latin America, 1900–1945*. Cambridge: Cambridge University Press, 1996.

Ochagavía Hurtado, Silvestre. *Dos causas de la ineficacia de nuestro sistema comunal*. Santiago: Universidad de Chile, 1920.

Olavarría Bravo, Arturo. *Chile entre dos Alessandri: Memorias políticas*. Vol. 1. Santiago: Editorial Nascimento, 1962.

Oppenheim, Lois Hecht. *Politics in Chile: Democracy, Authoritarianism, and the Search for Development*. 2nd ed. Boulder, CO: Westview Press, 1999.

Orrego Luco, Luis. *Casa Grande*. Santiago: Zig-Zag, 1908.

Ossandón Vicuña, Domingo. *Guía de Santiago*. 8th ed. Santiago: Editorial Universitaria, 1988.

Peña Otaegui, Carlos. *Santiago de siglo en siglo: Comentario histórico e iconográfico de su formación y evolución en los cuatro siglos de su existencia*. Santiago: Zig-Zag, 1944.

Pineo, Ronn, and James A. Baer, eds. *Cities of Hope: People, Protests, and Progress in Urbanizing Latin America, 1870–1930*. Boulder, CO: Westview Press, 1998.

Ramón, Armando de. "Estudio de una periferia urbana: Santiago de Chile, 1850–1900." *Historia* (Santiago) 20 (1985): 199–289.

———. *Santiago de Chile (1541–1991): Historia de una sociedad urbana*. Madrid: Editorial MAPFRE, 1992.

Rebolledo Hernández, Antonio. "La 'turcofobia': Discriminación antiarabe en Chile, 1900–1950." *Historia* (Santiago) 28 (1994): 248–72.

Remmer, Karen. *Party Competition in Argentina and Chile: Political Recruitment and Public Policy, 1890–1930*. Lincoln: University of Nebraska Press, 1984.

Robinson, Henry L. "American & Foreign Power Company in Latin America: A Case Study." Ph.D. diss., Stanford University, 1967.

Rodríguez Villegas, D. Hernán. "El Intendente Vicuña Mackenna: Genesis y proyección de su labor edilicia." *Boletín de la Academia Chilena de Historia* (Santiago) 51, no. 95 (1984): 103–60.

Rojas Flores, Jorge. *La dictadura de Ibáñez y los sindicatos (1927–1931)*. Santiago: Dirección de Bibliotecas, Archivos y Museos, Centro de Investigaciones Diego Barros Arrana, 1993.

———. *Los niños cristaleros: Trabajo infantil en la industria. Chile, 1880–1950*. Santiago: Dirección de Bibliotecas, Archivos y Museos, Centro de Investigaciones Diego Barros Arrana, 1996.

Romero, Alberto. *La viuda del conventillo*. Santiago: Ediciones Ercilla, 1932.

Rosemblatt, Karin Alejandra. *Gendered Compromises: Political Cultures and the State in Chile, 1920–1950*. Chapel Hill: University of North Carolina Press, 2000.

Ruhl, Arthur. "Santiago: The Metropolis of the Andes." *Scribner's Magazine* 43, no. 2 (February 1908): 139–55.

Sánchez, Luis Alberto. *Visto y vivido en Chile: Bitacura chilena, 1930–1970*. Lima: Editoriales Unidas, 1975.

Sater, William F. *Chile and the War of the Pacific*. Lincoln: University of Nebraska Press, 1986.

Scarpaci, Joseph. "Chile." In *Latin American Urbanization: Historical Profiles of Major Cities*, edited by Gerald Michael Greenfield, 122–27. Westport, CT: Greenwood Press, 1994.

Schteingart, Martha, and Horacio Torres. "Procesos sociales y estructuración metropolitana en américa latina: Estudio de casos." *Desarrollo Económico* (Buenos Aires), January–March 1973, 725–60.

Scobie, James R. *Buenos Aires: Plaza to Suburb, 1870–1910*. New York: Oxford University Press, 1974.

———. "The Growth of Cities." In *Latin American Economy and Society, 1870–1930*, edited by Leslie Bethell, 149–81. Cambridge: Cambridge University Press, 1989.

Scully, Timothy R. *Rethinking the Center: Party Politics in Nineteenth- and Twentieth-Century Chile*. Stanford, CA: Stanford University Press, 1992.

Siegfried, André. *Impressions of South America*. Translated by H. H. Hemming and Doris Hemming. New York: Harcourt, Brace, 1933.

Silva, Jorge Gustavo. *Nuestra evolución política-social (1900–1930)*. Santiago: Imprenta Nascimento, 1931.

Solberg, Carl. *Immigration and Nationalism: Argentina and Chile, 1890–1914.* Austin: University of Texas Press, 1970.

Sociedad Editora Internacional. *Baedeker de la República de Chile.* Santiago: Imprenta y Litografía "América," 1910.

Stevenson, John Reese. *The Chilean Popular Front.* Philadelphia: University of Pennsylvania Press, 1942.

Subercaseaux, Benjamín. *Chile: A Geographic Extravaganza.* Translated by Angel Flores. New York: Macmillan, 1943.

Szuchman, Mark D., and Eugene F. Sofer. "The State of Occupational Stratification Studies in Argentina." *Latin American Research Review* 11, no. 1 (1976): 159–72.

Tornero, Carlos. *Baedeker de Chile.* Santiago: Ministerio de Fomento, Sección Turismo, 1930.

Ugarte B., Rogelio. *Mi labor como alcalde y como regidor de la Municipalidad de Santiago durante el período 1918–1921.* Santiago: Imprenta Lathrop Hmnos., 1920.

———. *Por el progreso de Santiago: Proyecto de la reforma de la ley de municipalidades y razones en que el se fundamenta.* Santiago, 1923.

Urzúa Valenzuela, Germán. *Historia política de Chile y su evolución electoral (desde 1810 a 1992).* Santiago: Editorial Jurídica de Chile, 1992.

Valdebenito, Alfonso. *Historia del periodismo chileno (1812–1955).* 2nd ed. Santiago, 1956.

Valenzuela, Arturo. *Political Brokers in Chile: Local Government in a Centralized Polity.* Durham, NC: Duke University Press, 1977.

Van Dyke, Harry Weston. *Through South America.* New York: Thomas Y. Crowell Co., 1912.

Vega, Julio. "La clase media en Chile." In *La clase media en Bolivia, Brasil, Chile y Paraguay: Materiales para el estudio de la clase media en la américa latina,* vol. 3, edited and compiled by Theo R. Crevenna, 60–92. Washington, DC: Unión Panamericana, Departamento de Asuntos Culturales, 1950.

Vial Correa, Gonzálo. *Historia de Chile (1891–1973).* Vol. 1, *La sociedad chilena en el cambio del siglo (1891–1920).* Santiago: Editorial Santillana del Pacífico, 1981.

Violich, Francis. *Cities of Latin America: Housing and Planning to the South.* New York: Reinhold Publishing Corporation, 1944.

Viviani Contreras, Guillermo. *Sociología chilena: Estudio de sociología general aplicado a nuestro país.* Santiago: Editorial Nascimento, 1926.

Walter, Richard J. *Politics and Urban Growth in Buenos Aires, 1910–1942.* Cambridge: Cambridge University Press, 1993.

Wilkins, Mira. *The Maturing of Multinational Enterprise: American Business Abroad from 1914 to 1970.* Cambridge, MA: Harvard University Press, 1974.

Winn, Peter. *Weavers of Revolution: The Yarur Workers and Chile's Road to Socialism.* New York: Oxford University Press, 1986.

Wurth Rojas, Ernesto. *Ibáñez: Caudillo enigmático.* Santiago: Editorial de Pacífico, 1958.

Zeitlin, Maurice, and Richard Earl Ratcliff. *Landlords and Capitalists: The Dominant Class of Chile.* Princeton, NJ: Princeton University Press, 1988.

REFERENCE WORKS

Empresa Periodística "Chile," eds. *Diccionario biográfico de Chile, 1936.* Santiago: Empresa Periodística de Chile, 1936.

————. *Diccionario biográfico de Chile, 1946–1947.* Santiago: Empresa Periodística de Chile, n.d.

Figueroa, Virgilio, ed. *Diccionario histórico, biográfico y bibliográfico de Chile, 1800–1930.* 5 vols. Santiago: Establecimientos Gráficos "Balcells & Co.," 1931.

Fuentes, Jordi, and Lia Cortes, eds. *Diccionario político de Chile (1810–1966).* Santiago: Editorial Orbe, 1967.

Parker, William Belmont. *Chileans of To-Day.* Santiago: Imprenta Universitaria, 1920.

Valencia Avara, Luis, comp. *Anales de la república: Textos constitucionales de Chile y registro de los ciudadanos que han integrado los poderes ejecutivo y legislativo desde 1810.* Santiago: Imprenta Universitaria, 1951.

Index

Quezada, José L., 172
Quinta Normal, 35, 74, 145, 153
Quiroga, Bernardo, 90, 95–96

Radical Assembly of Santiago, 233,
    235–36
Radical Party, 25–26, 41, 55–58, 64,
    88–90, 100–102, 121, 182, 185–86,
    267–68; coalitions of, 102–3; and
    comerciantes, 231; and junta de vecinos,
    113–14, 177, 180. See also Chilean
    Popular Front; Radical Assembly
radio, 158, 184
Ramírez, Arturo, 90, 93
Ramírez Rodríguez, Enrique, 103
Ravinet de la Fuente, Jaime, 301n3
Recoleta, 217, 254
regidores, 24, 29–30, 42–46, 71, 218,
    268–69; and alcaldes, 214–15, 228–29;
    number of, 58, 181, 266; and regidoras,
    185
Retamales, Nicasio, 42–43, 46, 89–90, 98
Richard Barnard, Jorge, 186, 190, 197,
    200–201, 205–6, 211–12, 214, 247;
    and Canódromo, 193–94; and Con-
    treras, 227, 238
Rio de Janeiro, 1–2, 98
Ríos, Juan Antonio, 250
Ríos, Moisés, 248, 249
Rivas Vicuña, Carlos, 117, 120, 286n37
Rivera Vicuña, Jorge, 211–12, 229, 231,
    236, 238, 243, 247
Roca-Runciman pact, 268
Rockefeller, Nelson, 256
Rodó, José Enrique, 148–49
Roldán, Dario, 33
Romero, Alberto, 260
Ross, Gustavo, 177, 186, 196–97, 199,
    205; as presidential candidate,
    213–14, 217
Ross-Calder agreement, 196–97, 199,
    268
Rowe, Norman, 92
"Roxane" (Elvira Santa Cruz Ossa),
    100–101, 155–56

Rúa, Fernando de la, 270
Rubio Cuadra, Natalia, 183, 185, 190, 197
Ruhl, Arthur, 17–18

Salas, José Santos, 119, 286n45
Salas Rodríguez, Manuel, 120, 127,
    132–33, 136, 150, 162
Salinas, Rodolfo, 35
San Antonio, 1
Sánchez, José Manuel, 148
Sánchez, Luis Alberto, 257
Sánchez Vázquez, Leopoldo, 248
San Cristóbal, 2, 82, 127, 150, 154, 169,
    257, 281n53
Sanfuentes, Juan Luis, 65
sanitation, 18–19, 49–50, 161–62, 178,
    263; and strikes, 173
San Miguel, 74, 250–51
San Pablo (downtown), 8
Santa Lucía, 2, 16, 82–83, 127, 143, 236,
    238, 240, 259, 296n57; isolation of,
    207, 213
Santa María Sánchez, Alfredo, 167
Santa María Sánchez, Domingo, 108, 113,
    172
Santander Ruiz, Luis A., 43–44, 48
Santiago: city planning for, 79–81,
    147–56, 161, 186, 188, 254–55, 264;
    description of, 1–2, 18, 74–79,
    82–83, 257–61; population of, 1–3,
    74, 145, 250–51; sex ratio in, 5,
    145–46, 251
Santiago, Department of, xv, 74–75, 145,
    250
Santiago, Municipality of, 24, 29–31,
    48, 51–52, 58, 187–94, 198, 225,
    228, 265; appointment powers of,
    234; autonomy of, 246–47; internal
    struggles in, 228, 242, 249, 267;
    reforms of, 71–72; and restoration
    of elected government, 182, 265. See
    also elections; municipal government
Santiago, Province of, 2, 250–51
Schnake Vergara, Oscar, 221–22, 230,
    240–41, 297nn14, 15